Metrowerks CodeWarrior Programming

Second Edition

Dan Parks Sydow

M&T BOOK

M&T Books
A Division of MIS:Press, Inc.
A Subsidiary of Henry Holt and Company, Inc.
115 West 18th Street
New York, New York 10011
http://www.mispress.com

First Edition—1997

Library of Congress Cataloging-in-Publication Data

```
    p.        cm.
ISBN 1-55851-505-4
```

10 9 8 7 6 5 4 3 2 1

Associate Publisher: *Paul Farrell*

Executive Editor: *Cary Sullivan*
Editor: *Michael Sprague*
Copy Edit Manager: *Shari Chappell*

Production Editor: *Patricia Wallenburg*
Copy Editor: *Suzanne Ingrao*

Dedication

For Nadine...

Dan

Acknowledgments

Michael Sprague, Editor, M&T Books, for keeping things rolling along.

Patty Wallenburg, Production Editor, for a page layout effort that resulted in such a polished looking book.

The many Metrowerks people who were so readily accessible and quick to provide information. Among those at Metrowerks who answered questions or provided input:

Greg Galanos, President; Jim Trudeau, CodeWarrior Documentation; Ron Liechty, Middleman Extrordinaire; Joshua Golub, ZoneRanger; Eric Scouten, Constructor; Greg Dow, PowerPlant; Steve Nicolai, Profiler; and Greg Combs, CD Burnmeister.

Carole McClendon, Waterside Productions, for making this book happen.

Mike E. Floyd, for permission to use his Blue Angels picture in Chapter 12.

Table
of
Contents

Chapter 4: Debugging and MW Debug 99

Chapter 5: Fat Applications 135

Chapter 6: Java, Applets, and the World Wide Web   155

Introduction

Welcome to Macintosh programming using Metrowerks CodeWarrior! Over the course of reading the several hundred pages of this book you'll learn much about writing programs that run on the Macintosh and on the newer Power Macs. This won't just be a study of the theoretical, though—you'll be able to test out all the code that's described throughout this book.

If you already own one of the full-featured CD CodeWarrior packages (such as CodeWarrior Gold, CodeWarrior Academic, or Discover Programming), you'll be able to use the examples supplied on this book's CD. Or, you can use CodeWarrior to gain practice by creating you own version of each example project. If you aren't fortunate enough to already own a version of CodeWarrior, you aren't out of luck—this book's CD contains a special limited version of this *integrated programming environment*. The included copy of CodeWarrior doesn't do everything the full-featured version does, but it does allow you to open, view, edit, modify, and compile all the included source code files.

About the CD-ROM

The CD that accompanies this book contains a Lite, or limited, version of the CodeWarrior integrated development environment, or IDE. By "limited" I mean that while the IDE can be used to view, edit, and compile the source code for any of the over twenty included projects, you won't be able to create new projects of your own. For that, you'll have to order the full-featured version of CodeWarrior. The CD in the back of this book contains a file that holds more specific ordering information.

So what can you use the limited compiler for? As mentioned, you can open any of the numerous projects included on the CD—you'll find them in the folder named Sydow CW Book. You can use CodeWarrior to compile the included code and build applications from the projects. You can also go beyond the material covered in this book by typing in any new source code you want in an existing source code file. While you won't be able to save your work, you will be able to experiment with Macintosh programming and the features of the CodeWarrior editor and compiler.

The included CD comes with three Metrowerks utilities that can be used to help you in your programming endeavors. ZoneRanger is a memory-checker that allows you to examine how a program makes use of memory. The version of ZoneRanger that's included on this book's CD is a full-featured program that let's you see how the example programs—or any other programs—dynamically allocate memory. Constructor is another utility you'll find on the CD. Constructor is a graphical interface-building tool that can be used in conjunction with PowerPlant—Metrowerks exciting application framework. Finally, the Metrowerks Profiler is included on the CD. This code-profiling tool allows you to put a program through its paces, then obtain a detailed report of exactly how much processing time was spent in each of the program's routines. That's handy information for determining how to speed up and fine-tune a program. Like ZoneRanger and Constructor, the version of Profiler included on this CD isn't a limited version.

About This Book

In this book you'll find full descriptions of the elements of the CodeWarrior development environment. The book includes chapters on the CodeWarrior IDE application, the Metrowerks debugger, Java, PowerPlant, Constructor, ZoneRanger, and Profiler. You'll also find out how to get the most out of the CodeWarrior package to create stand-alone Macintosh applications for both older Macs and the new Power Macs.

Chapter 1 introduces you to the CodeWarrior development environment. CodeWarrior, as you'll find out, is more than just a compiler. The Metrowerks CodeWarrior package consists of several compilers, programming tools and utilities, example code, and documentation.

Chapter 2 explains why the full-featured CodeWarrior CD (and the CD that accompanies this book) comes with more than one compiler. Here you'll see that CodeWarrior allows you to write your programs in C or C++—whichever you're most comfortable with (Chapter 6 shows you that CodeWarrior makes it just as easy to program in Java as well). You'll find out how any program created with CodeWarrior starts out as a project consisting of source code files, resource files, and libraries.

Chapter 3 discusses the often times overlooked, and potentially troubling, topic of Apple's Universal interface header files. This collection of over one hundred header files define the function prototypes for each of the thousands of Toolbox routines. Without these function prototype, a Macintosh compiler will not compile code that includes a call to a Toolbox function. Here you'll see why Apple's occasional practice of updating the Universal interface header files can lead to headaches for a Mac programmer.

Chapter 4 introduces you to MW Debug, the CodeWarrior debugger included on this book's CD. Using Metrowerks' debugger you'll be able to easily step through the execution of a program, view memory, and change variable values in a running program—all without knowing a bit of assembly language. You'll also see how to use the debugger to gain a better understanding of Macintosh data structures.

Chapter 5 explains how CodeWarrior can be used to create fat binary applications. A fat binary is a version of a Mac program that is designed to run on both older Macs and the newer Power Macs. Not only will a fat binary run on either type of machine, it will know which type of computer it resides on. And that enables it to be compatible with the older 680x0 family of Macintosh microprocessors, and take advantage of the speed of the new PowerPC CPU.

Chapter 6 discusses CodeWarrior and Java applets. Metrowerks has made Java applet development as easy as Mac application development. CodeWarrior allows you to use the same environment—the one with which you'll now be quite familiar and comfortable with—to write, compile, and test out Java applets.

Chapter 7 is the start of a four-chapter journey that covers PowerPlant—the Metrowerks application framework that takes much of the drudgery out of programming. An application framework is code that handles the tasks common to all programs—such as working with menus. By using the Metrowerks-written code that is the PowerPlant framework, you can concentrate your programming efforts on the fun stuff—such as graphics. In this chapter you'll also see how to create the look of your program's windows by using the Metrowerks Constructor resource editor.

Chapter 8 continues with the description of PowerPlant programming. Here you'll move beyond the introductory topics of Chapter 7 to discover the details of how the C++ code that makes up the many PowerPlant files lets you forget about many of the details of creating a Mac program.

Chapter 9 carries on with PowerPlant and Constructor. In this chapter you'll see how to easily defined your program's menus, and, more importantly, how to get your program to work with these menus. Here you'll see how PowerPlant lets you ignore most of the menu-related Toolbox functions you've used so often.

Chapter 10 concludes the discussion of PowerPlant. In this chapter you'll learn all about panes—the self-contained drawing areas that hold all the text and graphics found in the windows of programs created from projects that use the PowerPlant framework. You'll see how a pane makes graphics-handling easy. You'll also find out how using panes allows you to easily add program features (such as allowing the user to click on a drawing area and drag it about a window) that would take a far greater programming effort using traditional programming practices.

Chapter 11 describes the use of ZoneRanger, the Metrowerks memory-checking tool. Because computer memory is something that's discussed in theory, rather than in practicality, it is a topic that includes many concepts that are difficult to grasp—topics such as pointers, handles, and memory allocation and deallocation. ZoneRanger is a software tool that provides a numerical and graphical look at how each running application is using memory. With this information you'll be able to move beyond theory and gain an understanding of Macintosh memory. You'll see how much memory an application uses, how much free space it leaves unused, and how it can be modified to make more efficient use of memory

Chapter 12 discusses programming timing and Profiler—the Metrowerks utility that keeps track of where a Mac's processor spends its time. By tracking the time spent in each routine of a program, you'll be able to decide where your programming efforts should be directed in order to speed up and optimize your code.

Appendix A is for readers who have little knowledge of C. Here you'll get an overview of this programming language, along with a thorough walk through of a simple source code example.

Appendix B is for readers who have little knowledge of C++. You won't need to know C++ in order to get a lot of use out of this book. But you will need to have at least a little knowledge of this language if you're going to use the PowerPlant application framework or if you're going to develop a Java applet.

Appendix C is useful for those of you who have programmed, but not on a Mac. This appendix provides an overview of what Mac programming is all about.

Appendix D is also of help to those new to Mac programming. This appendix describes the use of resources—a topic important to anyone writing a Macintosh application.

Appendix E is for readers who use the resource editor Resorcerer rather than ResEdit. Here you'll see how to set up CodeWarrior so that it better integrates with this resource editor.

Appendix F describes a special type of resource that's particular to programs written using the PowerPlant application framework.

Chapter 1

Introduction to CodeWarrior

The word *CodeWarrior* is often spoken as if it were merely a compiler. It is, in fact, much, much more than that. CodeWarrior is a programming package that consists of an editor in which you write your source code (in your choice of a number of programming languages), several compilers that allow you to compile the source code you just wrote, and a linker that turns your compiled code into a stand-alone, double-clickable Macintosh application. Most importantly, you control all these programming services from within a single application—the CodeWarrior integrated development environment, or *CodeWarrior IDE* as it's more often referred to. In this chapter you'll get an introduction to the CodeWarrior IDE.

Depending on which edition of CodeWarrior you buy, your CodeWarrior package will consist of one or two CD-ROMs. Regardless of whether you buy the one- or two-disc bundle, the fact that Metrowerks distributes CodeWarrior on CD-ROM makes it obvious that you're getting much more than the IDE. In this chapter you'll get an overview of the programming tools and utilities, example code, and documentation that is also a part of your CodeWarrior package. Before jumping in and writing some code, it's worthwhile to spend a few minutes exploring just what CodeWarrior consists of.

Some Terminology

Terminology usually appears in a glossary at the back of a book, right? Well, Metrowerks doesn't always follow conventions, so I won't either. There are a few words and phrases that will come up time and again throughout this book, so I think it makes sense to define them right up front.

Metrowerks and the CodeWarrior IDE

Metrowerks is a company that develops computer language software products. From its inception in 1986 Metrowerks has worked not only on the development of compilers, but also on the blending of compilers into a programming environment that makes the creation of applications easier for software developers. Such an *integrated development environment*, or *IDE*, allows a programmer to handle all programming tasks such as editing, compiling, linking, and debugging code from within a single environment. Metrowerks is now best known for its Macintosh IDE—the *CodeWarrior* for Macintosh IDE.

CodeWarrior Editions and Versions

CodeWarrior comes in a number of *editions*, each aimed at a different group of programmers. For example, CodeWarrior Gold is the all-encompassing edition that includes a wealth of compilers, several debuggers, and thousands of pages of online documentation, while the contents of the Discover Programming for Macintosh edition of CodeWarrior have been selected to include everything a beginning programmer needs to get started.

This section summarizes the features of each edition. To see the complete lengthy lists that describe all that's included in each CodeWarrior edition, visit the Products area of the Metrowerks World Wide Web site at *http://www.metrowerks.com*.

Metrowerks is constantly working to improve its products. As a result of those efforts, the company frequently releases enhanced *versions* of its compilers and other programming tools. Certain CodeWarrior editions are purchased as a subscription. Paying once for that edition entitles you to three versions of the CD: the one included in the package and two free versions. As new versions are created, they are sent to registered owners. As of this writing, CodeWarrior CW10 is available, and CW11 soon will be.

Metrowerks releases three new versions of its compilers each year. A new version adds enhancements to previous versions but doesn't make code you wrote using a previous version obsolete.

Ordering information and pricing for each of the editions can be found in a file on the CD-ROM included with this book.

CodeWarrior Gold

The contents of the two CD-ROMs in Metrowerks' top-of-the-line CodeWarrior Gold package provide the serious programmer with everything necessary to develop state-of-the-art Macintosh applications. Among the compilers included in the Gold edition of CodeWarrior are Java, C, C++, and Pascal compilers—enabling you to develop applications in any of these languages. Also included in the Gold edition are debuggers that allow you to track down programming errors, programming utilities such as a memory-watching tool, and thousands of pages of online documentation. The CodeWarrior IDE included in this edition runs on either 68K or PowerPC Macintoshes and generates applications that will run on both types of computers.

CodeWarrior Gold is one of the CodeWarrior editions that is sold as a subscription. You pay for the Gold edition once and receive two free updates within the year.

CodeWarrior Academic Pro

If you're a student or faculty member, this is the edition for you. You get all the features found in CodeWarrior Gold, including two updates. In fact, the Academic Pro edition is identical to the Gold edition—with the exception of its price. If you have proof of academic affiliation, Metrowerks offers you this edition at a *substantial* discount from the price of CodeWarrior Gold.

CodeWarrior Academic

CodeWarrior Academic is similar to CodeWarrior Academic Pro—except you don't get the two updates. Each year Metrowerks releases an annual academic version good for the current school year. As of this 1996 writing, the complete name of this edition of CodeWarrior is CodeWarrior Academic 96/97. CodeWarrior Academic is available at a cost that is even less than the inexpensive CodeWarrior Academic Pro edition.

Discover Programming for Macintosh

This inexpensive edition of CodeWarrior exists for those new to programming or new to programming on the Mac. Included with the same C, C++, and Pascal compilers and the same CodeWarrior IDE as all other editions of CodeWarrior are electronic (online) versions of four Macintosh programming books by authors notable in this field. To keep the price of this edition to a minimum, the two updates included in the Gold edition aren't included here. However, for those who take a liking to Mac programming, Metrowerks offers an upgrade path to the Gold edition.

Discover Programming with Java

Like the Discover Programming for Macintosh edition of CodeWarrior, this edition offers buyers a low-cost means of getting started in programming—only here, the emphasis is on Java programming. This edition features a Java compiler and the same CodeWarrior IDE used in all other CodeWarrior editions. Like Discover Programming for Macintosh, Discover Programming with Java includes online documentation (including an electronic version of a Java programming book) and a single version of CodeWarrior.

680x0, 68K, PowerPC, and PPC

Before Apple introduced Power Macintosh computers in 1994, all Macs had a central processing unit, or CPU, that was from the Motorola 680x0 family of microprocessors. That meant each Mac had either a 68000, 68020, 68030, or 68040 central processor unit chip. People often refer to a Macintosh that has one of these CPUs as a *680x0-based Macintosh* computer or a *68K-based Macintosh*.

Power Macs are driven by the new PowerPC chip—a chip developed jointly by Apple, Motorola, and IBM. The first Power Macs used the PowerPC 601 microprocessor. You'll sometimes see PowerPC abbreviated as *PPC*, and a Macintosh computer that has a PowerPC chip as a *PowerPC-based* or *PPC-based Macintosh*.

Native Code, Emulation, and Fat Applications

The PowerPC microprocessors and the 680x0 microprocessors use different instruction sets; code that is compiled to run on one family of chip isn't recognized by the other. So, along with the arrival of Macintosh computers based on the PowerPC chip came native PowerPC code. Here *native* simply means instructions that are part of the PowerPC instruction set.

Having a line of computers that use two very different CPUs, and thus two very different sets of instructions, presented special problems that needed to be addressed so that users of any type of Mac could enjoy the thousands of existing software titles that were already available for the Macintosh. Emulation and fat applications are the solutions to these potential problems.

EMULATION

PowerPC chips don't understand 680x0 instructions, and 680x0 chips don't understand PowerPC instructions. Apple considered this situation unacceptable, because it meant that programs developed to run on the newer, faster PowerPC machines wouldn't work on any of the 680x0-based Macs, and all older Mac applications developed before the arrival of the Power Macs would "break" in terms of running on the new PowerPC-based computers. So built into every Power Macintosh is a 680x0 *emulator*—code that translates 680x0 instructions into comparable PowerPC instructions that are recognized by the PowerPC chip in the Power Macintosh computer. The emulator makes it possible for a Power Macintosh to run just about any Mac application—even those written years before the PowerPC chip was designed.

Macs that include one of the microprocessors from the 680x0 family don't have an analogous PowerPC emulator. Thus these 680x0-based Macs can't run applications that were compiled for the newer PowerPC chip.

At first glance, this situation makes it seem advantageous to compile source code so that it ends up as an application consisting of 680x0 instructions; that way every Mac owner can run the resulting application. The drawback to this approach is that Power Mac owners will be running the program in *emulation mode*; the instructions that make up the application will be passed through the emulator before being processed by the PowerPC CPU. The result? A program that executes slower than it would if its instructions were native to the PowerPC chip.

The potential dilemma for a developer is whether he or she should compile his or her code so that the resulting application consists of 68K instructions (and is thus usable by every Mac owner, although Power Mac owners won't enjoy the speed advantage of the PowerPC chip in their machines) or PowerPC instructions (and is thus much faster than the same 68K application but is usable only by Power Macintosh owners). Again, Apple came up with a solution that eliminates this predicament—the fat application.

FAT APPLICATIONS

A *fat binary application* (or *fat application* or *fat app*) is a program that includes two complete sets of code; one set consists of 680x0 instructions, and the other consists of PowerPC instructions. Whenever a fat application is launched, only one of the two sets executes—the set that is appropriate for the computer running the program. That is, when the owner of a 680x0-based Macintosh double-clicks on the icon of a fat application, the set of 680x0 instructions will be loaded into memory and the PowerPC instructions will be ignored. When the owner of a Power Mac launches the same application, the other set of instructions, the PowerPC instructions, are loaded into memory instead.

The fat application solution is a powerful one—it pleases all Mac owners and all Mac software developers. Metrowerks has made the process of creating fat applications simple. In Chapter 5 you'll read all about how CodeWarrior does much of the work for you.

CodeWarrior Projects and Applications

To develop an application using CodeWarrior, you always start with a CodeWarrior project. As you'll see in Chapter 2, a *project* is a file designed to hold other files (namely, source code and resource files) and to keep track of preferences and settings particular to an application. The result of compiling the code in the files that the project keeps track of is an *application*.

CodeWarrior allows you to set up a project in a number of ways. If you choose to make use of a 68K project, then the application that is generated from that project will be a 68K application. Figure 1.1 shows that this type of application runs on any Mac, albeit in the slower emulation mode on a Power Mac.

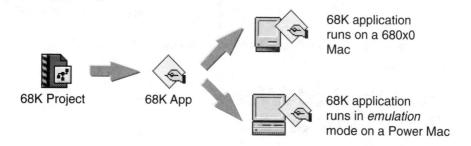

68K Project   68K App

68K application runs on a 680x0 Mac

68K application runs in *emulation* mode on a Power Mac

Figure 1.1 *A CodeWarrior 68K project generates a 680x0 application.*

If you set up a CodeWarrior project as a PPC project, the resulting application will be PowerPC-only. As shown in Figure 1.2, this means that the application won't run at all on a 68K Mac but will run in fast native mode on a Power Mac.

Figure 1.2 *A CodeWarrior PPC project generates a PowerPC application.*

If you want the best of both worlds, you'll set up your CodeWarrior project so that it generates a fat application. Figure 1.3 shows that such a program runs on both 68K Macs and Power Macs, with the benefit of running in fast native mode on Power Macintoshes.

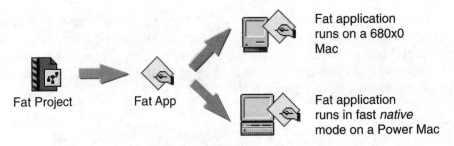

Figure 1.3 *A CodeWarrior fat project generates a fat application.*

About the CodeWarrior CD-ROM Package

This book comes with a CD-ROM that holds a trimmed-down version of CodeWarrior, some supporting files, and several example programs.

If you think that's a lot, double-clicking on the icons of two CD-ROMs that make up the full-featured Gold edition of CodeWarrior may prove downright intimidating. Figure 1.4 provides a partial view of the contents of these two discs.

NOTE If you have CodeWarrior Gold and the contents of your discs don't exactly match the ones pictured in the next few figures, don't become alarmed. I've used the CW10 version for the figures; you may have a newer version. You know from earlier in this chapter that Metrowerks releases a new version of CodeWarrior every four months. These subsequent versions of CodeWarrior (named CW11, CW12, and so forth) may have a slightly different folder hierarchy.

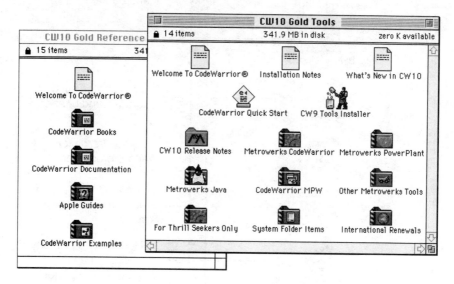

Figure 1.4   *A partial look at the contents of the CodeWarrior Gold CD-ROMs.*

As you traverse through the CodeWarrior folders you'll find a variety of applications, utilities, demos, documents, and more folders. Some things you'll immediately recognize, others won't make much sense to you—even after a close look. In this chapter you will learn about some of the main components of the CodeWarrior Gold package, with an emphasis on the software covered in this book.

The Metrowerks CodeWarrior Folder

The folder of most interest on the Tools CD-ROM is the one named **Metrowerks CodeWarrior**. As Figure 1.5 shows, this folder holds the CodeWarrior IDE, the application that serves as a control center from which all your programming tasks take place. This is the application sometimes simply referred to as *CodeWarrior*, and it's the application you double-click on each time you set to work programming.

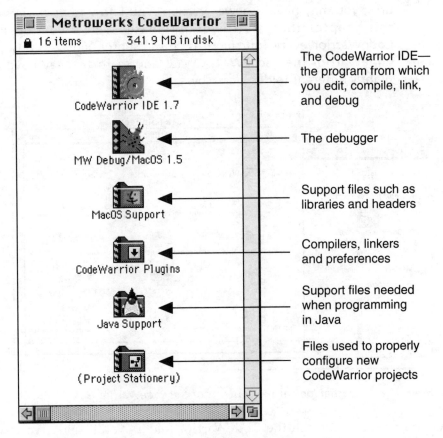

Figure 1.5 *The Metrowerks CodeWarrior folder on the Tools CD-ROM.*

The CodeWarrior IDE is the only file in the Metrowerks CodeWarrior folder that you'll ever work with directly. The other files in this folder are all used internally by the CodeWarrior IDE. For example, if a project you're currently working on isn't generating the code you expect it to, you can choose to run the code with the Metrowerks debugger. Instead of leaving the environment of the CodeWarrior IDE to double-click on the **MW Debug/MacOS** debugger, however, you'll simply make a menu selection from within the CodeWarrior IDE. It's then up to CodeWarrior to start the debugger for you.

CodeWarrior Gold comes with a variety of compilers; they're housed in the **Compilers** folder, which is located in the **CodeWarrior Plugins** folder. Figure 1.6 shows the many compilers available at the time of this writing. While some may not be familiar to you, you can see that CodeWarrior supports programming in the C, C++, Pascal, and Java languages. Each compiler exists as a plugin, meaning that any one of them can be "plugged into" the CodeWarrior IDE. Again, you won't be responsible for double-clicking on one of these files to run the desired compiler. Instead, the extension you include in your source code file name will automatically tell CodeWarrior which compiler to use. You'll find more on this topic in Chapter 2.

Another folder worth noting in the **Metrowerks CodeWarrior** folder is the one named (**Project Stationery**). When you start the development of a new Macintosh application you'll use the CodeWarrior IDE to create a new project that will serve to hold all the files related to what will eventually be your new program.

When you create this new project, CodeWarrior lets you specify what the target will be. The *target* is the end result of your programming efforts; it may be a 68K Mac application, a PowerPC Mac application, a Java applet, or one of a number of other types of programs. The files in the (**Project Stationery**) folder properly set up a new project based on the target you specify. Chapter 2 discusses project stationery and targets. Once again, I point out this folder only to give you a feel for the contents of the **Metrowerks CodeWarrior** folder—you won't ever have to open this folder or directly work with any of the files in it.

The Metrowerks PowerPlant Folder

The Tools CD-ROM holds a folder named **Metrowerks PowerPlant**. *PowerPlant* is the name of Metrowerks application framework. In general, an *application framework* is a set of files that hold the code that handles many of the repetitious programming tasks common to most Mac programs. By including this Metrowerks code in your own projects, you'll be able to devote your programming efforts to the fun areas of programming rather than the mundane parts. Figure 1.7 shows that the **PowerPlant** folder itself holds a number of other folders. Within each of these subfolders are several C++ source code files and header files. Collectively, these numerous files make up the application framework PowerPlant. Chapters 7 through 10 introduce you to PowerPlant.

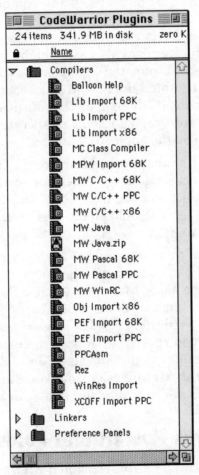

*Figure 1.6   The **CodeWarrior Plugins** folder from the **Metrowerks CodeWarrior** folder on the Tools CD-ROM.*

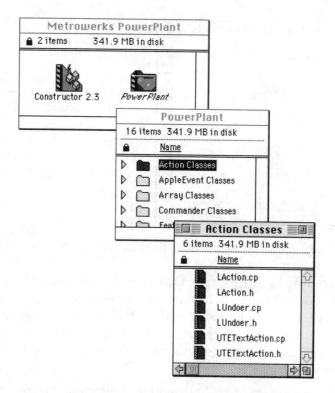

Figure 1.7   *PowerPlant is an application framework that consists of a number of source code and header files located on the Tools CD-ROM.*

As shown in Figure 1.7, the **Metrowerks PowerPlant** folder includes an application named Constructor. Constructor is a utility program that helps you create the special resources required by PowerPlant. In particular, Constructor helps you graphically lay out the contents of the windows used by the application you're developing. If you've ever used the resource editor ResEdit, the idea of a graphics editor like Constructor should make sense to you. Chapter 7 introduces you to Constructor.

The Other Metrowerks Tools Folder

The **Other Metrowerks Tools** folder (Figure 1.8) on the Tools CD-ROM holds several folders and applications—two of which are described in detail in this book.

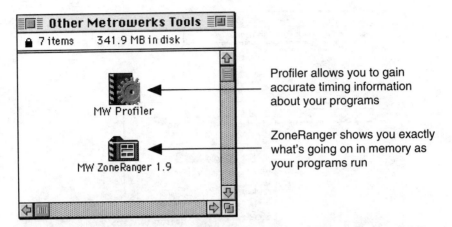

Profiler allows you to gain accurate timing information about your programs

ZoneRanger shows you exactly what's going on in memory as your programs run

*Figure 1.8   The **Other Metrowerks Tools** folder from the Tools CD-ROM.*

ZoneRanger is a neat program that runs unobtrusively in the background on your Macintosh. If you'd like to see how your own program manages memory, just launch it and look at the ZoneRanger windows. There you'll see specific information about the amount of memory your program uses and the way in which your program uses it. ZoneRanger is the topic of Chapter 11.

The *Metrowerks Profiler* allows you to determine the length of time it takes for different parts of your program to execute. Does your program seem to run sluggishly? Are graphics updated slowly? With the Profiler, you'll be able to find out exactly which lines of your code need fine-tuning, or *optimization*. Using MW Profiler on your own programs is the topic of Chapter 12.

Other Items of Interest on the CodeWarrior CDs

The **Cool Demos, SDKs, & Tools** folder on the Reference CD-ROM has a vast assortment of programming tools and utilities, most of them demos of the full-featured versions. One demo in particular is worth mentioning: the demo version of Resorcerer. *Resorcerer* is a resource editor that allows you to create and edit resources in a graphical manner, just as Apple's ResEdit program does. Resorcerer, however, is a much more powerful resource editing tool. In case you haven't bought CodeWarrior yet, I've included a copy of the demo on this book's CD-ROM.

Speaking of ResEdit, you'll find a working copy of this popular resource editor in the **Apple Development Tools** folder. You'll find a fully functional version of the resource editor ResEdit on this book's CD-ROM.

Chapter Summary

CodeWarrior is an integrated development environment that holds all the compilers, tools, and programming utilities that make it possible to write programs for both older 68K Macintosh computers and the new PowerPC-based Macs. At the heart of the CodeWarrior package lie Metrowerks fast, feature-laden compilers.

Chapter

CodeWarrior Projects

An application starts its life as a CodeWarrior project. Each project may consist of source code files, resource files, and libraries. Additionally, these files rely on several of Apple's Universal Header files. In this chapter you'll see how these different pieces of the puzzle fit together.

In this chapter you'll see how the CodeWarrior IDE, the integrated development environment introduced in Chapter 1, makes it easy to select the platform—such as a Macintosh 68K computer or a Power Mac computer—for which your new program will be targeted. The CodeWarrior IDE also makes it simple for you to select the language you want to program in—including C, C++, Pascal, or Java. Here you'll begin with a walkthrough of the creation of a short, simple application targeting the 68K Mac platform, and written in C.

Once you're familiar with the process of developing a Mac application, you'll see that setting up a project such that the resulting program targets a different platform (the Power Macintosh) or setting up a project to use a different language (such as C++) takes only seconds. Again, short, simple examples of each type of project appear in this chapter.

Introduction to Projects

A program developed using CodeWarrior always starts out as a project. In simplest terms, a project is a file that's used to hold the names of all of the files that will be compiled and linked together to become a Macintosh application. More descriptively, a project is your means of organizing the source code files, resource files, and libraries that will become your program, as well as the place where preferences are set and saved.

 CodeWarrior is capable of generating more than just Mac programs. A project can be used to create a code resource, a library, a shared library, or even a Windows application. However, this book focuses on the development of Macintosh applications.

In this section I'll create a new project that will be used to generate a 68K application—one that consists of 680x0 instructions, but which can run on either a Mac with a 680x0 CPU or on a Power Mac driven by a PowerPC CPU. The steps in creating a new project are simple enough, so along the way I'll add a little extra descriptive information so that you understand not only *what* you'll be doing, but also *why* you'll be doing it.

If you don't currently have the CodeWarrior integrated development environment running, start it up by double-clicking on the **CodeWarrior IDE** icon located in the **Metrowerks CodeWarrior** folder found in the main **CodeWarrior** folder on your hard drive.

Creating a New Project Using Project Stationery

Regardless of the type of program you're going to develop, you'll always begin by selecting **New Project** from the File menu. When you do that, CodeWarrior lets you select a project stationery and name the project file before it goes ahead and creates the new project.

CHOOSING A PROJECT STATIONERY

When you select **New Project** from the File menu, you'll encounter the New Project dialog box shown in Figure 2.1. This dialog box lists the various project stationeries that can be assigned to the project you're about to create. Click on the **arrow** icon to the left of the MacOS listing. When you do that, you'll see a couple of other categories. Click on the **arrow** icon to the left of the C/C++ listing. After you do that your New Project dialog box will look similar to the one pictured in Figure 2.1.

The list of project stationeries isn't static. That is, not only might it change from one version of CodeWarrior to another, you can change the contents of the list yourself. Metrowerks will add project stationery to new versions of CodeWarrior. Additionally, you're free to create your own stationery that can appear in this dialog box. After reading on and gaining a better understanding of project stationery you might want to create your own. If you do, refer to the *IDE User's Guide* electronic documentation that comes with each CodeWarrior package.

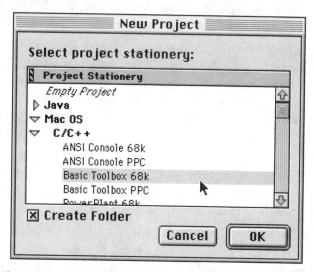

Figure 2.1   *The New Project box resulting from choosing* ***New Project*** *from the File menu.*

Before creating the new project, CodeWarrior requests that you choose a project stationery for the project. The project stationery is responsible for including the proper libraries in the new project. Because different types of projects require different combinations of libraries, it's easiest to let the project stationery determine which libraries are needed for your particular project.

Your selection of a project stationery will be based on a three factors:

- The type of application you'll be developing
- The platform the application is targeted for
- Whether or not you'll be using the PowerPlant application framework

CodeWarrior allows you to create two types of applications: ones that use the Macintosh Toolbox and ones that don't. If you're going to write a "real" Mac program that uses windows, menus, and other graphical user interface elements, you'll want to select one of the Basic Toolbox project stationeries. CodeWarrior also lets you write programs that rely on ANSI library functions and don't use any of the thousands of functions in the Macintosh Toolbox (refer to Appendix C if you're not familiar with the Toolbox). Such a program uses a console window to allow a user to supply input to the program and to display output. You'll read more about such programs (and see an example of one) later in this chapter.

The second factor to consider is the target platform—a topic discussed in Chapter 1. If you're writing a Macintosh 68K application, choose one of the 68k project stationeries. If you're writing a Macintosh PowerPC-only program, choose one of the PPC project stationeries. If you're developing a fat application, you can choose either a 68k or PPC project stationary—you'll find out why in Chapter 5, the chapter that deals with fat applications.

Finally, if you're going to make use of the classes that make up the Metrowerks PowerPlant application framework, you need to choose one of the PowerPlant project stationeries.

In Figure 2.1 I'm selecting the **Basic Toolbox 68k** project stationery. This tells you that the program I'm about to create will be a Mac program that makes use of Toolbox functions, targets the 680x0 family of Macs, and doesn't use the PowerPlant application framework.

After clicking once on a project stationery, check to make sure the
Create Folder checkbox is checked and then click the **OK** button.
Having this checkbox marked tells CodeWarrior to create a new folder
in which your project-related files will be stored.

NOTE Recall from Chapter 1 that an application that holds 68K code can
run on both 68K-based Macs and PowerPC-based Macs—it just
doesn't run as fast on the PowerPC-based Macs as it would if it
were specifically compiled with the Power Mac as the target platform. What I'm doing for this introductory example, then, is creating an application that's guaranteed to run on every reader's
Mac—regardless of the CPU it has.

NAMING THE NEW PROJECT

Clicking on the **OK** button dismisses the New Project dialog box and
posts another dialog box—one that prompts for a name for the project
that's about to be created (see Figure 2.2).

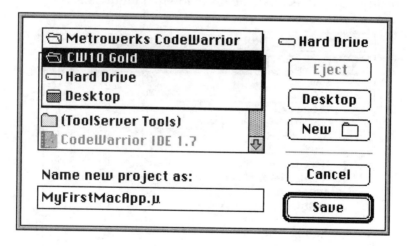

Figure 2.2   Changing folders and naming a new project.

You can give a project any name you wish, but it's common for a programmer to select a name that is the same or similar to the name that he
or she will give to the program that's about to be developed. It's also a
practice of programmers to a project name with an extension of μ. That

is, type a period followed by the **µ** character—a character you produce by typing the letter **m** while holding down the **Option** key. I'll be naming this book's first example program **MyFirstMacApp**, so as you can see in Figure 2.2 I've opted to name this book's first example project **MyFirstMacApp.µ**.

When you click the **Save** button, CodeWarrior will create a new folder to hold your project-related files (provided you left the **Create Folder** checkbox checked in the New Project dialog box, as suggested). By default, that folder will most likely end up in the **Metrowerks CodeWarrior** folder (simply because that's the folder that holds the CodeWarrior IDE application). Use the pop-up menu at the top of the Name Project dialog box if you want your project folder to be placed in a different folder. In Figure 2.2 I'm moving into the main **CodeWarrior** folder, which happens to be named **CW10 Gold** on my hard drive. Once you've supplied a name for the project and have the desired location for the project displayed in the dialog box pop-up menu, click the **Save** button to dismiss the dialog box. When you do that, CodeWarrior will create a new project like the one shown in Figure 2.3.

File	Code	Data	
▽ ✔ **Sources**	**0**	**0**	• ▾
✔ SillyBalls.c	0	0	• ▸
▽ ✔ **Resources**	**0**	**0**	▾
✔ SillyBalls.rsrc	n/a	n/a	▸
▽ ✔ **Mac Libraries**	**0**	**0**	▾
✔ CPlusPlus.lib	0	0	▸
✔ MacOS.lib	0	0	▸
✔ MathLib68K (2i).Lib	0	0	▸
▽ ✔ **ANSI Libraries**	**0**	**0**	▾
✔ ANSI (2i) C++.68K.Lib	0	0	▸
✔ ANSI (2i) C.68K.Lib	0	0	▸
✔ SIOUX.68K.Lib	0	0	▸
8 file(s)	0	0	

Figure 2.3   *The new project window that results from creating a new project based on the Basic Toolbox 68k project stationery.*

THE PROJECT WINDOW

A project window lists all the files that together will be used to generate a single Mac application. As Figure 2.4 shows, the project window is, however, much more than simply a file list.

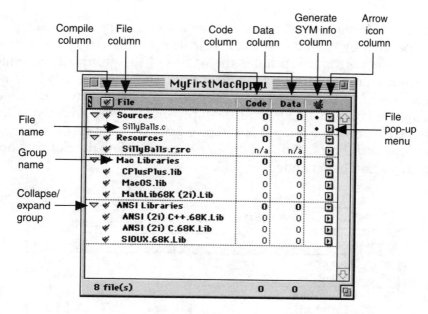

Figure 2.4 *A project window is composed of several areas.*

Groups

A project's files are organized into groups. A project always has at least one group, and can have any number of groups. Each group holds the name of one or more of the files that the project is tracking. Each group has a name, which, like groups themselves, serves only as a device to help you better organize a project's files. In Figure 2.4 you can see that the **MyFirstMacApp.µ** project is made up of four groups named *Sources, Resources, Mac Libraries,* and *ANSI Libraries.* These are the default names given by CodeWarrior to the groups—you're free to change a group name by double-clicking on it and typing in a new name in the dialog box that appears.

NOTE Technically, the term *group* is used for PPC projects, while the analogous organizational unit in a 68K project is referred to as a *segment*. However, you'll often hear (and read in Metrowerks documentation) the term *group* used regardless of the project type. I'll use *group* in this general sense too.

The list of file names that appears under a group name can be collapsed or expanded by clicking on the **arrow** icon to the left of the group's name. *Collapsing* a group hides the names of the group's files, while *expanding* a group redisplays the file names. These actions don't change the make-up of the project—the files within a group are unaffected. Collapsing and expanding groups simply provide you with two alternatives to viewing a project. In Figure 2.5 I've collapsed the groups named Mac Libraries and ANSI Libraries, and left the Sources and Resources groups expanded.

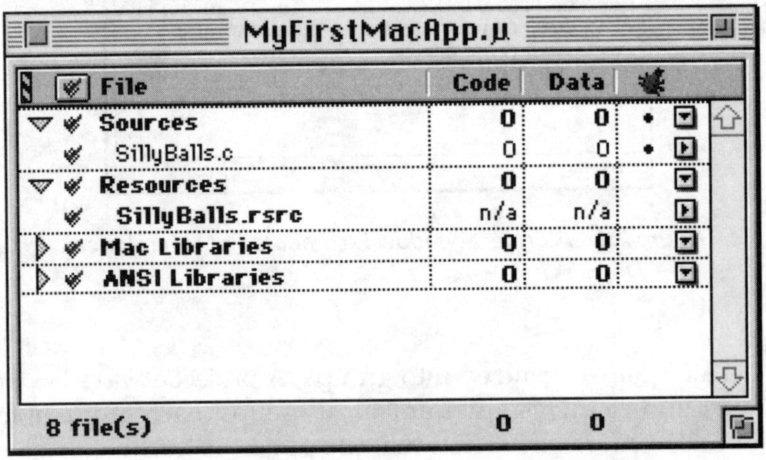

File	Code	Data	
▽ ✔ **Sources**	0	0	• ▾
✔ SillyBalls.c	0	0	• ▸
▽ ✔ **Resources**	0	0	▾
✔ **SillyBalls.rsrc**	n/a	n/a	▸
▷ ✔ **Mac Libraries**	0	0	▾
▷ ✔ **ANSI Libraries**	0	0	▾

MyFirstMacApp.µ

8 file(s) 0 0

*Figure 2.5   A project window with two of its groups
expanded and two of its groups collapsed.*

As mentioned, groups are a means of organizing a project's files. You can move a file name within a group, or from one group to another, by simply clicking on the file's name and, with the mouse button held down, dragging the file name to a new location.

You can move groups about in a project window, change their names, add new groups, remove existing ones, and so forth. For all the details of working with groups, consult the electronic version of the *IDE User's Guide* documentation that is included with each edition of CodeWarrior.

Compile Column

When you make a change to a file (such as editing source code in a source code file), that file needs to be recompiled so that the resulting application contains your changes. Normally, CodeWarrior knows when a file has been altered and recompiles that file when you build, or make, a new version of your application. Occasionally, however, CodeWarrior might not recognize a change you made. You can click on the small checkbox to the left of a file's name in the project window to force CodeWarrior to recognize that file as one that needs recompilation. Together, the checkboxes that are beside each group and each file in a group make up the Compile column.

File Column

The File column of the project window lists the name of each group and file in the project.

Code Column

The Code column shows the size of the executable object code for each group and file in the project. The size of a file is given in bytes, while the size of a group (representing the total size of each file in the group) is given in kilobytes.

Data Column

The Data column shows the size of the nonexecutable data for each group and file in a project. The values are presented in the same fashion as in the Code column—bytes for files, kilobytes for groups.

Don't expect the size of the resulting application to be the same as the sum of the Code column and Data column values. All the code in a library won't end up in the application—only the code for library routines that are referenced by your program is included in the application CodeWarrior builds from the project.

Generate SYM Info Column

Associated with each project is a SYM file—a file that holds information important to the Metrowerks debugger. This information includes function and variable names (these names are collectively referred to as *symbols*, from which comes the name of the debug file) and the location of these symbols within the source and object code. The Generate SYM info column allows you to include or exclude a file's code from contributing to the project's SYM file. By default, each source code file in a project has a mark in the Generate SYM info column—meaning that its code will be included in the project's SYM file. Click on this marker if you wish to exclude the code.

Arrow Icon Column

Each group and file in a project has a small arrow icon that appears in a column at the far right of the project window. Clicking on the icon for a group displays a pop-up menu that lists the files in that group—choosing an item from the menu opens that file. Clicking on the icon for a source code file displays a pop-up list of the names of files included in that file (as in the files brought into a C source code file using the #include directive); choosing an item from the menu opens that interface file.

Compiling and Running the Project's Code

Individual files in a project can be compiled by clicking once on the file's name in the project window to highlight the name and then selecting **Compile** from the Project menu. CodeWarrior also provides a simple means of compiling all the files in a project, *building* (also referred to as *making*) an application from the compiled code, and testing the resulting application. To perform all those tasks by making a single menu selection, choose **Run** from the Project menu.

As CodeWarrior compiles the files listed in the **MyFirstMacApp.µ** project, you'll see the numbers in the Code and Data columns of the project window get updated. A short time after that, the program will run—a window will open and randomly placed colored circles will start appearing in the window (see Figure 2.6). Click the mouse button to end the program. When the window closes, you'll find yourself back in the CodeWarrior IDE.

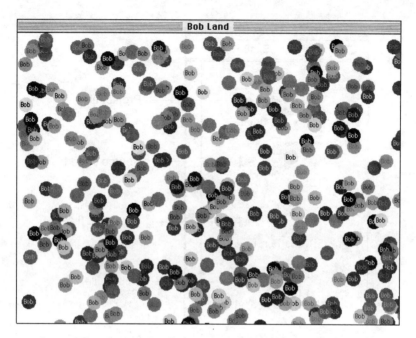

Figure 2.6   *The result of running the **MyFirstMacApp.µ** project.*

If you choose **Run** a second time, the window that displays the colored circles will appear sooner than it did the first time you selected **Run**. That's because all the project's files have already been compiled. CodeWarrior knows there's no need to recompile them, so the application starts up right away. Only if you make changes to the project (such as editing the source code in the **SillyBalls.c** file, adding resources to the **SillyBalls.rsrc** file, or adding or removing a library file) will CodeWarrior recompile any or all of the files.

After successfully running the program that CodeWarrior builds from the project, return to the desktop (you needn't quit the CodeWarrior IDE to do this). There, in the folder you designated when you created the project, you'll find a new folder with the same name as your project—less the **.µ** extension. For my **MyFirstMacApp.µ** project the folder is named **MyFirstMacApp**. Double-clicking on the folder reveals the files pictured in Figure 2.7.

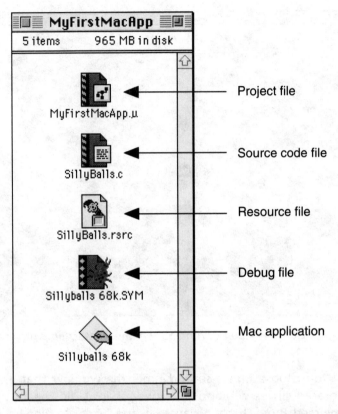

Project file

Source code file

Resource file

Debug file

Mac application

Figure 2.7 *The contents of the folder CodeWarrior creates to hold the files that are a part of the **MyFirstMacApp.μ** project.*

In the folder you'll find the project file, along with any source code files and resource files that are a part of that project. The folder, as well as these files, were created when the project was created. Additionally, you'll find a SYM file and an application file—these files were created when **Run** was selected from the Project menu. The SYM file holds information needed by the Metrowerks debugger.

It's important to note that the application that gets built from a project is a stand-alone program—in order to execute, it *doesn't* need any of the other files that appear in the folder. As a test, you can copy just the program (named **Sillyballs 68k** in this example) to any other Mac and double-click to run it.

What's Missing?

When I compiled and ran the code in the **MyFirstMacApp.µ** project, I didn't really create my own program—I simply compiled and ran sample code provided by Metrowerks. To turn this project into one I can truly call my own, I need to create my own source code file and add it to the project in place of the **SillyBalls.c** source code file. I then need to do the same with the project's resources—create a resource file using a resource editor such as ResEdit or Resorcerer and then add that file to the project in place of the **SillyBalls.rsrc** resource file.

The **MyFirstMacApp.µ** project includes the library files that hold all the compiled code that may be necessary for your source code to compile and link properly. The project also includes a single source code file and a single resource file. Every time you create a new project using the project stationery for a 68K Mac application, a new project window holding these same files will appear.

As you've just seen, you can compile and run a new project "as is." Of course, unless you really want the SillyBalls program, there's really no point in doing this. So, why does CodeWarrior include a source code file and resource file in a new project when, as it turns out, you'll need to use your own source code and resources? The **SillyBalls.c** and **SillyBalls.rsrc** files are included in each new project simply as placeholders of sorts. For example, the **SillyBalls.c** source code file reminds you that you need to add a source code file of your own to the project, and provides a group (named Sources) in which you can place your own file. The **SillyBalls.rsrc** file serves a similar purpose. In the future, when you create new projects you'll add your own files and remove these placeholders. You'll see an example of how to do that in the next section.

Creating an Application

In this section I'll walk through the process of developing a Macintosh application. While I will cover each step, I'll breeze though the first several steps—the ones that result in a new project window appearing on the screen. Those initial steps were just described in this chapter's introduction to projects, so a summary will suffice.

Because this chapter is about working with projects, I'll use only very simple examples to make sure the emphasis is on the process of working with projects rather than on explaining source code listings. Later in this book you'll encounter more examples that result in applications that do more than the ones developed in this chapter.

In the previous section you specified that your new project be set up as one that generates a 68K application. Additionally, without any input from you CodeWarrior used the C language plugin compiler with the project. In this section you'll see how to set up a project as one that instead generates a PowerPC-only application. You'll also see how to tell CodeWarrior which compiler to use. While this example will also be written in C, your understanding of how CodeWarrior selects a compiler will be applicable later in this chapter when you write a simple program using C++.

NOTE

If you're interested in building fat applications (a topic mentioned in Chapter 1), read the previous section and this section. While I don't create a fat application here, the techniques described in this chapter are directly applicable to the process for doing so. Chapter 5 completes the picture by thoroughly describing the fat application and how to develop one.

In keeping with this chapter's theme of developing only simple applications, the example program that I'll develop in this section does only one thing: it displays an empty window on the screen. There are no menus, and the window can't be moved. A click of the mouse button ends the program.

Creating a New Project

You've already taken a walk through the process of creating a new project, so here I'll only present a summary of the steps you'll take to do this:

1. Select **New Project** from the Project menu—the New Project dialog box appears.

2. Click on the appropriate project stationery for the type of application you're to develop.

3. Leaving the **Create Folder** checkbox checked, click the **OK** button to dismiss the New Project dialog box—the Name Project dialog box appears.

4. Enter a name for the project (end the name in **.µ** to go along with the generally accepted CodeWarrior project naming style).

5. CodeWarrior will create a new folder in which to hold your project and project-related files. Use the pop-up menu at the top of the dialog box to move to the folder in which you want this new folder placed.

6. Click the **Save** button to dismiss the Name Project dialog box— a new project window appears.

The project I'm creating will be a PowerPC-only project, so I'll select the **Basic Toolbox PPC** project stationery. I'll then give the project the very appropriate name **EmptyWindowPPC.µ**. When I do that, the resulting project window will look like the one shown in Figure 2.8.

File	Code	Data	
▽ 🖋 **Sources**	0	0	• ▾
🖋 SillyBalls.c	0	0	• ▸
▽ 🖋 **Resources**	0	0	▾
🖋 **SillyBalls.rsrc**	n/a	n/a	▸
▽ 🖋 **Mac Libraries**	0	0	▾
🖋 **InterfaceLib**	0	0	▸
🖋 **MathLib**	0	0	▸
🖋 **MWCRuntime.Lib**	0	0	▸
▽ 🖋 **ANSI Libraries**	0	0	▾
🖋 **ANSI C++.PPC.Lib**	0	0	▸
🖋 **ANSI C.PPC.Lib**	0	0	▸
🖋 **SIOUX.PPC.Lib**	0	0	▸
8 file(s)	0	0	

Figure 2.8   *The new project window that results from creating a new project based on the Basic Toolbox PPC project stationery.*

NOTE Merely looking at a project's icon or the icon of the resulting application won't tell you if a project or program is 68K or PowerPC-only. Starting here with the **EmptyWindowPPC.µ** project, and throughout the remainder of this book, I'll include "68K" or "PPC" in the names of projects and programs so that you'll readily know the difference. While not a requirement, doing so will be of benefit, especially when creating a fat application (as you'll see in Chapter 5).

Since the project stationery selected for the **EmptyWindowPPC.µ** project differs from the project stationery used with the **MyFirstMacApp.µ** project, you'd expect CodeWarrior to set up the projects differently. If you compare Figure 2.8 to Figure 2.3, you'll see that this is in fact the case—the libraries included in the projects differ.

Creating and Adding a Resource File to a Project

In Figure 2.8 you'll notice that once again CodeWarrior has added the **SillyBalls.c** and **SillyBalls.rsrc** files to the project. In developing your own program, you'll be replacing these two files with files of your own creation. I'll start by creating a new resource file and adding it to the project. The order in which you replace the two placeholder files is, however, unimportant.

The CodeWarrior integrated development environment includes just about everything you need to create a Macintosh application—except a resource editor. A resource editor isn't a simple utility—it's a complicated piece of software. There are already two good ones available—Apple's ResEdit and Mathemaesthetics' Resorcerer—so it wouldn't have made sense for Metrowerks to expend the time and effort creating another one. Instead, CodeWarrior lets you use the resource editor of your choice to create a resource file for your project's use.

Launching Your Resource Editor

CodeWarrior offers a neat trick in that you can double-click on the name of a resource file in a CodeWarrior project window and, if you haven't already launched your resource editor, CodeWarrior will start it up for you. If you use Apple's ResEdit (a free version of which comes on this book's CD-ROM and with any version of CodeWarrior from Metrowerks) as your resource editor, you're all set—double-clicking on the **SillyBalls.rsrc** file name in the project window will launch ResEdit and open the **SillyBalls.rsrc** file. When that happens, you'll see the window pictured in Figure 2.9.

Figure 2.9 *Launching ResEdit from the **EmptyWindowPPC.µ** project results in the **SillyBalls.rsrc** file opening.*

This trick doesn't just work for this one resource file in this particular project. Any time you double-click on the name of a resource file in any project window, ResEdit will be launched (if it isn't already running) and the clicked-on file will open.

If your preference in resource editors is the more sophisticated Mathemaesthetics' Resorcerer editor (a demo of which is provided on this book's CD-ROM and with each edition of CodeWarrior), you'll need to perform a one-time-only task to set up things so that CodeWarrior always launches Resorcerer rather than ResEdit. Refer to Appendix E to see how to set up your CodeWarrior environment so that it launches Resorcerer rather than ResEdit. After you follow the steps in Appendix E, double-clicking on the **SillyBalls.rsrc** file name in the project window will result in Resorcerer being launched and the **SillyBalls.rsrc** file being opened. You'll then see the resource file pictured in Figure 2.10.

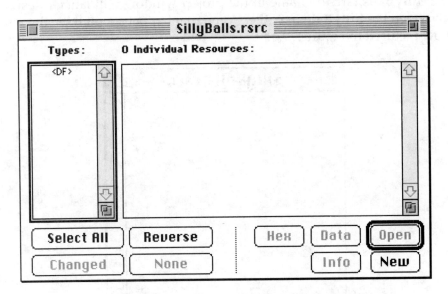

Figure 2.10 *Launching Resorcerer from the **EmptyWindowPPC.µ** project results in the **SillyBalls.rsrc** file opening.*

CREATING A RESOURCE FILE

Almost all Macintosh programs that have a graphical user interface are based on a project that includes a resource file. The resource file for the EmptyWindowPPC program is named **EmptyWindow.rsrc** and holds just a single resource, a WIND with an ID of 128.

 If you aren't familiar with resources, you can get an overview of this important topic by reading Appendix D.

N O T E

Double-click on the **SillyBalls.rsrc** file name in the **EmptyWindowPPC.µ** project if you haven't yet. That launches your resource editor and opens the **SillyBalls.rsrc** file. You won't be interested in this file—recall that its primary purpose is to serve as a placeholder in the project window. Instead, you'll be creating a new resource file that you'll add to the project in place of **SillyBalls.rsrc**.

While you can give a resource file any name you'd like, it makes sense to pick a name that shows that the file will be a part of a particular project. Ending the file name with an extension of **.rsrc** is a common practice, so for the resource file I'll soon be creating I'll use the name **EmptyWindow.rsrc**.

 I intentionally didn't include "PPC" in the resource file name because, unlike a project file, there is no 68K or PowerPC resource file. This same resource file can be used in the PowerPC-only CodeWarrior project that I've already created, and it could be used in a 68K version of the project.

If you use ResEdit as your resource editor, read on. If you prefer Resorcerer, skip the "Creating the Resource File with ResEdit" section and jump ahead a few pages to the "Creating the Resource File with Resorcerer" section.

Creating the Resource File with ResEdit

In ResEdit, select **New** from the File menu to create a new resource file. You'll see the New File dialog box pictured in Figure 2.11. Use its pop-up menu to move to the folder that holds the **EmptyWindowPPC.µ** project. Type in a name, then click the **New** button.

To add a WIND resource to the empty file, select **Create New Resource** from the Resource menu. Scroll to the **WIND** item in the list in the Select New Type dialog box that appears. Click once on **WIND**, then click the **OK** button, as shown in Figure 2.12.

For the EmptyWindowPPC program, it's not important what type or size window you use. Enter the values shown in Figure 2.13 or use window dimensions of your own choosing. When you're done, select **Save** from the File menu and return to the CodeWarrior IDE.

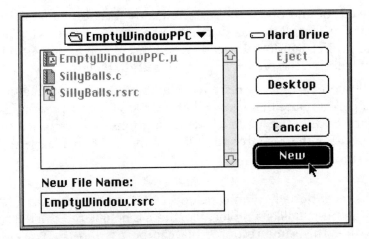

Figure 2.11 *Creating a new resource file in ResEdit.*

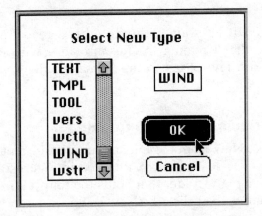

Figure 2.12 *Creating a WIND resource in ResEdit.*

Creating the Resource File with Resorcerer

If you use Resorcerer rather than ResEdit, go ahead and launch that resource editor now. Select **New File** from the File menu to open a new, empty resource file. Select **Save File As** from the File menu to enter a name for the file. In the dialog box that opens, use the pop-up menu to move to the folder that holds the **EmptyWindowPPC.μ** project. Type in a name, then click **Save** (see Figure 2.14).

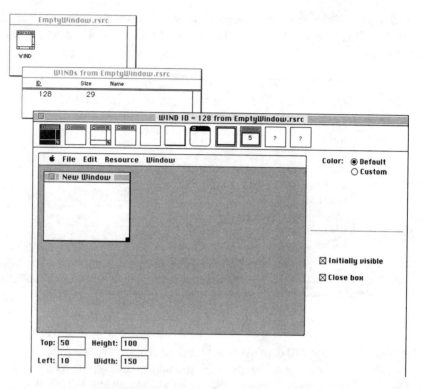

Figure 2.13 *The WIND editor in ResEdit.*

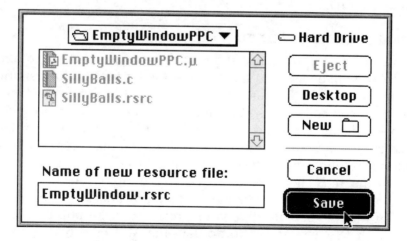

Figure 2.14 *Naming and saving a new resource file in Resorcerer.*

To add the WIND resource, select **New Resource** from the Resource menu. Scroll down to the **WIND** item in the dialog box and click once on the item. Then click the **Create** button, as shown in Figure 2.15.

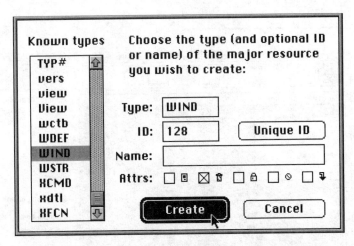

Figure 2.15   Creating a WIND resource in Resorcerer.

Select **Set Window Info** from the Window menu to change the size or type of the new window. Figure 2.16 shows the dimensions I've entered for the window—you're free to use your own values. When you're finished, select **Save File** from the File menu and return to the CodeWarrior IDE.

Adding a Resource File to a Project

A project only recognizes the files that are named in the File column of the project window, so you need to add the **EmptyWindow.rsrc** file to the project now. To do that, click on the name of the group that you want the resource file to end up in. Again, files can be placed in any group—CodeWarrior will compile and build the program regardless of which groups files are in. But for organizational purposes, you'll want to add the resource file to the group named Resources. Click on the that group name, then choose **Add Files** from the Project menu. If the pop-up menu at the top of the dialog box that appears isn't displaying the name of the folder that holds your project, use the pop-up menu to move to that folder. After you do that, the Add Files dialog box will look like the one pictured in Figure 2.17.

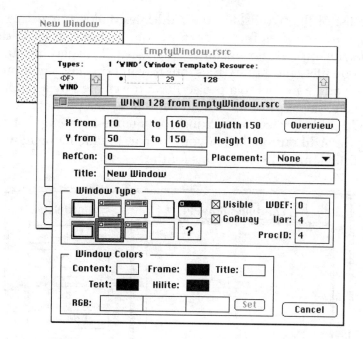

Figure 2.16   *The WIND editor in Resorcerer.*

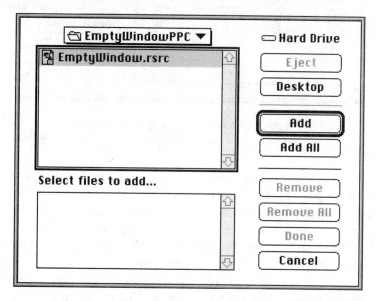

Figure 2.17   *Using the Add Files dialog box to add the resource file to a project.*

The top list of the two lists in the Add Files dialog box uses a filter to display only the files in the current folder that can be added to a CodeWarrior project. For instance, the list will display resource files, source code files, and library files, but it won't display, say, a project file (you can't add a project to a project) or a file created by a graphics program (again, this type of file would be useless to a project). You select a file to add to the project by clicking on its name in the top list and then clicking the **Add** button. When you do that, the file name moves to the bottom list. Figure 2.18 shows this for the resource file.

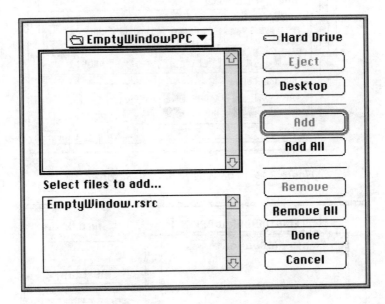

Figure 2.18   *After selecting a file to add,*
the file's name moves to the bottom list.

While this example only displays a single file, the top list is of course capable of displaying any number of files. And you can use the Add Files dialog box to add any number of files to a project. For instance, a project for what will be a large application may consist of several source code files and one or more resource files. When all the files that are to be added to the project appear in the bottom list, you click the **Done** button to dismiss the dialog box. Here I'm adding just the **EmptyWindow.rsrc** file to the project, so I'm ready to click the **Done** button now. When I do that, the project window shows that the resource file has been added to the Resources group, as pictured in Figure 2.19.

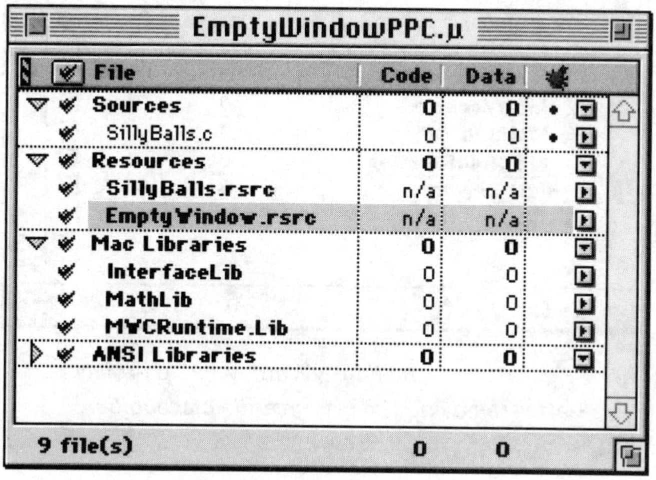

File	Code	Data	
▽ ✓ **Sources**	0	0	• ▽
✓ SillyBalls.c	0	0	• ▶
▽ ✓ **Resources**	0	0	▽
✓ **SillyBalls.rsrc**	n/a	n/a	▶
✓ **Empty Window.rsrc**	n/a	n/a	▶
▽ ✓ **Mac Libraries**	0	0	▽
✓ **InterfaceLib**	0	0	▶
✓ **MathLib**	0	0	▶
✓ **MWCRuntime.Lib**	0	0	▶
▷ ✓ **ANSI Libraries**	0	0	▽

EmptyWindowPPC.µ

9 file(s)   0   0

Figure 2.19   *The EmptyWindowPPC.µ project after adding the resource file.*

REMOVING THE RESOURCE FILE PLACEHOLDER FROM A PROJECT

The **SillyBalls.rsrc** file is simply a placeholder file. Now that the "real" resource file that the project will be using has been added, it's time to remove this placeholder. To do that, click once on the **SillyBalls.rsrc** file name and then select **Remove Files** from the Project menu. The **SillyBalls.rsrc** file name will then be removed from the list, as shown in Figure 2.20.

NOTE

If you remove the only file in any group, that group disappears from the project window. To avoid having the Resources group disappear, remove the placeholder after adding your new resource file. If you do inadvertently remove a group, consult the electronic *IDE User's Guide* documentation that comes with CodeWarrior to learn how to add a new group to a project.

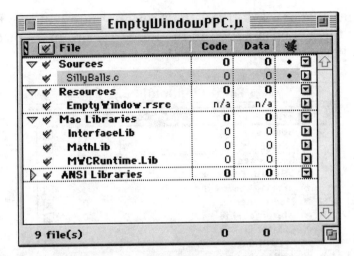

*Figure 2.20   The EmptyWindowPPC.µ project
after removing the resource file placeholder.*

Creating and Adding a Source Code File to a Project

A Mac program consists of resources and code, so the development of a Mac program typically requires that you create and add a resource file and create and add a source code file to a project. You're resource file is in place, so you're half-way there. Now it's time to work on the project's source code.

CREATING A SOURCE CODE FILE

You create a new source code file and add and edit source code in that file from within the CodeWarrior environment. To create a new, untitled, empty source code file, select **New** from the File menu. When you do that, an empty window will appear.

Next, select **Save** from the File menu to name the source code file and save it to disk. Typically, you'll give the source code file the same name as the project—without the 68K or PPC. For a C language program, give the source file a **.c** extension, as I've done in Figure 2.21.

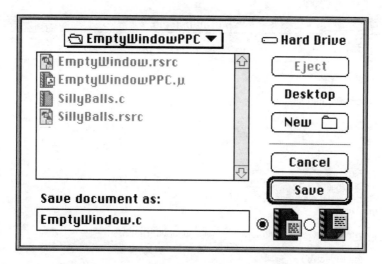

Figure 2.21 *Naming a new source code file.*

In the newly saved, empty window, type in the source code shown in Figure 2.22. Don't forget that C is a case-sensitive language. Type in the code exactly as it appears in Figure 2.22, without altering any of the capitalization. And don't forget to place a semicolon after every line in the body of the main() function—with the exception of the while statement line. After you've typed in the code, again select **Save** from the File menu to save your work.

NOTE If you haven't programmed in C, read Appendix A. That appendix provides a crash course in C—just enough to get you up and running. If you haven't programmed the Mac before, also read Appendices C and D—they provide similar summaries of the Macintosh Toolbox and resources. Figure 2.23 serves to provide a quick introduction to C programming on the Mac.

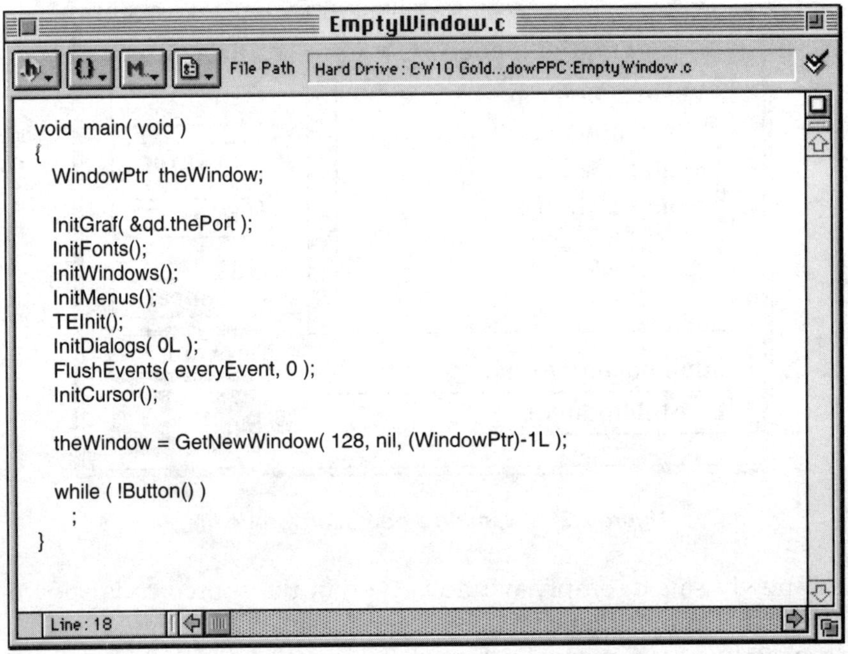

EmptyWindow.c
File Path
Hard Drive : CW10 Gold...dowPPC :Empty Window.c
void main(void)
{
WindowPtr theWindow;
InitGraf(&qd.thePort);
InitFonts();
InitWindows();
InitMenus();
TEInit();
InitDialogs(0L);
FlushEvents(everyEvent, 0);
InitCursor();
theWindow = GetNewWindow(128, nil, (WindowPtr)-1L);
while (!Button())
;
}
Line : 18

Figure 2.22 *The source code listing for the EmptyWindowPPC program.*

Every Macintosh C program must have a main() function
Declare a variable to reference a window
Initialize the Toolbox
Open a new window based on data from a WIND resource
Loop until user clicks mouse button
Do nothing
EmptyWindow.c
File Path
Hard Drive : CW10 Gold...dowPPC :Empty Window.c
void main(void)
{
WindowPtr theWindow;
InitGraf(&qd.thePort);
InitFonts();
InitWindows();
InitMenus();
TEInit();
InitDialogs(0L);
FlushEvents(everyEvent, 0);
InitCursor();
theWindow = GetNewWindow(128, nil, (WindowPtr)-1L);
while (!Button())
;
}
Line : 1

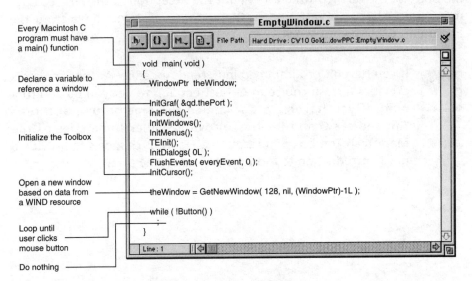

Figure 2.23 *What the source code in the **EmptyWindow.c** file does.*

Adding a Source Code File to a Project

Creating a new source code file and saving it doesn't make that file a part of your open project. To do that, you can select **Add File** from the project window, just as you did to add the **EmptyWindow.rsrc** resource file to the project. To add a single source code file to a project, however, CodeWarrior provides a shortcut that you'll probably want to take. First, click on the Sources group name in the project window so that the source code file gets added to the appropriate group. Then click once anywhere on the source code window to make it active (that is, to make it the frontmost window on the screen). Now choose **Add Window** from the Project menu. CodeWarrior then adds the **EmptyWindow.c** file to the project, saving you a trip to the Add Files dialog box. Figure 2.24 shows the results.

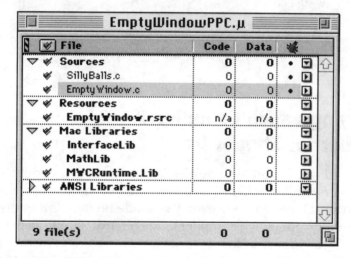

Figure 2.24   The EmptyWindowPPC.μ project after adding the source code file.

Removing the Source Code File Placeholder from a Project

As you did for the resource file placeholder, remove the source code file placeholder from the project window. Do this by clicking once on the **SillyBalls.c** file name in the project window and then selecting **Remove Files** from the Project menu. The **SillyBalls.c** file name will then be removed from the list. Figure 2.25 provides a final look at the **EmptyWindowPPC.μ** project window.

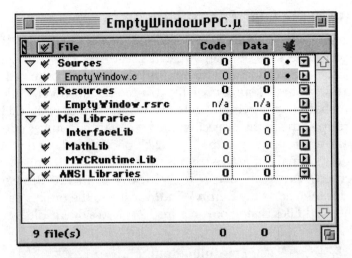

Figure 2.25   *The EmptyWindowPPC.μ project after removing the source code file placeholder.*

Specifying which Compiler CodeWarrior Should Use

As discussed in Chapter 1, CodeWarrior comes with a variety of different compilers (called *plugins*) that can each be used from within the CodeWarrior IDE. So far, however, I've made no mention of the way in which you indicate which compiler CodeWarrior should use. I've been able to skirt this issue because of the power of CodeWarrior to select the appropriate compiler to use for a project without any intervention from you.

How CodeWarrior Chooses a Compiler

The extension you give your project's source code file specifies which compiler plugin CodeWarrior should use to compile the file. For example, a file with a name that ends with an extension of **.p** or **.pas** is assumed to be a file that holds Pascal source code and will be compiled by one of the two CodeWarrior Pascal compilers (there's a separate Pascal compiler for 68K projects and PowerPC projects).

A file whose name ends with an extension of **.c**, on the other hand, will be considered a file that holds C language source code and will be compiled using one of the two CodeWarrior C/C++ compilers (again, there's a separate one for 68K projects and PPC projects). A file name that ends with an extension of either **.c++**, **.cc**, **.cp**, or **.cp** is considered a C++ language source code file and will be compiled by the same CodeWarrior C/C++ compiler used to compile a C language source code file. Because of the similarities between the C and C++ languages, this one compiler can compile both C and C++ files. Even though one C/C++ compiler is capable of compiling both C and C++ source code files, you still need to end your source code file's name with an extension that tells CodeWarrior whether the file holds C or C++ code. The compiler will base compilation decisions on this information.

In all the preceding cases, the selection of the compiler to use is automatic—you simply create a project using the project stationery of interest, add a source code file, and let CodeWarrior select the correct compiler for your project.

MATCHING FILE NAME EXTENSIONS TO COMPILERS

If you'd like to see which file name extensions are used for any language, select **Project Settings** from the Edit menu. In the Project Settings dialog box, click on the word **Target** in the scrolling list that appears to the left (see Figure 2.26). When you do that, the Target panel will fill the right side of the dialog box. You can scroll through the list in this panel to see which extension is paired with which compiler. If you click on a row in this list, more information will be displayed in the bottom of the panel.

Compiling and Running the Project's Code

Now it's time to compile the code and build an application. And, if you're working on a Mac that has a PowerPC CPU, you can also test your new application. If you're working on a Mac that has a CPU from the 680x0 family of chips, you'll be able to create the program, but you won't be able to run it—not from your computer anyway. If you have access to a Power Mac, you can copy the application to a floppy and test it by running it from the Power Mac.

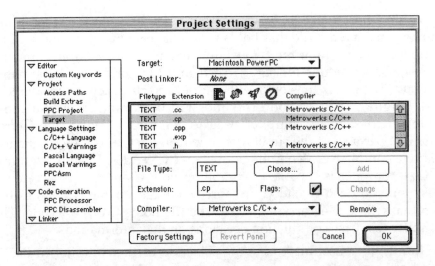

Figure 2.26 *The Target panel in the Project Settings dialog box.*

If you're using a Power Mac, select **Run** from the Project menu to compile the project's code, build an application, and give the new application a test run. If all went as planned, a small, empty window will appear on the screen. Click on the window to end the program and return to the CodeWarrior IDE.

If you're using a 68K-based Mac, the **Run** menu item in the Project menu will be dim. That's because you can't run a PowerPC-only application (the type you're about to create) on a 680x0 CPU. Instead, choose **Make** from the Project menu. This menu item compiles and links a project's code, building the PowerPC-only application in the process. The **Make** command doesn't, however, attempt to give the resulting application a test run.

If during compilation a window titled Errors & Warnings opens and displays an error message (or messages), look over your source code to make sure it matches the listing shown in Figure 2.22. Chapter 4 provides details on how to track down errors in your source code.

Supplying a New Name for the Application

When you create a new project that uses the Basic Toolbox PPC project stationery, CodeWarrior will always use **SillyBalls PPC** as the name for the stand-alone application that results from selecting **Run** from the Project menu. You'll of course want to supply this application with a name of your own choosing.

RENAMING THE APPLICATION FROM THE DESKTOP

You can give your program a new name by simply editing the file's name from the desktop, but this method has a drawback. Every time you work on this project (as in, say, editing its source code to add a new feature to the program) and then select **Run** from the Project menu, CodeWarrior builds a new version of the stand-alone application. The new version will once again be given the name **SillyBalls PPC**.

RESETTING THE NAME TO USE FOR THE APPLICATION

Rather than renaming one copy of an application, you should alter the name that CodeWarrior assigns the application it builds from your project. You can do this from within the Project Settings dialog box.

To see this dialog box, select **Project Settings** from the Edit menu. The Project Settings dialog box, shown in Figure 2.27, is a single dialog box that is capable of displaying a number of different panels of options. On the left side of the dialog box is a scrolling list. To the right of the list is the remainder of the dialog box, which Metrowerks refers to as a *panel*. Clicking on an item in the list changes the various settings displayed to the right of the list. That is, each item in the list displays its own panel of options.

To change the name CodeWarrior gives to applications it builds from the current project, click on the **PPC Project** item in the list. When you do that, the panel will change to include a number of settings that apply to the current project, including an edit box that lets you type in your choice of a name for the application. In Figure 2.27 you can see that the default name CodeWarrior uses is **SillyBalls PPC**. To change the name, highlight the contents of this edit box and type in the new name. The name I'll use is **EmptyWindowPPC**.

Click on an item in this list...   ...to change the settings displayed in this entire area

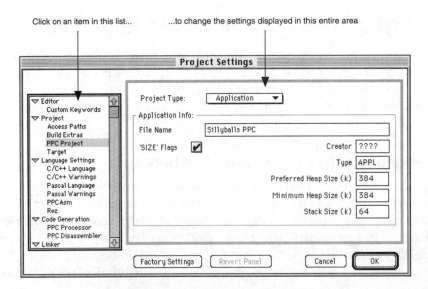

Figure 2.27 *Using the PPC Project panel of the Project Settings*
dialog box to change the name of an application.

NOTE Other settings in this panel, including the heap sizes, will be discussed in Chapter 11.

After typing in the new name, click the **OK** button. When you do that, CodeWarrior will respond by posting an alert that tells you the change you made requires that the project be linked again. The change you made concerns the name of the application CodeWarrior builds. Here CodeWarrior is telling you that the change of name won't affect the existing version of the **SillyBalls PPC** application that is on your hard drive. Instead, you need to again choose **Run** from the Project menu so that CodeWarrior can make a new stand-alone application with the newly entered name. Go ahead and click the **OK** button in this alert, and then choose **Run** to build a new version of the program.

NOTE If you're satisfied that your code is working as expected, you can choose **Make** rather than **Run** from the Project menu. Both menu items build a new stand-alone application. The **Make** command won't, however, take that application for a test run.

Examining the Results of Your Efforts

The **EmptyWindowPPC** folder that CodeWarrior created for you now holds a variety of files—Figure 2.28 shows the contents of this folder.

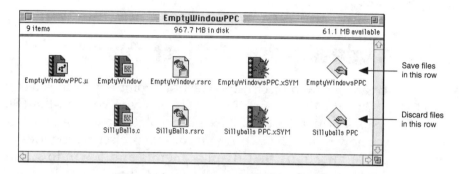

Figure 2.28 *The contents of the folder CodeWarrior creates to hold the files that are a part of the **EmptyWindowPPC.µ** project.*

Because I chose **Run** from CodeWarrior's Project menu twice (once before specifying a new application name in the Project Settings dialog box and once after), there's two debug files and two application files in the folder. Additionally, the two **SillyBalls** files that were initially a part of the project (courtesy of the project stationery) are present in the folder. As shown in Figure 2.28, none of these four files is needed—I can clean up things a lot by trashing them.

If you choose **Project Settings** just after you create a new project, you can set the application's name before you ever build a program. If you do that, the only extra unneeded files you'll have in your project folder are the ones named **SillyBalls.c** and **SillyBalls.rsrc**.

Earlier in this chapter you read a little about debug files. Recall that when a 68K project is compiled, CodeWarrior generates a SYM file that is used if you debug your program. Here you see that for a PowerPC project CodeWarrior creates a comparable debug file—one that ends with an **.xSYM** extension rather than a **.SYM** extension.

Congratulations—at this point you've successfully used CodeWarrior to create both a 68K and a PowerPC-only program! Now, to get a better understanding of the libraries that were added to the two projects, as well as a look at how header files are used in a project, continue on to the next section.

Other CodeWarrior Project Types

When you create a new project, CodeWarrior prompts you to select a project stationery for the project. In this chapter you've used the 68k and PPC versions of the Basic Toolbox project stationeries. In this section you'll see how to use the two ANSI Console project stationeries to create simple applications that display menus and a window, but require no resources and no calls to Toolbox functions.

So far the examples in this chapter have all been in C. If you're a C++ programmer, you can create projects that compile C++ code just as easily as you can create C projects. Here you'll see how.

Console Projects

If you're writing a simple program that doesn't need a Mac interface, you might consider using the standard CodeWarrior console window. If you use the console, your program will include the menus and the window pictured in Figure 2.29, without your having to write any supporting code.

To make use of the console, you need to include one of two *SIOUX* (*Standard Input Output User eXchange*) libraries in your project. As usual, CodeWarrior project stationery can be used to take care of determining which libraries should be included in the project; select either the **ANSI Console 68k** or **ANSI Console PPC** project stationery. Figure 2.30 shows the project window for a project set up using the ANSI Console 68k project stationery.

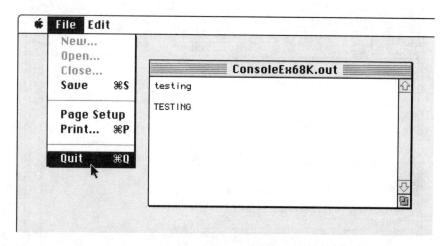

Figure 2.29 The output of the ConsoleEx68k program.

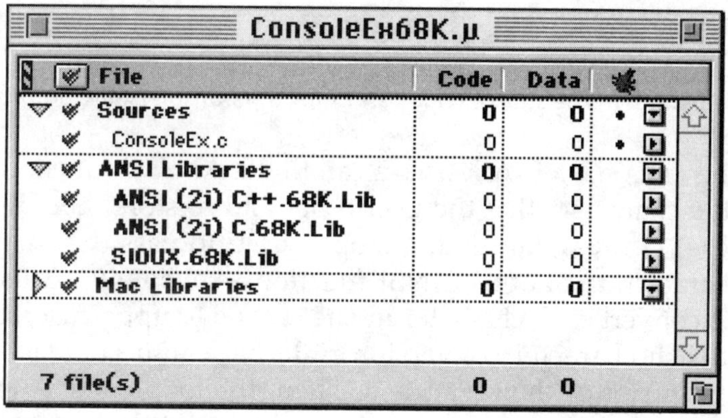

Figure 2.30 The project window of the **ConsoleEx68k.μ** project.

In the project pictured in Figure 2.31 I've replaced the **HelloWorld.c** source code file that CodeWarrior uses as a placeholder with my own source code file—**ConsoleEx.c**. Figure 2.31 shows the complete source code listing found in this file.

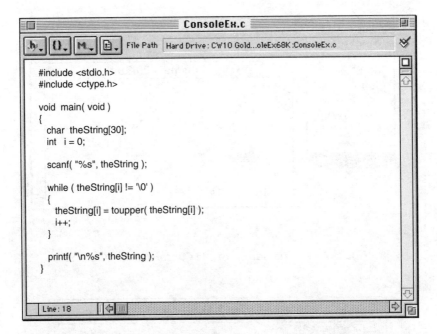

Figure 2.31 The source code listing for the ConsoleEx68k program.

The listing of ConsoleEx68k uses a call to the ANSI C function scanf() to read the characters that the user types and to store them in an array named theString. After that, a loop is used to pass the array, character-by-character, to another ANSI function—toupper(). This function is used to convert each character in theString to uppercase, storing the result of each character conversion right back into theString. When the last character of the string is reached, the loop ends. A call to one more ANSI C function, printf(), is used to print the newly converted string below the original string that was typed by the user.

Because the ANSI function toupper() is used, the ANSI header file **ctype.h** is included—that's the file that defines the function prototype for this function. And because the program calls the ANSI function printf(), the ANSI header file **stdio.h** is also included—it's the header file that defines what printf() looks like. CodeWarrior gets the project set up correctly through the use of project stationery, but it is up to you to use the necessary #include directives. To see the program's output, refer back to Figure 2.29.

C++ Projects

Earlier in this chapter you read that to let CodeWarrior know that your project uses C++ source code rather than C source code you should end the name of your source code file with an extension of **.cp** or **.c++**. Figure 2.32 shows a project that includes such a file. The **ObjectEx68k.µ** project is one that was created with the Basic Toolbox 68k stationery, but it could just as easily have been done using the Basic Toolbox PPC stationery.

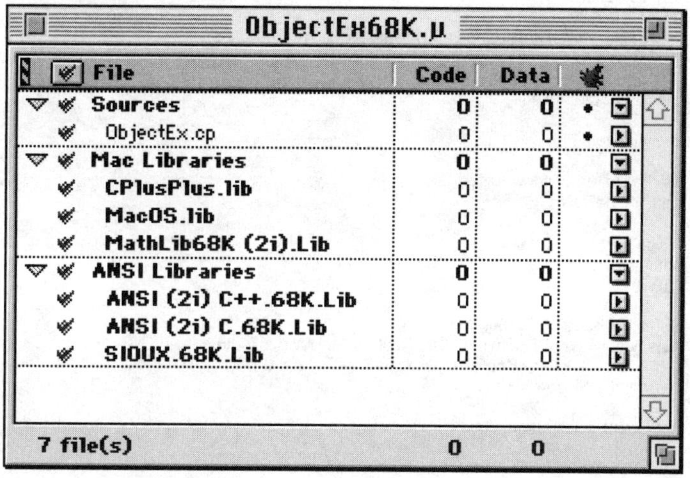

File	Code	Data	🍁
▽ ✔ **Sources**	0	0	• ▾
✔ ObjectEx.cp	0	0	• ▸
▽ ✔ **Mac Libraries**	0	0	▾
✔ CPlusPlus.lib	0	0	▸
✔ MacOS.lib	0	0	▸
✔ MathLib68K (2i).Lib	0	0	▸
▽ ✔ **ANSI Libraries**	0	0	▾
✔ ANSI (2i) C++.68K.Lib	0	0	▸
✔ ANSI (2i) C.68K.Lib	0	0	▸
✔ SIOUX.68K.Lib	0	0	▸

ObjectEx68K.µ — 7 file(s) — 0 0

Figure 2.32 *The project window of the **ObjectEx68k.µ** project.*

Figure 2.33 shows the complete source code listing for the ObjectEx68k program. When you select **Run** from the Project menu you'll see a single window like the one pictured in Figure 2.34.

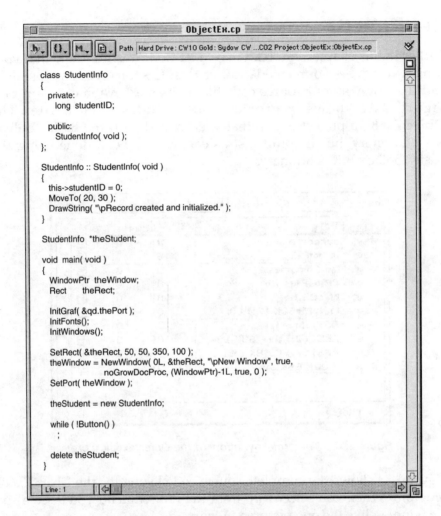

```
class StudentInfo
{
  private:
    long studentID;

  public:
    StudentInfo( void );
};

StudentInfo :: StudentInfo( void )
{
  this->studentID = 0;
  MoveTo( 20, 30 );
  DrawString( "\pRecord created and initialized." );
}

StudentInfo *theStudent;

void main( void )
{
  WindowPtr  theWindow;
  Rect       theRect;

  InitGraf( &qd.thePort );
  InitFonts();
  InitWindows();

  SetRect( &theRect, 50, 50, 350, 100 );
  theWindow = NewWindow( 0L, &theRect, "\pNew Window", true,
              noGrowDocProc, (WindowPtr)-1L, true, 0 );
  SetPort( theWindow );

  theStudent = new StudentInfo;

  while ( !Button() )
    ;

  delete theStudent;
}
```

Figure 2.33   *The source code listing for the ObjectEx68k program.*

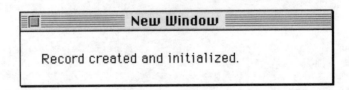

Figure 2.34   *The result of running the ObjectEx68k program.*

As you know, most Macintosh projects include a resource file, but the **ObjectEx68k.µ** project doesn't. This project can do without such a file because the ObjectEx68k application uses only one graphical user interface element—a window. In other examples you've seen that a window can be defined by a WIND resource. A window is a GUI element that can also be defined without the use of a resource. The **ObjectEx68k.c** source code calls the Toolbox function NewWindow() rather than GetNewWindow(). Whereas GetNewWindow() receives a window description via a WIND resource, NewWindow() receives this same information from the parameters that are passed to it. Same task, different means of accomplishing it.

If you don't know C++, don't be alarmed—no knowledge of C++ is expected for much of this book. The ObjectEx68k program is the only object-oriented programming example in these first few chapters. It's included for the benefit of those of you who do know C++ so that you can see how easy CodeWarrior makes it for you to work in a language other than C.

Chapter Summary

When using CodeWarrior to develop a Macintosh program, you always start by launching the CodeWarrior IDE and creating a new project. A project is a file that holds a list of all of the other files that, when compiled and linked, result in a stand-alone Macintosh program.

When you create a new project you specify a project stationery based on the target you've selected for your soon-to-be-developed program. The target is the type of machine your program will run on. The project stationery is responsible for ensuring that the proper library files get added to your new project. After that, you'll create a resource file that holds the resources your program will use and a source code file that holds your program's source code. When these files have been added to the project, you'll compile and link the files to create a stand-alone Mac application. You can perform both these steps, as well as give the resulting application a test run, by choosing a single menu item—the **Run** item from the Project menu.

Most editions of CodeWarrior come with a single CodeWarrior IDE program and a variety of compilers. When you write your source code, you can do so in a variety of languages, including C, C++, Java, and Pascal. The CodeWarrior ID knows which compiler to use to compile your source code based on the extension you use in the name of the source code file.

Chapter 3

Understanding the Universal Interface Files

The Universal Interface header files are a collection of more than 100 header files that define the function prototypes for each of the thousands of Toolbox routines. Toolbox function prototypes are of great importance—without a function prototype, the CodeWarrior compilers will not compile source code that includes calls to Toolbox functions.

For very small projects, a knowledge of what the Universal Interface header files are and how they work might not be necessary. But as your project grows, the chances of successfully compiling that project get smaller. That's because the more source code you write, the more Toolbox routines you call and the greater the likelihood that one of your function calls won't match the prototype listed in the header file. To add to the problem, Apple periodically modifies some of the Universal Interface header files. If you attempt to compile source code that was written using an older set of the Universal Interface header files, you'll find many incompatibilities that result in compiler errors.

In this chapter you'll learn all about the Universal Interface header files. You'll see that a knowledge of how these files work will eliminate countless compile-time headaches.

Header Files and the Toolbox

A CodeWarrior project consists of one or more source code files, one or more library files, and usually a resource file. And while you won't see the names of any header files in a project window, a project also uses several Universal Interface header files. The purpose of the Universal Interface header files is to let the compiler your project uses understand the format of the thousands of functions that make up the Macintosh Toolbox. In this section you'll see the relationship between the Universal Interface header files and the functions that make up the Toolbox.

Apple's Universal Interface Header Files

The Toolbox is a collection of Apple-written functions that have been compiled and placed in the ROM chips and the system software of each Macintosh. In order to include a call to one of the Toolbox routines, your source code must provide the compiler with the calling convention of the routine. That is, the compiler needs a function prototype for a called Toolbox function so that it can verify that the parameters and function return type you supply are correct. The Apple Universal Interface header files contain function prototypes for each Toolbox function. Figure 3.1 shows the names of a few of the more than 100 Universal Header files, along with the folder hierarchy in which Metrowerks stores these files.

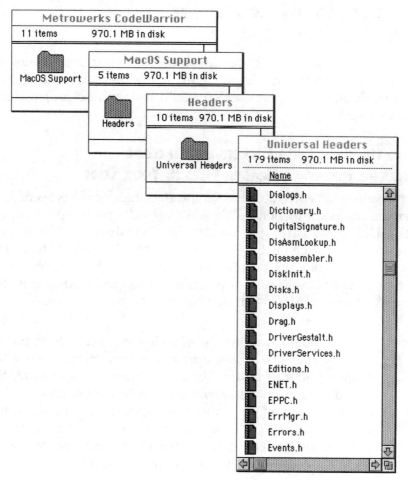

Figure 3.1   *Some of the many Apple Universal Interface header files.*

Apple occasionally adds new functions to the thousands of existing Toolbox routines. Additionally, as changes to the operating system are made, Apple may change the type of a parameter or the return type of some Toolbox functions. When that happens, these header files need to be updated. That's one reason there are different versions of the

Universal Interface header files. As of this writing, these Apple files have a version number of 2.1.

Universal Interface Header Files and Your Code

The Universal Interface header files don't do your project any good unless your project is made aware of them. There are two means of accomplishing this, both of which you'll use, and both of which are described next.

USING THE #include DIRECTIVE TO INCLUDE UNIVERSAL INTERFACE HEADER FILES IN YOUR CODE

As an example of when a Universal Interface header file is needed, consider the Toolbox function GetNewWindow(). Its prototype is supplied in the Universal Interface header file **Windows.h**. If one of my CodeWarrior projects includes a call to GetNewWindow(), then it will also need to include the **Windows.h** header file. That enables my project to use the GetNewWindow() function whose compiled code is stored in the ROM of each Macintosh (see Figure 3.2).

NOTE

Not all Toolbox routines have their compiled code in the ROM chips of your Mac. Some exist in the **System** file in your Mac's **System** folder. If all the Toolbox routines were in ROM, there would be no way Apple could get new Toolbox routines into your machine, short of having you replace the ROM chips. With the scheme now used, a new version of the operating system can include new Toolbox routines that will be available to any Mac, provided Mac owners upgrade to the new Mac OS.

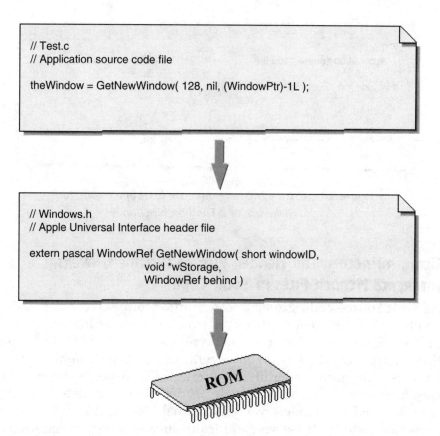

```
// Test.c
// Application source code file

theWindow = GetNewWindow( 128, nil, (WindowPtr)-1L );
```

```
// Windows.h
// Apple Universal Interface header file

extern pascal WindowRef GetNewWindow( short windowID,
                                      void *wStorage,
                                      WindowRef behind )
```

ROM

Figure 3.2   *The function prototype of a Toolbox function, necessary to use the Toolbox function located in ROM, is found in a Universal Interface header file.*

None of the more than 100 Universal Interface header files are a part of your project unless you specifically include them. One way to do that is to use the #include compiler directive. Figure 3.3 shows the **Windows.h** Universal Interface header file being included in a source code file.

```
// Test.c
// Application source code file

#include <Windows.h>

...
...
theWindow = GetNewWindow( 128, nil, (WindowPtr)-1L );
```

Figure 3.3 *Use a #include directive in a source code file to make use of a Toolbox function.*

USING A PRECOMPILED HEADER FILE TO INCLUDE UNIVERSAL INTERFACE HEADER FILES IN YOUR CODE

As your source code grows and you make more and more calls to Toolbox routines, keeping track of which Universal Interface header files are needed in a project would become a difficult chore. To simplify things, Metrowerks has taken several of the most commonly used Universal Interface header files and from them created a single *precompiled header file*. By using this single header file in a project, you eliminate the need to include several individual Universal Interface header files—the code for these several files is already a part of the precompiled header file.

There's a second advantage to using a precompiled header file as opposed to bringing the same header files into your project using #include directives—it saves time. When you compile a source code file that uses a #include directive to bring in a header file, as in the listing of Figure 3.3, the code in that header file needs to be compiled along with the code you've written for that source code file. If your project includes a large number of calls to Toolbox functions and requires, say, 30 of the Universal Interface header files, the compiler has to compile each of these files the first time you select **Run** from the Project menu. This compilation takes a little time. Including a single precompiled file that holds the already-compiled code from numerous Universal Interface header files doesn't involve any compile time—the code has, obviously, been compiled by Metrowerks and distributed to you in that form.

NOTE The compiling of each header file only needs to take place once. Subsequent selections of the **Run** command only results in the compiling of source code files that have been changed since the previous compilation. Since you won't be making changes to Apple's header files, the compiler wouldn't need to recompile them.

Metrowerks supplies you with a variety of precompiled header files—there are different versions for different project types. For example, a 68K project written in C uses the precompiled header file named **MacHeaders68K**, while a PowerPC project written in C++ uses the **MacHeadersPPC++** precompiled header file. Fortunately, Metrowerks has devised a simple scheme that allows you to forget all about which version of the MacHeaders files your project needs.

As a part of your CodeWarrior package, Metrowerks supplies a file named **MacHeaders.h**. This small file does nothing more than determine what type of project is currently being compiled (such as 68K or PPC, C or C++) and selects the appropriate MacHeaders file based on the project type. Figure 3.4 shows the listing of the **MacHeaders.h** file.

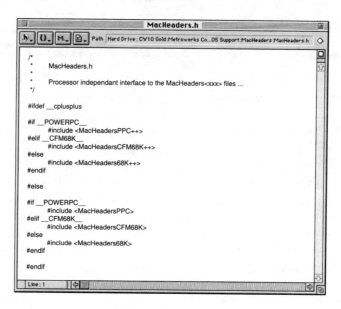

Figure 3.4 The **MacHeaders.h** file is used to determine which precompiled header file should be used by a particular project.

When you create a new project, by default, CodeWarrior uses the **MacHeaders.h** file as the project's *prefix* file. A prefix file is a single file that you tell CodeWarrior to include in your project. While in most cases you'll want to stick with **MacHeaders.h** as your project's prefix file, the C/C++ Language panel of the Project Settings dialog box does allow you to specify a different file, as shown in Figure 3.5.

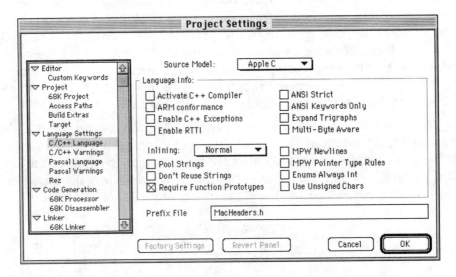

Figure 3.5   *The appropriate MacHeaders file is added to a project by naming the **MacHeaders.h** file as the project's prefix file.*

Once a MacHeaders file is included in a project, you'll seldom have to use #include directives for any of the Universal Interface header files. For example, each version of MacHeaders includes the compiled code for several Universal Interface header files, including **Windows.h**. That means your own source code won't have to use **Windows.h** in a #include directive, even if your source code calls GetNewWindow(), which is a Toolbox routine whose function prototype is defined in **Windows.h**. In Figure 3.6 you can see that I've commented out the inclusion of **Windows.h** in the **Test.c** source code listing I first presented in Figure 3.3.

```
// Test.c
// Application source code file

// #include <Windows.h>  Don't need this #include if
//                       a MacHeaders file is used as
//                       the prefix file

...
...
theWindow = GetNewWindow( 128, nil, (WindowPtr)-1L );
```

Figure 3.6 *With MacHeaders included in a project, few of
the Universal Interface header files will need to be included in source code.*

MacHeaders and the #include Directive

With a MacHeaders header file as your project's prefix file, you might
think that there'd be no need to use the #include directive for any
Universal Interface header file. Recall, however, that the MacHeaders files
contain the compiled code of the most commonly used header files—*not*
the code of *all* the header files. For example, **QuickDraw.h**, **Windows.h**,
Dialogs.h, **Events.h**, and **Resources.h** are a few of the header files that are
a part of MacHeaders, but the **Sound.h** header file is not. On occasion,
you'll make a call to a less commonly used Toolbox function that doesn't
have its prototype listed in MacHeaders, such as the SndPlay() Toolbox
routine, which is defined in **Sound.h**. In a project such as this, you must
use a MacHeaders file *and* a #include <Sound.h> directive. Another
example is a program that takes advantage of the Mac's speech capabilities. Such a program will use Toolbox routines that have prototypes listed
in the **Speech.h** header file. Like **Sound.h**, **Speech.h** isn't one of the
Universal Interface header files that were compiled into a MacHeaders
file. So, again like **Sound.h**, you'll need to explicitly bring **Speech.h** into
your source code by using a #include directive.

This chapter's SpeakPhrase program, discussed in just a bit, is an
example of a project that uses both a MacHeaders file (MacHeaders68K,
incidentally) and a #include directive to incorporate a Universal
Header file (**Speech.h**) into a project.

The SpeakPhrase Example Program

In this section we'll take a look at a very simple Mac program that exists for the purpose of demonstrating the last section's discussion about including Universal Interface header files in a CodeWarrior project. The SpeakPhrase program uses the Toolbox function SpeakString() to emit speech from the user's Macintosh speakers and the Toolbox function SpeechBusy() to make sure that the program doesn't "move on" before all of the words get spoken. Running SpeakPhrase produces no on-screen effects—you won't see any menus or windows (and thus the project needs no resource file). Instead, the program starts up, speaks a single sentence, and then quits.

NOTE To hear the SpeakPhrase program talk you'll need to make sure that the Speech Manager extension is in your **System** folder. Also make sure that the speaker volume of your Mac is set higher than 0.

The SetVolume Project

If you're using a 680x0-based Macintosh, create a new project using the Basic Toolbox 68k project stationery. If you're working on a Power Mac, you can use either the Basic Toolbox 68k or the Basic Toolbox PPC project stationery to create the SpeakPhrase project. You might, however, decide to go with the Basic Toolbox 68k stationery so that your efforts match the figures in this section. If you do that, and you name the project **SpeakPhrase68K.µ**, your project window will look like the one pictured in Figure 3.7.

Now, select **New** from the File menu to open a new, empty text file. Type in the source code shown in Figure 3.8. We'll take a look at the code a little later. For now, just select **Save** from the File menu and name the source code file. As you saw earlier, you'll typically give the source code file the same name as the project, without the 68K or PPC. Now that you've seen that the same source code file can be used in both a 68K and PPC project, it should make sense that the source code file name doesn't include a reference to either compiler. Because this is a C language program, I've added a **.c** extension to the file name, as shown in the title bar of the source code window pictured in Figure 3.8.

SpeakPhrase68K.µ
File
Code
Data
Sources
SpeakPhrase.c
Mac Libraries
CPlusPlus.lib
MacOS.lib
MathLib68K (2i).Lib
ANSI Libraries
ANSI (2i) C++.68K.Lib
ANSI (2i) C.68K.Lib
SIOUX.68K.Lib
7 file(s)

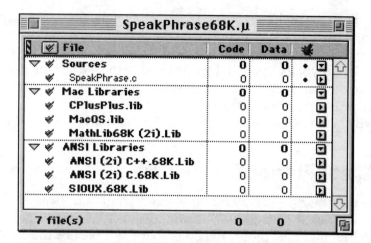

Figure 3.7 *The SpeakPhrase68K project window.*

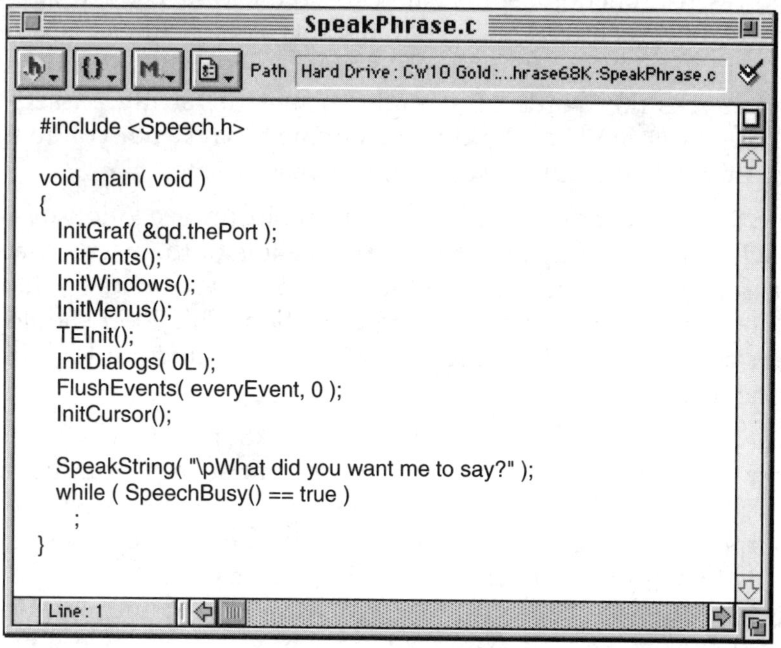

SpeakPhrase.c
Path
Hard Drive : CW10 Gold :...hrase68K :SpeakPhrase.c
#include <Speech.h>
void main(void)
{
InitGraf(&qd.thePort);
InitFonts();
InitWindows();
InitMenus();
TEInit();
InitDialogs(0L);
FlushEvents(everyEvent, 0);
InitCursor();
SpeakString("\pWhat did you want me to say?");
while (SpeechBusy() == true)
;
}
Line : 1

Figure 3.8 *The source code file for the SpeakPhrase project.*

Add the file to the project by first clicking once on the Sources group name in the project window, clicking once on the SpeakPhrase source code window to activate it, and then selecting **Add Window** from the Project menu. Remove the **SillyBalls.c** placeholder by clicking the file's name once in the project window and then selecting **Remove Files** from the Project menu. The project uses no resources, so you won't need a resource file. Remove the **SillyBalls.rsrc** placeholder as you did the **SillyBalls.c** placeholder.

The SpeakPhrase Source Code

The **SpeakPhrase.c** source code file has a single application-defined function, the main() function. To distinguish between functions written by a programmer and those functions that are a part of the Macintosh Toolbox, you'll see the phrase "application-defined function" used throughout this book.

The main() function begins with calls to the same eight Toolbox initialization routines found in most Mac source code listings. Next comes a call to the Toolbox function SpeakString(). As its name implies, this routine speaks the words of a single string—the string passed to it. Here I use the string "What did you want me to say?" but you're free to replace this text with any string of your own choosing.

The SpeakString() function doesn't hold up execution of a program while speech is emitted from the speakers of the user's Mac. For that reason, you must follow a call to SpeakString() with a "do nothing" loop that prevents further code execution. This loop should execute for as long as it takes the SpeakString() function to complete speaking its words.

When you write a program that calls SpeakString() you'll have no idea how long a pause is necessary to prevent speech from being cut off. So you'll leave it up to another Toolbox routine to determine that. The purpose of SpeechBusy() is to determine whether or not speech is currently taking place. If it is, the routine returns true. If no speech is taking place, SpeechBusy() returns false. By including a call to SpeechBusy() in a while statement, your program repeatedly invokes this routine until it returns a value of false. Once it *does* return false, the program moves on past the "do nothing" body of the loop (the semicolon), and the program ends.

The prototype for the SpeakString() and SpeechBusy() functions can be found in the **Speech.h** Universal Interface header file. The **Speech.h** file is *not* one of the many Universal Interface header files that gets compiled into a single MacHeaders file—and that's worth noting. This means that the **Speech.h** file needs to be included in the source code file. The SpeakPhrase program does that with the following line:

```
#include <Speech.h>
```

By including this line in **SpeakPhrase.c**, the SpeakPhrase program has access to any of the routines whose prototypes appear in the **Speech.h** file.

NOTE   If you'd like to know more about including speech in your own Mac programs, as well as other Macintosh multimedia programming topics such as sound playing and recording, offscreen drawing, animation, and QuickTime movie playing, consider picking up a copy of the M&T Books text *Graphics and Sound Programming Techniques for the Mac*.

Verifying that Header Files and Libraries are Necessary

In this section I'll do a couple of simple experiments with the MacHeaders precompiled header file and the Universal Header files to see the effect of omitting one or more of these elements from a project. In doing so, you should gain a better understanding of the purpose of these header files.

If the **SpeakPhrase68K.μ** project is not open, open it now by double-clicking on its icon in the desktop or by selecting it from the dialog box that appears when you choose **Open** from the File menu of the CodeWarrior IDE. Then open the **SpeakPhrase.c** source code file by double-clicking on its name in the **SpeakPhrase68K.μ** project window. Comment out the #include <Speech.h> line, then select **Run** from the Project menu to recompile and run the program. As you may have guessed, commenting out the inclusion of the **Speech.h** file prevents the project from successfully compiling. Before looking at Figure 3.9, try to guess what kind of error message might be displayed in the Errors & Warnings window.

Errors occur if Speech.h isn't included in the source code file

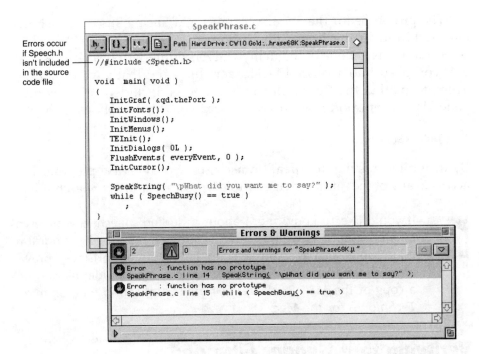

*Figure 3.9   Without the **Speech.h** header file, the compiler doesn't know what parameters should be passed to the* SpeakString() *and* SpeechBusy() *routines.*

N O T E   The Errors & Warnings dialog box can be collapsed to show only error messages or expanded to show both a list of error messages and the area in the source code file that holds an offending line. Click on the small **arrow** icon at the very bottom left of the dialog box to collapse or expand it.

The compiler informs you that without the **Speech.h** file, it can't determine what the Toolbox functions SpeakString() and SpeechBusy() should look like. Notice, however, that the compiler *didn't* report any errors regarding the other Toolbox function calls—the several initialization routines that make up the rest of the program. Why? They're commonly used routines, and the Universal Interface header files that define their prototypes are all a part of the MacHeaders precompiled header files.

To further investigate how Universal Interface header files are included in your project, open the Project Settings dialog box from the Edit menu. Then click on the **C/C++ Language** item in the list on the left of the dialog box. Next, cut or backspace over the string that's in the Prefix File edit box—**MacHeaders.h**. After clicking the **OK** button, again select **Run** from the Project menu. After you do that, you'll see a message window much like the one shown in Figure 3.10. Notice that without a MacHeaders precompiled header file in the project, the compiler doesn't recognize what *any* of the Toolbox routines look like.

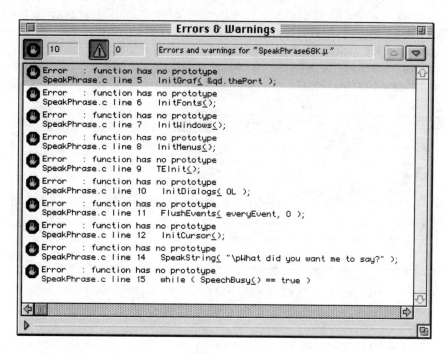

Figure 3.10 *Without MacHeaders and the **Sound.h** file, the compiler doesn't recognize any of the Toolbox functions.*

To return the **SpeakPhrase68K.μ** project to its initial state, remove the comment slashes from the front of the #include <Speech.h> line at the top of the **SpeakPhrase.c** source code file. Then select **Project Settings** from the Edit menu and again click on the **C/C++ Language** item in the dialog box list. Restore the Prefix File edit box contents by typing in the **MacHeaders.h** file name (refer way back to Figure 3.5 if you need to see a screen snapshot of how this dialog box should look). Click the **OK** button, then choose **Run** from the Project menu to recompile the project's code and test the program.

Errors and the Universal Header Files

Consider the following scenario. You buy a programming book, which of course includes example source code. Perhaps the author and publisher were even kind enough to provide project files and source code files on a CD-ROM. You attempt to compile the example code, following the book's instructions word-for-word. But instead of seeing a Mac program come to life on your screen, you end up looking at an Errors & Warnings window like the one pictured in Figure 3.11.

Figure 3.11 *The CodeWarrior Errors & Warnings window displaying a compiler error message.*

If you've attempted to compile even just a couple of examples that someone else has written, whether obtained from a disk in a book or downloaded from an online service library, you've no doubt encountered the above *cannot convert* error or the equally dreaded *type mismatch* error. If the example code came from a programming book, you of course immediately cursed the author's so-called competence and vowed to never purchase another book with his or her name on the cover. But wait! This incompatible code might not be the fault of the author; Apple and the Universal Interface header files may be to blame.

Fortunately, this chapter has so far supplied you with a thorough understanding of just what these header files are used for and why they are so important. Armed with that knowledge, you'll be able to get many projects up and running—projects that you had given up on and left dormant on your hard drive.

The PlaySound Project

The type mismatch errors can of course occur in your own projects as well as in those you've obtained from other sources. The reason I mentioned projects obtained from other sources is that there is a likelihood that a project you've received with a book or downloaded from an online service may be several months, or even a few years, old. In the time between the project's creation and your obtaining it, one important thing may have changed—Apple's Universal Interface header files. If these files have changed, the chances of the project successfully compiling are greatly diminished.

For the sake of this discussion on type mismatch errors, let's assume you're trying to compile a multimedia project that was included in a Macintosh programming book you've purchased. The book's disk also included a compiled, executable version of the program, which is named PlaySound68K. When double-clicked, the program plays the sound of a telephone ringing, then quits. No, it may not exactly be a multimedia showcase, but at least it does more than simply write "Hello, World!" to a window! Figure 3.12 shows what the CodeWarrior project window looks like for the **PlaySound68K.µ** project.

Like any CodeWarrior project, this one includes a number of libraries and a source code file. Like most projects, it also includes a resource file. To view the contents of the resource file, double-click on the file name in the project window. As mentioned in Chapter 2, doing that launches the resource editor that created the file (such as ResEdit or Resorcerer) and then opens that file within the resource editor. Figure 3.13 shows the **PlaySound.rsrc** file, as viewed from ResEdit.

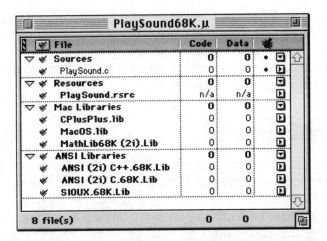

Figure 3.12 *The project window for the PlaySound68K program.*

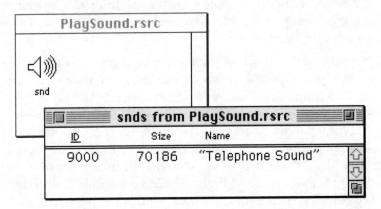

Figure 3.13 *The resource file for the PlaySound68K project.*

From Figure 3.13 you can see that the **PlaySound.rsrc** file holds a single resource: a snd resource with an ID of 9000. This resource holds the digitized recording of a telephone ringing and will be used by the code in the **PlaySound.c** source code file.

For obscure reasons that I won't delve into, snd resources that are not distributed by Apple should have IDs greater than 8191.

N O T E

Another fact about snd resources: All resource types have a four-character name, such as WIND, DLOG, and ALRT. The fourth character in the snd resource name is a blank space.

For the curious, a snd resource usually starts as a sound in a sound file. For a project to make use of it, it needs to be copied to the project's resource file. Figure 3.14 shows that the **Play Sound** folder found on this book's CD includes a sound file named **Telephone Sound**.

Figure 3.14   *A sound can be stored in a file,*
as is the telephone ringing sound here.

Where do sound files come from? Well, buying this book just got you one: the **Telephone Sound** file. That doesn't help if you're looking for more than a ringing telephone, though. Other sources of sounds are:

- Online services such as America Online and CompuServe have libraries of sound files that are yours for the downloading.

- You can buy a CD-ROM of a thousand sounds through a mail-order vendor for about $30.

- You can buy a sound digitizer for less than $200 and use your Mac to digitize your own sounds.

To copy the sound in a sound file, launch your resource editor. Use its **Open** menu item to open the sound file. Then open your project's resource file. Copy the sound from the sound file and paste it into the project's resource file. That's all there is to it. Figure 3.15 summarizes this process.

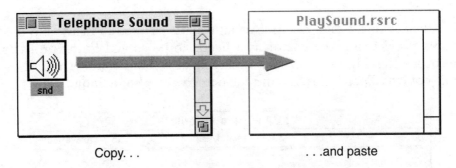

Copy. . .   . . .and paste

Figure 3.15 *A sound in a file is a resource that can be copied and pasted to a project's resource file.*

The Faulty PlaySound Source Code

Figure 3.16 shows the source code for the PlaySound68K program. Like the short programs in Chapter 2, about half of the code of **PlaySound.c** is devoted to Toolbox initializations. The rest of the code is explained in the figure.

Selecting **Run** from the Project menu starts the compile. A short way through, though, the compile will abruptly end and the Errors & Warnings window will open with the error shown in Figure 3.17.

The prototype for SndPlay() is in Sound.h, a file that's not a part of MacHeaders

Use this variable to keep track of a snd resource once it's loaded into memory

Load sound data in snd resource 9000 from disk to memory

Play the sound data that's in the area of memory referenced by the handle theSound

Free the memory that holds the sound data

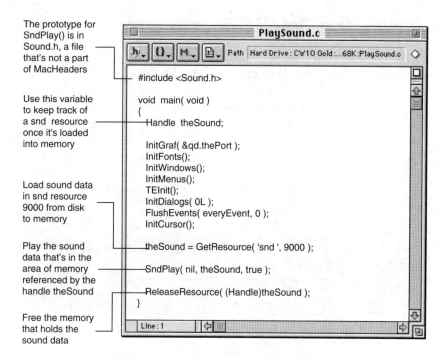

```
#include <Sound.h>

void  main( void )
{
    Handle  theSound;

    InitGraf( &qd.thePort );
    InitFonts();
    InitWindows();
    InitMenus();
    TEInit();
    InitDialogs( 0L );
    FlushEvents( everyEvent, 0 );
    InitCursor();

    theSound = GetResource( 'snd ', 9000 );

    SndPlay( nil, theSound, true );

    ReleaseResource( (Handle)theSound );
}
```

Figure 3.16 *The PlaySound source code has code to load and play a sound resource.*

```
Error   : cannot convert
'char **' to
'struct SndListResource **'
PlaySound.c line 18   SndPlay( nil, theSound, true );
```

Figure 3.17 *The CodeWarrior Errors & Warnings window displaying a cannot convert error.*

Correcting the Type Mismatch Error

The Errors & Warnings window pictured in Figure 3.18 shows that an error occurred while trying to compile the line of code that consists of the call to the Toolbox function SndPlay(). If you look at the call to SndPlay() as displayed in both the top and bottom parts of the Errors & Warnings window you'll notice that CodeWarrior has marked the code that it is having trouble with. Figure 3.18 shows that the compiler generates an error after compiling the second parameter in SndPlay().

An underscore in the top part of the window shows where the error lies

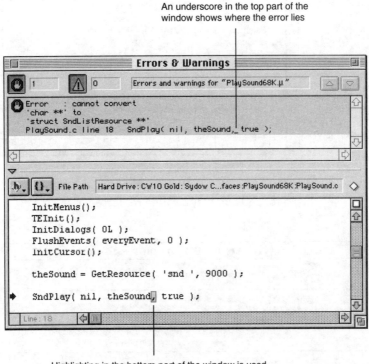

Highlighting in the bottom part of the window is used as a second means of indicating where the error is

Figure 3.18 *The CodeWarrior Errors & Warnings window marks the source code location of an error.*

While you might not be able to infer exactly what is meant by the error message in the top part of the Errors & Warnings window, you can safely guess that there is some problem involving the parameters in the call to SndPlay(). To see if you've used a value of the proper data type for each of the SndPlay() parameters, you'll want to compare the data types you've used with the data types the parameters should have, as defined in the Universal Interface header file that holds the prototype for the SndPlay() routine.

In some instances you'll know, or be able to quickly guess, which Universal Interface header file holds the prototype for a particular function. By its name, you'd guess that the SndPlay() routine is defined in the **Sound.h** file. The fact that **Sound.h** is used in a #include directive lends further support to this guess.

OPENING A UNIVERSAL INTERFACE HEADER FILE

There are two ways to open one of the project's header files. The traditional way to open a file is to select **Open** from the File menu, then use the dialog box pop-up menu to move to the folder that holds the file in question (refer back to Figure 3.1 to see the path of the **Universal Headers** folder). Scroll to the file of interest and open the file as you would any other type of file: either by clicking once on the file's name and then clicking the **Open** button or by simply double-clicking on the file's name in the list.

The second way to open a header file is more convenient, but there's a catch: the method is available to you only if you've successfully compiled a source code file that includes the header file in question. If that's the case, click on the **arrow** icon located to the far right of the row that holds the name of the successfully compiled file. When you do that, a pop-up menu will appear. In that menu is a list of header files included in the source code file. Selecting a file from this list opens that file, regardless of where it's located on disk. Figure 3.19 illustrates.

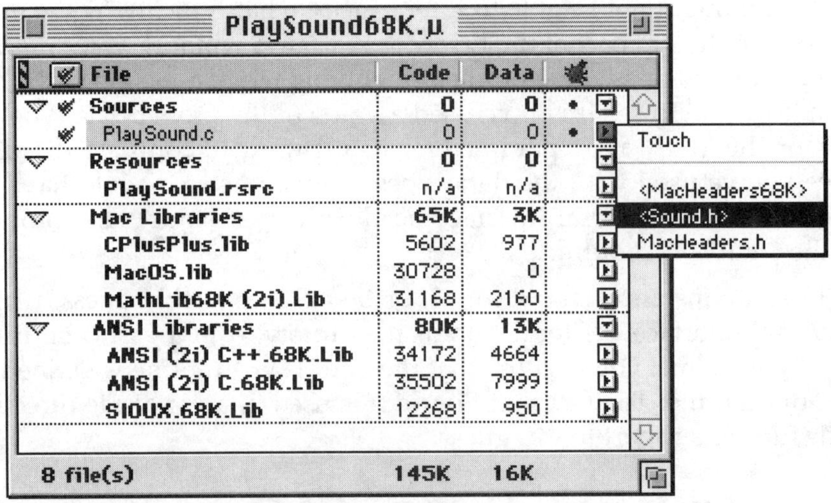

Figure 3.19 *Using the arrow icon to see a list of header files included in a source code file.*

Of what use is this method of opening a header file if it is available only *after* your source code has compiled without error? If your source code file doesn't compile and your project consists of more than one source code file—as many do—then you may still be able to open a header file as described here. You can open the header file from one of the successfully compiled files, provided it includes the same header file.

Another time when this method will work is if you've introduced an error *after* your source code file has already compiled successfully. As you write a program, you'll typically test it at different stages. If the project's source code file compiles just once, any header files named in #include directives in that file will then be available for opening at any time, even if you later attempt to run the project and the compile fails.

FINDING THE FUNCTION PROTOTYPE

With the **Sound.h** header file open, begin the search for the SndPlay() function. Select **Find** from the Search menu. Type **SndPlay** in the Find edit box, then click the **Find** button. In Figure 3.20 you can see I've done exactly that, and the search has taken me right to the function prototype for SndPlay() in the **Sound.h** file.

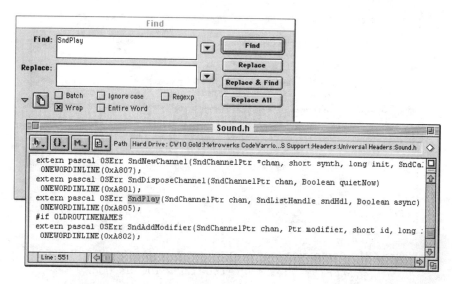

Figure 3.20 *Searching the **Sound.h** Universal Interface header file for the `SndPlay()` function.*

COMPARING PARAMETER DATA TYPES

Once you've found the prototype to the questionable function, note the data types of the parameters that should be used with it. For `SndPlay()`, the three parameter types are `SndChannelPtr`, `SndListHandle`, and `Boolean`. Now compare the parameter types found in your source code function call with the types listed in the header file. Here's how `SndPlay()` is listed in the **Sound.h** file:

```
SndPlay(SndChannelPtr chan, SndListHandle sndHdl, Boolean async)
```

Here's how the function is called from the **PlaySound.c** source code file:

```
SndPlay( nil, theSound, true );
```

In Figure 3.21 I've made a side-by-side comparison of the above. I've taken the liberty of inserting a little white space between parameters to make the comparison clear.

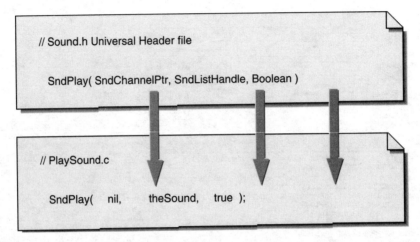

Figure 3.21 *Comparing the Universal Interface header file prototype of*
SndPlay() to a source code call to the function.

Let's examine each of the three parameters. The header file says the first should be of type SndChannelPtr. You may not be familiar with the SndChannelPtr type, but it should make sense to you that a value of nil won't lead to a type mismatch—any type of pointer can be assigned a value of nil.

The header file states that the second parameter to SndPlay() should be a SndListHandle. Looking back at Figure 3.16 you can see that **PlaySound.c** declares theSound to be of type Handle. When the compiler expects to see a particular kind of handle (such as a SndListHandle) and it instead finds a generic handle, it will consider it an error.

Correcting the Error

The solution is simple: cast the generic Handle variable theSound to a SndListHandle. Here's how:

```
SndPlay( nil, (SndListHandle)theSound, true );
```

In C, to cast a variable is to change its type—for the moment. By preceding a variable name with a data type, you're telling the compiler to view the variable as being of this type. In the preceding example, theSound will be considered again a variable of type Handle after the SndPlay() function call.

In the Errors & Warnings window, CodeWarrior gave an indication that the error involved the second parameter to SndPlay(). I'll play it safe and examine the final parameter to make sure that there isn't another discrepancy in data types in the call to SndPlay(). The header file states that the last parameter to SndPlay() should be of type Boolean. The PlaySound68K program passes SndPlay() a value of true as the third parameter, so this parameter won't cause a compile error.

WARNING

Don't make changes to any of the Universal Interface header files to get the function prototypes to match a Toolbox function call in your source code! Instead, change *your* source code to match the prototype. Apple may occasionally make changes to some of the prototypes in these files, but you shouldn't.

Now, go back to the source code file and make the change. After you do that, your **PlaySound.c** file should look like the one shown in Figure 3.22. Next, recompile the project by selecting **Run** from the Project menu. When you do that, you'll be rewarded by the sound of a telephone ringing!

NOTE

As an aside, the error I intentionally introduced in the **PlaySound.c** listing is one you may stumble across in the future. Older versions of the **Sound.h** Universal Interface header file did in fact define the second parameter to SndPlay() to be of type Handle rather than the more specific SndListHandle. So any older sound-playing example source code you encounter may include a call to SndPlay() that results in a compile-time error.

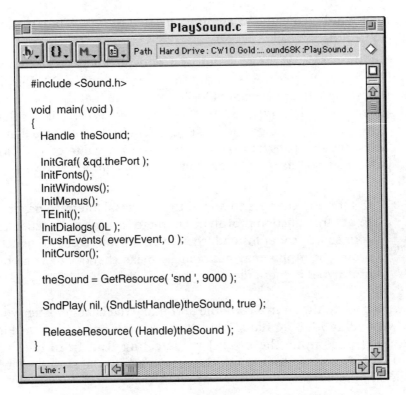

```
PlaySound.c

Path  Hard Drive:CW10 Gold:...ound68K:PlaySound.c

#include <Sound.h>

void  main( void )
{
  Handle  theSound;

  InitGraf( &qd.thePort );
  InitFonts();
  InitWindows();
  InitMenus();
  TEInit();
  InitDialogs( 0L );
  FlushEvents( everyEvent, 0 );
  InitCursor();

  theSound = GetResource( 'snd ', 9000 );

  SndPlay( nil, (SndListHandle)theSound, true );

  ReleaseResource( (Handle)theSound );
}

Line:1
```

Figure 3.22   The PlaySound.c source code file,
after the parameter to SndPlay( ) has been corrected.

Searching the Universal Interface Files

You've just seen how to solve an error for a Toolbox function that has its prototype in a *known* header file. What if an error occurs in a Toolbox function that you *aren't* as familiar with? If the error is in a call to a Toolbox routine, such as TickCount( ), GetDateTime( ), or Delay( ), which header file do you look at? The *cannot convert* error (and its close relative the *type mismatch* error) is a common error. Another error you'll see when making calls to Toolbox functions is the *function call does not match prototype* error. In this section I'll demonstrate a general technique for quickly tracking down the causes of any of these errors.

The Find Dialog Box and Search Sets

One of the features of the CodeWarrior Find dialog box is its ability to search multiple files. This in itself isn't extraordinary; other compilers offer this search option. What is helpful is the fact that you can save any number of files as a *search set* that can be saved and used in any and all projects you create.

If you create a file search set composed of all the Universal Interface header files, correcting compile-time errors that involve Toolbox functions becomes much easier. When the compilation of a project results in an error involving a call to a Toolbox routine, a single click of the mouse button causes a search that quickly results in the opening of the Universal Interface header file that holds the Toolbox function's prototype.

To create the file set, begin by selecting **Find** from the Search menu. When you do, you'll see a dialog box like the one pictured in Figure 3.23. This figure tells only half the story; for the rest, click on the small **arrow** icon, as shown in Figure 3.24. That expands the Find dialog box from its collapsed state. This lower half of the dialog box is used for multiple file searches. If the **Multiple File** icon appears as it does in Figure 3.23, click on it now. The icon will darken and have the appearance of a button that is pressed down, as shown in Figure 3.24. And, the items in the lower half of the dialog box will become enabled. Once enabled, click on the **Others** button, as shown in Figure 3.24.

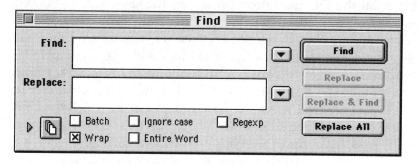

Figure 3.23   *The CodeWarrior Find dialog box, collapsed.*

Click the Triangle icon to expand
the bottom of the Find dialog box

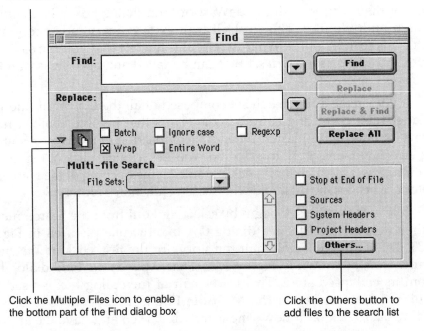

Click the Multiple Files icon to enable
the bottom part of the Find dialog box

Click the Others button to
add files to the search list

Figure 3.24 *The CodeWarrior Find dialog box, expanded—with
files about to be added to the search list.*

Clicking on the **Others** button brings up the same dialog box you see
when you select **Add Files** from the Project menu. Here, however, you
won't be adding files to the project. Instead, you'll be adding files to a
file set, that is, a collection of files used in a multiple-file search. Use the
pop-up menu in this dialog box to move to the folder that holds the
Universal Interface header files, as I've done in Figure 3.25. Refer back to
Figure 3.1 if you need to see the folder hierarchy in which the Universal
Interface header files are located. Once in the **Universal Headers** folder,
click the **Add All** button, then click on the **Done** button.

When you return to the Find dialog box, you'll notice that all the
Universal Interface header files now appear in the Multi-file Search list. It's
now time to save this collection of files to a file set. Click on the **File Sets**
pop-up menu located just above the scrollable list in the Find dialog box and
select the **Save this file set** item from the menu, as I'm doing in Figure 3.26.

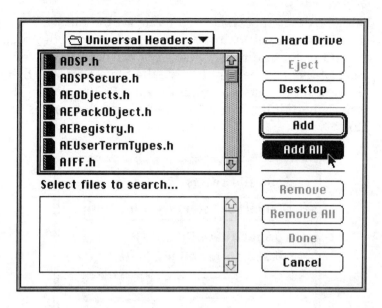

Figure 3.25   *Adding all the Universal Header files to the list of files to search.*

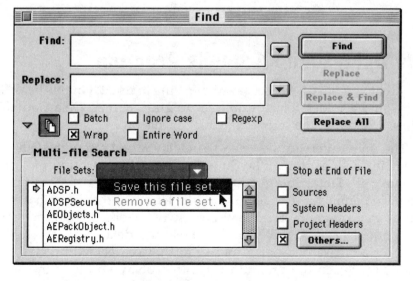

Figure 3.26   *Saving the Universal Interface header files
as a set of files that can be collectively searched.*

In the dialog box that appears, type a name for the file set. This set will be saved to disk and will be usable in any of your CodeWarrior projects, now and in the future. Because CodeWarrior allows you to save any number of file sets, be sure to give the file set a name that distinguishes it from future sets you might create. Before clicking the **Save** button, select the **Global, for all projects** radio button, as shown in Figure 3.27.

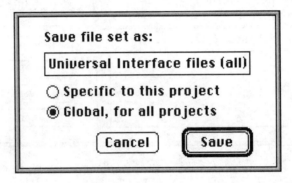

Figure 3.27 *Giving the search set a name and marking the set for use by any CodeWarrior project.*

The DelaySound Example Program

Now that you have a file set saved, it's time to use it. On this book's CD you'll find a folder for an example program named DelaySound68K. Figure 3.28 shows the source code file for this project.

The only difference between the **DelaySound.c** code and the code found in this chapter's **PlaySound.c** file is the addition of a single Toolbox call. **DelaySound.c** includes a call to Delay(). This function accepts a parameter that determines the length of the delay that should appear in a program. The delay is in sixtieths-of-a-second increments, so a parameter of 30 will yield a half-second delay, a parameter of 60 will give a one-second delay, and so forth. I've decided upon a 10-second delay. When the program runs, that delay will give me enough time to leave the room before the program plays the digitized telephone ring, removing suspicion from myself when everyone else in the room looks around to find the telephone.

```
DelaySound.c

Path  Hard Drive : CW10 Gold...Sound68K :DelaySound.c

    #include <Sound.h>

    void  main( void )
    {
      Handle  theSound;

      InitGraf( &qd.thePort );
      InitFonts();
      InitWindows();
      InitMenus();
      TEInit();
      InitDialogs( 0L );
      FlushEvents( everyEvent, 0 );
      InitCursor();

      theSound = GetResource( 'snd ', 9000 );

      Delay( 600 );

      SndPlay( nil, (SndListHandle)theSound, true );

      ReleaseResource( (Handle)theSound );
    }

Line : 1
```

Figure 3.28   *The source code file for the DelaySound program.*

After selecting **Run** from the Project menu, the Errors & Warnings window shown in Figure 3.29 will appear. Notice the error type—it's not a *cannot convert* error this time. Instead, it's a *function call does not match prototype* error.

Like SndPlay(), Delay() is a Toolbox function. Yet the error message isn't the same as the one I experienced when compiling the PlaySound project. That's because in this new example, the number of parameters in the source code function call doesn't match the number of parameters in the header file prototype. This error isn't the result of a change to the Universal Interface headers. Instead, I got my hands on a project that never compiled properly in the first place; the original programmer simply got it wrong!

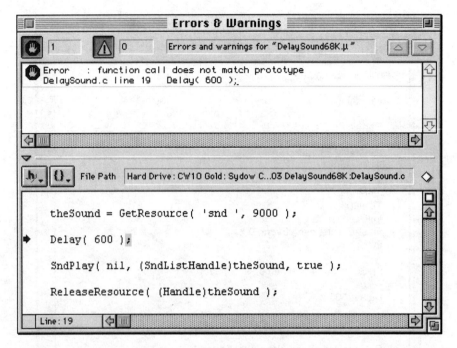

Figure 3.29 *The CodeWarrior message window displaying a compile error.*

Now, here's the dilemma: I don't know which Universal Interface header file holds the prototype for the Delay() function. The source code #include directive lists only the **Sound.h** header file, and I'm guessing that the Delay() function isn't a sound-related Toolbox function. Since there's no other header file given in a #include directive, and Delay() must have a prototype listed *somewhere*, what conclusion can I make? That the header file that holds the prototype for Delay() is one of those that is precompiled into the MacHeaders header file that is included in this project. (Page back to the start of this chapter if you have questions about the MacHeaders files.) Since the MacHeaders files are compiled code, I can't open the one used by this project to find any prototypes. Instead, the solution to my problem is, of course, to use the search set I created a little earlier.

Using the Search Set to Correct an Error

To find the prototype for the Delay() function, begin by selecting **Find** from the Search menu. Enter the phrase to search for in the Find dialog box. Because "delay" is a common computer term, it's bound to appear in at least a couple of the more than 100 Universal Header files, possibly as part of an Apple-defined constant. Because I'm looking for "Delay" as a function, I know an opening parentheses will follow the word; I can narrow the search by including an opening parentheses.

Before starting the search, make sure the bottom half of the Find dialog box is expanded and enabled. If it's not, click the **arrow** icon at the far left of the dialog box, and make sure that the **Multiple Files** icon looks as if it is pressed down. Then click on the **File Sets** pop-up menu and select the file set from the menu, as shown in Figure 3.30.

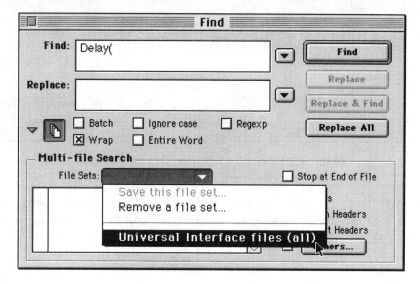

Figure 3.30 *Opening a saved file search set in the Find dialog box.*

Now click on the **Find** button to start the search. As the search takes place, the arrow at the left of the list at the bottom of the Find dialog box will move down the list of file names, always pointing at the file that is currently being searched. When **Delay(** is found, the search ends, the proper header file is opened, and CodeWarrior highlights the found text, as shown in Figure 3.31.

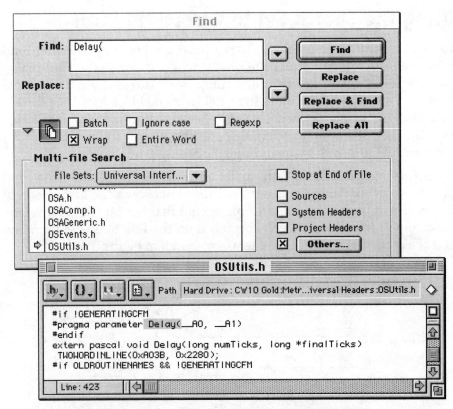

Figure 3.31 *Searching for the* Delay() *function*
in the Universal Interface header files search set.

Like SndPlay(), Delay() is a Toolbox function. Yet the error message isn't the same as the one I experienced when compiling the PlaySound project. That's because in this new example, the number of parameters in the source code function call doesn't match the number of parameters in the header file prototype. This error isn't the result of a change to the Universal Interface headers. Instead, I got my hands on a project that never compiled properly in the first place; the original programmer simply got it wrong!

NOTE

Searching more than 100 files to find a single function prototype? Don't worry about search time; the CodeWarrior search engine is fast. It only takes a few seconds to locate any Toolbox function prototype.

In Figure 3.31 you can see that the search took me to the words I was searching for, but not to the function prototype. I can see that the prototype happens to appear just below the found text, so I'm all set. If the prototype wasn't in sight, I would simply click the **Find Again** button in the Find dialog box and CodeWarrior would continue the search.

Figure 3.31 shows that the prototype for the Delay() function appears in the **OSUtils.h** Universal Header file—a fact that you probably would not have determined on your own. Looking at the prototype, you can see that Delay() requires two parameters, not the one parameter that appears in the incorrect code I'm attempting to compile. The first parameter is the length of the delay, while the second is a pointer to a long variable. When the Delay() function executes, the Toolbox fills this second parameter with the number of *ticks*—the number of sixtieths of a second—since the computer was turned on.

No, you probably couldn't deduce the purpose of the second parameter in Delay() from the Universal Interface header file prototype. But you *would* be able to see the correct number and type of parameters, even if you wouldn't know the purpose of each. For the Delay() function, you could simply declare a long variable and pass it in by reference.

NOTE Recall that in C the * operator in a function prototype means that a pointer is expected as the parameter. That is, rather than passing a variable (which has the effect of passing the value of the variable), you must preface the variable name with the & operator to pass a reference to the variable (that is, to pass the memory address that holds the value in the variable).

Now that I know the correct way to call the Delay() function, I'll make the changes to the **DelaySound.c** code. In Figure 3.32 you can see that I've added a long variable named finalTicks and passed its address to Delay().

Figure 3.32 *The **DelaySound.c** file after the parameters to the* Delay( ) *function have been corrected.*

If you've followed along with me, you can see if the change worked by again selecting **Run** from the Project menu. When it successfully compiles, expect a 10-second delay before the telephone sound plays and the program quits.

Chapter Summary

Apple's Universal Interface header files are a collection of more than 100 header files. Any compiler designed to generate Macintosh executables needs to have access to these header files. Without them, the compiler will not know if the parameters in your calls to Toolbox functions match the parameter list the Toolbox is expecting.

The CodeWarrior IDE allows you to save file search sets. A search set is a group of files that can be collectively searched with a single click of the mouse button. By creating a search set that consists of all the Universal Interface header files, you make it easy to find the function prototype for any one Toolbox function. Once you find a function's prototype, you can compare it to the call you're making in your own source code. That makes correcting function parameter errors fast and simple.

Chapter 4

Debugging and
MW Debug

MW Debug is the name of the CodeWarrior high-level debugger. A high-level debugger like MW Debug allows you to examine variable values as your program runs, without your having to know any assembly language. Because MW Debug allows you to view what's happening internally in your program, but from the comfort of working with the C or C++ source code that you're familiar with, this debugger is also referred to as a source-level debugger.

The MW Debug debugger includes a feature-laden Mac interface that allows you to use menu commands to slowly step through the execution of your program, view the contents of memory, and change the values of variables as your program runs. In this chapter you'll learn the basic terminology of MW Debug and walk through a short debugging session.

Macintosh data structures and their placement in memory are topics that can be explained in a book—but they only become clear when viewed in practice. Because MW Debug displays the address and contents of variables in an easy-to-understand format, the debugger is an excellent tool for understanding Macintosh memory. In this chapter you'll use MW Debug to examine memory to gain a better understanding of some of the common Macintosh data types.

Debugger Basics

During the course of writing a Mac program that has moved beyond the trivial stage in complexity, you're bound to discover a bug. When you make a syntax error (writing code that violates the programming language you're using), the compiler quickly catches it and reports back to you. This type of error doesn't require a debugger to locate—the compiler does that. When you make a semantic error (an error in logic), your code will compile successfully but won't run properly. This is the type of error that requires a debugger.

A *debugger* is a program that runs concurrently with your own program. MW Debug is such an application. It allows you to run your program line-by-line, observing changes in variable values at each step. By keeping a close watch over everything your program does and reporting this information back to you in a manner that's easy to understand, a debugger helps you pinpoint the section of code that isn't working as you intended.

Installing the Debugger

If you used the CodeWarrior Installer that comes on one of the CD-ROMs of every edition of CodeWarrior (including the Lite version supplied with this book), you already have MW Debug on your Mac. The installer software places the debugger in the **Metrowerks CodeWarrior** folder, as shown in Figure 4.1. In order for MW Debug to work properly, it must remain in this folder along with the CodeWarrior IDE application.

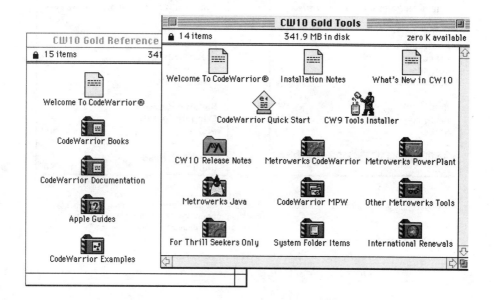

Figure 4.1   *The debugger is a separate application that's stored alongside the CodeWarrior IDE.*

This one version of MW Debug works for each of the many CodeWarrior plugin compilers.

N O T E

Enabling the Debugger for a Project

MW Debug is an application, but you don't have to double-click on it to start it up. Instead, you use this debugger from within the CodeWarrior IDE. To do that, first open the project that holds the code to debug and then select **Enable Debugger** from the Project menu, as shown in the menu pictured in the left of Figure 4.2. Doing that turns debugging on for that one project. It also toggles the text of the last two items in the Project menu, as shown on the right side of Figure 4.2.

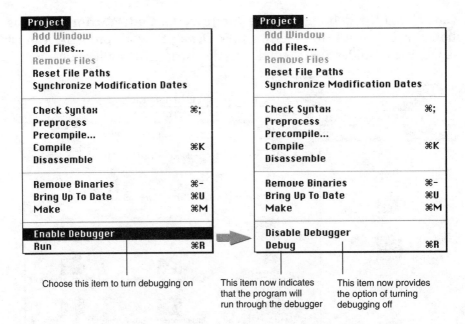

Project	
Add Window	
Add Files...	
Remove Files	
Reset File Paths	
Synchronize Modification Dates	
Check Syntax	⌘;
Preprocess	
Precompile...	
Compile	⌘K
Disassemble	
Remove Binaries	⌘-
Bring Up To Date	⌘U
Make	⌘M
Enable Debugger	
Run	⌘R

Project	
Add Window	
Add Files...	
Remove Files	
Reset File Paths	
Synchronize Modification Dates	
Check Syntax	⌘;
Preprocess	
Precompile...	
Compile	⌘K
Disassemble	
Remove Binaries	⌘-
Bring Up To Date	⌘U
Make	⌘M
Disable Debugger	
Debug	⌘R

Choose this item to turn debugging on

This item now indicates that the program will run through the debugger

This item now provides the option of turning debugging off

Figure 4.2   *To enable debugging for a project, select **Enable Debugger** from the Project menu.*

Now that debugging is on, you no longer simply run a program to test it. Instead, what used to be the **Run** menu item now is a **Debug** menu item. Selecting **Debug** has a similar effect to selecting **Run**—at first. If there is a file or files to compile, CodeWarrior will first do that. It will then build a stand-alone application (provided there were no compile errors that prevent it from finishing the compile and link, of course). After that, things change a bit. Whereas the **Run** menu item gives your program a test run, the **Debug** menu item lets the debugger steal the show. Instead of your program immediately executing, two debugger windows open. From within these windows you control the running of your program, and you observe what happens in memory as your program executes.

MW Debug Windows

With **Enable Debugger** now the second-to-last menu item in the Project menu, the Project menu's **Debug** command will start the debugger rather than your project's application. You'll then start your program from within the debugger. Figure 4.3 shows the two windows you'll see when you select **Debug** from the Project menu.

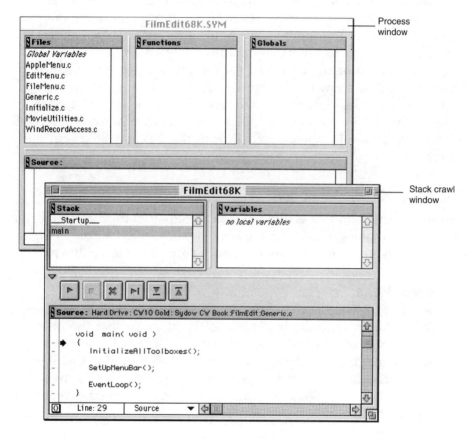

Figure 4.3 *Running the debugger results in two windows opening.*

The stack crawl window (also referred to as the program window) holds the source code from the file that holds the currently executing routine. Some projects, like the one shown in Figure 4.3, consist of more than one source code file. For projects such as these, the code for any of these other files can be viewed in the second debugger window—the process window.

THE BROWSER WINDOW

In Chapter 2 it was mentioned that when you build an application, CodeWarrior creates not one, but two files: the application itself and a *symbolic* file. For 68K projects the symbolic file has an extension of **.SYM**, while PowerPC projects generate a symbolic file with an extension of **.xSYM** file. The symbolic file holds information (such as variable names and variable locations within the code) that will be used by MW Debug when you debug a project. As you can see in the title bar of the browser window shown in Figure 4.3, the browser window makes use of the symbolic file. The browser window allows you to view the source code of any file in your project. The stack crawl window (described next) is used only for viewing code from the file that holds currently executing code.

THE STACK CRAWL WINDOW

The stack crawl window is divided into three panes: the Stack pane, the Locals, or Variables, pane, and the Source pane—you can see in Figure 4.4 that the window lists the name of each pane at the top of the pane.

The Stack Pane

The Stack pane lists the *call chain*. As one function calls another, each function's starting address is placed on the stack so that the program can "work its way back" to where it started. The Stack pane in Figure 4.4 shows that `AdjustAllMenus()` is highlighted, meaning that it is the currently executing function. Working up the call chain shows that `AdjustAllMenus()` was called from `EventLoop()`, a function that itself was called from `main()`.

The Locals Pane

The Locals, or Variables, pane lists variables and their values that are local to the currently executing routine. In Figure 4.4 the `AdjustAllMenus()` function is executing, so the variables listed in the Locals pane are the ones declared in `AdjustAllMenus()`.

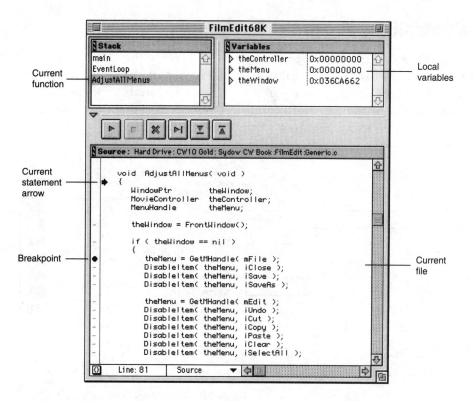

Current function

Local variables

Current statement arrow

Breakpoint

Current file

Figure 4.4 *The main features of the debugger's stack crawl window.*

The Source Pane

The Source pane holds the source code listing for the file that contains the currently executing function. As mentioned, in Figure 4.4 that function is AdjustAllMenus(). You can tell which line of code is about to execute by looking at the *current statement arrow* in the Source pane. Figure 4.4 shows that program execution has been halted at the start (the opening brace) of the AdjustAllMenus() routine. At this point you can have the program continue to run uninterrupted (as it would without the debugger turned on), you can have the program execute only the next line of code, or you can have the program execute an number of lines of code up to a *breakpoint*. You can specify a particular line at which the program should break by clicking on the **dash** by that line. This adds a breakpoint to the code.

Controlling Program Execution

To control execution of a program you use either the Control menu or the set of control buttons located in the center of the stack crawl window—whichever is easier for you. The functionality of the first six menu items in the Control menu is repeated in the six buttons in the stack crawl window. Figure 4.5 uses items in the Control menu to show the purpose of each control button.

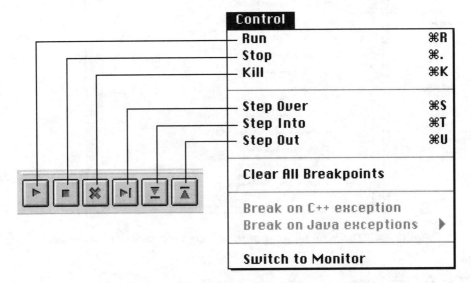

Figure 4.5 *Each program execution menu item*
has a corresponding button in the toolbar.

Once you've selected **Debug** from the CodeWarrior IDE and the debugger windows are on your screen, you'll start your program by either selecting **Run** from the Control menu or clicking the leftmost control button—the **Run** button. You can temporarily stop the program at any time by selecting **Stop** from the Control menu or by clicking on the **Stop** button—the control button second from the left. You can completely end program execution by instead selecting **Kill** from the Control menu or by clicking on the third control button from the left—the **Kill** button.

If you don't go with one of these options and you haven't set any breakpoints in the Source pane, your program will run on-screen as it normally would. If you've set a breakpoint, and the program reaches the line of code that is marked with that breakpoint, your program will stop executing and the current statement arrow in the stack crawl window Source pane will move to the breakpoint line. It's now up to you to decide what to do. Once your program has stopped, you have a number of options. You can:

- Look in the Variables pane of the stack crawl window to view the values of variables that are local to the routine your program stopped in.

- Click on **Global Variables** in the Files pane of the Process window, then look in the Globals pane of that same window to view the values of variables that are global to the program.

- Execute only the line of code currently pointed to by the current statement arrow.

- Restart your program (by again selecting **Run** from the Control menu or by clicking on the leftmost control button).

The three rightmost buttons are *step control* buttons. These buttons (or their corresponding menu items) all perform exactly the same when an application-defined function isn't involved. For example, if the current statement arrow was at the following line of code, clicking on any of these three buttons would execute the line of code and move the current statement arrow down to the next line of code:

```
squareValue = num * num;
```

If, on the other hand, the line of code at which the current statement arrow is pointing contains a function call, such as the following line, the buttons behave differently:

```
squareValue = SquareWholeNumber( num );
```

The **Step Over** button—the fourth control button from the left—would execute the line and move the current statement arrow down to the next line. If the **Step Into** button—the fifth button from the left—was instead clicked, the debugger would find the listing for the

SquareWholeNumber() function and would then move the current statement arrow to the start of this function. That allows you to "walk" through the function step-by-step. Once in SquareWholeNumber(), you could then use the **Step Over** or **Step Into** button repeatedly to execute this function one line at a time. Once inside this function, you could exit by clicking the **Step Out** button—the rightmost control button. That would have the effect of executing the remaining lines in the SquareWholeNumber() routine and then returning the current statement arrow to the line of code that follows the call to SquareWholeNumber().

Debugging an Example Program

There's no better way to learn about debugging than to walk through a debugging session. In this section you'll do that using the ChangingValues68K program. ChangingValues68K is a short, simple program—perfect for a quick look at how the MW Debug debugger works.

The ChangingValues68K Program

This chapter has a single example program, the ChangingValues68K application. When run, this program opens a window and draws a string to it, as shown in Figure 4.6. Figure 4.7 shows the project window for this program. You'll notice in Figure 4.7 that there is no resource file included in this project. Rather than obtaining window specifications from a WIND resource, the program's window is created based on information passed to the Toolbox in a call to NewWindow(). Figure 4.8 shows the source code listing for the ChangingValues68K program, including the call to NewWindow().

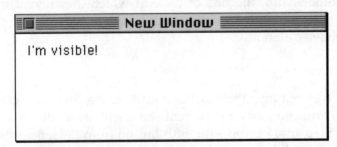

Figure 4.6   The window that's displayed when running ChangingValues68K.

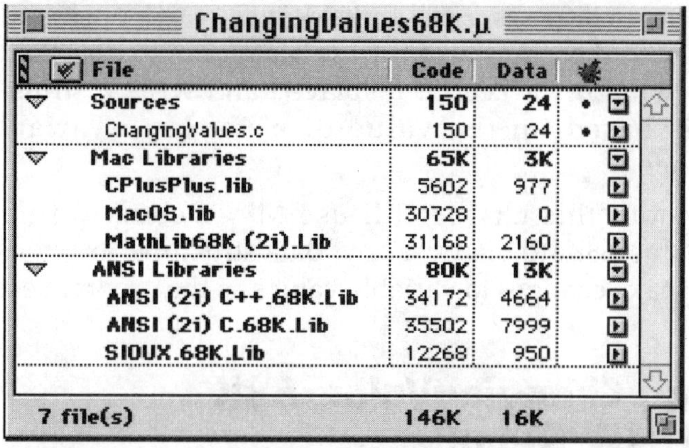

Figure 4.7 The **ChangingValues68K.µ** project window.

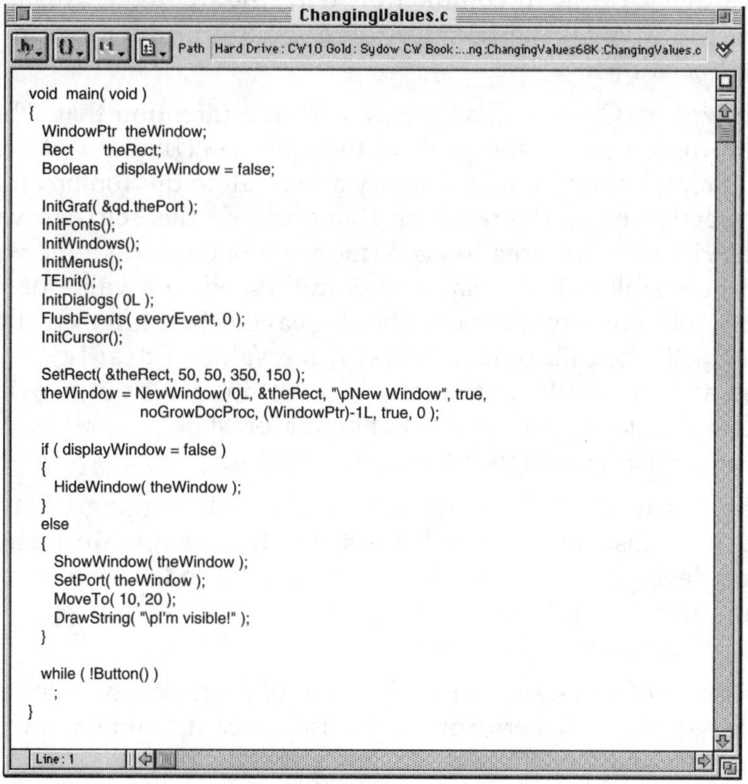

Figure 4.8 The ChangingValues68K source code listing.

ChangingValues68K uses a call to NewWindow() to open and display a new window. It then uses an if-else statement to determine whether to hide the window or keep it displayed and write a string to it. This decision is based on the value of a Boolean variable named displayWindow.

Throughout this chapter I'll use MW Debug to find a bug in ChangingValues68K, to discover how data structures are stored in memory, and to make changes to variable values as the program executes.

Executing ChangingValues68K without MW Debug

There's nothing special about the **ChangingValues68K.µ** project that requires that I run it in conjunction with the debugger. Instead, I'll make use of MW Debug because there's a bug in the program that I want to track down.

I've written ChangingValues68K with the intention that when the program runs, a call to the Toolbox function NewWindow() places window-defining information in memory and a call to the Toolbox function HideWindow() hides the window. I've declared the Boolean variable displayWindow to be used to keep track of whether or not the window should be visible. This variable gets initialized to a value of false, meaning the window shouldn't be displayed. Just after creating the window with the call to NewWindow(), the value of displayWindow is checked and the results of that check determine which of two Toolbox functions should be called HideWindow() or ShowWindow(). You can glance at the listing in Figure 4.8 to confirm this.

When I run ChangingValues68K without debugging (that is, the second-from-last item in the Project menu says **Enable Debugger**, meaning debugging is currently off), the source code compiles and the program runs. When it does, the application opens and displays a window—contrary to what I expected.

This type of situation, where the code of a project compiles but the resulting application performs in an unexpected manner, is one that calls for the use of MW Debug.

I've intentionally kept this example source code listing—and the problem I've introduced—simple. If you've already determined the nature of the bug, read along anyway so that you can become familiar with the MW Debug environment.

N O T E

Executing ChangingValues68K with MW Debug

Now it's time to rerun the ChangingValues68K program—this time with the use of MW Debug. If the second-to-last menu item in the Project menu says **Enable Debugger**, select this item to toggle it to its **Disable Debugger** state. Then choose **Debug** from this same menu. When you do, you'll see the MW Debug windows.

At this point the debugger is running, but the ChangingValues68K program isn't. Running a program from within the debugger is simple; just select **Run** from the Control menu or click the **Run** button on the toolbar. In this chapter I'll be using the handy control buttons in the stack crawl window rather than the menu items in the Control menu. Figure 4.9 shows the names of these buttons—use this figure as a reference throughout this section. I'll only be working with the stack crawl, or program window here—I'll be ignoring the second debugger window (the browser window).

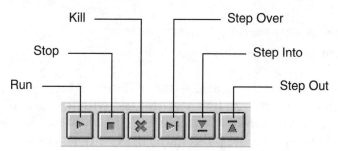

Figure 4.9 *The names of the control buttons that appear in the center of the stack crawl window.*

When you click on the **Run** button, program execution begins at the point of the current statement arrow. When I choose **Debug** from the Project menu of the CodeWarrior IDE, MW Debug starts up and places the current statement arrow at the first line of the program—the opening brace of main(). Figure 4.10 points this out.

Clicking the Run button starts execution from...

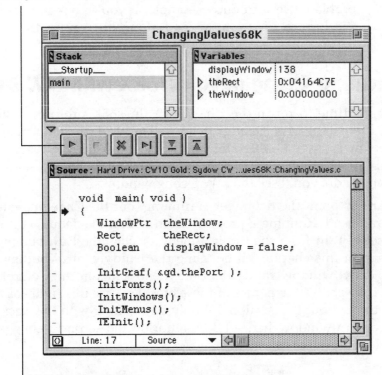

...the line of code pointed to by the current statement arrow

Figure 4.10 *Program execution always starts at the current statement arrow.*

If you run ChangingValues68K without setting a breakpoint, the program executes from start to finish as it would without the debugger present. What you'd rather do is set a breakpoint so that the debugger stops at a predictable spot in the program. What I've done is set a breakpoint *before* clicking on the **Run** button. When the **Run** button is then clicked, the program will execute up to the line that has the breakpoint. Now, where to set the breakpoint? Since the window is being displayed when I'm expecting it not to be, I'll want to monitor what's happening in the area of the source code that calls HideWindow() and ShowWindow(). For that reason I've decided to set a breakpoint at the if (displayWindow = false) line. To do that, I just click on the **dash** that appears to the left of that line in the stack crawl window. That causes a small stop sign to pop up at that line, indicating that if and when program execution reaches this line, the program will abruptly stop.

With the breakpoint set, I click the **Run** button and the ChangingValues68K program starts running. Only a few lines of code lie between the start of the program (the opening brace of the `main()` function) and the breakpoint, so after just a second the program reaches the breakpoint and stops. As indicated by the fact that the current statement arrow is on the same line as the breakpoint, I know that the program has indeed halted at the desired spot. Figure 4.11 shows that along with the debugger window, my screen now holds a new window—the window opened by the call to `NewWindow()` in the ChangingValues68K program.

This window was opened by a call to NewWindow() from the ChangingValues68K application—it's not a debugger window

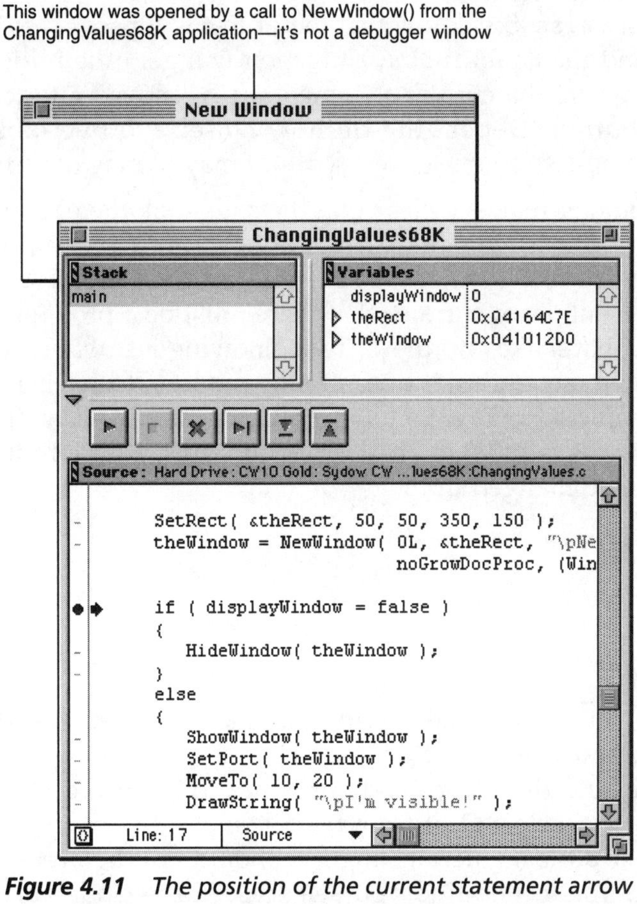

Figure 4.11 *The position of the current statement arrow shows that the program has stopped at the breakpoint.*

The current statement arrow always points to the line of code that is *about* to execute. In Figure 4.11 you can see that the if statement is about to execute. If I click on one of the Step control buttons in the stack crawl window, the program will perform the if test. The current statement arrow will then move down to the next line that is to be executed. Should the if test pass, the current statement arrow will end up at the HideWindow() line. Should the if test fail, the arrow will appear at the ShowWindow() line.

I know that the Boolean variable has a value of false; it was set to false when it was declared. After running the program up to the breakpoint, I can confirm that displayWindow is still false by looking at the Variables pane in the stack crawl window. There, displayWindow has a value of 0, or false. So I know that the if test will pass (displayWindow is false), and the HideWindow() function will get called. Right? Figure 4.12 shows where the current statement arrow moved after clicking the **Step Into** button. Depending on how closely you've looked at the ChangingValues68K source code, the result may or may not surprise you.

The debugger makes it clear that the code took the else path rather than the if path. Because the debugger clearly showed that displayWindow had a value of false at the time the program was at the if statement, I can surmise that there must be a problem within the line of code that makes up the if test. Knowing just where to focus my problem-solving energies, it doesn't take me long to realize that the if test is *assigning* displayWindow a value of false—it isn't *comparing* displayWindow *to* false as it should! To remedy the problem, the if test needs to be changed from:

```
if ( displayWindow = false )
```

to:

```
if ( displayWindow == false )
```

That changes the incorrectly used assignment operator to the desired equality comparison operator. This change needs to be made in the source code, and the source code then has to be recompiled. If you're following along, select **Quit** from the File menu to exit the debugger. If the debugger posts an alert asking if it should kill the process, click the **Kill** button. You'll then find yourself back in the CodeWarrior IDE. If the **ChangingValues.c** source code file isn't open, open it now. Type in the code change to correct the erroneous if statement; then rerun the program. Again step through the source code. This time you'll see that the HideWindow() call gets executed, and the window becomes hidden. Click the mouse button to end the program.

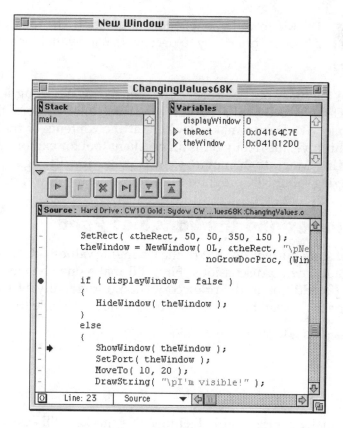

Figure 4.12   *The else section of code executes—not the if section.*

Variables, Data Structures, and the Debugger

Information about data structures and Macintosh memory can be found in several texts, including the Inside Macintosh series, this text, and other books by M&T Books. While the information found in these books is helpful, it can be greatly enhanced by using the MW Debug debugger to watch the changing values of variables as a program executes. This is especially true for a complicated concept such as the `WindowPtr`/`WindowRecord`/`GrafPort` relationship—a topic covered in this section.

N O T E

The Metrowerks ZoneRanger application, the topic of Chapter 11, is another great way to become familiar with Macintosh memory.

While the main purpose of a debugger like MW Debug is to help you correct faulty code, you shouldn't overlook another potential use for it. Because MW Debug makes looking at the contents of memory simple and intuitive, the debugger is an excellent tool for exploring and understanding Macintosh memory. In this section I'll again rely on the ChangingValues68K program to demonstrate the power of MW Debug.

Variables and the Variables Pane

To get some further use out of the ChangingValues68K project, I'll use it in the following discussions. First, I'll make one change to the source code (in addition to the prior correction of the faulty `if` statement). I'll change the declaration of the `displayWindow` variable from

```
Boolean  displayWindow = false;
```

to

```
Boolean  displayWindow = true;
```

After making sure **Enable Debugger** is checked, I'll select **Debug** from the Project menu to start up the debugger.

The upper-right corner of the debugger source window holds the Variables pane, an area that displays the variables declared in the routine currently being executed. Figure 4.13 shows the stack crawl window immediately after selecting **Debug** from the Project menu. In this figure you can see that the currently executing routine, `main()`, is highlighted in the Stack pane, and the three variables of `main()` are displayed in the Variables pane.

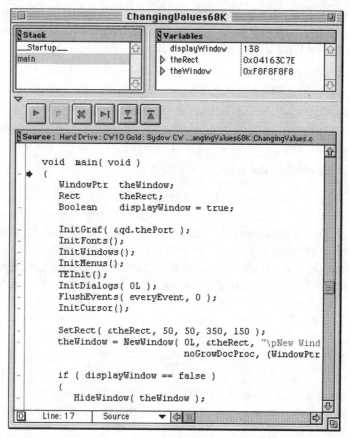

```
ChangingValues68K

Stack                          Variables
__Startup__                      displayWindow    138
main                           ▷ theRect          0x04163C7E
                               ▷ theWindow        0xF8F8F8F8


  ▶      ✖  ▶|  Ⅻ  ▲

Source: Hard Drive: CW10 Gold: Sydow CW ...angingValues68K:ChangingValues.c

    void   main( void )
→   {
         WindowPtr    theWindow;
         Rect         theRect;
         Boolean      displayWindow = true;

         InitGraf( &qd.thePort );
         InitFonts();
         InitWindows();
         InitMenus();
         TEInit();
         InitDialogs( 0L );
         FlushEvents( everyEvent, 0 );
         InitCursor();

         SetRect( &theRect, 50, 50, 350, 150 );
         theWindow = NewWindow( 0L, &theRect, "\pNew Wind
                               noGrowDocProc, (WindowPtr

         if ( displayWindow == false )
         {
             HideWindow( theWindow );

Line: 17      Source    ▼
```

Figure 4.13   *Program execution begins at the start of* main( ).

Figure 4.13 shows the values for the main() variables at the start of the program; note that the current statement arrow is at the start of main(). Here the variables in main() have values, but not necessarily the values they'll have once the program executes.

NOTE Because it's up to the Memory Manager where to place data structures in memory, the addresses you see when you run ChangingValues68K will differ from those shown in the figures in this chapter.

Some programs test to see if a window is open by checking to see whether the variable used to keep track of the window (a variable of type `WindowPtr`) has a value of `nil`:

```
if ( theWindow == nil )  // theWindow isn't open
  // so open the window
```

In Figure 4.13 the debugger shows that a `WindowPtr` variable isn't automatically assigned a value of `nil` when it's declared; you'll have to do this yourself when you declare the variable:

```
WindowPtr  theWindow = nil;
```

Next, I'll set a breakpoint at the `if` statement, then click the **Run** button in the stack crawl window. Figure 4.14 shows the state of the program at the time this breakpoint is reached. The value of the `Boolean` variable `displayWindow` is 1, or `true`—that occurred during the declaration of the variable. The rectangle variable `theRect` never gets assigned a new value, so its value remains the same. After the program reaches the breakpoint, the `NewWindow()` routine will have executed, and the `WindowPtr` variable `theWindow` will hold the memory address of the start of a `WindowRecord`—the data structure that holds the information that defines what a window looks like.

Compare the values of the three variables in Figure 4.14 with the values shown in Figure 4.13 to see the changes that took place.

Up to this point, the figures have shown addresses as the values for the `theRect` and `theWindow` variables. It's more likely that you'll want to see the contents of these variables, not the memory address where each is located. The Variables pane allows you to easily do that. But first, give yourself some room by slightly stretching out the Variables pane. To do that, click the mouse button on the double horizontal line that lies just beneath the Variables pane and, with the mouse button still held down, drag downward (see Figure 4.15).

After this line runs, displayWindow has a value of 1

After this line runs, theWindow has a value that is the address of the start of a WindowRecord data structure

Figure 4.14 *Variable values after the program reaches the breakpoint.*

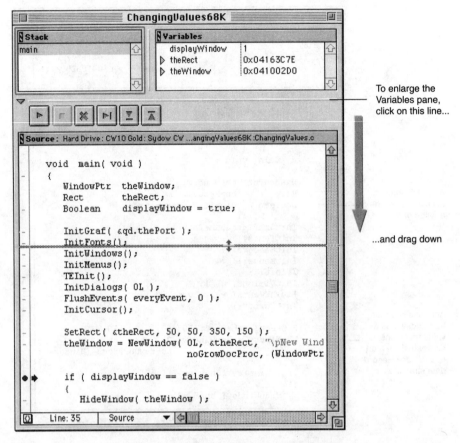

Figure 4.15 *The Variables pane can be enlarged with a click of the mouse button.*

Now, I'll take the remainder of this section to explore the data types of the theRect and theWindow variables. The topics I'll cover here will be useful in learning about any of the many data types unique to Macintosh programming.

The Rect Data Type

If a variable listed in the Variable pane has an arrow icon to the left of its name, then that variable has more data than is currently displayed. For example, a Rect is a structure with four fields: the top, left, bottom, and right pixel coordinates of a rectangle. Clicking on the **arrow** icon that's beside the variable's name in the Variable pane reveals the fields of the structure that's being pointed to. In Figure 4.16 the contents of `theRect` rectangle data structure have been displayed.

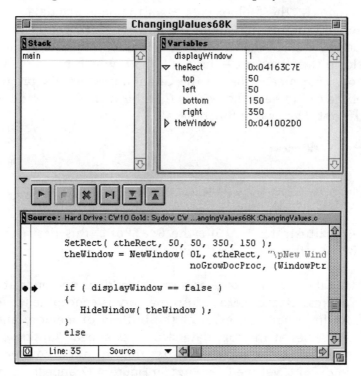

Figure 4.16 *A* Rect *variable is a data structure that holds the four coordinates of a rectangle.*

NOTE Notice from the placement of the current statement arrow in Figure 4.16 that at the time the data structure is being viewed, program execution has passed the call to the `SetRect()` Toolbox function. That's why the values of the rectangle coordinates match those provided as parameters to the SetRect() function. If you view `theRect` before the call to `SetRect()` is reached, you'll see entirely different numbers. Since no assignment is made to `theRect` initially, these values would be considered garbage—random "leftovers" from whatever program last used these memory locations.

The WindowPtr, WindowRecord, and GrafPort Data Types

When a window is created using a call to NewWindow() or GetNewWindow(), the Toolbox creates a WindowRecord data structure in which to hold information about the new window. The WindowRecord is a structure with 17 fields. The Toolbox then returns a pointer to the first field in this structure—the port field, which has a data type of GrafPort. That means that in the ChangingValues68K program, the result of the call to NewWindow() is that the variable theWindow points to a GrafPort. Here's that function call:

```
WindowPtr  theWindow;
...
...
theWindow = NewWindow( 0L, &theRect, "\pNew Window", true,
    noGrowDocProc, (WindowPtr)-1L, true, 0 );
```

Figure 4.17 illustrates that it's the GrafPort, this first field of the WindowRecord, that a WindowPtr points to.

A data structure starts at a smaller address and ends at a larger address. Because Macintosh memory is conceptually viewed as having small addresses at the bottom of memory and larger addresses at the top, data structures appear "upside down" in figures. For example, the first field of a WindowRecord is a GrafPort, yet the GrafPort in Figure 4.17 appears to be at the bottom of the WindowRecord.

So, does a WindowPtr hold the starting address of a GrafPort or of a WindowRecord? The answer is "both." Because the GrafPort is the first field in a WindowRecord, they share the same address. As you're about to see, it's the many fields of the GrafPort data structure that hold the window information commonly accessed by programmers, so it's the GrafPort that is accessed via the WindowPtr.

As it turns out, a GrafPort itself is a data structure consisting of several fields—more than two dozen, in fact. In Figure 4.18 I've expanded the GrafPort to show a few of these fields, the first three and the last two.

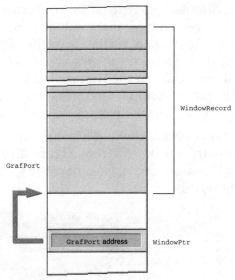

Figure 4.17 *A* WindowPtr *holds the address of a* GrafPort.

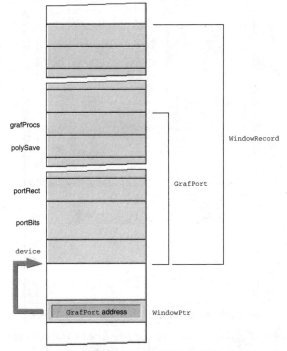

Figure 4.18 *A* GrafPort *is a data structure that consists of several fields.*

If the preceding discussion seems at all confusing, don't be alarmed. Window data structures is a topic that troubles many programmers. To see how MW Debug can help, again run the ChangingValues68K program with the debugger turned on. Make sure there's a breakpoint set at a line past the NewWindow() call, then click on the **Run** control button in the stack crawl window. When the program stops at the breakpoint, click on the **arrow** icon next to theWindow in the Variables pane of the stack crawl window.

Figure 4.19 shows part of the data structure that the pointer variable theWindow points to. You know from Figure 4.18 that the first three fields of the GrafPort are the device, portBits, and portRect fields. Figure 4.19 confirms this.

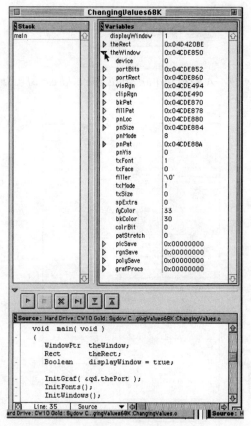

Figure 4.19 *The many fields of the GrafPort data structure can be viewed in MW Debug.*

Scrolling through the Variables pane reveals all the remaining fields in the GrafPort structure. A field that has a single value is displayed as that value. A field that is a data structure is displayed as a pointer; the address of the data structure is shown. You'll seldom have a reason to want to know the address of a variable or the address of a field of the data structure a variable points to. After all, you want to know what a variable is, not where the Memory Manager placed it in memory. You'll want to know the actual numerical (or string) contents of a variable or field. You can see that value by clicking on the **arrow** icon next to a pointer's name. In Figure 4.20 you can see that the pnLoc field is a data structure consisting of a v field and an h field, both of which have a value of 0.

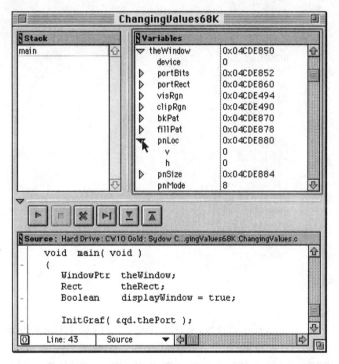

Figure 4.20 *A variable that is displayed as an address can also be viewed as the underlying data structure.*

Experimenting with the GrafPort

If you'd like to see the definition of any Toolbox data structure, refer to the Universal Interface header files. The structure that a WindowPtr points to—a GrafPort—is defined in the **QuickDraw.h** header file. I've listed it as follows.

```
struct GrafPort
{
    short       device;
    BitMap      portBits;
    Rect        portRect;
    RgnHandle   visRgn;
    RgnHandle   clipRgn;
    Pattern     bkPat;
    Pattern     fillPat;
    Point       pnLoc;
    Point       pnSize;
    short       pnMode;
    Pattern     pnPat;
    short       pnVis;
    short       txFont;
    Style       txFace;
    SInt8       filler;
    short       txMode;
    short       txSize;
    Fixed       spExtra;
    long        fgColor;
    long        bkColor;
    short       colrBit;
    short       patStretch;
    Handle      picSave;
    Handle      rgnSave;
    Handle      polySave;
    QDProcsPtr  grafProcs;
};
```

NOTE What if you didn't know that the GrafPort data type is defined in the **QuickDraw.h** header file? You'd open your Universal Header search set in the compiler Find dialog box and search for "GrafPort"!

Rather than have to memorize what each field of a GrafPort is and what each is used for, the Toolbox provides a number of Toolbox functions that allow you to indirectly change these fields. For example, the `pnLoc` field holds the current location of the graphics pen. When you call `DrawString()`, the starting point of the drawing is determined by the values in this field. To change the `pnLoc` field, you don't tamper with the field directly. Instead, you call `Move()` or `MoveTo()` to let the Toolbox change the values in `pnLoc` to those you specify. To satisfy yourself that this is indeed what happens, again run the ChangingValues68K program with the debugger turned on.

Set a breakpoint at the program's call to `MoveTo()`, then click the **Run** button. The program will stop at the `MoveTo()` call, before the call takes place. When it stops, click on the **arrow** icon by `theWindow` in the Locals pane. Then scroll down to the `pnLoc` field and click on its **arrow** icon. Note that both the vertical pen coordinate (v) and the horizontal pen coordinate (h) have a value of 0, as shown in Figure 4.21.

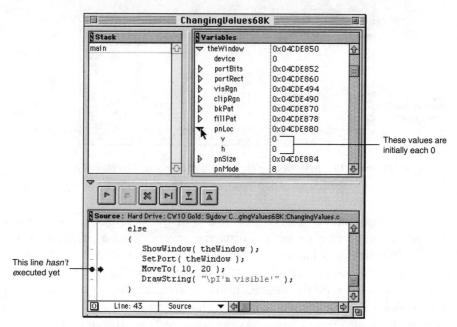

Figure 4.21 *MW Debug shows that the location of the graphics pen in a window is initially at the point (0,0).*

Now click the **Step Into** control button. When you do, the `MoveTo()` statement will execute and the current statement arrow will move down to the `DrawString()` line. More importantly, you'll notice that the values in the v and h fields of the `pnLoc` field of the `GrafPort` that `theWindow` points to will have changed (see Figure 4.22).

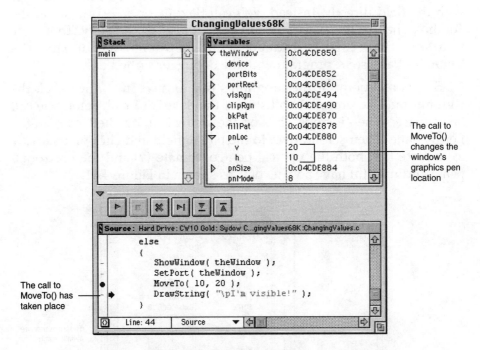

Figure 4.22 *MW Debug shows that after a call to* `MoveTo()`,
the graphics pen position has been changed.

An interesting feature of MW Debug is that the debugger allows you to change the value of a variable during the execution of a program. When you double-click on a variable's current value in the Locals pane, the value becomes surrounded by an edit box. To change the value of the variable, all you need to do is type the desired number. To gain a better understanding of how fields of a `GrafPort` work, try changing one or both of the `pnLoc` fields in this way. Rerun ChangingValues68K and step through the program until the current statement arrow stops at the `DrawString()` line. Because the `MoveTo()` call will have been made, the values of the `pnLoc` fields v and h will be 10 and 20, respectively. Double-click on the value of the h field (**10**) to surround the value with an edit box, as I've done in Figure 4.23. Then type in a new value. In the figure, I've entered a value of **150**. Before clicking the **Step Into** button, you should be able to accurately predict what will happen. Match your guess with the result shown in Figure 4.24.

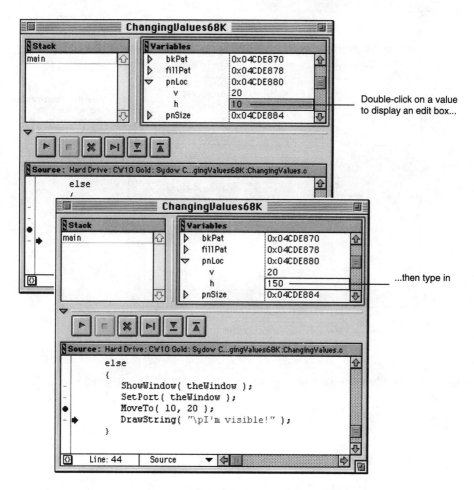

Figure 4.23 *A variable's value can be changed by double-clicking on the value and then typing a new number.*

The horizontal location of the pen was set to 150, so the DrawString() text now starts 150 pixels from the window's left edge

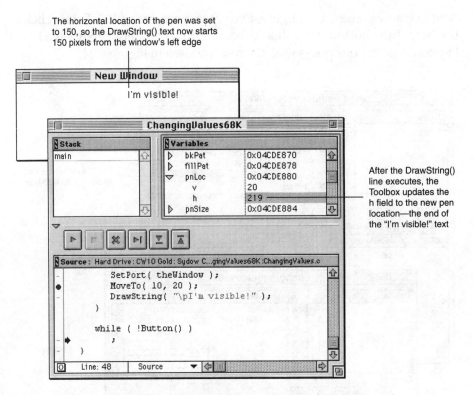

After the DrawString() line executes, the Toolbox updates the h field to the new pen location—the end of the "I'm visible!" text

Figure 4.24   Changing the graphics pen location affects subsequent text drawing.

Finally—the reason the program is named "Changing Values"!

NOTE

Further Investigation of the GrafPort

The pnLoc field of the GrafPort data structure isn't the only field you can alter, of course. The fgColor field is responsible for selecting which of eight colors foreground objects (such as text and graphics) will be drawn in. If you look in the **QuickDraw.h** Universal Header file you'll find that each of the eight colors has a corresponding constant defined for it:

```
blackColor      =    33
whiteColor      =    30
redColor        =   205
greenColor      =   341
blueColor       =   409
cyanColor       =   273
magentaColor    =   137
yellowColor     =    69
```

NOTE Color Macs are capable of using more than eight colors, of course, but only in color graphics ports (using the `CGrafPort` data type). The `fgColor` and `bkColor` fields of the `GrafPort` provide a quick and simple means of adding a minimal amount of color to basic graphics ports.

To see how the `GrafPort` affects window color, run ChangingValues68K again. Break at or before the `DrawString()` line of code. Then display the fields of the `GrafPort` data structure by clicking on the **arrow** icon by `theWindow` in the Variables pane. Scroll down to the `fgColor` field and note its current value—33. Looking back at the color constants, you can see that a value of 33 represents black. That's as you'd expect. By default, drawing takes place in black, so you know that the window foreground color is black. Double-click on the `fgColor` value to display an edit box, then type in one of the color constant values. In Figure 4.25 I've entered a value of **137**. This matches the `magentaColor` constant, so you'd expect writing and drawing to now take place in a purplish red color. Of course, the black-and-white figure can't illustrate this—all the more reason for you to try it on your color Mac!

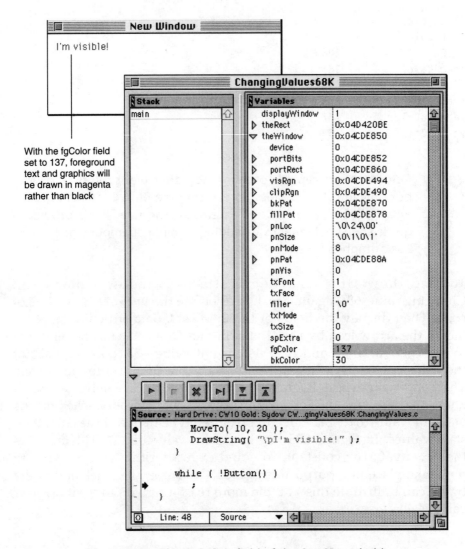

Figure 4.25 The fgColor field of the GrafPort holds
the foreground color for a window.

A few of the other GrafPort fields a program manipulates are listed as follows, along with the Toolbox routines your program can use to make the changes. Try adding calls to some or all of these routines and see how they affect the window. Then try changing these fields directly using MW Debug.

```
bkColor     BackColor()     // changes the window background color
txFont      TextFont()      // changes the text font
txFace      TextFace()      // changes the text style
txSize      TextSize()      // changes the text point size
```

NOTE

In the ChangingValues68K program, changing the background color won't have an effect on the window. That's because there's no event loop in the program, and the window never gets updated.

Chapter Summary

The CodeWarrior debugger, MW Debug, takes control of your program when you click **Enable Debugger** in the Project menu of the CodeWarrior IDE and then select **Debug** from that same menu. You use the debugger to execute your program up to a breakpoint and then to single-step through a part of your program. In this way you can carefully observe the effects each line of code has on variable values. Using this technique, you'll be able to accurately pinpoint where you've made mistakes in your source code.

Macintosh data structures and Macintosh memory can be topics that are difficult to master. If you devote some time to using MW Debug to examine memory, you'll gain a better understanding of how the Macintosh works with data. This investment in time will pay off in the future; the knowledge you gain will help you quickly track down bugs in future projects.

Chapter  5

Fat Applications

A program created using the Basic Toolbox 68k project stationery runs on either a 68K-based Macintosh or a Power Macintosh, but it has the disadvantage of running in emulation mode on the Power Macintosh. A program created using Basic Toolbox PPC project stationery runs in fast native mode on a Power Macintosh, but it has the disadvantage of not being executable at all on 68K-based Macs. If your application will be used by owners of 68K Macs, you'll need to supply them with a 68K version. If your application will be used by owners of PowerPC-based Macs, you should provide them with a faster, native PowerPC version. Rather than distribute two separate applications, wouldn't it be better if you could somehow combine the two versions into one program?

Better still, wouldn't it be ideal if this one program knew which type of computer was launching it—a 68K or a PowerPC Mac? A *fat binary application* is just such a program.

This chapter describes how executable code is stored in 68K, PowerPC-only, and fat binary applications. After that, you'll take a step-by-step journey through the creation of a fat binary application.

Executable Code and Resources

Before PowerPC-based Macs existed, all Macintosh applications stored a program's executable code within resources. With the arrival of PowerPC-only applications and fat applications, this is no longer true.

68K Applications and Code Resources

Macintosh files (and an application is a file) can consist of two *forks*: a resource fork and a data fork. For a 68K application file, both the program's executable object code and the resources that the program uses are stored in the resource fork. The data fork is generally empty. Figure 5.1 illustrates this.

NOTE

To programmers, the resource fork is the more familiar of the two forks. The resource fork holds the application resources that programmers edit with a resource editor such as ResEdit or Resorcerer. Programmers generally don't work directly with the data fork because in an application, this fork is empty. In document files, however, the situation is usually reversed—the data fork holds the document's text and graphics, while the resource fork has few or no resources.

Most of the resources shown in Figure 5.1 will be recognizable to you except, perhaps, the CODE resource. When a compiler builds a 68K application, it stores the compiled executable code in CODE resources. Because a single CODE resource is prohibited from exceeding 32K in size, most programs house more than one CODE resource.

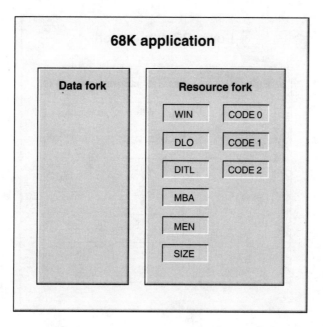

Figure 5.1 *The data fork of a 68K application is generally empty.*

When the user of a 68K program double-clicks the program's icon, it is the Segment Manager that finds the application's CODE 0 resource and loads the executable code that is stored in that resource.

PowerPC Applications and Data Fork Code

A PowerPC application, like a 68K program, consists of a data fork and a resource fork. There is a key difference in how executable code is stored in the two application files, however. In a PowerPC application, the executable code is stored in a code fragment in the data fork. The PowerPC code can be stored together like this because there is no 32K size limit on a fragment, as there is on a CODE resource.

The resource fork of a PowerPC application holds all the resources that you'll typically find in the resource fork of a 68K application, with the exception of the CODE resource. Additionally, you'll find a single resource not present in a 68K resource fork—a resource of type cfrg (for "code fragment"). Figure 5.2 illustrates.

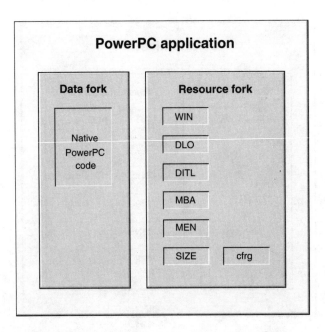

Figure 5.2 *The data fork of a PowerPC application*
holds the application's executable code.

When an application icon is double-clicked, it is the Process Manager that is responsible for launching that application. Before it does that, the Process Manager looks in the application's resource fork to see if there is a cfrg resource. If there is, it knows that the application it is about to launch is a PowerPC application. If there is no cfrg resource, the Process Manager knows to launch the program as a 68K application.

Fat Applications and Executable Code

A fat binary application contains two versions of executable code. One version is the native PowerPC code and is stored in the application's data fork. The other version is 68K code and is held in CODE resources in the application's resource fork. When this one application is copied to a PowerPC-based Macintosh and launched, the native PowerPC code gets loaded into memory. If this same application is copied to a 680x0-based Mac and launched, the 68K code will instead be loaded into memory.

How does the Process Manager know which set of code to use? The answer lies in the `cfrg` resource. When an application on a PowerPC-based Mac is double-clicked, the Process Manager first looks for a `cfrg` resource in the program's resource fork. If there is a `cfrg` resource, the Process Manager knows there's native PowerPC code to load. In this scenario the PowerPC code in the application's data fork gets loaded, while the 68K code in the `CODE` resources is ignored.

I'm generalizing a bit. Actually, a `CODE` resource could get loaded on a PowerPC-based Mac. If a `CODE` resource has its preload attribute set, it will always get loaded into memory, but on a PowerPC-based Mac, it won't ever execute. The code from the data fork will be used instead. So for all practical purposes, you can consider the `CODE` resources ignored on a PowerPC-based Macintosh.

Now consider this same fat binary application on the hard drive of a 68K Mac. The 68K Mac knows nothing of `cfrg` resources—they're defined only on PowerPC-based Macs. So when a fat binary is double-clicked on a 68K Mac, the `cfrg` resource is ignored, and the version of code that's housed in the `CODE` resources is used. Figure 5.3 shows how a fat binary application holds two versions of executable code, the resources that are common to both versions, and a `cfrg` resource.

What if an application that's on the hard drive of a PowerPC-based Mac doesn't have a `cfrg` resource? Then it is a 68K application—not a native PowerPC-only application or a fat binary application. A PowerPC-based Mac can run such programs, but they'll run in something called *emulation mode*. 68K code running in emulation mode is slower than native PowerPC code running directly on the PowerPC processor.

Building a Fat Binary Application

If you want to build an application that will run on older, 680x0-based Macs, you'll create an application from a project based on the Basic Toolbox 68k project stationery. If you'd rather your application be a fast, native PowerPC program that runs only on PowerPC-based Macs, you'll instead create an application from a project that uses the Basic Toolbox PPC project stationery. If you want your application to run on 68K Macs *and* in native mode on PowerPC-based Macs, you'll use both project types to create a fat binary application. This section describes the steps to carry this out.

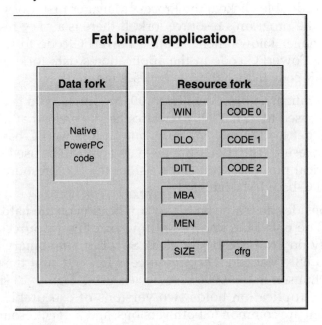

Fat binary application

Data fork

Native
PowerPC
code

Resource fork

WIN   CODE 0

DLO   CODE 1

DITL   CODE 2

MBA

MEN

SIZE   cfrg

Figure 5.3   A fat binary application holds two complete versions of an application's executable code.

Creating 68K and PowerPC Projects

Because a fat binary consists of both a 68K version and a PowerPC version of the same program, you'll want to compile and debug two separate projects. You'll first create and test a 68K version of the program and then do the same with a PowerPC version. When you're satisfied that each separate application runs as expected, you'll be ready to move to the creation of a fat binary.

In this section, I'll create a fat binary from a program that was developed in Chapter 3—the PlaySound68K application. In that chapter, I created only a 68K version of the program. That means I'll have to make a PPC version as well.

I'll begin by making a copy of the **PlaySound68K** folder—I'll be using much of its contents to create the fat application. I'll give the folder the name **PlaySoundFat**—a name that indicates what its final contents will contain. Then, from within the CodeWarrior IDE, I'll choose **New Project** from the File menu and then select the **Basic Toolbox PPC** project stationery. Before I click the **OK** button, I'll uncheck the **Create Folder** checkbox. Since I'll be using the source code file and the resource file from the **PlaySound68K.µ** project, I'll place the new PowerPC project in the same folder. When the next dialog box appears, I'll enter a name for the project and move to the **PlaySoundFat** folder. Figure 5.4 shows what my folder setup looks like after the new project has been created.

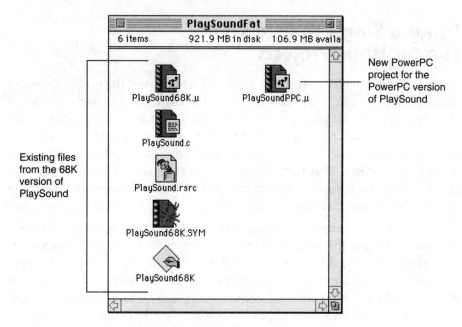

Figure 5.4   *The folder that holds both the 68K and PowerPC versions of the PlaySound project.*

In the new project window, I'll replace the **SillyBalls.c** and **SillyBalls.rsrc** placeholders with the same **PlaySound.c** and **PlaySound.rsrc** files used in the 68K project. Figure 5.5 shows the project window for both versions. It's important that you note that the two projects use the same source code file and the same resource file; only the libraries differ.

Figure 5.5   68K and PPC versions of the PlaySound project.

Using a Single Source Code File for Both Projects

PowerPC-based Macintosh computers are faster than 680x0-based Macs. Compared to some 68K models, the difference is very considerable. If you're developing on a Power Mac, you may end up adding certain features to your program that work fine on a PowerPC-based Mac but bog down a slower 68K model. You can resolve this dilemma by including conditional directives in your source code file. A *conditional directive* tells the compiler to compile the code that follows the directive only under certain circumstances.

The #ifdef powerc conditional directive tells the compiler to compile the code that follows the #ifdef powerc line *only* if the project is designated as a PowerPC project. If the project is marked as a 68K project instead, then the code following the #ifdef should be skipped. If the optional #else conditional directive appears, then the code that follows that line should be compiled for a 68K project and skipped for a PowerPC project. By using the #ifdef powerc directive, you can include sections of code that get compiled differently depending on which type of Mac is targeted by the project. Here's the format of the #ifdef conditional directive:

```
#ifdef powerc
    // code designed to run only if the user has a PowerPC-based Mac
#else
    // code designed to run only if the user has a 68K-based Mac
#endif
```

Just to prove to myself that the #ifdef powerc directive works, I've added one to the **PlaySound.c** source code file. Here's what it looks like:

```
#ifdef powerc
   SndPlay( nil, (SnListHandle)theSound, true );
#else
   SndPlay( nil, (SnListHandle)theSound, true );
   SndPlay( nil, (SnListHandle)theSound, true );
#endif
```

Remember, the same **PlaySound.c** file is a part of both the 68K project and the PPC project. When I compile and build my 68K version of the PlaySound program, I'll generate code that plays the telephone ring sound twice. When I compile and build the PowerPC version of PlaySound, I'll have a program that plays the sound only once. Figure 5.6 shows the complete listing for the PlaySound program, with the #ifdef directive in place.

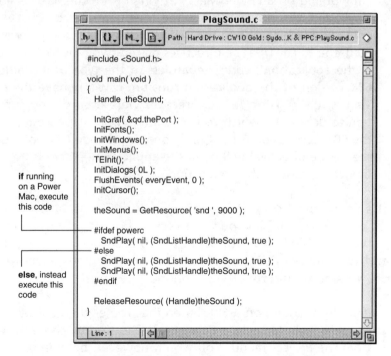

Figure 5.6   The **PlaySound.c** source code file, with the addition of a conditional directive.

In this book I just touch on the differences between PowerPC code and 68K code. For complete information on the particulars of programming the PowerPC-based Macintosh, refer to the *PowerPC System Software* volume of the *Inside Macintosh* series.

Building the Applications

While I already have a 68K version of PlaySound in my **PlaySoundFat** folder (the one I built in Chapter 3), I'll still want to open the **PlaySound68K.µ** project and rebuild a new application. That's because I've made changes to the source code. After selecting **Run** from the Project menu, the source code will recompile and the program will run. My **PlaySound.c** source code listing shows that the 68K version of the program should ring the telephone twice, so that's what I'll be expecting to happen.

I'm working on a Power Mac. Yet when I run the 68K version of PlaySound, the program rings the telephone twice—as it would on a 68K machine. When the 68K version of the program was created, the #ifdef/#else directives placed two calls to SndPlay() in the application's code. Regardless of the type of machine the 68K version of the application runs on, it will behave the same. That is, the #ifdef/#else directives were used during compilation to determine which code should go in the application. After the 68K application is built, only one set of code (the code under the #else directive) will be in the application—there is no if-else branching code in the application.

Now it's on to the PowerPC version of PlaySound. I'll open the PowerPC version of the PlaySound project and do the same as I did for the 68K project—I'll choose **Run** from the Project menu to compile the code and test the resulting application. When it does execute, this PowerPC version should ring the telephone only once.

If you're working on a 68K-based Mac rather than a Power Mac, you'll be able to build a PowerPC application by choosing **Make** from the Project menu. You won't, however, be able to run the program on your Mac. This is an inconvenience, but it won't prevent you from later creating the fat application.

Creating the Fat Application Project

To create the fat application of PlaySound, you'll create a third project—another PowerPC project. This one will be almost identical to the other PowerPC project, so you can start by simply making a copy of that project and renaming it on the desktop. I've named mine **PlaySoundFat.μ**. Then double-click this project to open it.

Because this new project was copied from an existing one, you'll want to change the name CodeWarrior assigns to the application that gets built from it. Choose **Project Settings** from the Edit menu, and then click on the PPC Project name in the scrolling list of the Project Settings dialog box to bring up the PPC Project panel. Type in a new, appropriate name in the File Name edit box, as I've done in Figure 5.7.

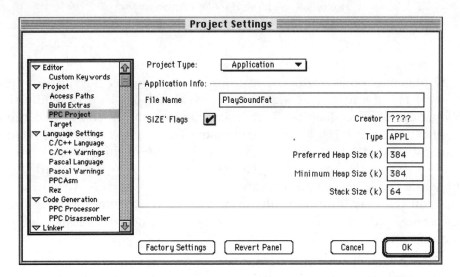

Figure 5.7 *Setting the name that will be used for the fat application.*

Now, add the PlaySound68K application to the PPC project. Yes, that's right. You'll be adding the *application* itself to the project window. Select **Add Files** from the Project menu, and then add the 68K application, as I'm doing in Figure 5.8.

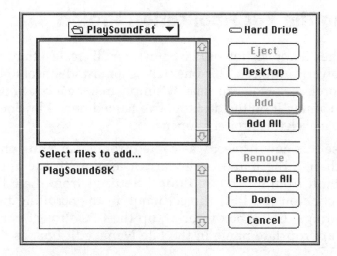

Figure 5.8 *Adding the 68K version of the*
PlaySound program to the fat binary project.

I've mentioned that CodeWarrior uses the concept of groups to organize files in a project window. An application doesn't fall neatly into
any of the groups that are already defined, so I've placed the
PlaySound68K application in its own, new group. If you added the
application without any group being selected, CodeWarrior will have
already created a new group and placed the file in this group. If you
had any of the existing groups selected when you added
PlaySound68K, then you'll create a new group yourself. To do that,
click on the **PlaySound68K** file name in the project window, drag the
file name beneath the last group in the project window, and release the
mouse button.

Regardless of how you created a new group, you can rename it by
double-clicking on its current name in the project window. In the dialog
box that opens, type in a new group name, as shown in Figure 5.9. Then
click the **OK** button.

After adding the application to its own group, your
PlaySoundFat.µ project window should look like Figure 5.10.

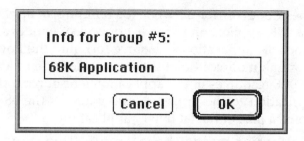

Figure 5.9   *Renaming a group in a project window.*

File	Code	Data	🍁
▽ Sources	0	0	• ▽
PlaySound.c	0	0	• ▷
▽ Resources	0	0	▽
PlaySound.rsrc	n/a	n/a	▷
▽ Mac Libraries	0	0	▽
InterfaceLib	0	0	▷
MathLib	0	0	▷
MWCRuntime.Lib	0	0	▷
▷ ANSI Libraries	0	0	▽
▽ 68K Application	0	0	▽
PlaySound68K	n/a	n/a	▷

PlaySoundFat.µ

9 file(s)   0   0

Figure 5.10   *The fat binary project after adding the
68K version of the PlaySound application.*

Creating the Fat Application

If your host computer is a PowerPC-based Mac, select **Run** from the
Project menu to build the fat binary. If you're working from a 68K-
based Mac, the **Run** command will be dim; use the **Make** menu item
instead. Regardless of which menu item you use, the result will be the
same—a fat binary version of PlaySound.

What does CodeWarrior do when it's building an application and it encounters a 68K application in the list of project window files? It simply copies the 68K application's resource fork into the PowerPC application during linking. Recall that the executable code of a 68K application lies in CODE resources in the application's resource fork. So adding the 68K application to the project window allows the 68K executable code to become a part of the fat binary application.

As CodeWarrior builds the fat application, you'll no doubt encounter the Errors & Warnings window shown in Figure 5.11. The 68K application holds the same snd resource as the one in the **PlaySound.rsrc** resource file—another file that is a part of the fat application project. Remember, the 68K application was built from a project that included this same resource file. CodeWarrior is smart enough not to attempt to add two versions of the same resource to an application it's building, so it's safe to ignore this warning.

Figure 5.11 *Duplicate resource warnings that occur during the building of a fat application can safely be ignored.*

NOTE

So, if the necessary resources for the fat application exist in the PlaySound68K application that becomes a part of the fat application, could you get away with removing the **PlaySound.rsrc** resource file from the fat application project? Yes. But it's good practice to leave the resource file in the project anyway. Your own projects may be much more involved than the PlaySound example, and they may not have an identical set of resources for both 68K and PPC projects. Perhaps one project may even have more than one resource file (a perfectly acceptable practice in Macintosh programming). For example, while both projects may share a common resource file, the PPC project may use its own additional resource file that holds some resources used only by the PPC version of the application.

If you're fortunate enough to have access to both a 68K Mac and a PowerPC-based Macintosh, try running the fat binary on both machines to verify that on a 68K Mac the program sounds the phone twice, while on a PowerPC-based Mac the program only rings it once.

Examining the Programs with a Resource Editor

Now that you have an honest-to-goodness fat app of your own, you can take a look inside it to see if this chapter's discussions of CODE resources, cfrg resources, and data forks hold true.

Using your resource editor, first open the PPC and 68K versions of the PlaySound program. Make sure to open the programs themselves, *not* the project resource files. Don't open the fat application just yet. If you're using ResEdit, as I am in this resource-viewing session, your screen should hold the windows shown in Figure 5.12.

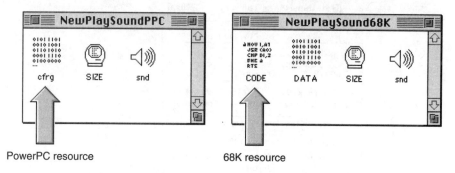

Figure 5.12   *The PPC version of PlaySound contains a cfrg resource, while the 68K version holds CODE resources.*

In Figure 5.12, you can see that the PPC version of the program has a cfrg resource, as any PowerPC-only application should. This resource was added to the program by CodeWarrior. Also notice that there are no CODE resources in the PPC version of the program, while there are in the 68K version. The executable code that holds the instructions that make up the PowerPC version of the program are held in the application's data fork—not in CODE resources in its resource fork.

The executable code for a 68K application is held in the application's CODE resources. The application's data fork is generally empty. You can verify this for yourself by clicking on the **PlaySound68K** window in ResEdit and then selecting **Get Info for This File** from the File menu of ResEdit. In the top window of Figure 5.13, you can see that the data fork of the 68K version of PlaySound is in fact empty.

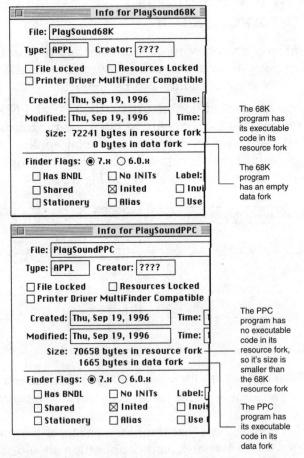

Figure 5.13 *Checking the size of the resource fork and data fork of both the 68K and PPC versions of PlaySound.*

The executable code for a PowerPC application is stored in the application's data fork. The resource fork isn't empty, though—it holds all the usual resources found in an application, such as WIND, DLOG, and so forth. You can check to see that the data fork of PlaySoundPPC isn't empty by making the ResEdit window that displays its resources active and then again selecting **Get Info for This File** from the File menu of ResEdit. In the bottom window of Figure 5.13, you can see that the data fork of the PPC version of PlaySound holds data.

Next, use your resource editor to open the fat binary application. In Figure 5.14, notice that the fat binary holds the resources from the 68K version of the program, including the CODE resources, as well as the cfrg resource that was added by CodeWarrior.

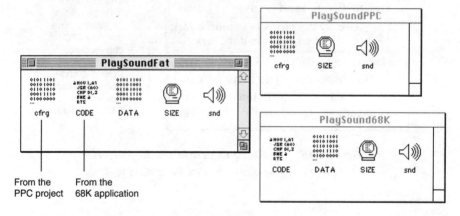

Figure 5.14   *The fat binary holds all the resources found in both the 68K and PPC versions of a program.*

Fat applications have two sets of executable code—one in the program's CODE resources, the other in the program's data fork. Figure 5.15 illustrates this for the fat version of PlaySound. In the figure, you can see that the fat binary version of this program has a resource fork that's a little larger than the 68K version of the program (see Figure 5.13 to make the comparison). The fat version holds all the resources found in the 68K version, including the CODE resources—and a cfrg resource. Further, Figure 5.15 shows that the fat version has a data fork with data. This data is the native PowerPC version of the PlaySound executable code. The data fork of the fat application holds the same thing that the

PowerPC-only version of PlaySound holds—the executable code for the PowerPC version of the program. You can use Figure 5.15 and the bottom window of Figure 5.13 to see that the data fork sizes of the fat application and the PowerPC-only version of PlaySound are the same.

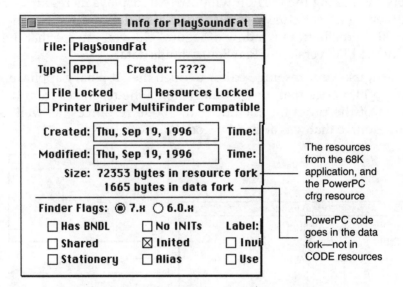

Figure 5.15 *The ResEdit Get Info window shows that a PPC application has data in its data fork.*

Summary

Making a fat binary version of one of your applications gives that application the "best of both worlds." A fat binary application is capable of running on both 68K-based Macs and PowerPC-based Macintoshes. And, when running on a PowerPC-based Mac, the program will run in fast, native PowerPC mode.

You create a fat binary by first making a 68K project and then building a 68K application from it. Next, use the same source code and resource files used in the 68K project in a new PowerPC project. Build a PowerPC application from this project. After testing both versions of the program, create another PowerPC project—a copy of the first will work fine. Add to the project the 68K application itself. Finally, build an application from this project. The resulting application will be a fat application—a program that holds two versions of the executable code for the same program.

Chapter 6

Java, Applets, and the World Wide Web

Java may very well eventually be the programming language that surpasses both C and C++ in popularity. Java is the language used to create applets—small, visual, dynamic mini-applications that can be readily added to any Web page.

In this chapter, you'll see how the CodeWarrior IDE is used to develop applets. You'll find comfort in the fact that an applet starts its life as a CodeWarrior project—just as a Mac application does. You'll also be pleased to know that from the CodeWarrior IDE you can com-

155

pile your Java language source code, build an applet, and then start up an applet viewer to test out your applet.

Web Browsers, Applets, and the Web

Like everyone else who is even remotely involved with computers, you've heard much about Java, applets, and the World Wide Web. Yet you might not be sure what all the fuss is about. The CodeWarrior programming environment makes it easy to create applets—but before you jump right in you should have a good understanding of why you're developing an applet and how it will be used! If you understand all of the following topics, and how they interrelate, you can skip the next several pages. If items in this list are unfamiliar to you, though, read on. The next sections discuss all of the following:

- Web browsers
- HTML
- Java programming language
- Java applets
- Java applications
- Bytecodes
- Java interpreters

About Web Browsers

A Web browser allows you to easily surf the Web—it does the work of transferring information from Web server computers to your Mac. The *Hypertext Markup Language*, or *HTML*, makes this possible. In the past, HTML was used to format both text and graphics on a Web page. Now it's also used to display applets on that same page.

WEB BROWSERS AND HTML

A Web site is nothing more than one or more files on the hard drive of a server—a computer that has a large capacity disk storage and is connected to the Internet. If you have your own Web site, then undoubtedly you've been assigned a few megabytes of disk space from someone else's server. That "someone else" could be your Internet provider, such as an *ISP* (*Internet Service Provider*) or an online service such as America Online or CompuServe. A Web browser is capable of accessing files stored on servers. A Web browser is also capable of recognizing the contents of those files. A browser knows how to read files on any Internet server because each file holds HTML tags.

HTML is the programming language of the World Wide Web. An HTML file is made up of HTML *tags*—commands that specify the layout and formatting of the text and graphics that are to appear on that Web page. For example, to indicate that a graphic image should appear on a page, the HTML file will use the `<img>` tag. This tag has *attributes*—parameters that provide the details about the graphic image. One detail is the name of a separate file (also located on the server along with the HTML file itself) that holds the graphic image that is to be displayed.

WEB BROWSERS AND APPLETS

The fact that a Web site keeps its graphic images in files separate from the HTML file is important: that's similar to how applets work. As an HTML file uses a tag (the `<img>` tag) to reference a graphic image contained in a separate file, so too does the HTML file use a tag (the `<applet>` tag) to reference an applet contained in a separate file. If you have your own Web page and you want it to display a picture on that page, you'll upload a graphic file (such as a GIF or JPEG file) to the directory on the server that holds the files that make up your Web page. If you want that same page to display an applet, you'll upload the applet to the directory on the server.

NOTE Not all Macintosh Web browsers are capable of understanding the HTML `<applet>` tag. Browsers that do recognize the `<applet>` tag are referred to as Java-capable (or Java enabled, or Java-aware, or Java compatible). As of this writing, Netscape Navigator 3.0 or later is Java-capable—and Microsoft's Internet Explorer soon will be.

When a user's browser encounters the `<applet>` tag in the HTML file of a Web page, the browser finds the applet file on that Web site's server and actually downloads the applet to the user's computer. For that reason it's best to keep the size of an applet small—that makes the transfer of the applet quick. Besides being small in size, there's one other thing an applet should be—nonstatic. That is, an applet should be dynamic—it should do something! An applet should be animated, or should interact with the user. If an applet does nothing more than display some text or display a picture, then the same effect could have been achieved without the use of an applet.

Applets and Platform Independence

Java applets are *platform-independent*. That is, if you have a Java-capable Web browser you'll be able to see and interact with applets that appear on Web pages—regardless of the platform—the operating system—you run your browser from.

WEB PAGES AND PLATFORM INDEPENDENCE

As someone who has browsed the World Wide Web, you're already familiar with platform-independent Web pages. Web pages have been viewable by users running browsers on any number of computer systems. A Webmaster (one who manages the files that make up a Web site) didn't keep separate sets of files on a server—one set for users browsing from a Windows machine, another set for users browsing from a Macintosh, and so forth. Instead, a single HTML text file could be placed on the server, along with a single GIF file for each graphic image that was to appear on the page.

So, why all the excitement about the ability to develop a single applet for use by any number of Web browsers? Because an applet isn't just text, and it isn't just graphics. An applet, as its name implies, is a small application. If you've programmed at all—in any computer language—you've heard of cross-platform applications. And you've also heard that creating such a program is normally difficult and time-consuming. The Java language and applets change that.

Java Source Code and Bytecodes

When a programmer compiles a C or C++ source code file, the result is an executable file that can be run on one type of computer. More specifically, the executable will run on a machine that is driven by a processor from a single family of processors—usually the same family as the computer that hosts the development environment. For instance, if you do your programming on a computer with an Intel 80486 CPU, the programs you develop will run on machines with an 80x86 CPU. If you do your programming on a Power Macintosh that has a PowerPC 603 CPU, your programs will run on other Power Macintosh computers.

If it were only a matter of recompiling the same source code to generate different versions of the same application, the effort necessary to create a program usable by owners of different platforms wouldn't be too bad. Unfortunately, when a program is developed from source code written in languages such as C, C++, or Pascal, the same source code can't be used. That's because when writing a program, a programmer relies on code that is specific to one platform. For example, when you write a program designed to run on a Mac, you make use of many of the functions that are a part of the Macintosh Toolbox. This source code can't be compiled for a different platform (such as Windows 95) because other platforms won't recognize the calls to Toolbox routines.

The Java language is different than other programming languages in that it isn't platform-specific. One Java source code file will compile on a Macintosh compiler or a Windows 95 compiler. Just as importantly, the resulting executable will be able to run on a wide variety of machines—regardless of which platform is used for development. The bytecode file that each Java compiler generates is identical, so this file can run on any number of machines.

When you compile a source code file written in a traditional language, such as C or C++, the resulting binary file (the executable, or application) holds machine code. This machine code consists of instructions which are particular to a processor (or family of processors). When you compile a Java source code file, the result is also a binary file (an executable, or applet). And the contents of this binary file are very similar to the machine code found in the executable that results from the compilation of a C++ file. The distinction is that the Java binary code—which is called bytecode—holds instructions that are not specific to any one machine.

Java Interpreters and Bytecode

While I've mentioned that bytecode files can be executed on different types of computers, I've glossed over one very important point—how this is possible.

READYING AN APPLET FOR THE WEB

After you've created an applet by compiling your Java source code into a Java bytecode file, it's time to add the applet to your Web page in order to let others enjoy the amazing things the applet is capable of doing! You'll do a few things to make that happen:

1. You'll add an `<applet>` tag to your Web page's HTML file so that the file references the applet.

2. You'll re-upload the modified HTML file back to your server that holds your Web page documents (such as this HTML file and any graphics files).

3. You'll upload the applet to the server that holds your other Web page documents.

Once you've performed these steps, anyone with a Java-capable Web browser will be able to view your Web page and, of course, the applet that appears on the page. As you're about to read, what makes a browser Java-capable is the fact that it has a built-in Java interpreter.

JAVA INTERPRETERS

How is it that the instructions in a single binary file can be meaningful to processors that normally recognize instructions from very different instruction sets? The answer is that the instructions aren't meaningful to the processor—they're meaningful to an intermediary piece of software—the Java interpreter. When an applet runs, the instructions that make up the applet's code aren't processed directly be the CPU. Instead, they're fed through software called a Java interpreter.

A *Java interpreter* is responsible for translating the instructions that make up the bytecode file to instructions recognizable by the CPU the applet is to run on. That means that while one version of an applet can run on any of several platforms, the interpreter itself can't. There's one version of the Java interpreter that runs only on a Mac—it knows how to translate bytecode instructions to instructions that are usable by the CPU in a Macintosh. There's another version of the Java interpreter that runs only on a Windows 95 machine—it knows how to translate bytecode instructions to instructions that are usable by the CPU in a computer running Windows 95.

 You'll see the Java interpreter also referred to as Java runtime, Java virtual machine, or JVM. These terms all mean the same thing.

Browsers and Java Interpreters

Just where does an interpreter come from, and how does a user get one on his or her computer? If a Web browser claims to be Java-capable, then it has a Java bytecode interpreter built into it. For instance, version 3.0 and higher of Netscape Navigator for Macintosh has a built-in Java interpreter. When a Macintosh user running Netscape Navigator is browsing the Web, and a Web page that includes an applet is encountered, the browser is able to properly access the page, download the applet bytecode, and execute that code.

Java Interpreters and Java Applications

While the focus of this introduction to Java has been on applets, the fact is that the Java programming language can be used to write platform-independent *applications* as well. Like a Java applet, a Java application starts as a single version of source code that gets compiled to a bytecode file. And, again like a Java applet, a Java application can run—without modification—on a number of different types of computers. That means that a Java application requires the presence of a Java interpreter in order to execute. Because a Java application has nothing to do with a Web browser, the Java interpreter built into a Web browser is of no help here. Instead, anyone wishing to run a Java application must have a Java interpreter program on his or her computer. Stand-alone Java interpreters exist for many platforms, including the Macintosh.

If you've purchased a version of CodeWarrior (such as CodeWarrior Gold or Discover Programming with Java), you have such an interpreter—the Metrowerks Java application that's placed on your Mac when you install CodeWarrior.

Now that you know all the theory behind Java, bytecodes, applets, and interpreters, it's time to move on to the application of that theory—it's time to start developing Java applets!

The Java Applet Project

In Chapter 2, you were introduced to projects and the CodeWarrior integrated development environment. There you saw that the CodeWarrior IDE truly is integrated—it looks the same and works the same whether you program in C or C++. By no accident, the CodeWarrior IDE allows you to work with Java source code in the same manner as you do with other languages. From the now-familiar comfort of this one IDE you can create an applet using the same techniques you use to create a traditional application: You'll start with a project, write source code and save it to a file in the project, and then compile the source code to generate an executable. If you run into problems along the way, you can use MW Debug to debug your Java source code—just as you debugged C source code in Chapter 4.

In the first example in Chapter 2, I left in place the default files that CodeWarrior adds to a new project—the **SillyBalls.c** source code file and the **SillyBalls.rsrc** resource file. Then I compiled the code and ran the resulting application. I'll do the same here—though the files CodeWarrior adds to a Java project are different than the ones added to a Basic Toolbox project, and the resulting executable will be a bytecode file (an applet) rather than an application.

After taking a look at the applet, I'll discuss just how it came to pass that you just easily ran an applet—without the aid of a Web browser and without being connected to the Web. Here I'll take a look at how the applet, the HTML file, and the Metrowerks Java application interact.

The CodeWarrior-supplied Java source code is intentionally trivial—it's the minimal code that allows you to quickly create and test an applet. While the source code is too trivial to result in a useful, exciting applet, it does demonstrate many of the basic properties all Java source code files share. So instead of skipping the source code walkthrough as I did for the Chapter 2 SillyBalls example, I'll examine and comment on the Java source code found in the CodeWarrior-supplies **TrivialApplet.java** file that is a part of each Java project.

Creating a Java Applet Project

A Java applet starts out just as a Macintosh application does—as a CodeWarrior project. From the CodeWarrior IDE, select **New Project** from the File menu to create a new Metrowerks CodeWarrior project. Choose the **Java Applet** project stationery, as I'm doing in Figure 6.1.

Figure 6.1   *Creating a Java applet project by selecting the Java Applet project stationery.*

 Once built, an applet can execute on any machine that has a Java interpreter or a Java-capable Web browser on it. That means the same applet can be used on a Macintosh, a Power Macintosh, or even a computer running Windows 95. That's why there's no separate 68k and PPC project stationery for Java-related projects.

Leaving the **Create Folder** checkbox checked, click the **OK** button to dismiss the New Project dialog box and to bring on the dialog box that prompts you to enter a project name. In Figure 6.2 I'm doing just that.

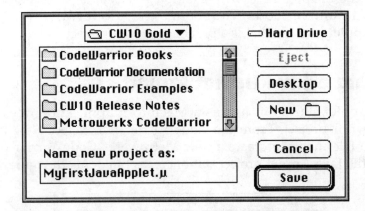

Figure 6.2   *Name the applet project as you would any other CodeWarrior project.*

In Figure 6.2, you see that I've given the project a name appropriate to the program I'll be developing. After then clicking the **Save** button, a new project window appears, as shown in Figure 6.3.

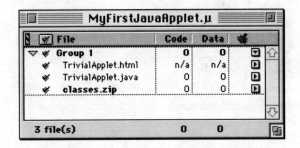

Figure 6.3   *The project window for a project based on Java Applet project stationery.*

The Files in a Java Project

Looking at Figure 6.3, you'll notice that a project based on Java Applet project stationery consists of files not found in a project based on Basic

Toolbox project stationery. Figure 6.4 provides an overview of the purpose of each of the three files that appears in a new Java project.

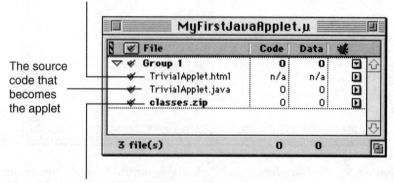

Used only to test the applet—nothing
in this file becomes a part of the applet

The source
code that
becomes
the applet

Numerous Java classes, some of
which become a part of the applet

*Figure 6.4   A project based on Java Applet
project stationery consists of three files.*

THE TRIVIALAPPLET.JAVA

Just as a program written in C has its source code stored in a file with an extension of **.c**, an applet written in Java has its source code stored in a file with an extension of .java. When you create a project based on the Java Applet project stationery, CodeWarrior always adds the **TrivialApplet.java** file to the project—just as CodeWarrior adds the **SillyBalls.c** file to a project based on one of the Basic Toolbox project stationaries. And, like the **SillyBalls.c** file, you'll modify or replace the **TrivialApplet.java** file when developing your own applet. To simplify the walkthrough of the process of building and testing an applet, however, I'll leave the **TrivialApplet.java** file unchanged.

Double-click on the **TrivialApplet.java** file name in the project window to take a look at the Java source code for the applet you're about to build. Figure 6.5 shows the complete source code listing for the applet that will be named TrivialApplet.

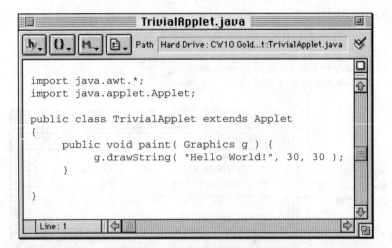

Figure 6.5   *The complete source code listing for the TrivialApplet applet.*

No matter how little or how much experience you have with the Java language, you can certainly guess that the very short source code listing shown in Figure 6.5 will result in a rather simple applet (of course the name of the file might lead you to this conclusion as well). As you may suspect, this applet does nothing more than write the string "Hello World!" to a Web browser window. A little later in this chapter, I'll return to this file and take a closer look at the Java code in it.

THE CLASSES.ZIP FILE

A Mac application that you develop consists of your own compiled source code as well as code written by others—every call to a Toolbox function that your program makes relies on code written by Apple engineers. A somewhat analogous situation exists for a Java applet. Just as one could say that Macintosh C is the C language and a set of prewritten functions, one could also describe Java as the Java language and a set of prewritten classes. While the Macintosh Toolbox functions exist in the ROM and system software of a Mac, the prewritten Java classes exist in the **classes.zip** file. When you install CodeWarrior onto your hard drive, the installer places this large (it's close to 1 MB in size) **classes.zip** file in the System Folder of your Mac.

NOTE If you aren't familiar with the Java language or with C++, take a detour to Appendix B. That appendix provides an overview of C++—the language on which Java is based. There you'll see a description of what a class is.

Your Java source code file, no matter how simple, will make use of at least some of the classes defined in the **classes.zip** file. Consider the **TrivialApplet.java** file. In order to write a string to the window of a Web browser, a call is made to a Java function named drawString(). Because drawString() is defined in a class in the **classes.zip** file, the source code in the **TrivialApplet.java** file is making use of the **classes.zip** file, as illustrated in Figure 6.6. Because of this dependency, CodeWarrior always adds the **classes.zip** file to a project based on the Java Applet project stationery.

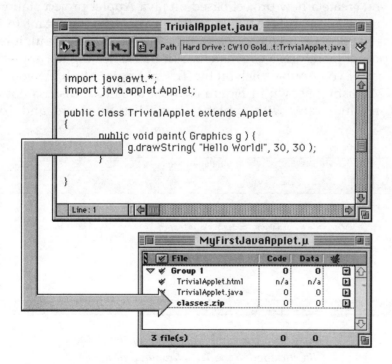

Figure 6.6 *Your Java source code can make use of Java classes and methods defined and stored in a file named **classes.zip**.*

If you're familiar with C++, you know that a class consists of data in the form of data members and functions in the form of member functions. A Java class also consists of data and functions. In Java, data exists as instance variables and functions exist as methods. So while I referred to drawString() as a function, it is more correctly said to be a method.

In C++ a member function doesn't exist on its own—it's part of a class. The same is true for a Java method—it's part of a class. In the case of the drawString() method, it's a part of a Java-defined class named Graphics.

THE TRIVIALAPPLET.HTML FILE

When you create a new project based on Java Applet project stationery, CodeWarrior adds an HTML file to the project. It's important to note that this file doesn't become a part of the applet itself. Instead, it exists in the project merely as a convenience—it makes testing the applet you build easy. If you double-click on the **TrivialApplet.html**, file you'll see the HTML listing shown in Figure 6.7. Just ahead I'll discuss how the HTML file integrates with applet testing, Web browsers, and applet viewers.

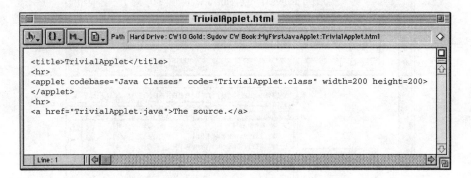

Figure 6.7 *The complete listing for the HTML file included in the **TrivialApplet.μ** project.*

Running the Default Applet

The CodeWarrior IDE lets you build an applet in the same manner as you build an application—just select **Run** from the Project menu. Before doing that, read on to see what you'll encounter when you use CodeWarrior to run an applet.

Applets and the Metrowerks Java Applet Viewer Application

To create an applet without running it, you can select **Make** from the Project menu. Doing that causes CodeWarrior to compile any .java files in the project and then link the compiled code with any needed code from the **classes.zip** file to build the applet. If you instead choose **Run** from the Project menu, as I'm about to do, CodeWarrior performs the same steps as Make—and one additional step. After building the applet, CodeWarrior launches a program named Metrowerks Java.

The Metrowerks Java application is an applet viewer. As its name implies, an *applet viewer* is an application that allows you to run, and thus view, an applet. To do that, you provide the applet viewer with an HTML file. The applet viewer ignores all HTML tags (commands) in the file except for the <applet> tag. Think of an applet viewer as a simplified Java-enabled Web browser—its only purpose is to execute an applet as if it were on a Web page.

Without making any changes to either the **TrivialApplet.java** source code file or the **TrivialApplet.html** HTML file, go ahead and select **Run** from the Project menu of the CodeWarrior IDE. When you do, CodeWarrior will launch the Metrowerks Java program. Before viewing the applet, you'll most likely see a dialog box displaying a copyright notice, as shown in Figure 6.8.

After reading and agreeing to the disclaimer in the dialog box, click the **Accept** button. After doing that, you won't see this dialog box ever again.

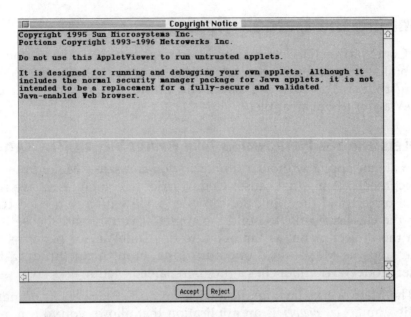

Figure 6.8   *The Copyright Notice dialog box that appears the first time you run Metrowerks Java.*

NOTE The text in the dialog box simply implies that it's best to use an applet viewer to test *your own* applets (or the applets of someone or some company you trust—like Metrowerks). A Java-enabled Web browser will be encountering and executing applets from anywhere on the World Wide Web—so it has safeguards built in to perform certain validation tests. A Java applet viewer is a simpler program, so it doesn't have these safeguards.

After dismissing the Copyright Notice dialog box, a Java Output window will open and then, a moment later, another window will appear. This second window will display the applet. An applet viewer knows which applet to load and display by reading an HTML file. When launched from the CodeWarrior IDE, the Metrowerks Java application uses the HTML file listed in the project window. Recall that for this example the HTML file in the **MyFirstJavaApplet.μ** project is named **TrivialApplet.html**. Figure 6.9 shows that the CodeWarrior-supplied applet simply writes the string "Hello World!" to the window.

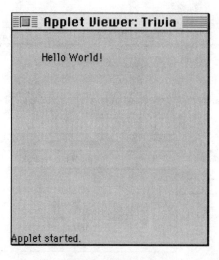

Figure 6.9 *The TrivialApplet applet, as viewed in the Metrowerks Java applet viewer.*

The Java Output window will display the name of the applet that's executing, and will list error messages if errors occur during the applet's execution.

After viewing the applet, choose **Quit** from the File menu of the Metrowerks Java application.

The Results of Building an Applet

After quitting the Metrowerks Java applet viewer, you'll find yourself back in the CodeWarrior IDE. Click on the desktop of your Mac, then open the folder that CodeWarrior created for you when you created the new project. If you named the project **MyFirstJavaApplet.µ**, as I did, then the folder will be named **MyFirstJavaApplet**.

In the **MyFirstJavaApplet** folder you'll find the Java project and two of the three files that are in that project—the **TrivialApplet.java** source code file and the **TrivialApplet.html** file. Recall that the third file—the **classes.zip** file—is kept in the System Folder. You'll also find a folder in the **MyFirstJavaApplet** folder. As shown in Figure 6.10, this folder holds a single file—the applet itself.

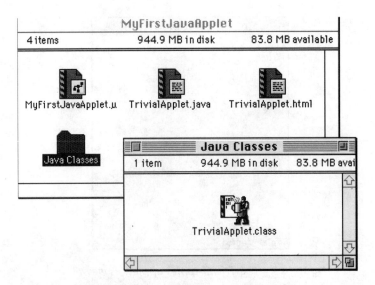

Figure 6.10 *The files that are a part of an applet project—including the applet file.*

 After CodeWarrior builds an applet, it always places the applet in its own folder within the project folder. By default this folder is named **Java Classes**. If for some reason you aren't happy with this name, you can change it from within the CodeWarrior IDE. To do that, select **Project Settings** from the Edit menu (the CodeWarrior project from which the applet is built must be open, of course). Click on **Java Project** in the list of the Project Settings dialog box to display the Java Project panel shown in Figure 6.11. Then type in a new folder name in the File Name edit box. Now, each time you rebuild the applet, it will end up in a folder with this new name.

While you have the applet folder open, take a look at the size of the **TrivialApplet.class** applet. You can do that as you would any file—click once on the file's icon, then select **Get Info** from the File menu. When you do that, you'll see that the applet is quite small—only 420 bytes (see Figure 6.12).

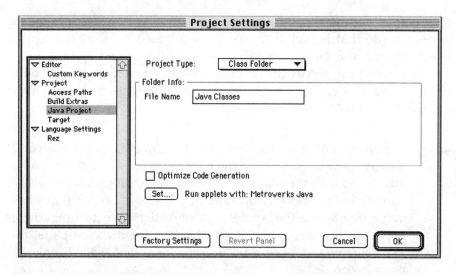

Figure 6.11 *The name of the folder that holds the applet class file can be changed from within the CodeWarrior IDE.*

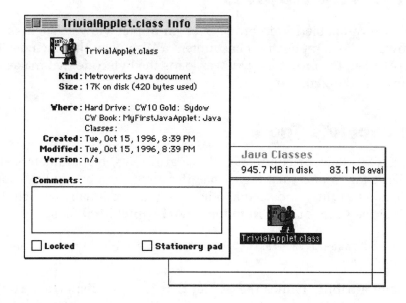

Figure 6.12 *Examining the size of the TrivialApplet.*

You'll notice that the size of the applet is well under 1K. Recall that the **classes.zip** file that is included in a project based on the Java Applet project stationery is close to 1 MB in size. Quite obviously that whole file is not becoming a part of the Java applet. When an applet is built, only the pertinent code from the **classes.zip** file gets included in the code that makes up the applet.

NOTE   The amount of disk space the applet occupies (17K in Figure 6.12) is dependent on the size of the hard drive the applet is on—it has little to do with the size of the applet. The smallest space my 1 GB hard drive can allocate for a file of any size is 17K, so that's how much disk space the applet occupies. If I were to upload this applet to the server that holds the files for my Web page, this 17K value would be of no concern—the applet really is only 420 bytes in size.

HTML and Applets

When a Java-enabled Web browser or an applet viewer (such as the Metrowerks Java application) encounters a Web page that includes the `<applet>` tag, the browser or viewer loads the bytecode that makes up the applet and executes it.

The `<applet>` Tag

Some HTML tags, or commands, have attributes, or parameters. The `<applet>` tag is one such tag. It has three required attributes—`code`, `width`, and `height`—and several others that can optionally be included. Consider the `<applet>` tag from the **TrivialApplet.html** file:

```
<applet codebase="Java Classes" code="TrivialApplet.class" width=200
    height=200>
```

The `code` attribute names the applet that is to be displayed. You've already seen that an applet is always stored in a file that ends with a **.class** extension. This extension must be included in the name supplied to the code attribute, and the entire applet name must be enclosed in quotes. In the above example, the applet that is to be displayed is the **TrivialApplet.class** applet.

The second and third `<applet>` attributes specify the size of the applet. The size is the amount of Web page pixel space that the applet will occupy. In this example the applet will be displayed in an area 200 pixels wide by 200 pixels high. Figure 6.13 illustrates that the Metrowerks Java applet viewer adjusts the size of the display window depending on the values of the `width` and `height` attributes. On the left of this figure is the window the applet viewer opens when it encounters the `<applet>` tag shown above. On the right is the window the applet viewer would open if the same `<applet>` tag was modified such that the `height` attribute had a value of 50 rather than 200.

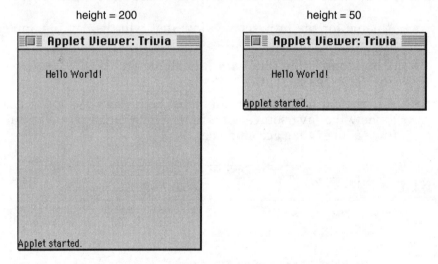

height = 200   height = 50

Figure 6.13   *Changing the value of the height attribute*
of the `<applet>` tag changes the area an applet occupies.

The `<applet>` example I've given above also includes one optional attribute—*codebase*. The codebase lists the path to the directory, or folder, that holds the applet. If the applet (the **.class** file) appears in the same folder as the HTML file that holds the `<applet>` tag, then the codebase attribute need not be included in the `<applet>` tag. If the applet is held in a subdirectory, however, then codebase needs to be included so that the browser or applet viewer knows where the applet is located. Because the **TrivialApplet.html** file is in one folder and the applet appears in the **Java Classes** folder within that folder, the codebase attribute is included in the `<applet>` tag and is given a value of "Java Classes." Like the name of the applet itself, the name of the path must be enclosed in quotes.

Applets and Web Browsers

When the Metrowerks Java applet viewer processes an HTML file, it ignores all tags except the `<applet>` and `</applet>` tags. You can verify this by looking at the **TrivialApplet.html** file, which is shown in Figure 6.14. Notice that while the applet viewer displays one the applet, the HTML code in the **TrivialApplet.html** file specifies all of the following:

- A name for the browser window that will display the applet (the `<title>` tag does that).

- A horizontal rule (line) appears above and below the applet (the `<hr>` tags do that).

- A hypertext reference, or link, must be present to allow a user to view the Java source code from which the applet was built (the `<a href>` tag accomplishes this).

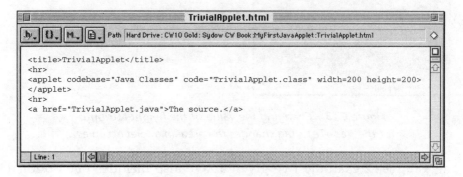

Figure 6.14 *The complete listing for the **TrivialApplet.html** HTML file.*

The HTML code that is ignored by an applet viewer isn't ignored by a Web browser. If you own a Web browser, you see this demonstrated by first launching the browser. There's no need to connect to the Web for this test—you can use your browser to open an HTML file that resides on your hard drive. Choose the **Open File** menu item from the File menu, then select the **TrivialApplet.html** file. Figure 6.15 shows the browser window when this is done using the Macintosh version of Netscape Navigator.

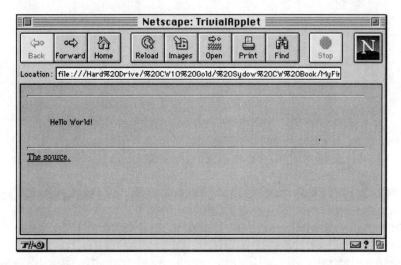

Figure 6.15 *The TrivialApplet as viewed in Netscape Navigator for the Macintosh.*

Clicking on the source hypertext link causes the browser to load the **TrivialApplet.java** source code file and display the files code in the browser window. Figure 6.16 again uses Netscape Navigator to illustrate this.

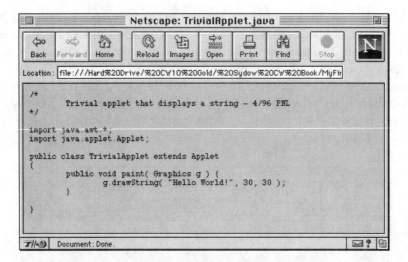

```
/*
        Trivial applet that displays a string – 4/96 PNL
*/

import java.awt.*;
import java.applet.Applet;

public class TrivialApplet extends Applet
{
        public void paint( Graphics g ) {
                g.drawString( "Hello World!", 30, 30 );
        }

}
```

Figure 6.16   *The TrivialApplet source code listing as viewed in Netscape Navigator for the Macintosh.*

Java Source Code and the TrivialApplet

While a teaching of the Java language is well beyond the scope of this book, a look at the few lines of Java code found in the **TrivialApplet.java** file will serve as a good introduction to readers unfamiliar with this new language. Figure 6.17 provides a look at the complete listing found in the **TrivialApplet.java** file.

If you're going to write your own applets, you'll need a good reference to the Java programming language. If you need such a book, consider picking up a copy of Brian Overland's *Java in Plain English* also published by M&T Books.

Import Statements

Sun Microsystems, the developer of the Java language, supplies Java programmers such as yourself with a huge base of code that can be used in any of your own applets. This code exists in classes. These classes are organized into *packages*—collections of related classes. In order for your applet to make use of the classes in a package, that package must be imported. In Java, the import statement is used in a manner similar to a C or C++ #include directive. The **MyFirstJavaApplet.java** listing includes two import statements:

```
import java.awt.*;
import java.applet.Applet;
```

The asterisk in the first import statement means that all of the classes in a package named **java.awt** are to be made available to this applet. The second import statement designates that only one particular class (the Applet class) from the java.applet package be made available to the applet.

The classes stored in the **java.awt** package provide you with the methods (functions) that allow you to easily include graphics in your applets. The Applet class in the **java.applet** package defines the code that makes it possible for an applet to execute within a Web browser.

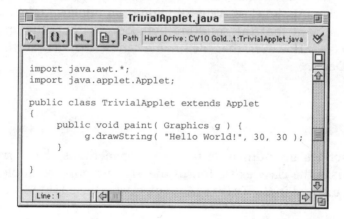

Figure 6.17 *The complete source code listing for the TrivialApplet applet.*

The Applet Class

All applets must define a class that is extended, or derived, from the Java class named Applet. Such an extended class is said to be a *subclass*. Thus the TrivialApplet class is a subclass of the Java Applet class. As such, the TrivialApplet class inherits all of the code defined in the

Applet class. In other words, any of the methods defined in the Applet class now become available for use in the TrivialApplet class.

```
public class TrivialApplet extends Applet
{
    public void paint( Graphics g ) {
        g.drawString( "Hello World!", 30, 30 );
    }

}
```

The applet class begins with the Java keyword public, followed by the Java keyword class. After that comes the name of the applet class. Next comes the Java keyword extends, followed by the Java class being extended—the Applet class.

NOTE The name of the applet class must be the same as the name of the applet. For instance, because the applet class in this example is named TrivialApplet, the resulting applet must be named **TrivialApplet.class.** When building an applet, CodeWarrior will see to it that the resulting bytecode file gets the appropriate name. However, that file's name can be changed at the desktop. Don't.

Methods

A class defines any number of functions, or methods, that carry out the task or tasks the class exists for. In the TrivialApplet example, there is only one method in the TrivialApplet class—the paint() method:

```
public void paint( Graphics g ) {
    g.drawString( "Hello World!", 30, 30 );
}
```

The paint() method is special—it's a function that gets invoked automatically when the applet needs to be redrawn, or painted. That occurs when the window that holds the applet is obscured or partly obscured, and then comes back into view. When such an event occurs, the browser running the applet will know enough to invoke the paint() method defined in the applet class so that the applet can redraw itself. In the case of the TrivialApplet applet, redrawing the applet simply involves redrawing the string "Hello World!" to the browser window.

When the browser invokes paint(), it passes along a reference to an object of the Java class type Graphics. This object is something the browser creates when it encounters a Web page that holds an applet. In short, the Graphics object is a drawing area.

The Graphics class defines dozens of methods. Because the browser passes the paint() method a reference to a Graphics object, the paint() method is free to invoke any of these Graphic classes—provided it specifies the name of a Graphics object upon which the invoked method should operate. The call to the drawString() method of the Graphics class is such an example:

```
g.drawString( "Hello World!", 30, 30 );
```

Summary

To use CodeWarrior to develop an applet, launch the CodeWarrior IDE—the same integrated development environment you've been using to develop Mac applications. Then create a new project based on the Java Applet project stationery. Replace or supplement the source code listing found in the **TrivialApplet.java** file that CodeWarrior includes in each Java project. To build the applet and then test it, choose **Run** from the Project menu. Doing that will launch the Metrowerks Java applet viewer—an application that allows you to view and test applets without having to connect to the Web.

Chapter 7

Getting Started with PowerPlant and Constructor

PowerPlant is used to create Macintosh applications. But it's not a compiler or any other type of application. It's an application framework. That means it's a set of C++ classes that are used in conjunction with your own C++ object-oriented code. These classes—written by Metrowerks programmers—provide a great deal of the interface functionality common to all Mac applications.

In this chapter, you'll see how to set up a CodeWarrior project so that it makes use of PowerPlant. You'll then compile the example source code that CodeWarrior adds to this project. The resulting application will be one that you'll use in this and the next three chapters.

Like any Mac application, a program that is generated from a PowerPlant project starts out as source code and resources. In this chapter, you'll learn about Constructor—Metrowerks's own resource editor that was designed specifically for editing the resources of a PowerPlant-based project. In the following three chapters, you'll learn about both the PowerPlant source code and the source code you'll write to work in conjunction with the PowerPlant code.

The PowerPlant Project

In Chapter 2, I introduced projects and the CodeWarrior IDE by creating a new application using project stationery. In that chapter's first example I left in place the default files that CodeWarrior adds to a new project—the **SillyBalls.c** source code file and the **SillyBalls.rsrc** resource file. Then I compiled and ran the resulting program. Because the two SillyBalls files generally serve as placeholders and are normally replaced by your own files, I didn't bother to examine them.

In this chapter, I'll take an approach similar to the one presented in Chapter 2. I'll use project stationery to set up a project, compile the default source code file and link it with the default resource file to create an application, and then give that application a test run. After that, my approach will differ from that taken in Chapter 2. In this chapter, I'll take a long look at the resources that CodeWarrior places in a project that is based on PowerPlant project stationery. In doing that I'll lightly touch upon a few of the many classes that make up the PowerPlant source code. The next three chapters will be spent fully exploring the source code. I'll take the approach of working with the example resources and source code that CodeWarrior supplies to a PowerPlant-based project because unlike the placeholder files included in a project based on Basic Toolbox project stationery, the source code and resource files CodeWarrior includes in a project based on PowerPlant project stationery are *very* useful.

TIP

If you become familiar with the source code in the **PP Basic Starter.cp** and **PP Basic Starter.h** files that CodeWarrior supplies as the starting point for each PowerPlant project, you'll acquire an excellent background in PowerPlant basics. This chapter, as well as Chapters 9, 10, and 11, use these two files as the starting point for PowerPlant applications. While you *can* replace these files with your own PowerPlant code, it makes the most sense to start with the code Metrowerks supplies for you.

What the Example PowerPlant Application Does

In this chapter, I'll examine the project file and resource files for an example program I've named PowerPlantIntro68K. The next three chapters will carry on with this same example. When you run the PowerPlantIntro68K application, your screen will look like the one shown in Figure 7.1. A menu bar with three menus will appear, and a single window that holds a line of text will open. A stand-alone version of this program already exists on this book's CD, so you can take a look at PowerPlantIntro68K before you spend your time on these next few chapters learning about its project, source code, and resources.

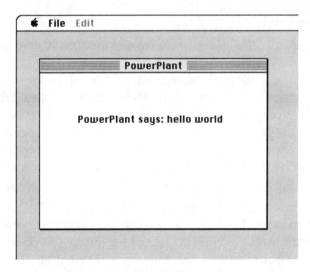

Figure 7.1 *The PowerPlantIntro68K program displays a window and menu bar.*

Figure 7.2 shows the items you'll find in the three menus used by PowerPlantIntro68K. The Apple menu allows the user to select the **About** menu item or any of the items found in the user's Apple Menu Items folder. The File menu lets the user create a new window, close an existing one, or quit the application. While several other items appear in this menu, each is disabled. Because PowerPlantIntro68K doesn't support the editing of the text that's displayed in its windows, the items in the Edit menu are disabled.

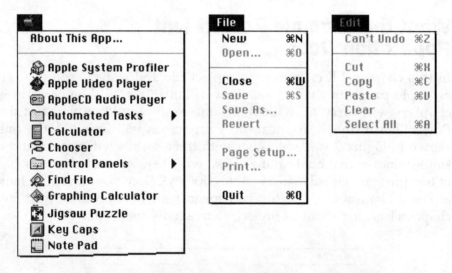

Figure 7.2   *The menus of the PowerPlantIntro68K program.*

The window that opens can be moved, and it can be closed. Any number of new windows can be created by selecting **New** from the File menu (or by typing **Command-N**). Each new window will appear in the same screen position as the first window, but you can freely drag any window about and position each wherever you want. Figure 7.3 shows PowerPlantIntro68K running with several windows open.

The following three chapters discuss the source code that makes up the project's main source code file—a file named **PP Basic Starter.cp**. You'll want to note that this file includes no code to handle a mouse click in a menu and no code to handle a menu selection such as the Apple menu **About** item or the File menu **Quit** item. There's also no code for moving the windows about the screen. Yet the program readily handles these tasks. The trick to this, of course, lies in the code that makes up the many PowerPlant source code files.

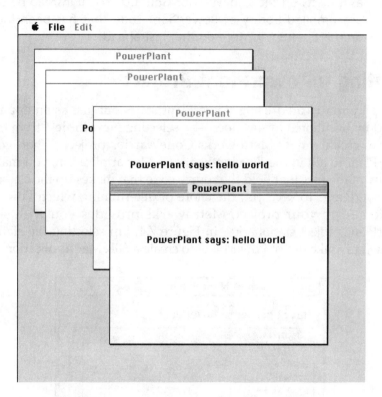

Figure 7.3 *The PowerPlantIntro68K program allows any number of windows to be opened.*

If you're using a version of CodeWarrior that you purchased (that is, if you're using a version other than the one included on this book's CD), make sure that you have PowerPlant installed. PowerPlant *isn't* a part of every option provided in the installer program on the CodeWarrior Gold Tools CD. If you aren't sure if you have PowerPlant installed, open the **Metrowerks CodeWarrior** folder that's located in your main **CodeWarrior** folder. In that folder, open the **MacOS Support** folder. There you should find a folder named **PowerPlant**. If it's not there, you'll want to rerun the tools installer, check the **Metrowerks**

PowerPlant checkbox, and then do an install. If you're using CodeWarrior Lite from this book's CD, you don't have PowerPlant as it exists on the CodeWarrior Gold CD. You'll instead be using a precompiled library of PowerPlant code that has been included on this book's CD. More on that just ahead.

Creating a PowerPlant Project

An application created using PowerPlant starts out just as an application created by traditional means does—by selecting **New Project** from the File menu to create a new Metrowerks CodeWarrior project. When you use PowerPlant to aid in the development of a Mac application, you make use of many of the files that hold the source code that makes up the classes that are PowerPlant. To save you the chore of determining which PowerPlant files to add to your project, Metrowerks provides you with several PowerPlant project stationeries. In Figure 7.4, I'm selecting the stationery designed to make use of PowerPlant to create a 68K Mac application.

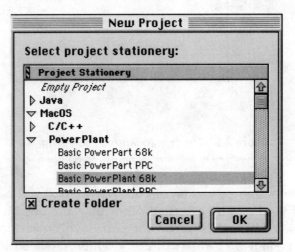

*Figure 7.4   Create a PowerPlant project by selecting **PowerPlant project stationery**.*

As is typical of the examples in this book, I'm going with a 68K project. Recall that programs generated from a 68K project will run on either a 68K-based Mac or a Power Macintosh. And that nables every reader to give each example program a test run on his or her computer.

Leaving the **Create Folder** checkbox checked, click the **OK** button to dismiss the New Project dialog box and to bring on the dialog box that prompts you to enter a project name. In Figure 7.5, I'm doing just that.

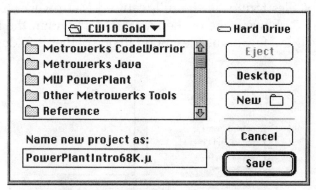

Figure 7.5   *Name the PowerPlant project as you would any other CodeWarrior project.*

In Figure 7.5, you see that I've given the project a name appropriate to the program I'll be developing. After then clicking the **Save** button, a new project window appears (see Figure 7.6).

File	Code	Data	
▽ ✓ **Application**	0	0	• ▣
✓ PP Basic Starter.cp	0	0	• ▣
✓ **PP Basic Resource.rsrc**	n/a	n/a	▣
✓ **PP Basic Resource.ppob**	n/a	n/a	▣
✓ **PP Action Strings.rsrc**	n/a	n/a	▣
✓ PP DebugAlerts.rsrc	n/a	n/a	▣
▷ ✓ **Commanders**	0	0	• ▣
▷ ✓ **Features**	0	0	• ▣
▷ ✓ **Panes**	0	0	• ▣
▷ ✓ **File & Stream**	0	0	• ▣
▷ ✓ **Apple Events**	0	0	• ▣
▷ ✓ **Lists**	0	0	• ▣
▷ ✓ **Support**	0	0	• ▣
▷ ✓ **Utilities**	0	0	• ▣
▷ ✓ **Libraries**	0	0	• ▣
72 file(s)	0	0	

Figure 7.6   *The project window for a project based on PowerPlant project stationery.*

PowerPlant Projects and PowerPlant Classes

Looking at Figure 7.6, you'll notice that a project based on PowerPlant project stationery consists of several more groups than a project based on Basic Toolbox project stationery. Remember, PowerPlant is not an application; it's a collection of classes. The definitions of these classes are held in dozens of files found on the full-featured Metrowerks CodeWarrior CD. Figure 7.7 shows some of the many folders within the **PowerPlant** folder, as well as a few of the files found in one of theses folders.

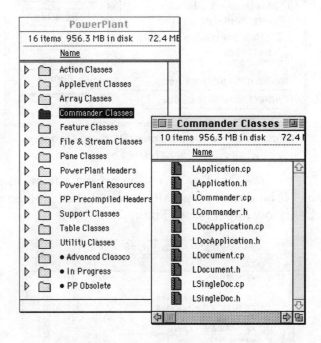

Figure 7.7 *A few of the files that hold PowerPlant source code.*

Looking at the **PowerPlantIntro68K.µ** project file will give you a better idea of how the contents of a project that uses PowerPlant differs from a project that doesn't. Figure 7.8 shows this project file.

Figure 7.8 shows the same project window as pictured back in Figure 7.6. Here, in Figure 7.8, I've clicked on the **arrow** icon beside each of two groups to provide an indication of just how many files are in a project based on PowerPlant project stationery.

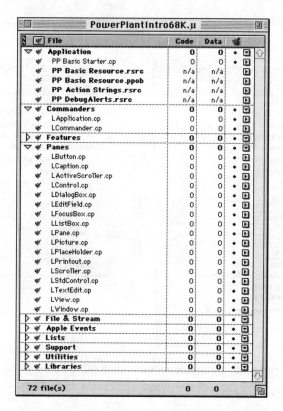

File	Code	Data	🐛	
Application	**0**	**0**	•	▽
PP Basic Starter.cp	0	0	•	▶
PP Basic Resource.rsrc	n/a	n/a		▶
PP Basic Resource.ppob	n/a	n/a		▶
PP Action Strings.rsrc	n/a	n/a		▶
PP DebugAlerts.rsrc	n/a	n/a		▶
Commanders	**0**	**0**	•	▽
LApplication.cp	0	0	•	▶
LCommander.cp	0	0	•	▶
Features	**0**	**0**	•	▽
Panes	**0**	**0**	•	▽
LButton.cp	0	0	•	▶
LCaption.cp	0	0	•	▶
LActiveScroller.cp	0	0	•	▶
LControl.cp	0	0	•	▶
LDialogBox.cp	0	0	•	▶
LEditField.cp	0	0	•	▶
LFocusBox.cp	0	0	•	▶
LListBox.cp	0	0	•	▶
LPane.cp	0	0	•	▶
LPicture.cp	0	0	•	▶
LPlaceHolder.cp	0	0	•	▶
LPrintout.cp	0	0	•	▶
LScroller.cp	0	0	•	▶
LStdControl.cp	0	0	•	▶
LTextEdit.cp	0	0	•	▶
LView.cp	0	0	•	▶
LWindow.cp	0	0	•	▶
File & Stream	**0**	**0**	•	▽
Apple Events	**0**	**0**	•	▽
Lists	**0**	**0**	•	▽
Support	**0**	**0**	•	▽
Utilities	**0**	**0**	•	▽
Libraries	**0**	**0**	•	▽
72 file(s)	0	0		

Figure 7.8 *Many of the groups of a PowerPlant project
hold several PowerPlant class source code files.*

NOTE

If you're using the Lite version of CodeWarrior, you won't be able to compile **PowerPlantIntro68K.µ**—not this version, anyway. Instead, look in the **C07 PowerPlant Intro** folder for a folder aptly titled **CW10 Lite Users Use This**. There you'll find another version of this same project—a version created just for you. For copyright reasons, the numerous individual files that make up the PowerPlant application framework have not been included on the CD that accompanies this book. In place of the many individual PowerPlant files, you'll find one precompiled library named **BookPowerPlantLib68K**. For you CodeWarrior Lite users this one library is used in place of all of the PowerPlant files normally included in a project. Figure 7.9 shows the two versions of this project.

Project for full-featured version of CodeWarrior   Project for Lite version of CodeWarrior

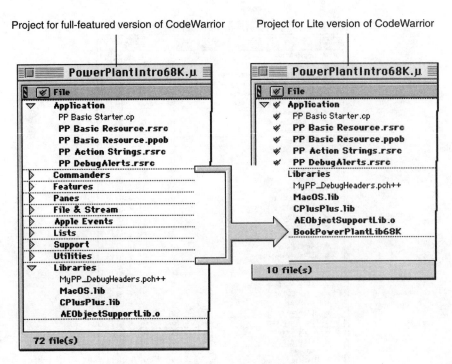

Figure 7.9   *A precompiled library can be used in place of individual PowerPlant source code files.*

Running the Default Program

Like a project created from Basic Toolbox project stationery, a project based on PowerPlant stationery includes source code and resources. The remainder of this chapter is dedicated to describing the resources. If you want to gain a sound understanding of everything in the **PowerPlantIntro68K.µ** project, try running the PowerPlantIntro68K program now. You can go ahead and compile the files in the project now. Without making any changes to either the code or the resources, choose **Run** from the Project menu to compile the code and run the resulting application. When you do, you'll see the window and menus shown back in Figure 7.1.

N O T E

If you get a slew of errors like the ones pictured in Figure 7.10, then your project doesn't have C++ exceptions enabled. Exceptions are covered later in this chapter. To remedy this problem, choose **Project Settings** from the Edit menu and click on **C/C++ Language** in the list. Then check the **Enable C++ Exceptions** checkbox, as shown in Figure 7.11.

Figure 7.10 *Attempting to compile a PowerPlant-based project when exceptions aren't enabled.*

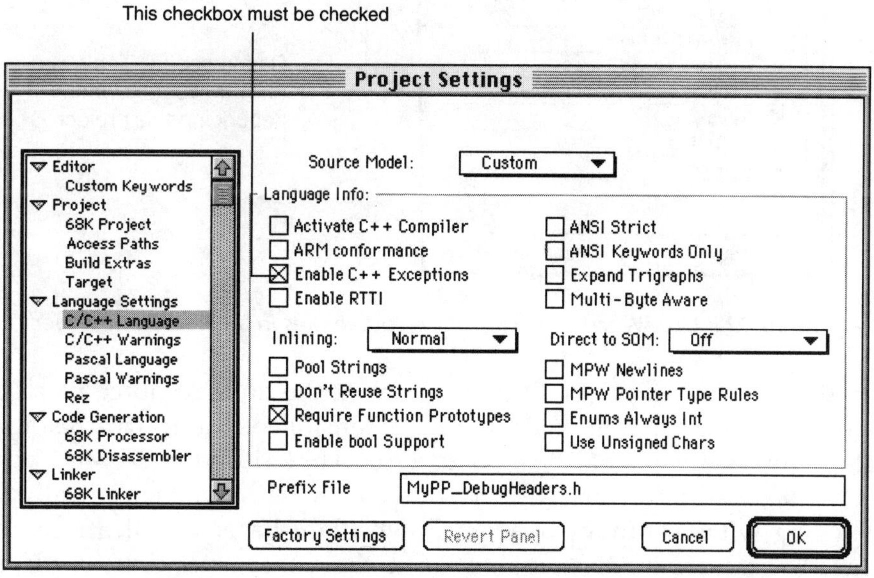

This checkbox must be checked

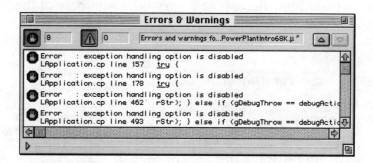

Figure 7.11 *If "exception handling option is disabled" errors occur during compilation, make sure that exceptions are enabled.*

PowerPlant Resource Files

A Mac application that is built using PowerPlant classes includes resources of the types you're already familiar with—and a couple of new types. When you create a project that's based on PowerPlant stationery, CodeWarrior adds four resource files to the new project. Figure 7.12 shows these files, along with a very brief summary of the purpose of each.

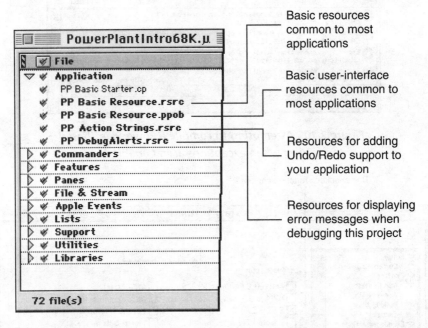

Figure 7.12   CodeWarrior places four resource files in a PowerPlant project.

On the next few of pages, I'll take a look at the three resource files that end with an extension of **.rsrc**. The extension of the fourth resource file—**.ppob**—is probably new to you. That file was created with Constructor—Metrowerks own resource editor designed specifically for working with resources used in PowerPlant-based applications. I'll want to spend extra time looking over the Constructor-created file, so I'll reserve the examination the **PP Basic Resource.ppob** file for later in this chapter—in the section devoted to Constructor.

The four files shown in Figure 7.12 hold the basic resources you'll need to get your project started. Metrowerks has included many resources that are either required or handy to have in a PowerPlant project—but they of course couldn't include *everything* your program will need. For instance, if your program displays a company logo in a window, Metrowerks obviously couldn't include a PICT resource that holds this logo. As you develop your program, you'll add new resources to the project. In Chapter 10, you'll see how and when to do that.

The PP Basic Resource.rsrc File

Double-clicking on the **PP Basic Resource.rsrc** file name in the **PowerPlantIntro68K.µ** project window launches ResEdit and opens the resource file pictured in Figure 7.13.

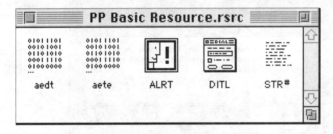

Figure 7.13   The resource types found in the PP Basic Resource.rsrc file, as viewed in ResEdit.

The resources in **PP Basic Resource.rsrc** are the most basic resources necessary for a Macintosh application that is built using PowerPlant. The ALRT, DITL, and STR# resource types should be recognizable, but the aedt and aete types may not be.

Some of the PowerPlant code that becomes a part of your application may be expecting one or more of the resources that are defined in the **PP Basic Resource.rsrc** file to be present in your application. Keep all of these resources as a part of your project, even if you don't think your program will need them!

ALRT and DITL Resources

One of the two ALRT resources defined in the **PP Basic Resource.rsrc** file is used by your program if memory runs low. The ALRT is used to display an alert box that informs the user of the low memory condition. Figure 7.14 shows this ALRT resource. One of the two DITL resources in **PP Basic Resource.rsrc** is used to define the items that appear in this alert.

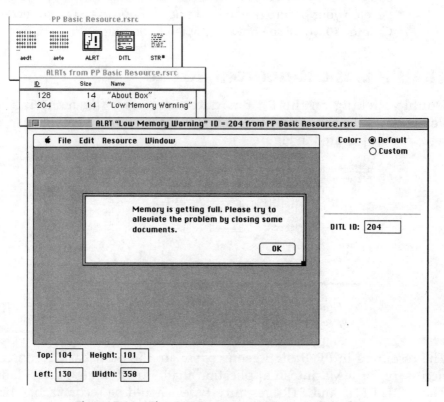

Figure 7.14   *The memory error ALRT resource in the*
PP Basic Resource.rsrc file, as viewed in ResEdit.

The second ALRT and second DITL in **PP Basic Resource.rsrc** are used by PowerPlant code in your program to display a simple About box when the user selects the **About** item from the Apple menu of your program. Figure 7.15 shows the ALRT resource. You can edit DITL 128—the DITL that defines the look of the About alert box—to make this About box specific to your own application.

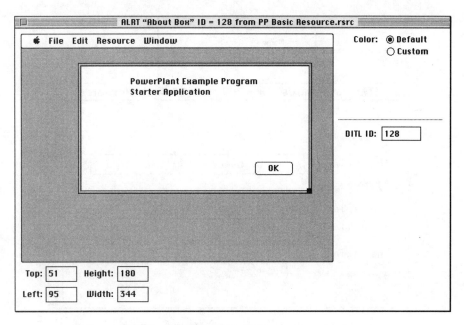

Figure 7.15 *The About ALRT resource in the*
PP Basic Resource.rsrc file, as viewed in ResEdit.

STR# RESOURCE

A STR# resource is a string list. The one string list in **PP Basic Resource.rsrc** holds a few strings that are commonly used by PowerPlant—Figure 7.16 shows the strings in this resource. You'll leave the second and third string untouched, but the first string in the list should be changed to match the name of your program. As your program executes, PowerPlant code that is a part of your program may have occasion to display a warning alert (for instance, if your application creates documents, and the user elects to quit the program without saving an open document). When it does that, it will insert the name of your application in the alert. PowerPlant gets the program name from the first string from STR# 200 in the alert.

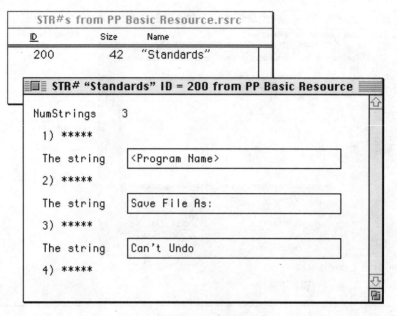

*Figure 7.16   Commonly used strings held in a STR# resource
in the PP Basic Resource.rsrc file, as viewed in ResEdit.*

AEDT AND AETE RESOURCES

An aedt resource is an Apple Event Description Table. This is a custom resource used by PowerPlant to help in the support of Apple events. PowerPlant classes rely heavily on Apple events, so you'll always want your project's resource file to include the three aedt resources that are defined in this resource file. PowerPlant's use of aedt resources is internal. This means that although you'll need to include the three aedt resources in your own projects, you won't need to be concerned with their usage.

For the curious, here's a little background information on the aedt resource. The Macintosh Toolbox uses two 32-bit numbers when working with a single Apple event. In PowerPlant, this two-number system is inconvenient. So Metrowerks uses an aedt resource to create a single 32-bit number that points to the two numbers used by a particular Apple event.

An `aete` resource is another Apple Event-related resource; it's an Apple Event Terminology Extension resource. The information in such a resource defines the human language (as opposed to a computer language) of the program, and is used by Apple script editors. If the application you're creating is scriptable, then this resource is used by a script editor. The `aete` resource that is a part of the **PP Basic Resource.rsrc** file specifies that information in your program is displayed in the English language.

The PP Action Strings.rsrc File

The **PP Action Strings.rsrc** file in the **PowerPlantIntro68K.µ** project is a Resorcerer file that holds only one type of resource. Figure 7.17 shows the resource file when opened in ResEdit rather than Resorcerer.

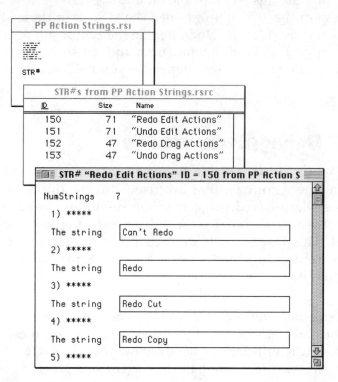

Figure 7.17 *Some of the strings found in one of four STR#*
*resources in the **PP Action Strings.rsrc** file, as viewed in ResEdit.*

Metrowerks resource files that you may have occasion to edit (such as the just-described **PP Basic Resource.rsrc**) are supplied as ResEdit documents. Everyone has ResEdit—it's Apple's free resource editor and it's included on this book's CD and as a part of every CodeWarrior package—so Metrowerks knows that when you double-click on the name of such a file in a project window, ResEdit will be guaranteed to launch and to open the file. Other Metrowerks resource files—ones that are less likely to be edited by a programmer—are supplied as Resorcerer documents. That's the resource editor preferred by many (including, obviously, some folks at Metrowerks). If you want to view or edit a Resorcerer file from ResEdit, you can do so—just run ResEdit and then open the file.

The **PP Action Strings.rsrc** file holds four STR# resources—Figure 7.17 shows some of the strings from one. The strings in these string lists supply the text used for the **Undo** item in the Edit menu of an application that support an **Undo** menu command. In such a program, the text of this menu item changes depending on the last action taken by the user.

The PP DebugAlerts.rsrc File

The **PP DebugAlerts.rsrc** file is another Resorcerer resource file. It holds a few resources that are used during the debugging of your PowerPlant-based project. When debugging, and an exception is thrown or a signal is raised, an informative alert will be displayed. This resource file defines a pair of alerts that provides you with debugging feedback. Figure 7.18 provides a ResEdit view of this file.

Exceptions and signals, as used by PowerPlant, are discussed near the end of Chapter 8. If you aren't familiar with these terms, for now it is sufficient to simply know that they refer to types of errors that occur during the running of your program.

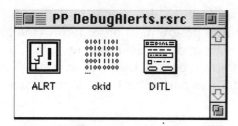

Figure 7.18 *The resource types found in the*
PP DebugAlerts.rsrc file, as viewed in ResEdit.

The PP Basic Resource.ppob File

The fourth resource file that CodeWarrior includes in a PowerPlant-based project is **PP Basic Resource.ppob**. The **.ppob** extension gives you an indication that this file might be different than other resource files—and it is. It's a file that was created by, and is edited in, a program named Constructor—Metrowerks's own resource editor. I'll discuss this file in detail in the next section. For now, be aware that it holds the graphical interface resources for the PowerPlantIntro68K program. Some of these resources, such as the MENU and MBAR resources, you're already familiar with. Others, such as the PPob resource, will be new to you.

Constructor and PowerPlant Resources

A CodeWarrior project that uses PowerPlant project stationery generates a Macintosh program—just as a CodeWarrior project that uses one of the Basic Toolbox project stationeries does. The difference isn't in the final application, it's in the source code used to create the application. A project that uses PowerPlant project stationery includes the source code from some or many of the PowerPlant files that holds the classes that make up the PowerPlant application framework. So it makes sense that a PowerPlant project can include all the same resources you'll find in any other project. In addition to the traditional resource types such as MENU, MBAR, DLOG, and DITL, though, a PowerPlant project includes resources of a few types that aren't found in other projects. In particular, PowerPlant defines its own resource type that's used to define the characteristics of the windows used in a program. In order to provide programmers with an easy means to create and edit their own resources, as well as resources of most of the common types, Metrowerks includes Constructor, its own visual resources editor, as part of the CodeWarrior package.

Constructor—The Resource Editor

Just as you can launch ResEdit and open a ResEdit resource file by double-clicking on the resource file name in a CodeWarrior project window, so too can you launch the Constructor application and open a Constructor-created resource file by double-clicking on its name in a project window. The **PowerPlantIntro68K.µ** project introduced earlier in this chapter contains just such a file—the **PP Basic Resource.ppob** file that CodeWarrior placed in the project. If you double-click on that file's name in the **PowerPlantIntro68K.µ** project window, Constructor will launch and you'll see the contents of the file displayed in a project window like the one pictured in Figure 7.19.

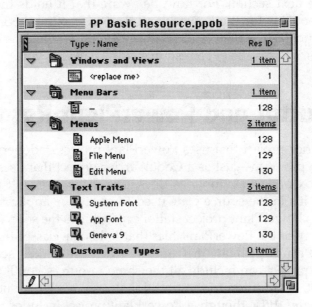

Figure 7.19   The resources held in the
***PP Basic Resource.ppob** file, as viewed in Constructor.*

Like the CodeWarrior IDE, Constructor also uses the term *project window*. In Constructor, the window that holds the list of resource types in a file is called a project window.

In the *Constructor Manual* (a very useful electronic document found on the Reference CD of the Metrowerks CodeWarrior Gold package), Constructor is referred to as "a visual interface builder for PowerPlant." Constructor is just that—it allows you to create the graphical user interface elements of your program—such as menus, windows, and dialog boxes—and to do so in a visual manner. If that sounds similar to the task you employ a visual resource editor like ResEdit or Resorcerer for, then you're thinking of Constructor in the correct light. If you're new to PowerPlant and Constructor, it might help if you think of Constructor as a resource editor much like ResEdit.

VIEWING A CONSTRUCTOR FILE RESOURCE IN RESEDIT

If you want proof that the contents of a Constructor file are in fact resources, close the **PP Basic Resource.ppob** file in Constructor, launch ResEdit, and reopen this same file. When you do that, you'll see a window like the one pictured in Figure 7.20.

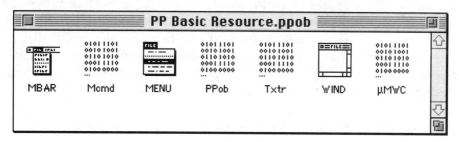

Figure 7.20 *The resource types held in the*
PP Basic Resource.ppob *file, as viewed in ResEdit.*

You'll recognize some of the resource types displayed in ResEdit. And if you double-click on the icon of one of these types, such as the **MENU** resources icon, the resulting display of the resources of this type will also look familiar. Figure 7.21 shows how ResEdit displays the three MENU resources found in **PP Basic Resources.ppob**.

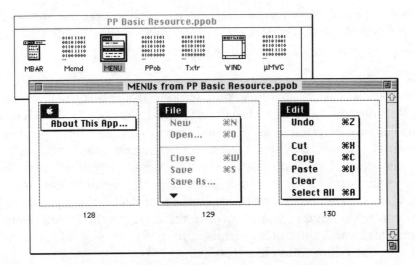

Figure 7.21 *The MENU resources held in the*
PP Basic Resource.ppob file, as viewed in ResEdit.

Some of the resources in the Constructor resource file won't look familiar to you—and they won't be recognizable to ResEdit either. ResEdit
can display the hexadecimal contents of any type of resource, but it can
display in a graphical form the contents of only resource types for
which a template is defined. For example, Apple has a MENU template
built into ResEdit so that menu data can be viewed graphically, as
shown in Figure 7.21. Apple hasn't defined any such template for the
resource type Mcmd, however. When you try to view an Mcmd resource in
ResEdit, you'll see only hexadecimal data (see Figure 7.22).

Viewing a Constructor File Resource in Constructor

The Mcmd was established by Metrowerks as resource type that is to be
used in conjunction with MENU resources. As you'll see in Chapter 9, the
source code you write for your PowerPlant-based project will reference
Mcmd resources. Because the Mcmd resource type is one created by
Metrowerks and designed for use with PowerPlant projects,
Metrowerks of course included a means of working with Mcmd
resources in Constructor. To see this, quit ResEdit and reopen the **PP
Basic Resource.ppob** file in Constructor.

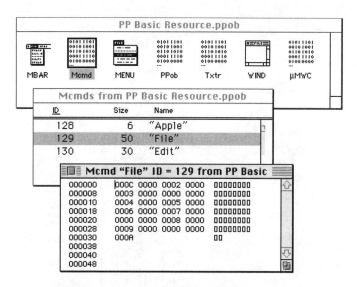

Figure 7.22   *An Mcmd resource from the*
PP Basic Resource.ppob *file, as viewed in ResEdit.*

In the Constructor project window, you see a list of the resource types and resources in the file. For the **PP Basic Resource.ppob** file, there is a resource type named Menu (and three resources of that type), but there is no Mcmd resource type or resources listed. To investigate, double-click on one of the Menu resources. In Figure 7.23, I've double-clicked on the small icon to the right of the Menu resource named **File Menu**. The window that opens provides a graphical look at what this one menu will look like. Notice that to the right of each menu item in the menu is a number. Together, the numbers in this column labeled Cmd ID make up a single Mcmd resource.

Constructor makes it easy to change the characteristics of a menu item—just double-click on the menu item to edit. I did that for the **New** menu item pictured in Figure 7.23, and the results are shown in Figure 7.24. In Figure 7.24, you can see that this new window is where the menu item name can be edited, as well as the shortcut key (also referred to as the menu item command key equivalent). In this window, you can also edit the menu item's command number—the number your source code will use when referring to this one menu item. If you edit the menu item's command number, you are in fact editing an Mcmd resource.

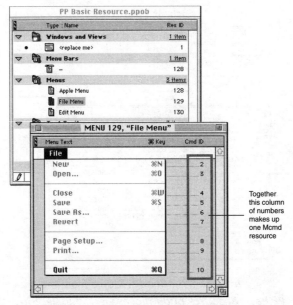

Figure 7.23 *When a Menu resource is displayed in Constructor, the contents of an associated Mcmd resource are also seen.*

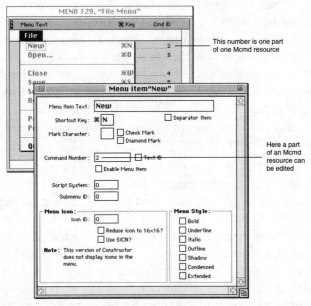

Figure 7.24 *Editing a Menu resource in Constructor.*

So, just where *are* the Mcmd resources displayed in Constructor? They aren't—not directly. The Constructor project window doesn't list Mcmd resources separately. Notice too that the Constructor project window doesn't list MENU resources. Instead, it lists three menu-related resources in a group titled Menus. What Constructor calls a Menu is actually a MENU resource along with an Mcmd resource. As you've just seen, when you edit a Menu resource, you may be editing both a MENU and an Mcmd resource.

CONSTRUCTOR IS *THE* RESOURCE EDITOR FOR POWERPLANT

This integration of standard resources types with PowerPlant resource types is common in Constructor. That's intentional, of course—Constructor was created specifically as a resource editing tool for PowerPlant-based projects. It's this integration of resource types, and the ability to display both standard and PowerPlant-specific resources in a visual manner that make Constructor the tool you should use when working with the resources used by your own PowerPlant-based projects.

The PPob Resource Type

While a traditional Mac program can use a WIND resource to adequately describe a window, a program created using PowerPlant requires more information in its window descriptions. Enter the PPob resource. The PPob is one of the resource types designed by Metrowerks specifically for use in PowerPlant-based applications. Embedded within a PPob resource is a WIND resource and other information descriptive of a window. Specifically, the PPob resource contains information about a window's pane or panes.

The PowerPlant framework supports the concept of window panes. In short, a *pane* is a self-contained drawing area within a window. This simple definition makes a pane sound much like a port, a Macintosh programming idea you're already familiar with. There is a substantial difference between the two, however. While a window has a single port associated with it, a PowerPlant window can contain one, two, or many panes. These individual drawing areas can be stationary or resizable and movable. Chapter 10 describes panes in much greater detail.

Since the PPob resource type isn't common to applications other than those created using the Metrowerks compilers, ResEdit provides no editor that makes PPob creation and editing easy. While the previous pages described the merging of the MENU and Mcmd resources into one easily editable resource that can be viewed graphically as one of the advantages of working with Constructor, the primary reason why Metrowerks developed their own resource editor was so that programmers would have an intuitive, visual means of working with PPob resources.

NOTE

The resource editor Resorcerer includes a PPob template, so it understands what a PPob resource is. That means that Resorcerer can be used to create and edit PPob resources. Constructor, however, was designed specifically for work with PPob resources, so Constructor is your best bet. Using Constructor and Resorcerer to create PPob resources is covered in Chapter 11.

THE LAYOUT EDITOR

As is the case with other resource editors, Constructor is really a number of separate editors—there's one for each type of resource that it recognizes. In Figure 7.23, you saw the menu editor that is used to edit MENU resources (and, indirectly, Mcmd resources). For a PPob resource you use the *layout editor* (also referred to as the layout window). Double-clicking on the PPob resource named **<replace me>** under the heading Windows and Views brings up the layout editor with the **<replace me>** PPob resource displayed in it (see Figure 7.25).

NOTE

Because some of the PowerPlant-specific resources that Metrowerks has defined actually consist of multiple resources, the Constructor project window lists resources under category names. For instance, a menu is defined as a Menu, which is made up of both a MENU and an Mcmd resource. Another example is the PPob. This resource is made up of the PPob resource itself and a standard WIND resource. Constructor lists such resources under the heading Windows and Views.

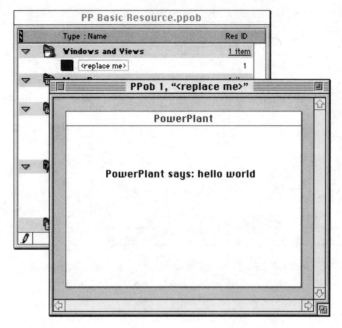

Figure 7.25 *A PPob resource being edited in Constructor.*

As mentioned, a pane is a self-contained drawing area. For now, suffice it to say that a window, and each individual element in the window (including text, pictures, icons, and controls) is a type of pane. It also turns out that the window that holds all of these panes is itself a pane. To get a better idea of the area a pane occupies, select **Show Pane Edges** from the Layout menu. This draws a dashed line around each pane in a window. In Figure 7.26, you see that the window displayed in the layout editor has only one pane in it—a pane that holds a string of text. Each pane has its own pane ID. Choose **Show Pane IDs** from the Layout menu so you can also view that information. Figure 7.26 shows that the window that the PowerPlantIntro68K application will display is itself a pane with a pane ID of 1. The text area is a pane with a pane ID of 2.

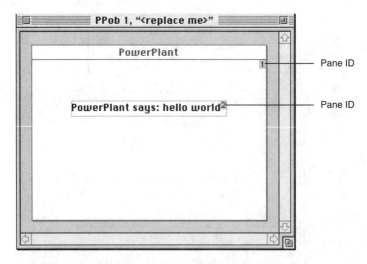

Figure 7.26   *Each pane in a PPob resource has an ID*
that can be displayed in the layout editor.

N O T E

Because a window is a pane, and elements within a window are panes, you might not be surprised to read that there is a hierarchy of panes. Chapter 10 delves into this concept.

PANES AND PROPERTY INSPECTORS

Constructor makes it easy to add a new pane and to edit an existing one. Here you'll edit some information that defines one pane. In Chapter 10, you'll create new panes.

To open a pane's *property inspector*—the window that holds the information that defines the pane—double-click on the pane. In Figure 7.27, you see that I've done that for the window pane.

A property inspector window is used to examine and, if desired, edit a pane's data. I'll be working with the property inspector for window panes in Chapter 10, so I'll click on this inspector window's **close** box without making any changes to the data.

Different types of panes require different data to define the panes—so Constructor supplies separate property inspectors for each pane type. In Figure 7.28, I've double-clicked on the text pane to display its property inspector.

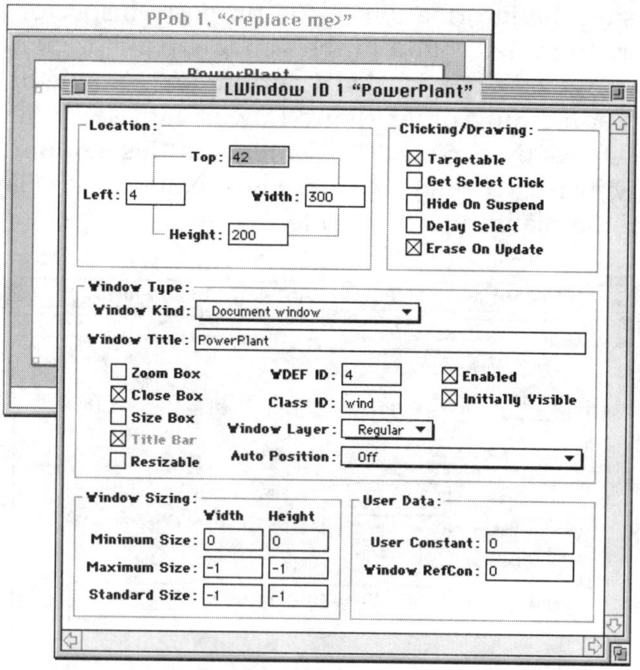

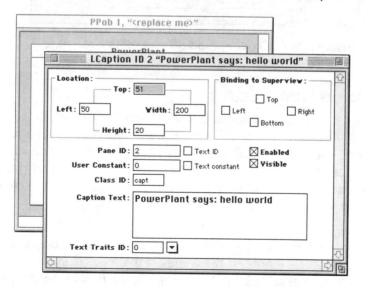

Figure 7.27 The property inspector for a window pane.

Figure 7.28 The property inspector for a text pane.

After perusing the information in the property inspector and noting that it differs from that found in the window pane property inspector, click in the large edit box labeled **Caption Text**. Now edit the text so that it says something other than "PowerPlant says: hello world." Figure 7.29 shows the new text I've entered in this edit box. Now click the property inspector window's **close** box. Note that the layout editor now reflects the change you just made.

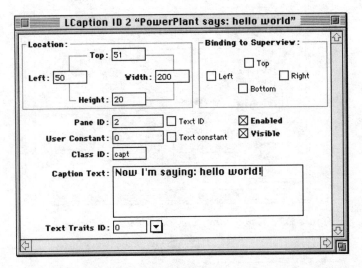

*Figure 7.29 Using the property inspector of a text pane
to change the text that's displayed in a window.*

PANES AND THE LAYOUT EDITOR

Each property inspector includes Location edit boxes that allow you to enter the pixel coordinates that define the placement of a pane within a window (or, more technically, within another pane). You can also arrange panes from within the layout editor by clicking and dragging them. In Figure 7.30, I'm dragging the text pane from near the center of the window to near the upper-left corner of the window.

Before moving a pane, double-click on it to bring up its property inspector. Take note of the values in the four Location edit boxes. Then, with the property inspector still open, click on the pane in the layout editor and drag it to a new location. When you release the mouse button, note that the values in the Location edit boxes of the property inspector are updated to reflect the new pixel location of the pane.

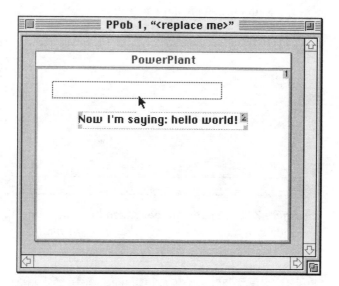

Figure 7.30 *A pane can be moved about in a window by using standard drag-and-drop techniques in the layout editor.*

You can change the size of a pane from within the layout editor by clicking on its lower-right corner and then, with the mouse button still down, dragging the mouse. In Figure 7.31, I'm making the window pane smaller. When I release the mouse button, the result will be a window pane the size of the one shown in Figure 7.32.

If you've followed along in your own version of **PP Basic Resource.ppob**, go ahead and test your changes. Return to the CodeWarrior IDE and choose **Run** from the Project menu to rebuild and rerun the PowerPlantIntro68K program. When it runs, the program will now display a smaller window with the new text in it, as shown in Figure 7.33. Choosing **New** from the File menu of this program opens an identical window. The changes to the PPob resource affect each new window.

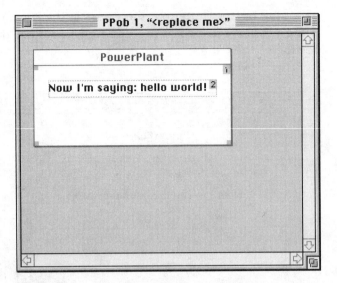

Figure 7.31 *A pane can be resized by clicking on its lower-left corner and then dragging the mouse.*

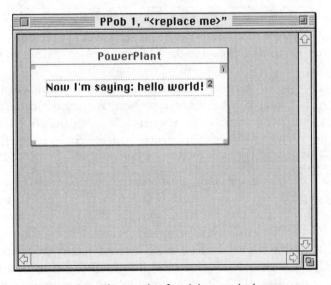

Figure 7.32 *The result of resizing a window pane.*

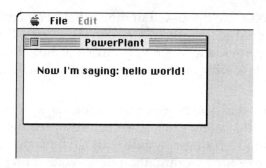

Figure 7.33 The results of editing a project's *PPob* resource
and then recompiling and rerunning the application.

PANES AND POWERPLANT CLASSES

A pane is always based on a PowerPlant class. As shown in Figure 7.34, a window is an instance of the LWindow class and a string of text is an instance of the LCaption class. You'll use Constructor to create and lay out the panes that make up your program's window or windows. Then, your source code can use class member functions to access and to work with these panes.

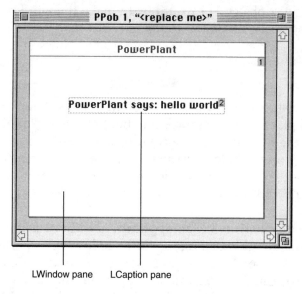

Figure 7.34 Each pane has a corresponding PowerPlant class type.

PowerPlant classes are discussed in the next chapter and, as mentioned, panes are covered at length in Chapter 10—but I'll jump ahead of myself a bit to provide a concrete example of how PowerPlant uses a resource. If the following isn't crystal clear now, it will be after you read Chapter 10.

You just saw that a PPob resource defines a window. More specifically, the panes that are a part of a PPob resource define the window and its contents. Defining a window in Constructor isn't enough to make it useful to your program, though. In your source code, you need to declare an LWindow class pointer variable and then use that variable in the creation of an LWindow object. That works something like this:

```
const   ResIDT    window_Sample = 1;

Window   *mDisplayWindow;
mDisplayWindow = LWindow::CreateWindow( window_Sample, this );
```

CreateWindow() is a member function of the LWindow class. window_Sample is a constant—it's the ID of the PPob resource on which a new window should be modeled. After the code executes, any of the member functions of the LWindow class can be invoked from the mDisplayWindow object. For example, to make the window visible, you call the LWindow class member function Show():

```
mDisplayWindow->Show();
```

NOTE The value assigned to the constant window_Sample is given in a few places in the resource file that holds the PPob resource. Look for the number 1 to the right of the <replace me> resource in the project window pictured in Figure 7.19, in the title bar of the layout editor shown in Figure 7.25, or in the property inspector window for the LWindow pane in Figure 7.27.

If you were developing a Mac application without using PowerPlant, this scenario is roughly analogous to the following. Use ResEdit to create a WIND resource. Then, in your source code, declare a WindowPtr variable. Next, call GetNewWindow() to create the new window based on the WIND resource and to assign the WindowPtr variable to point to that window. Finally, call the Toolbox routine `ShowWindow()` to make the new window visible:

```
WindowPtr    theWindow;
theWindow = GetNewWindow( 128, nil, (WindowPtr)-1L );
ShowWindow( theWindow );
```

Other Resource Types

Looking back at Figure 7.19 shows that the Constructor project window lists resources besides the ones discussed to this point—the `PPob` and `Menu` resources. The default Constructor file that CodeWarrior adds to each PowerPlant-based project also holds a single Menu Bar resource and three Text Trait resources. Because Constructor supplies your project with these resources, I'll concentrate on these two types here—even though Constructor is capable of creating and editing many other resource types.

MENU BAR RESOURCES

In Constructor, a Menu Bar resource is a standard `MBAR` resource—a resource type you can easily create and edit in a resource editor such as ResEdit. Constructor's menu bar editor is much nicer than that supplied by ResEdit. When you double-click on a Menu Bar resource in Constructor, the menu bar editor opens to display the menus currently in the menu bar resource. In this editor, you can add new menus or view and edit existing individual menus. Clicking once on a menu name in the menu bar editor displays the items in that menu. Double-clicking on a menu name brings up a menu property window that allows you to rename the menu or provide the ID of a different Menu resource. If you instead double-click on a menu item in one of the menus, a menu item property window appears. This window allows you to edit this one menu item. Figure 7.35 shows all three of these windows.

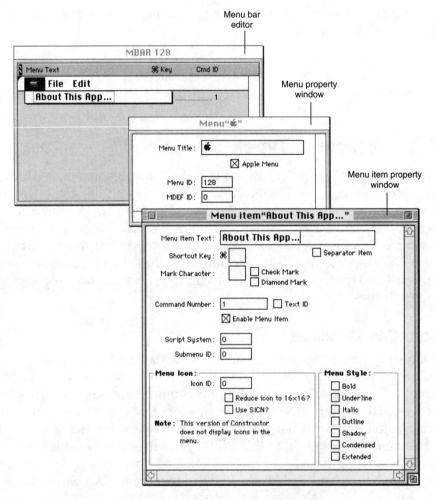

Figure 7.35 *The Constructor windows that can be used when editing a Menu Bar resource.*

Text Trait Resources

The Text Trait resource holds a single Txtr resource—a PowerPlant-specific resource. This powerful resource allows you to specify a font, size, style, and other text characteristics and then package these traits into a single resource. When you then apply such a resource to a specified text object, all the characteristics held in the resource are applied to that text.

Figure 7.36 shows the text traits editor for one of the three text trait resources that are included in the **PP Basic Resources.ppob** file.

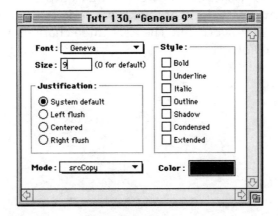

Figure 7.36 *The text trait editor allows you to set the characteristics of the text that will be displayed in a pane.*

N O T E One example of this was shown in Figure 7.28. At the bottom of the property inspector window for an LCaption pane, you see an edit box (and pop-up menu) that allows you to set the text traits for the text in that pane.

Summary

PowerPlant is an application framework. An application framework is simply a set of C++ classes that contain the code that handles many of the more mundane tasks common to all Macintosh programs. The PowerPlant classes will take care of tasks such as menu handling and window updating, dragging, and resizing.

To use PowerPlant, you create a project using PowerPlant project stationery. That has the effect of adding several files holding PowerPlant classes to the new project. CodeWarrior also adds a single example source code file and a few resource files to the project. These files compile into a very simple Mac application, and can be used as a starting point for your own application—just add the resources and C++ source code to implement the features unique to your program.

In this chapter, you received an overview of Constructor, the Metrowerks resource editor designed specifically for editing the resources that are a part of a PowerPlant-based project. You also got a very quick glimpse at a little of the source code that goes into a project that makes use of PowerPlant. The next three chapters will expose you to much more of PowerPlant.

Chapter  8

PowerPlant Classes

PowerPlant consists of dozens of classes that are used in conjunction with your own source code to create Macintosh applications. The PowerPlant code supplies the functionality that takes care of tasks common to most Mac programs. By incorporating PowerPlant source code into your CodeWarrior projects, you'll spend less time writing interface code. That allows you to devote your programming efforts to the parts of your project that will make your application different from existing programs.

In this chapter, you'll get an overview of the most important PowerPlant classes. Using the project that was created in Chapter 7, you'll see how your own source code works with PowerPlant code.

PowerPlant Classes

The numerous classes that make up the PowerPlant application framework can be found in files in the **PowerPlant** folder. If you've purchased an edition of CodeWarrior, you'll find this folder in the **MacOS Support** folder inside the **Metrowerks CodeWarrior** folder. Within the **PowerPlant** folder are several folders, each used to hold the files that make up a family of classes. Figure 8.1 illustrates the class folder hierarchy. This figure shows some of the many files found in the Pane family.

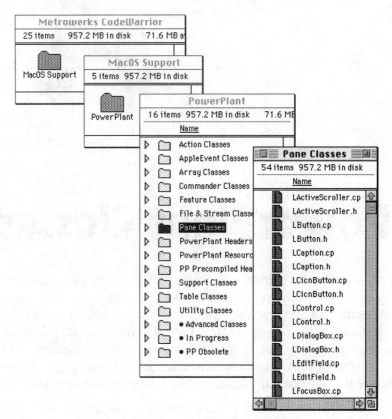

Figure 8.1 *PowerPlant is a collection of dozens of files that hold class definitions.*

In Figure 8.1, you'll note that each PowerPlant class has two files associated with it—a header file and a source code file. Each PowerPlant class uses a header file to define the class and a source code file to define the member functions of that class. Figures 9.2 and 9.3 provide an example. Figure 8.2 shows a part of the **LApplication.h** header file. This file defines the LApplication class. Figure 8.3 shows a little of the **LApplication.cp** source code file. In this figure, you can see that the Run() function, a member function of the LApplication class, is defined in the source code file.

The LApplication class is defined
in the LApplication.h header file

```
                         LApplication.h
 h,  {},  M,  b,   Path  Hard Drive : CW10 Gold :Metrowerks Co...t :Commander Classes :LApplication.h  ◇

    class   LApplication :  public LCommander,
                       public LEventDispatcher,
                       public LModelObject {
    public:
                    LApplication();
         virtual      ~LApplication();

         EProgramState    GetState() const        { return mState; }
         void           SetSleepTime(
                          Int32         inSleepTime)
                     {
                        mSleepTime = inSleepTime;
                     }

         virtual void     Run();
         virtual void     ProcessNextEvent();
         virtual void     ShowAboutBox();

         virtual Boolean    ObeyCommand(
                          CommandT       inCommand,

 Line : 1       ◁
```

Figure 8.2   A PowerPlant header file holds one or more class definitions.

Looking at a few of the primary PowerPlant classes results in a discovery of many of the key concepts involved in writing a PowerPlant-based application. So at many points along the way to the end of this chapter I'll make reference to the source code of an application created using PowerPlant—the PowerPlantIntro68K program. Recall from Chapter 78 that this program is nothing more than a compilation of the example source code that CodeWarrior adds to a new PowerPlant-based project. This code can be found in the **PP Basic Starter.cp** file that is a part of the **PowerPlantIntro68.µ** project (or any other project you create using PowerPlant project stationery) and in the **PP Basic Starter.h** header file that CodeWarrior placed in the folder that holds the **PowerPlantIntro68K.µ** project.

Run() is one of the LApplication member functions,
so it's listing is found in the LApplication.cp file

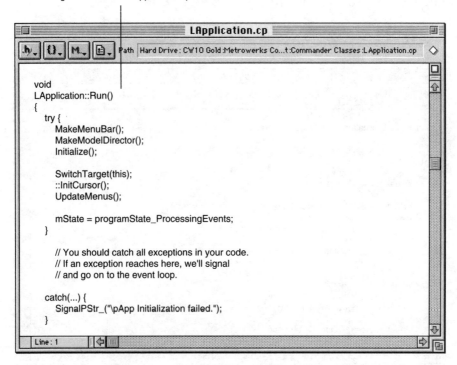

```
void
LApplication::Run()
{
    try {
        MakeMenuBar();
        MakeModelDirector();
        Initialize();

        SwitchTarget(this);
        ::InitCursor();
        UpdateMenus();

        mState = programState_ProcessingEvents;
    }

        // You should catch all exceptions in your code.
        // If an exception reaches here, we'll signal
        // and go on to the event loop.

    catch(...) {
        SignalPStr_("\pApp Initialization failed.");
    }
```

Figure 8.3   A PowerPlant source code file holds member function definitions.

PowerPlant Naming Conventions

PowerPlant uses a naming convention that makes it easy to recognize PowerPlant classes, data members, member functions, and constants.

Class Names

For classes, you'll see that each begins with *L*, *U*, or *C*. A class that begins with an *L*, like LApplication, is a PowerPlant library class. Figure 8.4 highlights this fact.

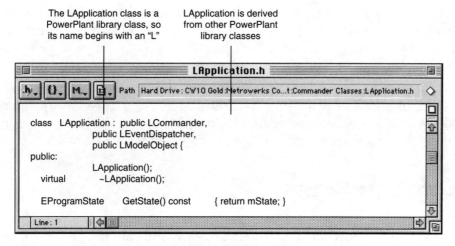

The LApplication class is a PowerPlant library class, so its name begins with an "L"

LApplication is derived from other PowerPlant library classes

Figure 8.4   PowerPlant library classes begin with the letter L.

Classes that begin with a *U* are PowerPlant utility classes. This type of class, while important, is used more infrequently than a library class. A utility class also has no dependencies on other PowerPlant classes. An example of a utility class is UQDGlobals.

You'll encounter the UQDGlobals class later in this chapter. This class defines a member function named InitializeToolbox().

Your PowerPlant projects will define a class (or classes) of its own. To make it obvious that a class is an application-defined class and not a part of the PowerPlant application framework, you should begin the class name with a *C*. This chapter's **PowerPlantIntro68K.μ** project does that for the one class the application defines, CPPStarterApp.

Variable Names

Variables found in PowerPlant code follow the PowerPlant variable naming convention. Class data members will begin with the letter *m*. For example, consider that your application needs to keep track of a window. You might define a data member in an application-defined class for this purpose. While working on a nonapplication framework project you might name this variable `displayWindow`. In your PowerPlant application framework project, you should instead give this variable a name such as `mDisplayWindow`.

Local variables begin with *the* and use an uppercase letter for each word break. Three examples are: `theCount`, `theWindow`, and `theGrandTotal`. To generalize, all PowerPlant variable names begin with a lowercase letter and use an uppercase letter for a word break.

Data Type Names

For integral values, PowerPlant uses a few of its own data types. These PowerPlant-defined data type names clearly indicate the bit (and thus byte) size of each type. The most common types are the `Int8` (equivalent to a `char`), `Int16` (equivalent to a `short`), and `Int32` (equivalent to a `long`).

Related to these integer types are a few other types that are merely synonyms for the PowerPlant-defined types. The `CommandT` type and the `MessageT` type—both used in the defining of constants—are the same as the `Int32` type. You'll see more of these types in other PowerPlant chapters. The `ResIDT` type is the same as the `Int16` type.

Constant Names

The just-described `ResIDT` data type is used in defining resource ID constants. For example, your code used in a PowerPlant project might define a constant that represents the resource ID of a `PICT` resource. Here, that constant is named `PICT_logo`:

```
const  ResIDT  PICT_logo = 500;
```

Because the ResIDT type is the same as the Int16 type, the above example is the same as this constant definition:

```
const  Int16  PICT_logo = 500;
```

Since an Int16 is defined to be a short, the above two definitions are also the same as this constant definition:

```
const  short  PICT_logo = 500;
```

While variable names use uppercase characters to denote word breaks, as in theTotalScore, constants contain an underscore for the first break and uppercase for subsequent word breaks:

```
const  ResIDT  ALRT_aboutBox = 128;
```

This difference—the inclusion of an underscore—is simply to highlight the fact that something like ALRT_aboutBox is a constant and not a variable. Finally, when a constant is used as a resource ID (as are PICT_logo and ALRT_aboutBox), it should begin with the four characters that make up the resource type (as do, obviously, PICT_logo and ALRT_aboutBox).

Function Parameter Names

PowerPlant variables that are used as function parameters will begin with *in*, *out*, or *io*. The first is for variables used as input to the function—variables that hold values to be used in the function to which they are passed. The second is used for output—variables that will have their values set by the function for use outside the function. Figure 8.5 shows the header for a function named FindCommandStatus(). This function is a PowerPlant class member function used when working with menus. From the figure, you can see that the function's first parameter, inCommand, will be used by FindCommandStatus(). The four other parameters will have their values set by FindCommandStatus().

```
FindCommandStatus( CommandT  inCommand,              Input parameter,
                                                     used by the function
          Boolean   &outEnabled,

          Boolean   &outUsesMark,                    Output parameters,
                                                     filled in by the function
          Char16    &outMark,

          Str255    outName );
```

Figure 8.5   *PowerPlant function parameters follow a naming convention that indicates the use of each parameter.*

Select PowerPlant Classes

While PowerPlant consists of dozens of classes, there are only a few that you'll need to be familiar with when writing a very simple PowerPlant-based application. As your PowerPlant-based projects grow in complexity, you'll want to know about more and more of the useful classes defined by PowerPlant. Even then, however, the primary classes that you will soon learn about will be the ones you rely on most.

The LApplication Class

Your PowerPlant-based project will make use of a few, or perhaps many, of the dozens of PowerPlant classes. *All* PowerPlant projects, however, will use the LApplication class.

THE PURPOSE OF THE LAPPLICATION CLASS

The LApplication class contains about three dozen member functions. Member functions such as EventMouseDown() and EventUpdate() provide a hint that LApplication takes care of event handling. The LApplication member function ObeyCommandStatus() tells you that the application class also handles menu item selections (in PowerPlant, menu items are also known as commands).

The application class is, obviously, a powerful class. In fact, it is the class that coordinates and manages the flow of control of a program created with PowerPlant. When an event occurs, it is the application class that determines which member function should handle that event. That member function may in turn invoke other member functions belonging to other classes.

CREATING THE CLASS DERIVED FROM THE LAPPLICATION CLASS

Any PowerPlant project must define a class derived from the LApplication class. As a refresher, here's the format for the definition of a derived class in C++:

```
class keyword    derivedClassName  :  public keyword    baseClassName
```

As noted earlier, classes that you define in a project that uses PowerPlant should have names that begin with a C. When CodeWarrior creates a PowerPlant-based project it adds a starter source code file to the project—**PP Basic Starter.cp**. That file includes a header file named **PP Basic Starter.h** (another file supplied by CodeWarrior). This header file defines a class derived from the LApplication class—the CPPStarterApp class. Note that this class name begins with an upper-case C. Here's that class definition:

```
class    CPPStarterApp : public LApplication {
public:
                          CPPStarterApp();
   virtual                ~CPPStarterApp();

   virtual Boolean        ObeyCommand(CommandT inCommand, void*
                                  ioParam);

   virtual void           FindCommandStatus(CommandT inCommand,
                              Boolean &outEnabled, Boolean
                              &outUsesMark,
                              Char16 &outMark, Str255 outName);
protected:

   virtual void           StartUp();
};
```

From this definition you can see that the PP Basic Starter version of the class derived from the LApplication class contains five member functions. These are, of course, in addition to the numerous member functions and data members inherited from the LApplication base class. We'll have more to say about these functions throughout this chapter and the next.

CREATING AN APPLICATION OBJECT

One of the first things a PowerPlant program needs to do is define an instance, or object, of the application class. In the `main()` function listed in the **PP Basic Starter.cp** file, you'll find the declaration of a variable of the class type defined in the **PP Basic Starter.h** file:

```
CPPStarterApp    theApp;
```

Figure 8.6 shows that this line of code creates an object that consists of the data members and the dozens of class member functions (a few of which are named in the figure) inherited from the `LApplication` class, as well as the member functions defined by the `CPPStarterApp` class.

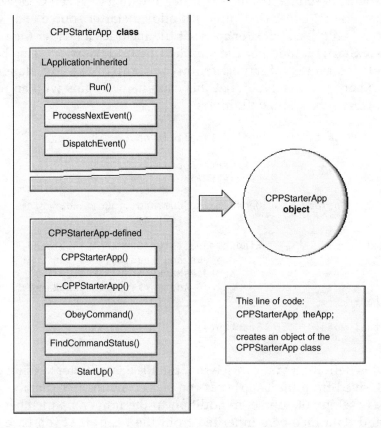

Figure 8.6 *The application object consists of application-defined member functions as well as all of the `LApplication` member functions and data members.*

Using the Application Object to Start the Program

With an object created, any of its class member functions can be invoked. As mentioned, the LApplication class consists of about three dozen member functions. Just after the program declares the variable theApp, the LApplication member function to call is Run():

```
theApp.Run();
```

The LApplication member function Run() begins by doing some preliminary setup work, such as putting up the program's menu bar and setting the cursor to the arrow. It also sets the LApplication data member mState to a constant value, and then enters a while loop. From the PowerPlant **LApplication.cp** source code file, here's the definition of the Run() member function:

```
void
LApplication::Run()
{
    try {
        MakeMenuBar();
        MakeModelDirector();
        Initialize();

        SwitchTarget(this);
        ::InitCursor();
        UpdateMenus();

        mState = programState_ProcessingEvents;
    }

    catch(...) {
        SignalPStr_("\pApp Initialization failed.");
    }

    while (mState != programState_Quitting) {
        try {
            ProcessNextEvent();
        }

        catch(...) {
            SignalPStr_("\pException caught in LApplication::Run");
        }
    }
}
```

Keep in mind that you aren't required or expected to fully understand the code in the PowerPlant files. Getting a feel for the purpose of some of the more commonly used PowerPlant member functions, however, will make you feel more comfortable with the process of creating an application based on this application framework.

Setting the data member `mState` to the PowerPlant-defined constant `programState_ProcessingEvents` means that the `while` loop test will pass and the loop body will execute. This loop will repeatedly execute until `mState` is set to the constant `programState_Quitting` elsewhere in PowerPlant code.

You can verify that `mState` is an `LApplication` data member by examining the definition of the `LApplication` class in the **LApplication.h** header file. Or, because you know PowerPlant's naming convention (listed earlier in this chapter), you can just assume it's a data member because it begins with an *m*.

THE MAIN EVENT LOOP

The `Run()` while loop acts as the application's main event loop—something you're used to writing yourself. If you look at the `main()` routine in the **PP Basic Starter.cp** file, you'll see that there is no application-defined main event loop:

```
void main(void)
{
   SetDebugThrow_(debugAction_Alert);
   SetDebugSignal_(debugAction_Alert);

   InitializeHeap(3);

   UQDGlobals::InitializeToolbox(&qd);

   new LGrowZone(20000);

   CPPStarterApp    theApp;
   theApp.Run();
}
```

The code that precedes the declaration of theApp and the call to Run() is standard initialization code you'll want to include in the main() function of any of your own PowerPlant-based projects. Near the end of this chapter, I discuss the purpose of these few lines.

From C++, you should recall that one class member function can invoke another member function of that same class. The LApplication member function Run() does just this. At the center of the while loop is a call to a routine named ProcessNextEvent(). Like the Run() routine itself, this function is an LApplication member function. ProcessNextEvent() calls the Toolbox routine WaitNextEvent()— just as the main event loop does in any program you've written in the past. ProcessNextEvent() then takes the event information and passes it to another member function—DispatchEvent().

You'll notice that while I highlighted what the LApplication member function ProcessNextEvent() does, I didn't show its listing. Here's still one more reminder that while it never hurts to know what's going on in a PowerPlant class, it isn't necessary to know everything about each class. As you begin to make the adjustment to working with an application framework, don't attempt to determine exactly how a class handles things. Instead, take the easier route of learning what the class handles. Eventually, as you work with PowerPlant, you'll become familiar with its intricacies.

DispatchEvent() serves as nothing more than a branching station. It compares the event type to the Apple-defined event constants (also called *event codes*) and, based on this comparison, invokes the appropriate PowerPlant routine to handle the event. Mac programs that you've created in the past no doubt have a routine much like DispatchEvent(). The difference will be in the number of event types handled. While your own application probably handled just a few types (mouseDown, keyDown, and updateEvt are the most notable), the PowerPlant DispatchEvent() function must be able to take care of any event type you want your application to handle. Because DispatchEvent() should remind you of code you've written in the past, it warrants a listing here:

```
void
LEventDispatcher::DispatchEvent(const EventRecord &inMacEvent)
{
    switch ( inMacEvent.what )
    {
        case mouseDown:
            AdjustCursor( inMacEvent );
            EventMouseDown( inMacEvent );
            break;

        case mouseUp:
            EventMouseUp( inMacEvent );
            break;

        case keyDown:
            EventKeyDown( inMacEvent );
            break;

        case autoKey:
            EventAutoKey( inMacEvent );
            break;

        case keyUp:
            EventKeyUp( inMacEvent );
            break;

        case diskEvt:
            EventDisk( inMacEvent );
            break;

        case updateEvt:
            EventUpdate( inMacEvent );
            break;

        case activateEvt:
            EventActivate( inMacEvent );
            break;

        case osEvt:
            EventOS( inMacEvent );
            break;

        case kHighLevelEvent:
            EventHighLevel( inMacEvent );
            break;
```

```
    default:
        UseIdleTime( inMacEvent );
        break;
    }
}
```

 DispatchEvent() is a member function of the LEventDispatcher class—not the LApplication class. A member function of the LEventDispatcher class can be called by a member function of the LApplication class because one of the classes that the LApplication class is derived from is LEventDispatcher.

THE IMPORTANCE OF THE LAPPLICATION CLASS

You've seen quite a bit of the LApplication class, so it's time for a summary. All Metrowerks projects that use PowerPlant *must* define a class derived from the PowerPlant LApplication class. The derived class will, of course, inherit all the member functions and data members of the LApplication class. The derived class will also include its own application-specific member functions and data members. The CPPStarterApp class defined in the source code listing supplied by CodeWarrior as a starting point for your own applications defines five member functions and no data members. More detail of these application-specific parts of this important class will be provided later in this chapter. The main() function creates an object of this derived class, then calls the object's Run() member function to kick off the program. The Run() function, defined in the LApplication class (and thus inherited by the application class derived from LApplication) includes a loop that serves as the application's main event loop. Figure 8.7 illustrates what goes on when the LApplication Run() member function is invoked.

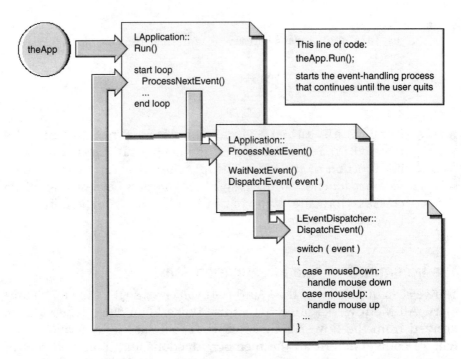

Figure 8.7 *When the application object invokes*
Run ( ), the event loop is entered.

The LWindow Class

The PowerPlant LWindow class exists so that your application can work with windows in much the same way you're used to. In a PowerPlant project, you'll work with a pointer to an LWindow class object instead of the WindowPtr you're used to working with in nonapplication framework projects.

The LWindow class consists of more than 50 member functions. And, because the LWindow class is itself derived from other PowerPlant classes (two of which, LPane and LView, are discussed in Chapter 10), the number of member functions that can be accessed by an LWindow object is actually far greater.

If you look through the class definition of LWindow in the **LWindow.h** header file, you'll see that many of the member functions—such as CreateWindow(), Show(), and DoClose()—are analogous to

Toolbox routines that work with the `WindowPtr` data type. Since you'll be working with an object of the `LWindow` class, you'll use the `LWindow` member functions and not their Toolbox counterparts. For example, to create and display a window, you'll use the `LWindow` member functions `CreateWindow()` and `Show()`—not the Toolbox routines `GetNewWindow()` and `ShowWindow()`.

PowerPlant Classes and Static Member Functions

From your experience programming in C++ you should recall that the member functions of a class can usually only be accessed through an object, as shown in Figure 8.8. In this figure, a class named `UQDGlobals` holds one data member and four member functions. If the `InitializeToolbox()` member function is to be accessed, there must first be a `UQDGlobals` object. In Figure 8.8, that object is named `QDobject`.

In contrast to Figure 8.8, the snippet in Figure 8.9 shows that if a class member function is declared `static`, that function can be accessed without the use of an object. Instead, the class name is listed, followed by the scope resolution operator (`::`). Finally, the member function name is given.

Related data and functions that are used for utility purposes such as Toolbox initialization can be neatly packaged together in a class. Then, because the `static` keyword is used, this information can be used without first creating an object of the class type. For such tasks as Toolbox initialization, the creation and use of an object doesn't make sense.

The version of the `UQDGlobals` class used in Figure 8.9 is an actual utility class that is a part of PowerPlant. Because the class name begins with *U*, you'll recognize it as a utility class. The member functions of PowerPlant utility classes are declared `static` and can therefore be invoked without first creating a class object. One of the first lines of code you'll encounter in the `main()` function of a source file that uses PowerPlant is the call shown in Figure 8.9:

```
UQDGlobals::InitializeToolbox( &qd );
```

If you look at the `main()` function that appears in the **PP Basic Starter.cp** file, you'll see the above call to `InitializeToolbox()`.

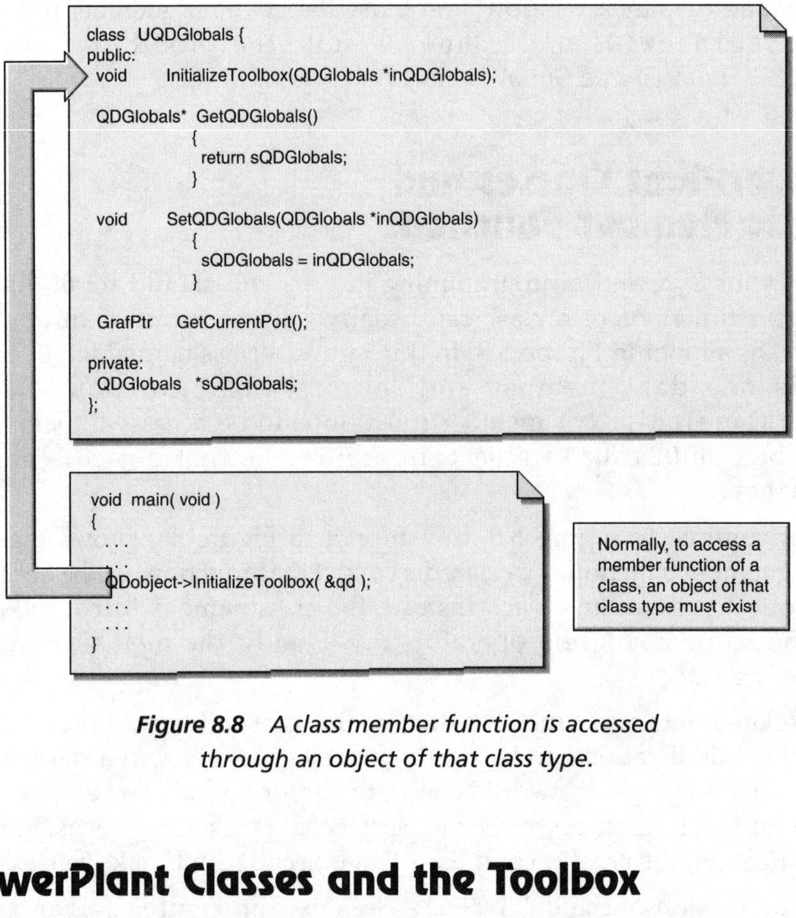

```
class  UQDGlobals {
public:
  void       InitializeToolbox(QDGlobals *inQDGlobals);

  QDGlobals*  GetQDGlobals()
              {
                return sQDGlobals;
              }

  void       SetQDGlobals(QDGlobals *inQDGlobals)
              {
                sQDGlobals = inQDGlobals;
              }

  GrafPtr    GetCurrentPort();

private:
  QDGlobals  *sQDGlobals;
};
```

```
void  main( void )
{
    . . .
    . .
    QDobject->InitializeToolbox( &qd );
    . . .
    . . .
}
```

> Normally, to access a member function of a class, an object of that class type must exist

Figure 8.8 *A class member function is accessed through an object of that class type.*

PowerPlant Classes and the Toolbox

Since thousands of Toolbox routines exist to make life easier for Mac programmers, it makes sense that an application framework, which exists to make life easier still, uses the Toolbox.

If you examine code found in PowerPlant source code files, you'll see the names of many Toolbox calls with which you're familiar. Consider as an example `InitializeToolbox()`—a member function of the `UQDGlobals` class. Here's a look at the definition of that routine:

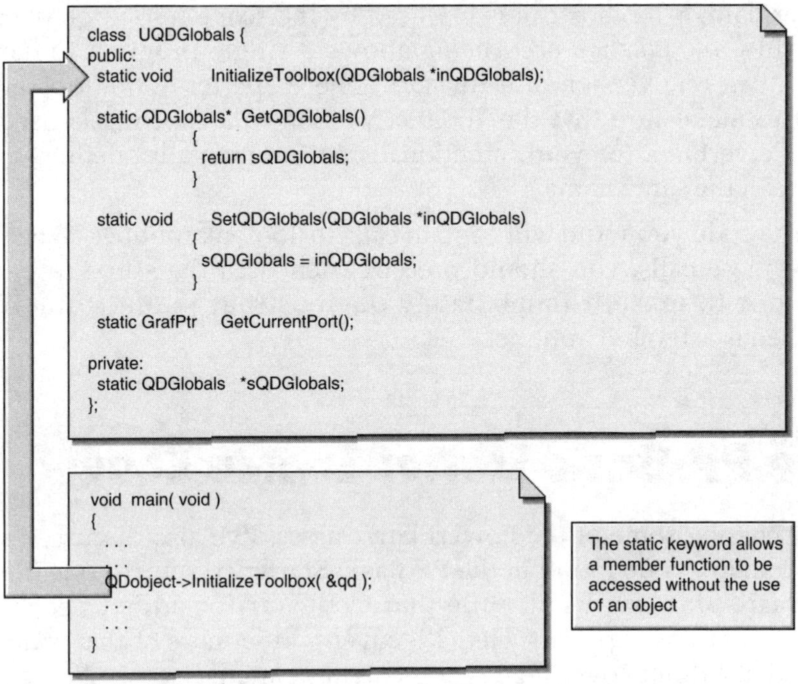

```
class  UQDGlobals {
public:
  static void      InitializeToolbox(QDGlobals *inQDGlobals);

  static QDGlobals*  GetQDGlobals()
          {
            return sQDGlobals;
          }

  static void      SetQDGlobals(QDGlobals *inQDGlobals)
          {
            sQDGlobals = inQDGlobals;
          }

  static GrafPtr    GetCurrentPort();

private:
  static QDGlobals  *sQDGlobals;
};
```

```
void  main( void )
{
  . . .
  . . .
  QDobject->InitializeToolbox( &qd );
  . . .
  . . .
}
```

The static keyword allows
a member function to be
accessed without the use
of an object

Figure 8.9 *Member functions declared* static *can be accessed without the use of a class object.*

```
void
UQDGlobals :: InitializeToolbox(QDGlobals *inQDGlobals)
{
    sQDGlobals = inQDGlobals;

    ::InitGraf((Ptr) &sQDGlobals->thePort);
    ::InitFonts();
    ::InitWindows();
    ::InitMenus();
    ::TEInit();
    ::InitDialogs(nil);
}
```

InitializeToolbox() makes calls to six Toolbox functions—the same functions you've called in Toolbox initialization routines for applications you've written in the past. The difference here is that in

PowerPlant, a Toolbox call is prefaced by the scope resolution operator (::). In C++, *function overloading* allows a single program to contain more than one version of a function. The scope resolution operator is used to make sure that the Toolbox version of a function is used—in case PowerPlant (or you) intentionally (or accidentally) defines a routine with the same name.

The code you write will contain calls to Toolbox routines. When you make these calls, you should precede each with the scope resolution operator to make it immediately obvious that the function being invoked is a Toolbox routine.

The PP Basic Starter Source Code

In discussing some of the PowerPlant classes, I've also discussed some of the source code found in the **PP Basic Starter.cp** source code file and **PP Basic Starter.h** header file that CodeWarrior adds to each new PowerPlant-based project. Here I'll cover a little more of that code. The code that I don't cover here will be menu-related. Because PowerPlant and menus are the topics of Chapter 9, I'll wrap up the discussion of the PP Basic Starter code in that chapter. In Chapter 10, I'll finally add my own code to this file to come up with my own application.

The main() Function

In this chapter, you saw how `main()` calls the `UQDGlobals` class member function `InitializeToolbox()` to perform standard initializations. You also read that `main()` is used to create an instance of the `CPPStarterApp` class—an application object—and to then kick off the application by invoking the `LApplication` class member function `Run()`. Not yet described are the debugging, heap initialization, and grow zone code. Here's a look at `main()`:

```
void main(void)
{
    SetDebugThrow_(debugAction_Alert);
    SetDebugSignal_(debugAction_Alert);
```

```
InitializeHeap(3);

UQDGlobals::InitializeToolbox(&qd);

new LGrowZone(20000);

CPPStarterApp    theApp;
theApp.Run();
}
```

ENABLING POWERPLANT DEBUGGING

SetDebugThrow_() and SetDebugSignal_() are macros that allow your source code to include calls to PowerPlant's powerful debugging features. When a serious error occurs, your program is said to *throw* an error. When an unusual situation occurs, your program is said to *raise* a signal. By including the following code at the start of main(), your source code can optionally use PowerPlant macros to enhance your ability to debug your application:

```
SetDebugThrow_(debugAction_Alert);
SetDebugSignal_(debugAction_Alert);
```

NOTE

You don't have to know anything about throwing errors or raising signals to use MW Debug on your PowerPlant project. That is, you can still select **Enable Debugger** from the Project menu, select **Run**, and step through your program at the source code level in an MW Debug window. To read more about PowerPlant debugging, refer to the electronic documentation *The PowerPlant Book* on the Reference CD of CodeWarrior Gold.

INITIALIZING THE HEAP

When an application is launched, the operating system reserves a section of RAM to be devoted to that application. This application heap will hold the program's executable code, as well as data that the program may create or load from resources as it executes. Calling InitializeHeap() near the start of main ensures that the application gets the full amount of RAM that it needs for its application heap. The one parameter that's passed to InitializeHeap() specifies how many blocks of master pointers should be allocated on the heap. In the **PP Basic Starter.cp** file CodeWarrior supplies a value of 3:

```
InitializeHeap(3);
```

The application heap is covered in detail in the ZoneRanger chapter—Chapter 11. That chapter also discusses master pointers.

NOTE

SETTING THE GROW ZONE

While the application heap will most likely be all the memory your application needs, some unusual situation may necessitate that your program temporarily require extra RAM. PowerPlant has a comprehensive memory management scheme designed to ensure that your application will not run into such memory-related problems.

By creating a new LGrowZone object near the start of main(), your application tells PowerPlant to allocate a memory reserve that can be used by your program in emergency situations. The one parameter to the LGrowZone constructor specifies the size in bytes of this memory reserve. As shown below, the code provided by CodeWarrior sets this reserve to about 20 KB, which should be adequate:

```
new LGrowZone(20000);
```

The LApplication Derived Class

As discussed earlier in this chapter, every PowerPlant project must define a class derived from the LApplication class. While this class can contain any number of member functions, it should at least contain a constructor. For the CPPStarterApp class defined in the CodeWarrior example file **PP Basic Starter.cp**, the class derived from LApplication contains a constructor, a destructor, and three other member functions. The three functions other than the constructor and destructor are inherited from the LApplication class and overridden. That is, these three CPPStarterApp class member functions that are listed in the **CPPStarterApp.h** file and defined in the **CPPStarterApp.cp** file can also be found listed in the PowerPlant **LApplication.h** file and defined in the PowerPlant **LApplication.cp** file. The CPPStarterApp class overrides, or redefines, what each of these five functions does.

CPPStarterApp() Constructor Member Function

Typically, the purpose of a constructor function is to take care of initialization matters. The CPPStarterApp class defines its simple constructor as follows:

```
CPPStarterApp::CPPStarterApp()
{
    RegisterAllPPClasses();
}
```

In PowerPlant, a class that relies on a PPob resource must be registered. In short, the registering of a class tells PowerPlant which of its own creator functions it should associate with a particular PPob resource. That's information that's necessary for the creation of an object based on a PPob resource. The RegisterAllPPClasses() function handles the registering of all the basic classes that PowerPlant itself defines. Your application will need to specifically register its own classes. Chapter 10 discusses the registering of such classes.

CPPStarterApp() Destructor Member Function

A class destructor function typically performs any cleanup that may be necessary when an object of the class type is destroyed. The one object of the CPPStarterApp class type (declared as the variable theApp) represents the application itself. When the user quits, this object is destroyed by PowerPlant. In this simple example program, there are no tasks to perform at that time—so there's no need for a destructor function. Still, the CPPStarterApp defines an empty destructor to provide you with a "shell" to possibly fill in if your own more sophisticated PowerPlant-based application could benefit from one:

```
CPPStarterApp::~CPPStarterApp()
{
}
```

StartUp() Member Function

The StartUp() function is automatically invoked when your application launches. While this sounds much like the case of your application's constructor function, there is a difference. Your application class constructor will always execute when your program runs (it's invoked when the line that declares theApp executes), whereas the StartUp() function will only execute under certain circumstances.

If your application creates and saves its own documents, then the user can launch your application from the desktop by double-clicking on the icon of one of the application's existing documents (something that's true with any well-designed Mac application—not just PowerPlant-based ones). In such a case, the StartUp() function will *not* execute—even if your application class defines a version of it. If your application creates and saves documents, but the user chooses to launch the application directly by double-clicking on the application's icon, then StartUp() *will* execute. And if your application doesn't save documents, then StartUp() *will still* execute. The best use for StartUp() is as a means to open a new document:

```
void
CPPStarterApp::StartUp()
{
    ObeyCommand(cmd_New, nil);
}
```

ObeyCommand() is a routine used to handle the selection of any menu item. For that reason I'll reserve coverage of the function until the next chapter. Rather than leave you entirely in the dark, though, I will say this much. While ObeyCommand() is invoked automatically when the user makes a menu selection, it can also be called from any member function of the derived application class. Here the CPPStarterApp function StartUp() calls it to simulate the selection of the **New** menu item from the File menu. In this application, the **New** menu item is used to open a new window. So the result of calling ObeyCommand() here is the appearance of a new window—the window that the program displays upon starting up.

ObeyCommand() and FindCommandStatus() Member Functions

ObeyCommand() and FindCommandStatus() are member functions of the LApplication class. A PowerPlant-based application that includes menus will want to override these two functions so that they act appropriate to the menu items in the application. You'll read all about these two very important PowerPlant functions in the next chapter.

What's Left?

Once you compile and run PowerPlantIntro68K, you'll see that you can drag the window about the screen and click its **go away** box to close it. These tasks are handled by PowerPlant code—there's no window-handling code in the **PP Basic Starter.cp** file. You'll also notice that the menu bar will be properly drawn at the top of the screen—without **PP Basic Starter.cp** making calls to Toolbox routines like SetMenuBar(), AddResMenu(), and DrawMenuBar().

For the PowerPlantIntro68K program, the only task left for the source code is the handling of menus. As you'll see in Chapter 10, menu-related tasks are easily taken care of by the ObeyCommand() and FindCommandStatus() member functions.

Summary

PowerPlant is Metrowerks's application framework that consists of dozens of C++ classes. These classes hold the code that handles many of the basic tasks that all Mac programs are expected to perform.

One of the most important of the many PowerPlant classes is the LApplication class. This class oversees the flow of control that takes place in a program. Every CodeWarrior project that uses PowerPlant must create an application-defined class that is derived from LApplication.

The main() routine of a project that uses PowerPlant should create an object from the derived application class. This act will initiate the object's constructor function. This function can be used to perform initializations. Next, the Run() member function should be invoked. When it is, and if your application launches without opening any documents, the StartUp() member function will execute. After that, Run() invokes other functions to start the application's event loop.

Chapter 9

PowerPlant and Menus

An application framework will not reduce the total amount of code in an application you write, but it will reduce the amount of code you have to write. The handling of menus is one area where PowerPlant does just that. With PowerPlant files in your project, you'll be able to forget about most of the menu-related Toolbox functions you've used so often.

A menu selection, whether **Quit**, **Save**, or an application-specific item, always acts on something. What that "something" is varies depending on the menu item. The **Quit** menu item (or command) acts on the application itself. The **Save** command acts on a document. An application-specific menu item (such as, say, a **Draw Circle** item) might act on the active window. In any case, there will always be a target object that receives the action of the command. In this chapter you'll see how PowerPlant keeps track of the target object and how PowerPlant knows which target should receive the action of a menu item selection.

The previous chapter highlighted, but didn't describe in detail, two resource types that are particular to PowerPlant projects—the Mcmd and the PPob resources. This chapter covers the first of these two types, the Mcmd, which is the menu command resource. Chapter 10 provides details on the PPob resource.

Menu Resources and PowerPlant

CodeWarrior projects that use PowerPlant need to include an MBAR resource and MENU resources as do projects that don't use PowerPlant. Additionally, PowerPlant projects must also include resources of the type Mcmd. Fortunately, the Metrowerks Constructor resource editor that was introduced in Chapter 8 makes it easy to work with all three of these resource types.

The PowerPlantIntro68K Program

The **PowerPlantIntro68K** program introduced in Chapter 8 has the menu and menu items shown in Figure 9.1.

In this section, you'll see the menu-related resources that are needed to add the menus shown in Figure 9.1 to a PowerPlant project. When you create a new PowerPlant-based project, CodeWarrior adds a Constructor resource file to the project. This file holds all the resources necessary to implement the menus and menu items shown in Figure 9.1. Later in this chapter you'll see specific examples of how you can use Constructor to add menu resources of your own.

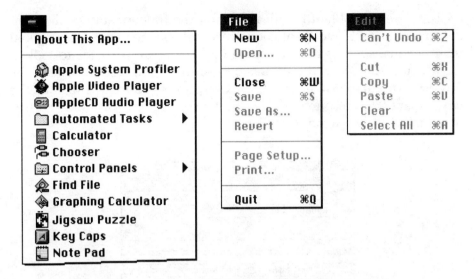

Figure 9.1 *The menus of the PowerPlantIntro68K program.*

MENU and MBAR Resources

In Chapter 8, you saw that programs developed using PowerPlant use the same MENU and MBAR resources used by a program developed using a traditional compiler—they just happen to be saved under different names in a Constructor resource file (Constructor calls an MBAR Menu Bar, and groups an Mcmd with a MENU and calls it a Menu). What wasn't mentioned in that chapter is that PowerPlant requires that some of these resources have certain specific IDs. The Apple, File, and Edit menus, which Apple calls the standard menus (and which Apple suggests should appear in all Macintosh programs), must have these ID numbers:

- The Apple menu must have an ID of 128.
- The File menu must have an ID of 129.
- The Edit menu must have an ID of 130.

Also, the MBAR resource that defines which MENU resources will appear in the application's menu bar must have an ID of 128.

Because PowerPlant handles much of the functionality of the standard menus, the PowerPlant code must make some assumptions about these menus, such as their resource IDs. Using Constructor to look at the Menu resources in the **PP Basic Resource.ppob** resource file of the **PowerPlantIntro68K** example in Chapter 8, you can see that the PowerPlant MENU resource ID numbering convention was followed (see the title bar of each window in Figure 9.2).

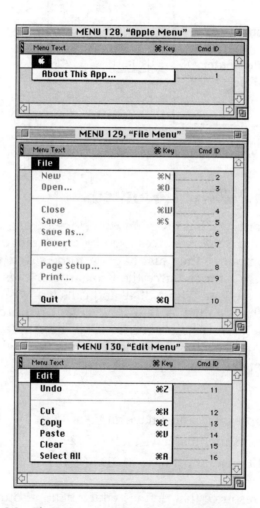

Figure 9.2 *The Menu resources for the PowerPlantIntro68K project have ID numbers that match PowerPlant conventions.*

Menu Items and the Mcmd Resource

In a Macintosh project that doesn't use an application framework, you typically add a #define directive to a source code file (or header file) for each menu item that will appear in the program's menus. Figure 9.3 gives an example using the standard Edit menu.

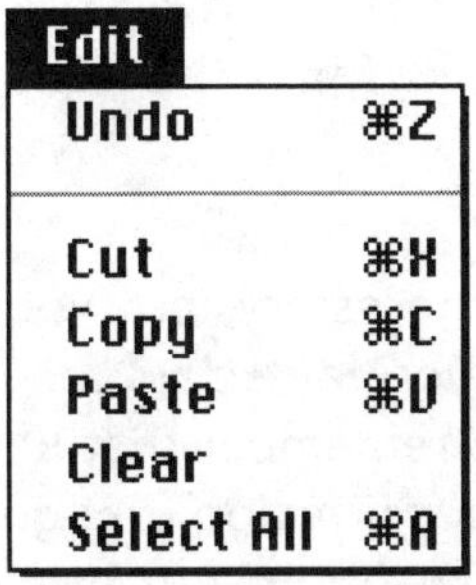

```
Edit
Undo        ⌘Z

Cut         ⌘H
Copy        ⌘C
Paste       ⌘U
Clear
Select All  ⌘A
```

Figure 9.3   Macintosh programs usually define constants for each menu item.

When your program's event loop determines that a mouseDown event is menu related, it makes a call to the Toolbox routine MenuSelect() in order to determine which menu, and which menu item, was selected. The menu item number is then compared to the item constants (like the ones in Figure 9.3) that were defined using the #define directive. After that, your code takes the proper action necessary to handle the menu choice.

The preceding scheme works fine for a program written without the aid of an application framework. An application framework, however, exists to eliminate your need to write the code common to all Macintosh programs, including much of an application's menu handling code. In an application framework like PowerPlant, a class and its member functions are meant to handle a programming task without the programmer making major alterations to the code. Making changes to class definitions and member function code each time you write a program defeats the purpose of PowerPlant. That's why defining menu item constants that specify exactly where in a menu a menu item appears is counterproductive. If at a later time you make program changes that involve rearranging menu items, changes will also have to be made in your source code.

To eliminate the need to define as a constant the menu position of each menu item, PowerPlant obtains menu item numbers by relying on resources rather than source code constants. If each MENU resource has a corresponding resource of a different type (and with the same ID as the MENU), it's a simple matter for a PowerPlant class member function to read in menu item information for each menu. Specifically, the PowerPlant LMenu class has a member function named ReadCommandNumber() that handles this task. The resource that ReadCommandNumber() looks for is the Mcmd resource—a resource type specific to PowerPlant.

NOTE As always, it isn't necessary, but you're free to browse through the code of a PowerPlant class member function. In fact, you don't even have to remember that ReadCommandNumber() is the name of the member function that gets menu item numbers from resources. Having to figure out exactly how each class member function works isn't important.

If you're using Constructor for your resource editing, when you add a Menu resource to your project's resource file, you'll be adding both a MENU resource and an Mcmd resource. The Mcmd resource will have the same resource ID as the MENU resource—that's how the PowerPlant code knows which Mcmd holds information about a MENU. In Figure 9.4, I've opened the **PP Basic Resource.ppob** file using ResEdit rather than Constructor. While ResEdit doesn't allow me to easily view the contents of a single Mcmd resource, this resource editor does make it clear that there is one Mcmd resource for each MENU resource, and that there is a one-to-one correspondence between Mcmd resources and MENU resources.

Each Mcmd resource holds a command number for each menu item in a single MENU resource. For instance, in the **PP Basic Resource.ppob** file, Mcmd 130 holds seven command numbers—one for each of the six editing items (Undo, Cut, Copy, and so forth) and one command number for the one dashed line item.

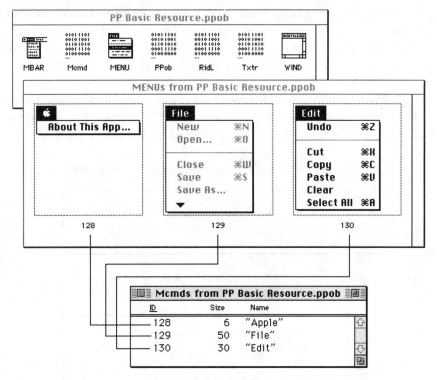

Figure 9.4 *Each MENU resource requires an Mcmd resource that has the same ID as the MENU.*

NOTE

The Mcmd is one of the PowerPlant resource types that isn't common to other Mac applications. Because of this, resource editors such as ResEdit and Resorcerer don't have Mcmd editors built into them. While Constructor makes the display of the contents of Mcmd resources easy and intuitive (the values in such a resource are listed in the menu editor), you may have occasion to view these resources in an editor other than Constructor. In such a case, you'll want to make sure your resource editor (whether it be ResEdit or Resorcerer) is set such that it can display resources of this type. To use templates to do this, refer to Appendix F.

For any one program, each command number is unique; that is, no two menus in a single program share any of the same command numbers. Because the Apple, File, and Edit menus hold many of the same items from program to program, Metrowerks was able to define constants to represent many of these menu items. The PowerPlant header file **PP_Messages.h** lists the predefined command numbers, as well as other constants. Table 9.1 lists the command number constants as well.

The exception to the scheme of using a unique number for each command is the dashed divider line. This menu item always has a command number of 0 regardless of how many times it appears.

Table 9.1   PowerPlant Command Number Constants

```
                    All menus Mcmd constant

              cmd_Nothing      =   0


                    Apple menu Mcmd constant

              cmd_About        =   1


                    File   menu Mcmd constants

              cmd_New          =   2

              cmd_Open         =   3
              cmd_Close        =   4
              cmd_Save         =   5
              cmd_SaveAs       =   6
              cmd_Revert       =   7
              cmd_PageSetup    =   8
              cmd_Print        =   9
              cmd_Quit         =  10

                    Edit   menu Mcmd constants


              cmd_Undo         =  11

              cmd_Cut          =  12
              cmd_Copy         =  13
              cmd_Paste        =  14
```

The PowerPlant menu command number constants are only useful for the standard menus. Of course your application will also include menu items that are specific to your application. For simplicity, the PowerPlantIntro68K example doesn't use any application-specific menu items. An example of how to add a new menu and new menu items appears later in this chapter.

Table 9.1 helps you to easily find the command numbers that will be needed for the menu items in the three menus of the PowerPlantIntro68K example program. Figure 9.5 shows the command numbers in the three Mcmd resources. The constant names are shown in parentheses.

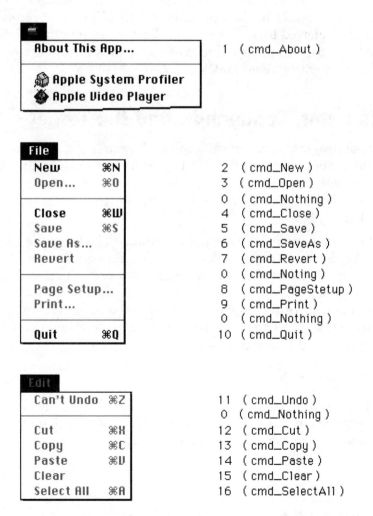

Figure 9.5 *The command number constants for the menu items in the PowerPlantIntro68K program.*

As you'll see later in this chapter, the command name (such as cmd_Quit) will be used in your application source code, while the command number (such as 10 will be used in the Mcmd resource.

Menus, Commands, and Commanders

When the user makes a menu selection, PowerPlant sends a command to one of the objects in the application. The object that receives this command is referred to as a *commander*. Understanding this relationship between menus, commands, and commanders is an important part of programming with PowerPlant.

Menu Items, Commands, and the Target

Macintosh programs are typically menu driven. It is a menu command that brings about some action. In PowerPlant nomenclature, a menu choice (whether invoked by a menu selection or command key) is called a *command*. To carry out a command, the command must be directed at an object.

When a menu item is selected, the command is directed at the target object. Application frameworks, including PowerPlant, are typically based on object-oriented programming. A PowerPlant-created program consists of at least one, and usually many more, objects. All PowerPlant programs consist of the application object—the object created from the class derived from LApplication. The Chapter 8 PowerPlantIntro68K program named that object theApp:

```
CPPStarterApp theApp;
```

Once the preceding line of code executes, other objects, such as window objects, can be created. PowerPlantIntro68K does just that by invoking ObeyCommand() from its version of StartUp():

```
void
CPPStarterApp::StartUp()
{
    ObeyCommand(cmd_New, nil);
}
```

Recall from Chapter 8 that the New menu item of the PowerPlantIntro68K program results in a new window opening. Also recall that such a menu selection automatically invokes a call to the `CPPStarterApp` class version of the `ObeyCommand()` function, with a parameter of `cmd_New` being passed. In addition to relying on a menu selection, the PowerPlantIntro68K program can (and does) call `ObeyCommand()` directly.

Don't worry if you don't fully understand this relationship between menus, `ObeyCommand()`, and the appearance of a window on the screen. The details will be filled in throughout this chapter.

NOTE

From the preceding explanation you can see that PowerPlantIntro68K initially consists of two objects. When a menu command (such as Quit) is made in PowerPlantIntro68K, it will be directed at the window—the target object. The window is the target object because it is active. If the user closes the window by clicking in the window's close box, the application object will become the active object, and thus the target object. With the window closed, the same menu item selection (such as Quit) that was previously directed at the window object will now be directed at the application object.

Figure 9.6 shows a look at the screen for three scenarios in a hypothetical Mac program. Assuming the same menu item is selected, each of the three screens will have a different target object. In the top view, the application object, which is the only object at this point in the running of the program, will be the recipient, or target, of a menu command. In the middle view, the window will be the target—it's active. In the bottom screen, the edit text item object with the I-beam will be the target—it's now the active object.

Commands and the Chain of Command

While some menu items are useful to more than one object type, a menu item doesn't typically have a use to every object in a program. For example, the Copy menu item in the Edit menu may work for either an active edit text item object or an active picture object, but won't make sense for a window object or application object. As a second example, the Quit menu item from the File menu is meaningless to all objects except the application object. Regardless of this, each and every menu command is always directed at the object that is the target at the time the menu selection is made. What happens next, however, depends on whether the command can be used by that object.

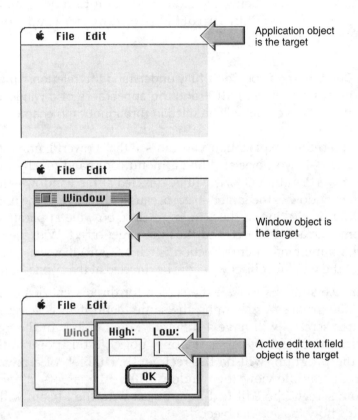

Figure 9.6   *The target object in an application changes as the program executes.*

If a menu command applies to the target object, the target object will handle the command. Consider the case of a program that has a window open and active when the user selects **Close** from the File menu. Because the Close command applies to windows, the window object will be able to handle the command. If, on the other hand, a menu command doesn't apply to the target object, the command will be *passed* to a different object for handling.

The passing of a command isn't indiscriminate. Every target resides at the bottom of a chain of command, and commands are always considered to be passed upwards along the chain. The application itself is always the top object in the chain. Windows and documents lie beneath the application, and window contents are lower still. Figure 9.7 gives an example of the chain of command for a program that has two open windows—one empty, and one with text in it.

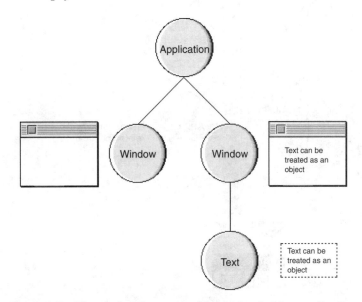

Figure 9.7   The chain of command for a simple Mac application.

If the user of the program shown in Figure 9.7 selects the **Close** menu item while the leftmost window is active, that window is the target and will handle the command. Figure 9.8 shows this.

If the user selects the **Quit** menu item while the rightmost rather than the leftmost window is active, the command again starts at the window. Since a window is only responsible for window-related commands, it passes the command up the chain to the application, as shown in Figure 9.9.

Again referring back to Figure 9.7, if the text in the rightmost window is active (perhaps the text is an object that the user can click on and edit), then the text is the target. Since a Close command doesn't apply to the text, the text object will pass the command up the chain to the window object. Here the Close command applies, and the window will handle the command by closing itself. Figure 9.10 shows this scenario.

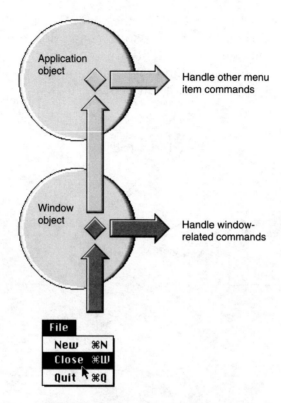

Figure 9.8 *A window as the target object can handle a Close menu item.*

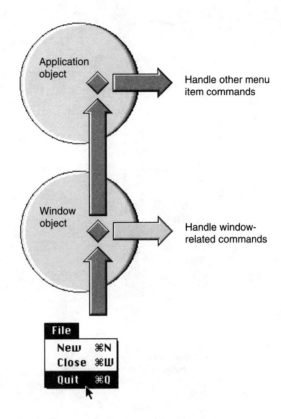

Figure 9.9   *A window as the target object passes a*
Quit command up the chain of command.

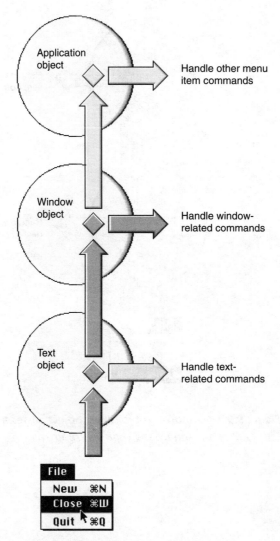

Figure 9.10   *A window with an active pane in it as the target object passes a Close command up the chain of command.*

The Target and the LCommander Class

A target object—an object that is capable of handling a menu command—is referred to as a commander object. That's because the class of which the target is an instance of is derived from the LCommander class.

A program's chain of command changes as the program runs. As windows and dialog boxes open, become active, inactive, and close, the chain of command changes. The LCommander class keeps track of these changes. It is also responsible for routing commands to the appropriate object in the chain.

In C++, multiple inheritance allows a class to be derived from more than one base class. PowerPlant makes extensive use of multiple inheritance, as the following lines of code from a few PowerPlant header files show. These definitions show which classes the LApplication, LWindow, and LEditField classes are derived from. You've already encountered LApplication and LWindow in the PowerPlantIntro68K example in Chapter 8. The LEditField class is used to add an edit text field to a window.

```
class    LApplication : public  LCommander,
                        public  LEventDispatcher,
                        public  LModelObject

class    LWindow      : public  LView,
                        public  LCommander,
                        public  LModelObject

class    LEditField   : public  LPane,
                        public  LCommander,
                        public  LPeriodical
```

While the preceding three classes are each derived from a different set of base classes, they have one thing in common: The LCommander class is one of the base classes. That means that an object of any one of these classes (and numerous other PowerPlant classes) can be a target; it can be a commander that resides in the chain of command. There it can handle a menu command or pass it upwards in the chain.

Handling Menu Selections

Your PowerPlant-based application relies on two member functions to take care of the task of handling a menu selection. Both these functions are defined in LApplication—but your own application class will override these routines and implement its own version of each.

ObeyCommand() and the Chain of Command

Before describing exactly how the PowerPlant chain of command operates, it's time for a quick diversion. If you haven't used an application
framework before, you'll appreciate this example—it has nothing to do
with frameworks or PowerPlant! From object-oriented programming,
you know that a derived class inherits the member functions of the class
on which it is based. You also know that a derived class can override
member functions of the base class. Figure 9.11 shows a base class named
`Vehicle` and a class named `Automobile` that is derived from `Vehicle`.
Note that both classes have a member function named `WriteInfo()`.

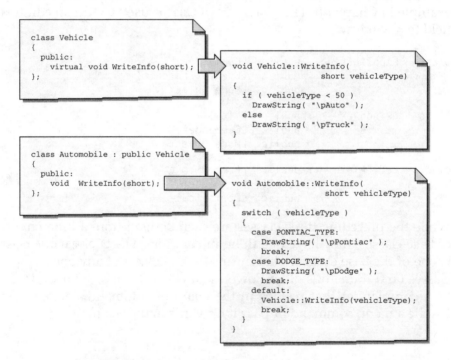

Figure 9.11 *In C++ both a base class and a derived
class may have identically named functions.*

If you aren't familiar with object-oriented programming, refer to
Appendix B for an overview of the primary features of C++.

NOTE

When a derived class overrides a base class member function, as the `Automobile` class overrides `WriteInfo()`, it is the derived class version of the member function that gets invoked by a derived class object. In the following snippet, the `Automobile::WriteInfo()` function gets invoked:

```
Automobile  *theObject;

theObject = new Automobile;
theObject->WriteInfo( 2 );
```

 N O T E Recall that in C++ if a base class member function is to be made available for overriding by a derived class, the base class member function must be declared using the `virtual` keyword.

When a derived class overrides a member function, the base class version of the function is still accessible to the derived class. To differentiate between the two versions of the function, however, the base class name must be included in the call to the base class version. In Figure 9.12, you can see that the derived class version of `WriteInfo()` uses this technique to invoke the base class version of the function with the same name.

```
void Vehicle::WriteInfo(short vehicleType)
{
  if ( vehicleType < 50 )
    DrawString( "\pAuto" );
  else
    DrawString( "\pTruck" );
}
```

```
void Automobile::WriteInfo(short vehicleType)
{
  switch ( vehicleType )
  {
    case PONTIAC_TYPE:
      DrawString( "\pPontiac" );
      break;
    case DODGE_TYPE:
      DrawString( "\pDodge" );
      break;
    default:
      Vehicle::WriteInfo(vehicleType);
      break;
  }
}
```

Figure 9.12 *A derived class version of a function may invoke the base class version of the same function.*

A closer examination of the derived class version of `WriteInfo()` shows that the function examines `vehicleType` to see if its value matches any of the auto types that `WriteInfo()` recognizes, namely, Pontiac or Dodge. If the passed-in value does match, `WriteInfo()` handles things by printing out the vehicle type. If the passed-in value doesn't match, `WriteInfo()` defers the handling of things to the base class version of `WriteInfo()`. Here is the code that does that:

```
default:
    Vehicle::WriteInfo(vehicleType);
    break;
```

In essence, the `Automobile` class version of `WriteInfo()` function takes first crack at handling `vehicleType`. If the `Automobile` class version of `WriteInfo()` can't handle the information in `vehicleType`, it passes control up to the base class version of `WriteInfo()`. We'll assume this program defines vehicle types in the 0 to 49 range to be different car types, and vehicle types greater than 49 to be different truck types. The base class version of `WriteInfo()` simply checks the value of `vehicleType` and writes out a generic vehicle type string ("Auto" or "Truck") based on this value. Figure 9.13 shows this.

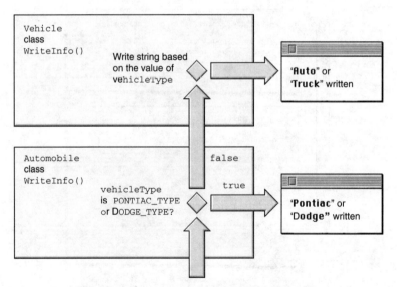

Figure 9.13 *Information not handled by the derived class is passed up to the base class.*

Now it's time to tie the preceding example to PowerPlant. In the preceding example, an `Automobile` class object attempts to handle `vehicleType` using a member function named `WriteInfo()`. If the object doesn't know how to handle `vehicleType`, it passes it up to the `Vehicle` class, where the identically named `WriteInfo()` member function handles it. In PowerPlant, menu commands are passed about just as the `vehicleType` parameter is. In PowerPlant, this menu command parameter is named `inCommand`.

Like the vehicle example, PowerPlant uses identically named member functions to handle a command. In the vehicle example, this routine was named `WriteInfo()`. In PowerPlant, this routine will always be named `ObeyCommand()`.

When the `Automobile` class member function `WriteInfo()` can't handle a vehicle command, it relinquishes control to the `Vehicle` class version of the `WriteInfo()` function. In PowerPlant, if an object's `ObeyCommand()` function can't handle a menu command, it too lets another class handle the command. In a simple PowerPlant program, the target object attempts to handle a menu command. If a window object—based on the `LWindow` class—is the target, it will try to handle the command. If the `LWindow` class `ObeyCommand()` member function has no provision for handling the particular type of menu command selected, the command will be passed up the chain of command to the application object. The application object—based on the `LApplication` class—will then handle the command using its own version of `ObeyCommand()`. Table 9.2 summarizes how my own trivial vehicle example compares to a simple PowerPlant program.

Overriding ObeyCommand()

Every class that is derived from the `LCommander` class must override the `ObeyCommand()` member function. Since (as you saw earlier) several PowerPlant classes, including `LApplication` and `LWindow`, are derived from `LCommander`, the code that makes up PowerPlant includes several versions of the `ObeyCommand()` function.

NOTE

Control objects, such as buttons, are the exception to the previous statement. They don't use the chain of command, and they don't have an `ObeyCommand()` member function.

Table 9.2 *The Vehicle Example is Analogous to the PowerPlant Way of Handling Menu Commands*

	Vehicle example	PowerPlant program
Command that gets passed	vehicleType	inCommand (a menu command)
Functions that handle command	WriteInfo()	ObeyCommand()
Classes that handle command (chain of command)	Automobile ==> Vehicle	LWindow ==> LApplication

Any of your own application-defined classes that are derived from LCommander should also override ObeyCommand(). In Chapter 8, you learned that all PowerPlant programs define a class derived from the LApplication class. Since LApplication is itself derived from LCommander, then the application-defined class too should override ObeyCommand(). Recall that the CPPStarterApp class defined in the CodeWarrior-provided **PP Basic Starter.h** file does this:

```
class    CPPStarterApp : public LApplication {
public:
                    CPPStarterApp();
    virtual         ~CPPStarterApp();

    virtual Boolean     ObeyCommand(CommandT inCommand, void*
    ioParam);

    virtual void        FindCommandStatus(CommandT inCommand,
                        Boolean &outEnabled, Boolean
    &outUsesMark,
                        Char16 &outMark, Str255 outName);
protected:

    virtual void        StartUp();
} ;
```

The CPPStarterApp class also overrides a second LApplication function: FindCommandStatus(). You'll read about this member function later in this chapter.

N O T E

If an application class *doesn't* override ObeyCommand(), the application object is capable of handling only standard menu commands that PowerPlant knows of—menu items such as About and Quit. When such a program receives one of these commands, and a window isn't open, the application itself is the target. The LCommander class (the overseer of commands) will first check to see if the application object, based on the application class, has an ObeyCommand() function. Since the class doesn't, the command is sent up the chain of command to the class the application class is derived from—LApplication. LApplication does have an ObeyCommand() function, so this PowerPlant-defined function is the routine that attempts to, and does, handle the command.

For an application to handle anything but the most common menu commands, its class must include an ObeyCommand() member function. Then, when a menu command is issued and the application object receives it, the application object can handle it. The New menu item is one example. The New menu item in the File menu usually means that a new window should be created. But what kind of window? That's an application-specific issue, so PowerPlant can't handle this menu item on its own. Its handling will be governed by the ObeyCommand() function defined in the class derived from LApplication. Figure 9.14 shows the sequence of ObeyCommand() functions in the chain of command for a simple PowerPlant program that implements a New command.

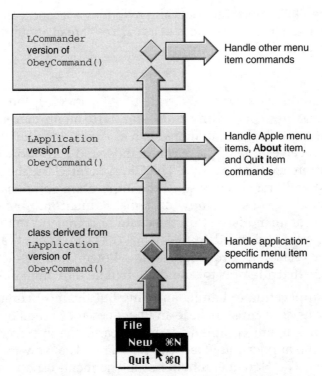

Figure 9.14 *An example of the chain of command*
*for a selection of the **New** menu item.*

In Figure 9.14, you see that because a project's application class is derived from the `LApplication` class, it is the `LApplication` class version of `ObeyCommand()` that handles menu commands that the derived class can't handle. Further, if the `LApplication` class can't handle the command, it is up to the class that `LApplication` is derived from—`LCommander`—to handle the command.

Because PowerPlant knows how to handle standard menu commands, any `ObeyCommand()` function you write shouldn't also attempt to handle these same items. While the application-defined `ObeyCommand()` will handle the File menu's New command, it won't handle the same menu's Quit command. Instead, any command that isn't application-specific should be sent up the chain of command, as shown in Figure 9.15.

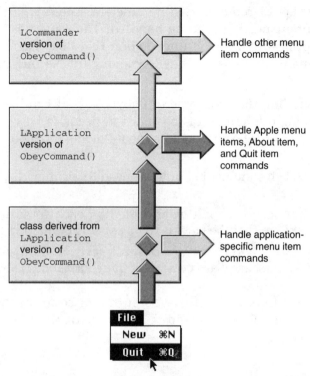

Figure 9.15 *An example of the chain of command for a selection of the **Quit** menu item.*

A Look at the ObeyCommand() Member Function

When writing the LApplication-derived class that's required for each PowerPlant project, include an ObeyCommand() member function. The prototype for the ObeyCommand() function will always be the same:

```
virtual Boolean  ObeyCommand( CommandT  inCommand,
                              void*     ioParam );
```

To allow ObeyCommand() to be overridden by other classes, it must be a virtual function. The return type for ObeyCommand() is Boolean so that the function can report as to whether or not the command it received was handled.

ObeyCommand() requires two parameters. The first, inCommand, is the menu command that is to be handled. The second is a pointer to any extra application-specific information that ObeyCommand() might require. In many versions of ObeyCommand() this second parameter is ignored.

After including the prototype of ObeyCommand() in the application class definition, a definition of the function needs to be written. When you do, it will always be written with the following three points in mind:

1. A switch statement should be used to examine the inCommand parameter.

2. A case section should be included for each application-specific menu item that the class is to be capable of handling.

3. The switch statement's default section should be used to invoke the base class version of ObeyCommand().

Once again I'll look at Metrowerks-supplied code. In the **PP Basic Starter.cp** file, the ObeyCommand() function for the CPPStarterApp class looks like this:

```
Boolean
CPPMenuApp::ObeyCommand(
    CommandT    inCommand,
    void        *ioParam)
{
    Boolean        cmdHandled = true;

    switch (inCommand) {

        case cmd_New:
            LWindow     *theWindow;
            theWindow = LWindow::CreateWindow(window_Sample, this);
            theWindow->Show();
            break;

        default:
            cmdHandled = LApplication::ObeyCommand(inCommand, ioParam);
            break;
    }

    return cmdHandled;
}
```

This version of `ObeyCommand()` is able to handle one application-specific menu item—the New item. Recall from earlier in this chapter that each menu in a program has a `Mcmd` resource associated with it. The `Mcmd` resource has an value—a command number—that is associated with each menu *item* in that menu. Because each menu item in a menu bar must have an `Mcmd` value that's unique to all other menu item `Mcmd` values, this one number is enough to specify both the menu item and the menu that item is in.

In Figure 9.16, I show the resource for the File menu from the **PP Basic Resource.ppob** file. In this figure, you see that the New menu item has a Cmd ID of 2—that's the value in this menu's `Mcmd` resource. If you want to refer to the New menu in your source code, you can use the number 2, or, more appropriately, the PowerPlant-defined constant `cmd_New`. In Figure 9.16, I've provided a view of part of the **PP_Messages.h** PowerPlant file so that you could see that using `cmd_New` is in fact the same as using the number 2 in your source code.

You can tell how many menu items a program implements in its own way by looking at the number of constants used in the switch statement in `ObeyCommand()`. In the above version, there's only one— `cmd_New`.

NOTE Selecting **New** from the File menu of a program that uses the above version of `ObeyCommand()` (such as the PowerPlantIntro68K example application) results in a new window appearing on the screen. The few lines of code under the `cmd_New` constant take care of that. In Chapter 10, we'll look at the details of this window-creating code.

If a menu selection other than the one application-specific menu item is made, the `CPPStarterApp` class version of `ObeyCommand()` that's shown above uses the default section of the `switch` statement to invoke a *different* version of `ObeyCommand()`—the version found in the `LApplication` base class.

```
default:
    cmdHandled = LApplication::ObeyCommand( inCommand, ioParam );
    break;
```

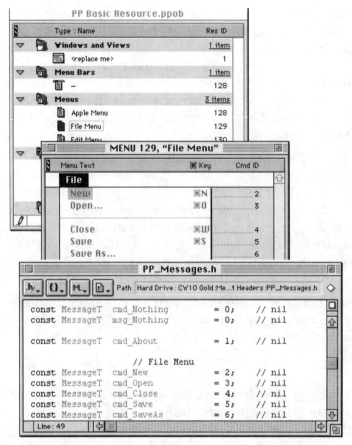

Figure 9.16 *The command number of many commonly used menu items can be found in* **PP_Messages.h***.*

NOTE
Recall from C++ that preceding a call to a member function with a class name followed by the scope resolution operator (::) tells the program to use the version of the function defined by the named class.

LApplication is a PowerPlant class, so you won't have to write its version of ObeyCommand()—it already exists. You'll find the LApplication version of ObeyCommand() in the PowerPlant file **LApplication.cp.** Listed as follows is a part of that function.

```
Boolean
LApplication::ObeyCommand(
    CommandT    inCommand,
    void        *ioParam)
{
    Boolean  cmdHandled = true;

    ResIDT    theMenuID;
    Int16     theMenuItem;

    if ( IsSyntheticCommand( inCommand, theMenuID, theMenuItem ) )
    {
        ...
        // menu command is from a synthetic menu, handle here
        ...
    }
    else
    {
        switch ( inCommand )
        {
            case cmd_About:
                ShowAboutBox();
                break;

            case cmd_Quit:
                SendAEQuit();
                break;

            default:
                cmdHandled = LCommander::ObeyCommand( inCommand, ioParam );
                break;
        }
    }
    return cmdHandled;
}
```

The first part of the LApplication version of ObeyCommand() handles
synthetic menu commands. For menus that hold a variable number of
menu items, such as the Apple menu and a Font menu, PowerPlant
uses a concept called *synthetic menu commands*. These are menu command numbers that are determined at run time—not in Mcmd resources.

NOTE Examples in this book won't use synthetic menus, except for the Apple menu, which holds a variable number of Apple menu items. If you think your application requires other menus of this type, and you're an owner of the full version of Metrowerks CodeWarrior, you'll find synthetic menu commands thoroughly described in the comprehensive electronic document *The PowerPlant Book*.

If a menu command isn't a synthetic command (and most won't be), the LApplication version of ObeyCommand() follows the pattern discussed earlier. A switch statement examines the menu command, and case sections handle the commands the class is familiar with. For LApplication, that means there is a case section to handle the About and Quit menu items. The actual handling of these two menu items is performed by other PowerPlant functions, namely, ShowAboutBox() and SendAEQuit(). For any other menu item, a different version of ObeyCommand() must be called. The LApplication class is derived from the LCommander class, so it's the LCommander version of ObeyCommand() that gets invoked here:

```
case cmd_About:
    ShowAboutBox();
    break;

case cmd_Quit:
    SendAEQuit();
    break;

default:
    cmdHandled = LCommander::ObeyCommand( inCommand, ioParam );
    break;
```

These last few pages have shown how a menu command can work its way up the chain of command from the LApplication-derived class to the LApplication class and finally to the LCommander class. Depending on what objects are on the screen when a menu item is selected by the user, an application can of course have a different chain of command. What's important to keep in mind is that PowerPlant already includes many ObeyCommand() member functions—you're responsible for writing only the versions that accompany your own application-defined derived classes.

Overriding FindCommandStatus()

As a program runs, menu items may need to be updated. A menu item might have a checkmark beside it that gets toggled on and off as the item is selected. Or, a menu item may need to be disabled under certain circumstances. For example, the Close item in the File menu should become disabled after the user closes the last open window. PowerPlant eliminates much of the confusion associated with keeping track of the state of menu items through the use of the FindCommandStatus() member function.

When an event occurs, a PowerPlant routine named UpdateMenus() is called. The purpose of this routine, obviously enough, is to see if the event that just occurred gives rise to a need to update any items in any of the menus. UpdateMenus() in turn calls the LCommander class member function FindCommandStatus() several times—once for every menu item that has an Mcmd resource (only a menu item created on the fly, and thus represented by a synthetic command number, *doesn't* have an Mcmd resource). FindCommandStatus() determines the status of a menu item. That is, it determines the following:

- If the item has a mark
- What that mark is (such as a checkmark)
- Whether the item should be marked at the current point in time
- Whether the menu item should be enabled or disabled at the current point in time

Like ObeyCommand(), the FindCommandStatus() function can be found in several of the PowerPlant classes. That's because the FindCommandStatus() function, again like ObeyCommand(), can be overridden by other classes. Any of your application-defined classes that will be capable of handling menu item selections should override FindCommandStatus(), just as they do with ObeyCommand().

In the Chapter 8 PowerPlantIntro68K example, the LApplication-derived CPPStarterApp class provides the functionality for a selection of the **New** menu item. Therefore this class has both an ObeyCommand() and a FindCommandStatus() member function. The CPPStarterApp class version of ObeyCommand() contains the code that does something in response to a selection of the **New** item (it opens a new window), while the CPPStarterApp class version of FindCommandStatus() contains the code that properly updates the New menu item (more on that just ahead).

When UpdateMenus() calls a FindCommandStatus() routine, it passes the command number of the menu item that is to be updated. The FindCommandStatus() function is then responsible for filling in some or all of the other four parameters for use by UpdateMenus(). Figure 9.17 shows the information held in each of the FindCommandStatus() parameters.

The FindCommandStatus() routine of an application-defined class should have a switch statement with a case section for each menu command handled by the ObeyCommand() member function of that same class. Within each case section, you'll specify the status of one menu item. Here's the CPPStarterApp class version of FindCommandStatus():

```
void
CPPStarterApp::FindCommandStatus(
    CommandT    inCommand,
    Boolean     &outEnabled,
    Boolean     &outUsesMark,
    Char16      &outMark,
    Str255      outName)
{

    switch (inCommand) {

        case cmd_New:
            outEnabled = true;
            break;

        default:
            LApplication::FindCommandStatus(inCommand, outEnabled,
                            outUsesMark, outMark, outName);
            break;
    }
}
```

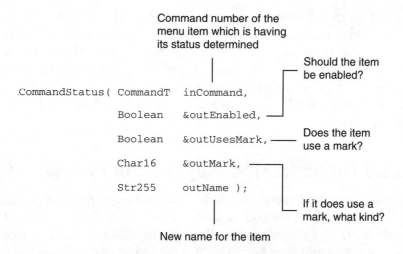

Command number of the
menu item which is having
its status determined

Should the item
be enabled?

.CommandStatus(CommandT   inCommand,

  Boolean   &outEnabled,

  Boolean   &outUsesMark, ——

Does the item
use a mark?

  Char16   &outMark, ——

  Str255   outName);

If it does use a
mark, what kind?

New name for the item

*Figure 9.17 The information held in each of
the* FindCommandStatus() *parameters.*

If FindCommandStatus() is passed an inCommand value of cmd_New, the
routine will set outEnabled to true. This will tell the calling routine
that the **New** menu item should be enabled. Since this menu item uses
no mark, there is no need to give outMark a value. And since the New
menu item doesn't have its text changed (the item will always appear as
"New" in the menu), there is no need to assign outName a string value.

If FindCommandStatus() is passed an inCommand value of anything
other than cmd_New, the function will pass inCommand on to the version
of FindCommandStatus() that is next up in the chain of command—the
LApplication version of this same function. There, the LApplication
version of FindCommandStatus() will update the status of the menu
item—or it too will pass inCommand on to yet another version of
FindCommandStatus().

Adding Application-Specific
Menu Items

Applications usually have more than just the three standard menus
(Apple, File, and Edit), and more than just the standard menu com-

mands found in those menus. To interact with any of these items, PowerPlant needs additional information—information that you will supply. Here I'll provide an overview of the steps you'll take to add a new menu (and of course, its new menu items) to a program being built from a PowerPlant project. After this section, the walkthrough of the development of an example program named PowerPlantMenu68K will provide the specifics.

Command Numbers and Application Menus

For application-specific menu items, you'll provide your own command numbers. These numbers should be outside the PowerPlant reserved range of -999 to 999. While negative values in the -1000 to -65535 range can be used as command numbers, you'll want to stick with the 1000 to 65535 positive range. That's because a command number that is negative results in a menu item that can't have its appearance altered.

Adding Resources for a New Menu

If you're using Constructor to define your application's resources, each application-specific menu will require a new Menu resource (which internally holds one new MENU resource and one new Mcmd resource), and a mention in the Menu Bar resource (which holds an MBAR resource). Except for the Mcmd resource, this is the same as you would do for a menu addition in a project that didn't rely on PowerPlant.

When you create a new Menu resource, Constructor gives you the opportunity to enter a command number for each menu item in the new menu. Together, these command numbers become an Mcmd resource.

Adding the resources for a new menu is the first step to letting PowerPlant in on your intentions. After that, you'll need to add some code to a project's source code file.

Defining Menu Item Constants

For standard menu items such as New, Quit, Copy, and Cut, your source code need not include definitions of the menu item command numbers—they're already defined in the **PP_Messages.h** header file. For menu items that are specific to your application, though, you'll need to add constant definitions. For instance, if I were developing a program that would be used to edit pictures, I might have a Transform menu that held three menu items: Scale, Rotate, and Distort. In Constructor, I would have assigned each of these items a command number—say, 1055, 2003, and 1165, respectively. In my source code, I'd now define a constant for each:

```
const  CommandT   cmd_ScalePicture   =  1055;
const  CommandT   cmd_RotatePicture  =  2003;
const  CommandT   cmd_DistortPicture =  1165;
```

Earlier in this chapter, you read that one of the advantages of using PowerPlant was that you wouldn't have to make changes to your project's source code if you rearranged menu items. To stress this point, I've intentionally given the three menu command numbers values that do not give any indication of the order in which the items appear in the Transform menu (or even that they appear in the same menu). I *could* have given them consecutive numbers, though—like this:

```
const  CommandT   cmd_ScalePicture   =  1001;
const  CommandT   cmd_RotatePicture  =  1002;
const  CommandT   cmd_DistortPicture =  1003;
```

All that matters is that the number in the source code match the command number in the Menu resource.

Writing the ObeyCommand() Function

For each new menu item that has been added to the Constructor resource file, an appropriate `case` label and section needs to be added to the version of `ObeyCommand()` that your application class defines. That's how your program knows what to do in response to a selection of one of these new menu items—PowerPlant code invokes your application's `ObeyCommand()` function. In brief, for this example you'd use the above three constants and add the following sections to the `switch` statement in `ObeyCommand()`:

```
case cmd_ScalePicture:
   // code to handle scaling of the active picture
   break;

case cmd_RotatePicture:
   // code to handle rotation of the active picture
   break;

case cmd_DistortPicture:
   // code to handle distortion of the active picture
   break;
```

Assuming that the program being worked on handled the New menu item as well as the three newly added items, ObeyCommand() would look like this:

```
Boolean
CPPMenuApp::ObeyCommand(
   CommandT    inCommand,
   void        *ioParam)
{
   Boolean      cmdHandled = true;

   switch (inCommand) {

      case cmd_New:
         LWindow     *theWindow;
         theWindow = LWindow::CreateWindow(window_Sample, this);
         theWindow->Show();
         break;

      case cmd_ScalePicture:
         // code to handle scaling of the active picture
         break;

      case cmd_RotatePicture:
         // code to handle rotation of the active picture
         break;

      case cmd_DistortPicture:
         // code to handle distortion of the active picture
         break;

      default:
         cmdHandled = LApplication::ObeyCommand(inCommand, ioParam);
         break;
   }
```

```
    return cmdHandled;
}
```

Writing the FindCommandStatus() Function

Every application-specific menu item that you add to your program should have a case section in both the `ObeyCommand()` and `FindCommandStatus()` member functions of the application-defined class. The `ObeyCommand()` member function provides for the handling of these menu selections, while the `FindCommandStatus()` function describes the appearance of the menu items. For simplicity, I'll assume this version of `FindCommandStatus()` is written such that each of the three new menu items is always enabled. Figure 9.18 shows that the three application-specific menu items in my hypothetical picture-editing program appear in the `ObeyCommand()` and `FindCommandStatus()` routines.

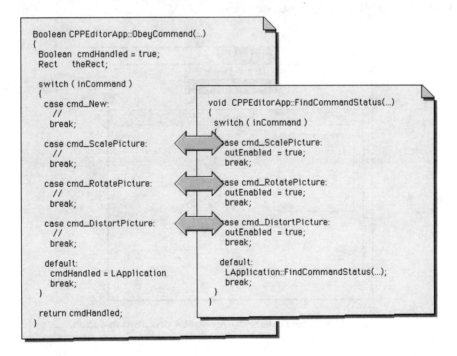

Figure 9.18 *Application-specific menu items should be listed in both the* `ObeyCommand()` *and* `FindCommandStatus()` *member functions.*

The PowerPlantMenu68K Example Application

The PowerPlantIntro68K program in Chapter 8 demonstrates the use of menus in an application created using PowerPlant, but only to a limited extent. PowerPlantIntro68K only implemented the standard menus found in all Mac programs. Typical Mac applications will also add menus and menu items not common to all other programs. The PowerPlantMenu68K example includes the standard menus that PowerPlant knows about (the same three that are present in PowerPlantIntro68K—the program that is simply the compilation of the files CodeWarrior places in every new PowerPlant-based project). In addition, PowerPlantMenu68K has one new application-specific menu—a *Draw* menu that holds two menu items. In Figure 9.19, you can see that the **Draw Square** item has already been selected and the **Draw Circle** item is about to be chosen.

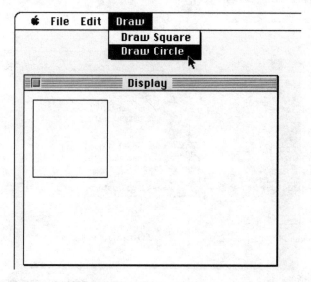

Figure 9.19   *The **PowerPlantMenu68K** program in action.*

The PowerPlantMenu68K Project

You can create the **PowerPlantMenu68K.µ** project in the same manner as last chapter's **PowerPlantIntro68K.µ** project—choose **New Project** from the File menu of the CodeWarrior IDE, select the **Basic PowerPlant 68k** project stationery, then provide a name for the project. After that, a project window like the one shown in Figure 9.20 appears.

If you select **Run** from the Project menu right now, CodeWarrior will build and run the default starter application—the one I named PowerPlantIntro68K in Chapter 8. Instead of doing that, I'll add both resources and source code to the files that CodeWarrior has supplied so that I'll get a new program—one that does just a little more than the starter program. In Figure 9.20, you see that I've pointed out the two files that I'll be working with—all the other files will be included "as is."

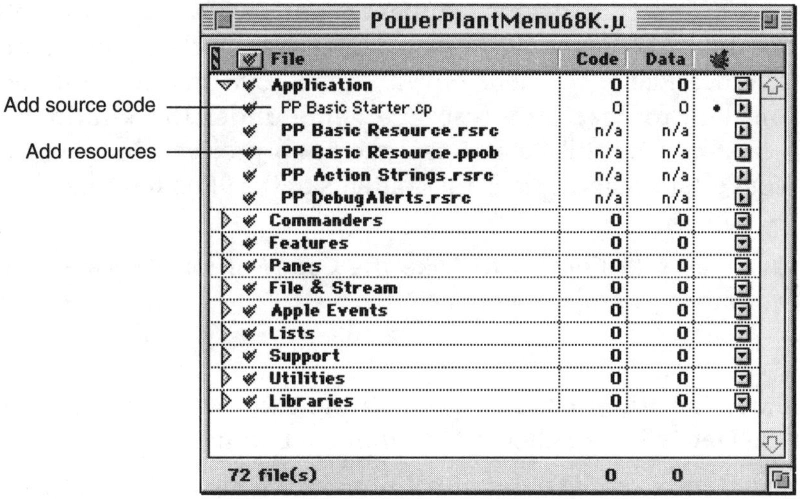

Figure 9.20   The project window of the PowerPlantMenu68K.µ project.

The PowerPlantMenu68K Resources

The **PowerPlantMenu68K.µ** project has all of the same resources that were found in Chapter 8's **PowerPlantIntro68K.µ** project. These are the resources supplied to the project in the four resource files CodeWarrior adds to any PowerPlant-based project. Additionally, the **PowerPlantMenu68K.µ** project will have a new Menu resource not found in the supplied files. I'll use Constructor to:

- Create this new Menu resource.
- Add a couple of menu items to it.
- Specify a command number for each of these two menu items.

If you don't have the project's **PP Basic Resource.ppob** file open at this time, double-click on the file name in the **PowerPlantMenu68K.µ** project window to launch Constructor and to open this file.

EDITING THE PPOB RESOURCE

My PowerPlantMenu68K program will use a window like the one CodeWarrior provides in the PPob resource of the **PP Basic Resource.ppob** file. I can't, however, get away with leaving this resource untouched—it holds a pane (an LCaption class pane) with the words "PowerPlant says: hello world." To remove this pane, I'll double-click on the **<replace me>** resource name under the Windows and Views listing in the **PP Basic Resource.ppob** project window to open the layout editor that displays the contents of the PPob resource.

NOTE

Recall that Constructor, like the CodeWarrior IDE, calls its main window a project window.

To remove the text, first click once on the text pane to select it. Then press the **Delete** key, or choose **Cut** from the Edit menu.

While I'm in the layout editor I'll make a couple of trivial changes as an excuse to gain a little experience with Constructor and the PPob resource. I begin by double-clicking anywhere within the window that's displayed in the layout editor. That opens the property inspector for the window pane. As shown in Figure 9.21, this inspector displays quite a bit of information about the window. Some of this information will be described in Chapter 10. For now, I'll just type in a new title for the window—Figure 9.21 shows that I've typed "Drawing" in the **Window**

Title edit box. Now, each new window created from this PPob resource will have this title displayed in its title bar.

With the window title changed, click on the property inspector window's **close** box. Then click on the close box of the layout editor to close it too—it's time to move on to the creation of a new menu.

N O T E

The Constructor property inspector for a window pane lets you enter the same descriptive information for a window as a ResEdit lets you make to a WIND resource. For instance, you can see that the four edit boxes in the upper-left corner of the property inspector allow you to set the window's initial screen location and size—window characteristics the ResEdit lets you set as well.

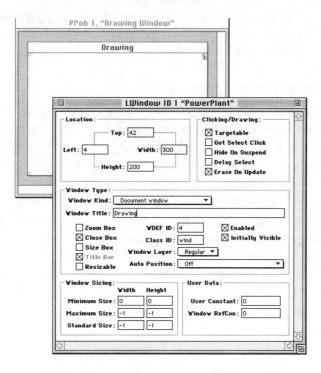

Figure 9.21 *The property inspector for a window pane.*

EDITING THE MENU BAR RESOURCE

There's nothing special about the Constructor Menu Bar resource—it holds an MBAR resource. What is special is the way in which Constructor implements its menu bar editor. While this editor of course lets you add and remove menus from a menu bar, it also allows you to edit the items in any one menu, and to establish the command numbers that each item in a menu needs. In being able to do all that, the Constructor menu bar editor will most likely serve as the only editor you'll use for working with your project's menu bar, menus, and menu item. That is, you might use the menu bar editor as your menu-editing "command center" and forego ever double-clicking on any one Menu resource. To begin your menu editing, double-click on the unnamed Menu Bar resource in the **PP Basic Resource.ppob** project window. As shown in Figure 9.22, you'll see the menu bar that CodeWarrior uses to start off each PowerPlant-based project. In this figure, the one item in the Apple menu is shown. If you want to display the items in the File or Edit menu, you can click once on either of those menu names.

ADDING A NEW MENU RESOURCE

Back in Figure 9.19, you saw that the PowerPlantMenu68K program has one new menu added to the three supplied by CodeWarrior—a Draw menu with two items in it. To add this new menu to the existing Menu Bar resource, you'll use the Edit menu. As shown in Figure 9.23, the Edit menu offers you the means to do quite a bit with menu resources.

To create the new Draw menu, first click on the **Edit** menu in the menu bar editor (not on the Edit menu in the Constructor menu bar!). Next, choose **New Menu** from the Edit menu. When you do that, a new menu like the one shown in Figure 9.24 will be added to the menu bar. Constructor adds the new menu after the selected menu in the menu bar editor—that's why I clicked on the **Edit** menu first.

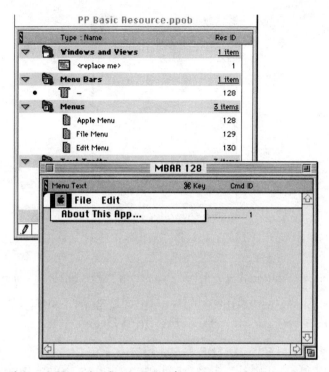

Figure 9.22 *Viewing a menu bar resource in Constructor.*

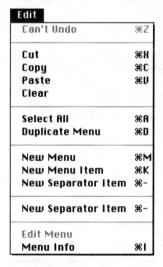

Figure 9.23 *With a Menu Bar resource open, Constructor's Edit menu holds several menu-editing items.*

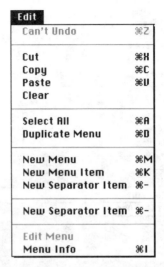

Figure 9.24 *Adding a new menu to a Menu Bar resource in Constructor.*

To change the name of the new menu, just start typing. To make the new menu a Draw menu, type in the word **Draw**.

Adding Menu Items to the New Menu Resource

The new menu is initially devoid of menu items. To create a new item, choose **New Menu Item** from the Edit menu. Then, as I've just done in Figure 9.25, type the name of the new menu item. For this example, type **Draw Square**. The results are shown in Figure 9.25.

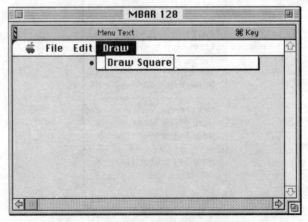

Figure 9.25 *Adding a new menu item to a menu in a Menu Bar resource in Constructor.*

Now, again select **New Menu Item** from the Edit menu to add the second menu item. In the new, empty item, type in the words **Draw Circle**, as shown in Figure 9.26.

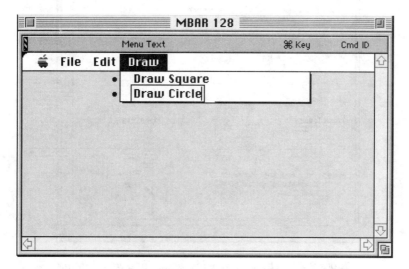

Figure 9.26   *Adding a second new menu item to a menu in a Menu Bar resource in Constructor.*

ASSIGNING COMMAND NUMBERS TO THE NEW MENU ITEMS

For a project that didn't rely on PowerPlant for much of its code, you'd consider the new menu complete. PowerPlant, however, relies on the fact that each menu item has its own command number by which it can be identified. To assign a menu item such a number, double-click on it to bring up its property inspector. When you do that for the Draw Square item, you'll see the property inspector pictured in Figure 9.27. Here you can assign a shortcut key (a command key equivalent), change the look of the text of the item, and so forth. You can also assign the menu item a command number. As you see in Figure 9.27, I've entered the number **1006** as the command number for the Draw Square menu item. Do the same, then close the property inspector. Note that the menu bar editor now displays the command number to the right of the menu item (see Figure 9.28).

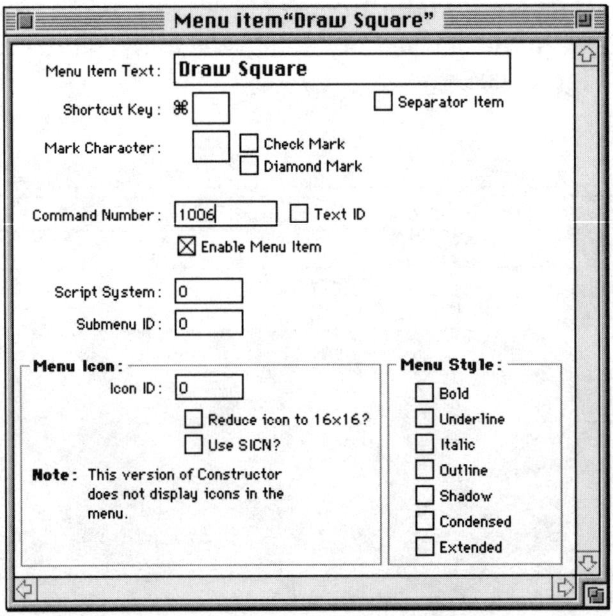

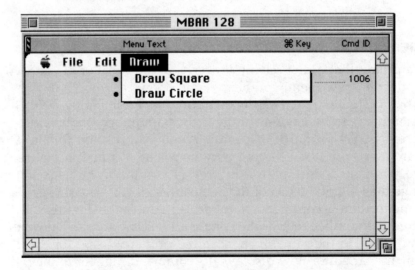

Figure 9.27 *The property inspector for a menu item.*

Figure 9.28 *If a menu item in the displayed menu has been assigned a command number, Constructor lists it in the menu bar editor.*

NOTE Recall from the *Adding Application-Specific Menu Items* section that values assigned to the command numbers of menu items are arbitrary. There are two points you should abide by. First, a command number must be unique compared to all other command numbers used by items in this application's menu bar. Second, the PowerPlant numbering convention for command numbers for application-specific menu items states that command numbers should be given values greater than 999. Beyond that, the choice is yours.

Next, assign a command number for the second menu item—the Draw Circle item. Figure 9.29 shows that I've opened that item's property inspector and entered a value of 2005 as the command number.

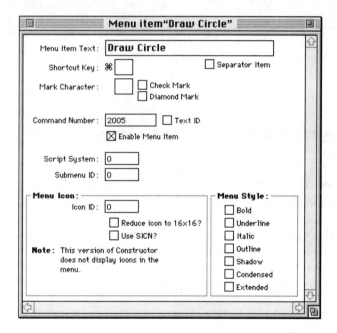

Figure 9.29 The property inspector for a second menu item.

After closing the Draw Circle menu item's property inspector, the new Draw menu is complete. As shown in Figure 9.30, this menu now has two items, each with a unique command number. You'll see these numbers again when I describe the additions you'll make to the project's source code.

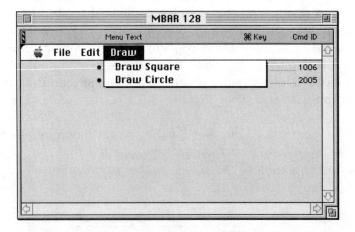

Figure 9.30 *The completed Draw menu, its menu items, and its menu item command numbers are all displayed in the menu bar editor.*

The PowerPlantMenu68K Source Code

For the PowerPlantMenu68K project, I'll start with the source code in the **PP Basic Starter.h** and **PP Basic Starter.cp** files that have been supplied to the project by CodeWarrior. No, that's *not* cheating! Metrowerks supplies this code to programmers as another way of reducing the effort necessary to write a Mac application. Remember, PowerPlant exists to minimize your programming efforts.

RENAMING THE STARTER HEADER FILE

In the Chapter 8 PowerPlant example, I simply compiled all the files in the project created using PowerPlant stationery and gave the resulting application a name—PowerPlantIntro68K. Here, I'll be making some changes (albeit minor ones) to the CodeWarrior-supplied code that is a part of each new PowerPlant project.

In keeping with the convention of defining a class in one file and its member functions in another file, a newly created PowerPlant-based project provides the definition of an application class in a header file—the CPPStarterApp class defined in the **PP Basic Starter.h** file. I'll give this class a name that's a little more descriptive of the purpose of the class (which is to be the main class for a program that demonstrates adding a new menu to a program). CodeWarrior calls this application class CPPStarterApp—I'll rename it CPPMenuApp.

You'll find that most projects that use PowerPlant store application-specific code in a source code file and header file that each bear the same name as the application class. Consider the code for this example—the PowerPlantMenu68K program. Because I'm naming the class derived from the LApplication class CPPMenuApp, I'll define that class in a header file named **CPPMenuApp.h** and define each of the class member functions in a source code file named **CPPMenuApp.cp**.

I'm modifying the CPPStarterApp class in the existing **PP Basic Starter.h** file, so I'll simply rename that file to match the file naming convention that I just mentioned. From the CodeWarrior IDE, I'll select **Open** from the File menu to open the **PP Basic Starter.h** file, as shown in Figure 9.31. When the file opens, I select **Save As** from the File menu and rename the file **CPPMenuApp.h** (see Figure 9.32).

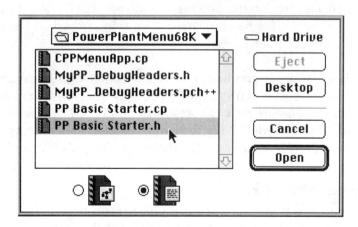

Figure 9.31 *Opening the **PP Basic Starter.h** header file from within the CodeWarrior IDE.*

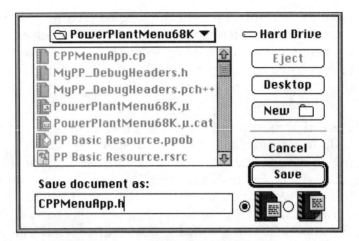

*Figure 9.32   Renaming the **PP Basic Starter.h** header
file from within the CodeWarrior.*

N O T E

You don't have to rename the basic starter files, but you'll want to. It makes keeping track of files from different projects easier, and it abides by a convention that's generally followed for PowerPlant-based projects. For this example, I'll take my time walking through the process. In Chapter 10, I'll leave it up to you to make the file naming changes (or to peek back at this example if you need a refresher).

N O T E

As an aside, if you like this idea of renaming CodeWarrior-supplied files that you've edited, you may also want to rename the Constructor file **PP Basic Resource.ppob** to, say, **PPMenu.rsrc**. If you do that, you'll have to remove **PP Basic Resource.ppob** from, and add **PPMenu.rsrc** to, the project in the CodeWarrior IDE.

EDITING THE HEADER FILE

I've changed the name of the **PP Basic Starter.h** header file—but I haven't changed any code within the file. I'll do that now. The only thing I'll change in this header file is the name of the application class. In Figure 9.33, you can see that this change necessitates editing the old class name (`CPPStarterApp`) in three places.

I've given the file a new name because I've made changes to it. On

the other hand, the changes are so trivial that I really should give
Metrowerks credit for the code. In Figure 9.33, you see that my comment at the top of the file reflects this.

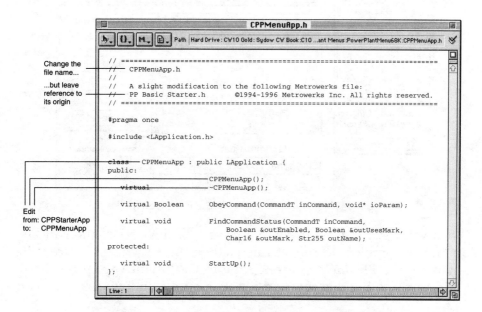

Figure 9.33 *Changing the file name comment and
the name of the application class in the application header file.*

With the changes to the header file complete, select **Save** from the File
menu and then close the file.

RENAMING THE SOURCE CODE FILE

The real additions to the source code come in the **PP Basic Starter.cp**
file. Before jumping right in, rename the file to match the convention
mapped out above. In the project window, double-click on the name of
the **PP Basic Starter.cp** file to open it. Then select **Save As** from the File
menu. As I'm doing in Figure 9.34, rename the file **CPPMenuApp.cp**,
and then click the **Save** button.

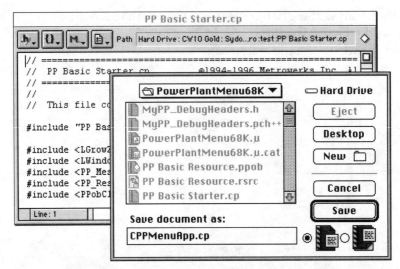

Figure 9.34 *Renaming the **PP Basic Starter.cp** file.*

When you rename a file that's in a project, CodeWarrior automatically updates the project to reflect this change. As shown in Figure 9.35, renaming the **PP Basic Starter.cp** file to **CPPMenuApp.cp** results in CodeWarrior using this new name in the project window.

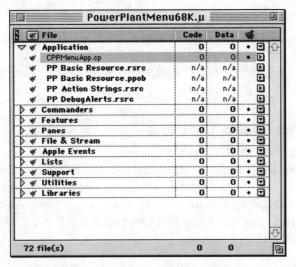

Figure 9.35 *The **PowerPlantMenu68K.µ** project after the **PP Basic Starter.cp** file name has been changed.*

EDITING THE SOURCE CODE FILE

Now it's time to make the changes to the source code. I'll start with the easy stuff—the changes that don't involve new code, but rather involve only the updating of code to match the change of the name of the header file and the change of the name of the application class.

Because I've changed the name of the included header file from **PP Basic Starter.h** to **CPPMenuApp.h**, I'll need to change the first #include directive. It was #include PP Basic Starter.h, I'll change it to #include CPPMenuApp.h. Then, while I'm at the top of the source code file, I'll make a change to the comment—a change that's similar to the one I made at the top of the **CPPMenuApp.h** file. Figure 9.36 shows these changes.

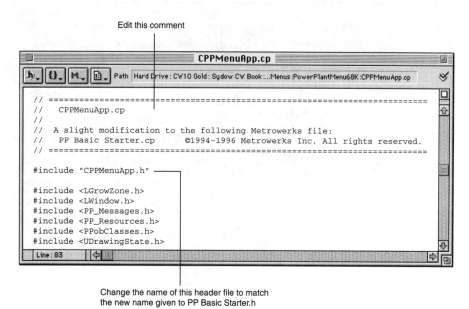

Edit this comment

Change the name of this header file to match
the new name given to PP Basic Starter.h

*Figure 9.36 Changing the file name comment and
the name of the included application header file.*

Now I need to change each occurrence of "CPPStarterApp" to "CPPMenuApp." Each class member function definition includes the class name, so there'll be a few changes to make. As shown in Figure 9.37, I can use the Find dialog box to facilitate this type of change.

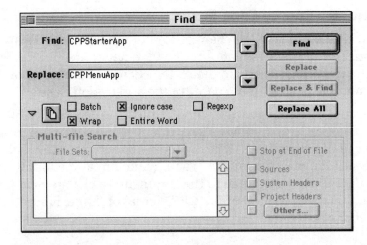

Figure 9.37　*The Find dialog box set up to perform a search and replace on the old application class name.*

After clicking the **Replace All** button in the Find dialog box, the changes will be made. In Figure 9.38, you see that main() now declares theApp to be a variable of the class type CPPMenuApp—as expected.

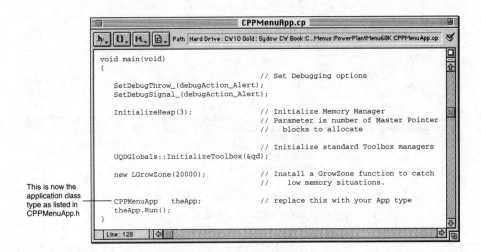

Figure 9.38　*The search and replace will change the declaration of theApp in* main( ).

My search and replace also resulted in changes to the first line of the class constructor, destructor, and the `StartUp()` member functions. Figure 9.39 points this out.

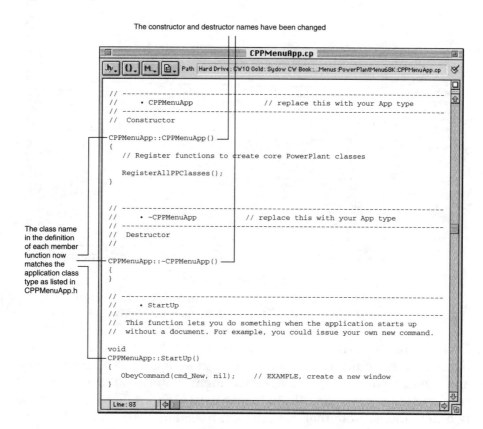

Figure 9.39 *The search and replace will change the class name in the definitions of the application class constructor, destructor, and* StartUp() *member functions.*

The last two occurrences of `CPPStarterApp` that have been changed to `CPPMenuApp` are in the function definitions for `ObeyCommand()` and `FindCommandStatus()`. Figure 9.40 shows these changes.

Adding the Command Number Constants

Now it's time to make *real* changes to the code—changes that implement the behavior that is expected of the new menu and menu items.

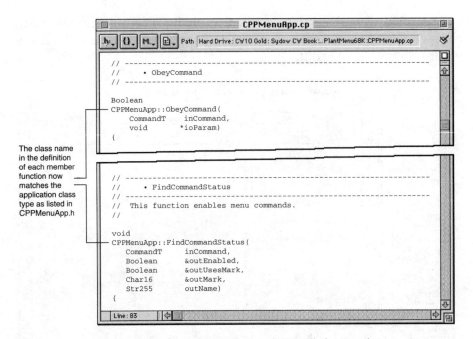

The class name in the definition of each member function now matches the application class type as listed in CPPMenuApp.h

```
// ------------------------------------------------------------
//     •  ObeyCommand
// ------------------------------------------------------------

Boolean
CPPMenuApp::ObeyCommand(
    CommandT     inCommand,
    void         *ioParam)
{
```

```
// ------------------------------------------------------------
//     •  FindCommandStatus
// ------------------------------------------------------------
//  This function enables menu commands.
//

void
CPPMenuApp::FindCommandStatus(
    CommandT     inCommand,
    Boolean      &outEnabled,
    Boolean      &outUsesMark,
    Char16       &outMark,
    Str255       outName)
{
```

Figure 9.40   *The search and replace will change the
class name in the definitions of the application class* ObeyCommand()
and FindCommandStatus() *member functions.*

Each application-specific menu item should have its own constant defined in the source code. That provides the link between source code and menu resources. I've added two menu items, so I'll need to add two constants to the one that already exists. Figure 9.41 shows these two definitions. Note that the numbers 1006 and 2005 match the command numbers assigned to the new menu items in the new menu resource that I created and edited using Constructor.

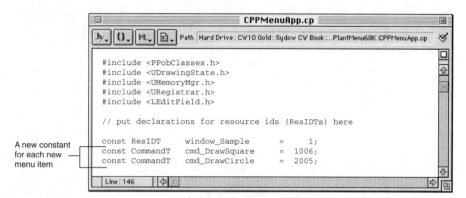

Figure 9.41   *Adding a constant for each of the two new menu items that were added in the new menu in the Constructor resource file.*

ADDING TO THE OBEYCOMMAND() MEMBER FUNCTION

In order for the program to respond to user selections of new menu items, each application-specific menu item needs a case section in the ObeyCommand() routine. Figure 9.42 shows the additions I made to the ObeyCommand() function.

The **PowerPlantMenu68K** application will be able to handle two application-specific menu items. The first, Draw Square, does just that— it draws a square in the program's window. The second, Draw Circle, draws a circle. Both menu commands are implemented using calls to QuickDraw Toolbox routines. As discussed in Chapter 8, the scope resolution operator (::) is used to make it clear to anyone reading the code that SetRect(), FrameRect(), and FrameOval() are Toolbox routines.

As the program is now written, drawing takes place in the ObeyCommand() routine that is a member function of the application class. Since menu commands that perform drawing always apply to a *window*, not to the application itself (recall that menu commands such as New and Quit apply to an application), it would make more sense to have these two commands handled by an ObeyCommand() routine written for a window class derived from the PowerPlant class LWindow. Not only would it make more sense, it would make window updating work (you'll see that the circle or square doesn't get properly redrawn in a window that needs refreshing). In Chapter 10, I'll remedy this situation.

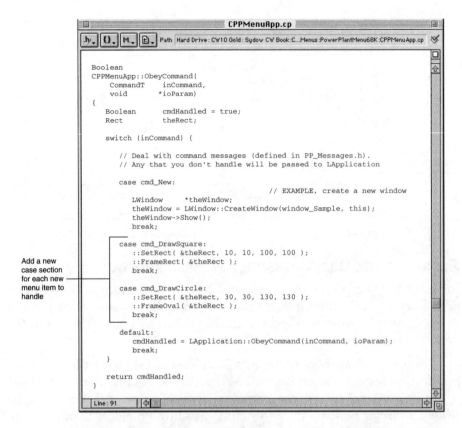

Add a new
case section
for each new
menu item to
handle

*Figure 9.42   Adding a case section for each new menu
item in the* ObeyCommand() *member function definition.*

In Figure 9.42 you can see that the two constants that I just recently
added near the top of the source code file are used in my new
ObeyCommand() code. Here are the two constants you'll find at the top
of the source code:

```
const  CommandT  cmd_DrawSquare  =  1006;
const  CommandT  cmd_DrawCircle  =  2005;
```

The constants are then used in the switch statement in
ObeyCommand():

```
case cmd_DrawSquare:
   // draw a square
```

```
case cmd_DrawCircle:
   // draw a circle
```

ADDING TO THE FINDCOMMANDSTATUS() MEMBER FUNCTION

Each new menu item should have a corresponding section of code in
the application's FindCommandStatus() member function. Figure 9.43
shows the code that has been added to FindCommandStatus().

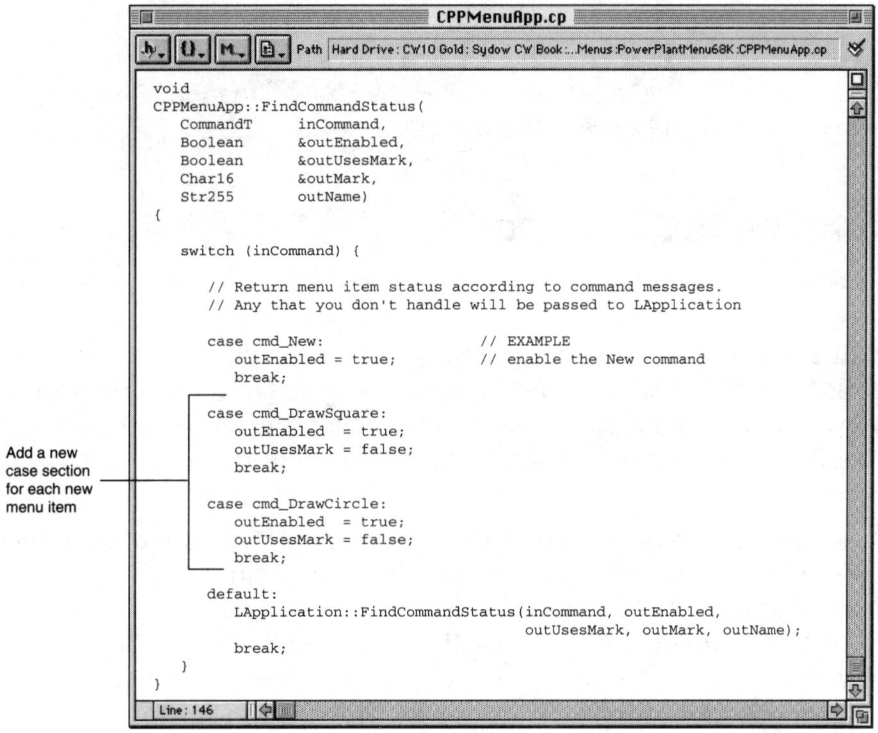

```
void
CPPMenuApp::FindCommandStatus(
    CommandT    inCommand,
    Boolean     &outEnabled,
    Boolean     &outUsesMark,
    Char16      &outMark,
    Str255      outName)
{

    switch (inCommand) {

        // Return menu item status according to command messages.
        // Any that you don't handle will be passed to LApplication

        case cmd_New:                // EXAMPLE
            outEnabled = true;       // enable the New command
            break;

        case cmd_DrawSquare:
            outEnabled  = true;
            outUsesMark = false;
            break;

        case cmd_DrawCircle:
            outEnabled  = true;
            outUsesMark = false;
            break;

        default:
            LApplication::FindCommandStatus(inCommand, outEnabled,
                                outUsesMark, outMark, outName);
            break;
    }
}
```

Add a new case section for each new menu item

CPPMenuApp.cp

Path Hard Drive : CW10 Gold : Sydow CW Book : ...Menus :PowerPlantMenu68K :CPPMenuApp.cp

Line : 146

Figure 9.43   *Adding a case section for each new menu item in the*
FindCommandStatus() member function definition.

Once again the two command number constants that I defined near the
start of the source code listing are used to let PowerPlant communicate
with the new Menu resource. If FindCommandStatus() is passed an
inCommand value of cmd_DrawSquare, the routine will set outEnabled

to `true` and `outUsesMark` to `false`. This will tell the calling routine that the **Draw Square** menu item should be enabled and should not have any kind of mark beside it. Since this menu item uses no mark, there is no need to give `outMark` a value (recall that `outMark` specifies the *type* of mark that should appear to the left of a menu item). And since the Draw Square menu item doesn't have its text changed (the item will always appear as "Draw Square" in the menu), there is no need to assign `outName` a string value.

If `FindCommandStatus()` receives an `inCommand` value of `cmd_DrawCircle`, `outEnabled` will again be set to `true` and `outUsesMark` will again be set to `false`. This is because the Draw Circle menu item behaves the same as the Draw Square menu item: It is always enabled and doesn't use a mark.

Running the Program

After implementing the changes to the source code, select **Run** from the Project menu to compile the code and to give the program a test run. With PowerPlantMenu68K running, verify that the new menu items work by first choosing **Draw Square** from the Draw menu, and then **Draw Circle** from the same menu. Next, select **New** from the File menu to open a new, empty window. Again make selections from the Draw menu.

After successfully compiling and running PowerPlantMenu68K, return to the source code and try your hand at making a few changes to `ObeyCommand()`. If you question the use of Toolbox calls in a PowerPlant project, try changing the code under the `cmd_DrawSquare` case label. Alter the values of the parameters to `FrameRect()`. Or, change the calls to the drawing routines. Substitute the call to `FrameRect()` with a call to the Toolbox function `FrameRoundRect()`. To draw a line rather than a square, replace the `SetRect()` and `FrameRect()` calls with calls to the Toolbox routines `MoveTo()` and `Line()`.

Summary

PowerPlant classes greatly reduce the amount of menu-handling code you'll need to write for an application. You will, however, still need to create menu-related resources for your programs. Fortunately Constructor makes this task simple.

When the user makes a menu selection from a program created from a PowerPlant-based project, PowerPlant code sends a command to one of the objects in the application. The object that receives this command is referred to as a commander, or target. Through the use of the ObeyCommand() member function, the target object gets the first opportunity to handle the menu command. If the command doesn't pertain to the target, the target will pass the command up to the next higher object in the chain of command.

To keep track of the current state of each menu item, PowerPlant relies on the FindCommandStatus() member function. You can use this routine to tell PowerPlant under what conditions menu items should be enabled or disabled, or checked or unchecked.

Chapter 10

PowerPlant and Panes

An application framework takes care of much of the drudgery of programming. Its job is to handle the tasks common to all programs. Drawing is a big part of any Mac program—it's usually the graphics and text that are drawn to a window that makes one Mac program different from all other Macintosh applications. Because drawing varies with each program, you might suspect that this is the point where an application framework loses its effectiveness. Not so! Easing the task of drawing, and working with drawn objects, is where PowerPlant really shines.

In a PowerPlant project, you'll rely on panes to serve as areas of a window that hold drawn objects. Each pane will have the ability to draw itself (as in response to an update), and will have other features not found in a traditional Mac programming environment—like the ability to allow the user to drag a pane about a window. In this chapter, you'll learn all about panes—the theory behind what they are, the creation of them using the Metrowerks Constructor, and an example program that uses a draggable pane.

Windows, Panes, and Views

Anything that is drawn in a PowerPlant-created program is drawn in a *pane*. A view is a special type of pane that can hold other panes within it.

About PowerPlant Panes and Views

A pane is a rectangle that occupies part or all of a window. One important property of a pane is that it is capable of drawing itself. A pane is an object that is derived from the PowerPlant LPane class. As one of its many member functions, the LPane class (and thus any class derived from LPane) includes a member function named DrawSelf(). This routine, as you probably have just guessed, draws the contents of the pane.

To create a self-contained drawing area in a window, a program creates a class derived from LPane or LView. The LView class is itself derived from LPane. A class derived directly from the LPane class is a pane, while a class derived from the LView class is considered a specialized type of a pane—PowerPlant calls it a *view*. Objects derived from either class are *drawing areas*. The difference is that a view may contain other views or panes, while a pane may not. Figure 10.1 elaborates on this somewhat tricky notion. In this figure, I show a part of the PowerPlant class hierarchy. Here you see the classes derived from the LPane class and from the LView class (which, as mentioned, is itself derived from the LPane class). Note that this figure doesn't show all of the PowerPlant classes derived from the LPane class—it just shows some of the more commonly used classes.

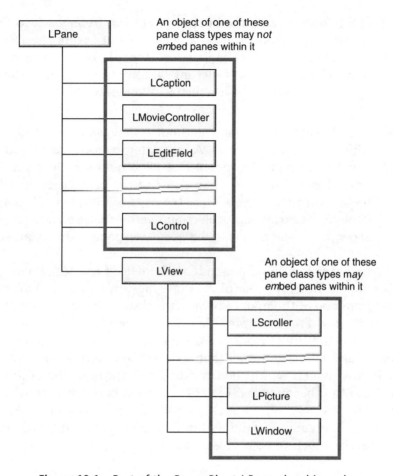

Figure 10.1   *Part of the PowerPlant* LPane *class hierarchy.*

From Figure 10.1, you see that an object of one of the class types derived from LView can contain other panes or views within it. You've already seen this to be the case with the LWindow class. Back in Chapter 7, I used Constructor to examine the **PP Basic Resource.ppob** file that was a part of that chapter's **PowerPlantIntro68K.µ** project. (refer to Figure 7.27 in that chapter). There, when I double-clicked on the window in the PPob layout editor, the title bar in the property inspector that opened let me know that the selected item was a pane of type LWindow. When I next double-clicked on the text that was in the window (the "PowerPlant says: hello world" string), the property inspector that opened let me know that this text was a pane of type LCaption (refer back to Figure 7.28). Obviously, the LCaption pane was present inside the LWindow pane. While LWindow *can* be called a pane, it would be more descriptive and more accurate if I restated that last sentence to say that the LCaption pane was present inside the LWindow view.

N O T E Since LCaption is a pane, and not a view, you can't add a pane within an LCaption pane. A little later in this chapter, you'll see how to add panes (or views) to a PPob resource. Once you know how that's done, you can use Constructor to open the **PP Basic Resource.ppob** file from the Chapter 7 example **PowerPlantIntro68K.µ** project and verify that Constructor won't allow you to add a pane to the LCaption pane in the layout editor.

If a drawing area is to hold a standard element of the Macintosh interface, such as a button or scroller, the program can create an object derived from one of the many PowerPlant classes that are derived from the LPane class. For example, the LScroller class is derived from LView (which is derived from LPane) and is used to add a scroll bar to an area *inside* a window (rather than as a scroll bar along the outer edge of a window, which would be used to scroll through the entire window). Note that because the LScroller class is derived from LView (rather than directly from LPane), a scroll bar object is a view. As such, it may contain a view or pane within it. Typically, a scroller object will contain text or a picture object inside it.

N O T E Looking back at the class hierarchy shown in Figure 10.1 you see that the LPicture class is a view. That means that if an LPicture is placed inside an LScroller (which is often the case), the LPicture itself could have a pane or panes within it. Thus there could be a picture within a picture, or text within the picture, or even another scroll area with a picture *within* another picture. If you're curious, you can peek ahead to Figures 10.11 and 10.12 to see a scroller and picture in a window.

A pane doesn't exist on its own; it is always inside something else. Typically, that "something" is a window. Thus a scroll bar in a window would be an `LScroller` in an `LWindow`. So that you realize the "pane connection" here, it's important to take note of the fact that both the `LScroller` and `LWindow` classes are derived from the `LView` class, which, in turn, is derived from the `LPane` class.

You've just read that a view can hold other views or panes. When a view *does* hold still another view or pane, it is said to be the *superview* of the held view or pane. For instance, a window is the superview of a scroll bar that appears in the window. From the scroll bar's perspective, it is considered a *subpane* of the window. This hierarchy doesn't carry on infinitely, of course. At the top is the window, which has no superview. A view that doesn't have a superview is called a *top level container*.

Panes and Constructor

Panes can be created and edited with the resource editor Resorcerer or with the Metrowerks Constructor. Because Constructor provides a more graphical look at the panes you're creating, I'll describe its use in this chapter.

Creating Panes

A pane (or view, or collection of panes and views) can be defined in a `PPob` resource. In Chapter 8, you read that Constructor exists primarily to create `PPob` resources. Using Constructor you can easily create a single `PPob` resource that defines a window and all of its views and panes. This collection is referred to as a *containment hierarchy*. Once you're satisfied with the look of a window and its subpanes, you save the results to the `PPob` resource that's stored in a resource file (typically, but not necessarily, a Constructor file with an extension of **.ppob**). When you create your CodeWarrior project, you'll include this file in your project window. When you build an application from this project, the `PPob` resources in the resource will become a part of that program—they'll be saved along with other resources in the program's resource fork. The source code that you write will include code that reads the `PPob` data from the resource fork and then creates an object (or objects) based on this information.

The **PP Basic Resource.ppob** file that's a part of each PowerPlant-based project initially holds one PPob resource. You're free to modify this resource so that its contents match what you have in mind for your own program. To do that, you just double-click on this resource under the Windows and Views heading in the Constructor project window to display the PPob in the Constructor layout editor. To add a pane to the window, begin by selecting **Display Classes** from the Window menu. When you do that, the window appears, as shown in Figure 10.2.

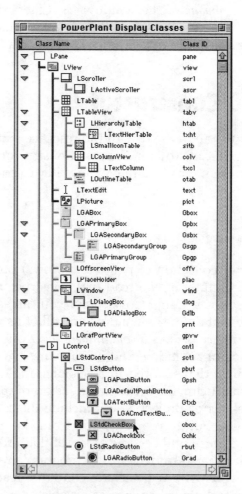

Figure 10.2 *The Display Classes window is used to add any type of pane to the layout editor.*

To add a pane of any of the listed types to a PPob resource, drag and drop. Click on the icon of a pane type in the Display Classes window and, with the mouse button still held down, drag the mouse until the cursor is over the approximate spot in the PPob resource where the new pane should be place. When you release the mouse button, the outline of a rectangle will appear in the PPob. In Figure 10.2, I have a standard checkbox (an LStdCheckBox) highlighted. In Figure 10.3, I've dragged and dropped the LStdCheckBox in the window pane of the PPob resource.

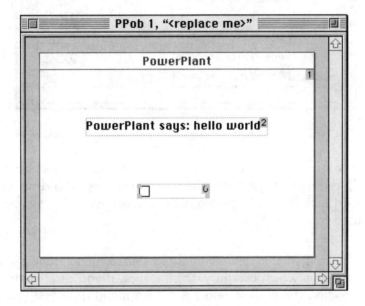

Figure 10.3 *Adding a standard checkbox pane to a* PPob *resource.*

Creating a PPob Resource with Constructor

The PowerPlant examples you've seen to this point have all used a PPob resource to define a window, but you've had no exposure to creating one of these PowerPlant-specific resources. So far I've relied on the one PPob resource that's in the **PP Basic Resource.ppob** file which CodeWarrior places in a new PowerPlant-based project. If your application has more than one type of window, you'll want to add other PPob resources to this file.

You can add a new PPob resource to an existing resource file, or create a new file and add the PPob resource to it. To create a new file, choose **New Project File** from the File menu. When you do that, you'll see a project window like the one pictured in Figure 10.4.

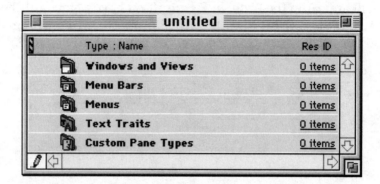

Figure 10.4   A new, empty Constructor project window.

To create the new PPob resource, click on the **Windows and Views** heading in the project window and then select **New Window Resource** from the Edit menu. In response, Constructor will display the dialog box pictured in Figure 10.5.

 The text of the New Window Resource menu item will change based on which category. For instance, if you click on the **Menus** heading the New Window Resource menu item text will change to **New Menu Resource**.

The dialog box pictured in Figure 10.5 allows you to enter specifics about the resource that is to be created. In that figure I've left untouched all but one of the values Constructor places in this dialog box—in the **Resource Name** edit box I've entered an optional resource name. After clicking the **Create** button, the project window displays the newly added PPob resource under the Windows and Views heading (see Figure 10.6).

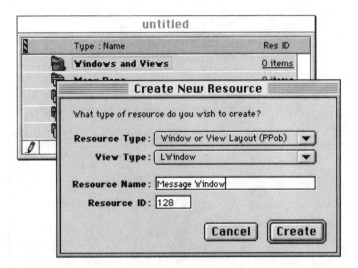

Figure 10.5 *Adding a new window resource (an LWindow) to a PPob resource.*

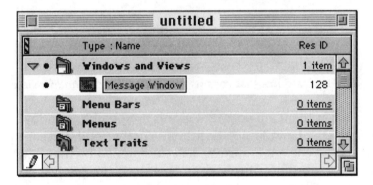

Figure 10.6 *Changing the name of a resource in the Constructor project window.*

Double-clicking on the name of the new resource opens the layout editor and displays the only pane in the new PPob resource—the view that defines a window. Figure 10.7 shows this untitled window.

The name that I entered for the resource, Message Window, is only used within Constructor—it's not a name that will be shown in the title bar of a window created from this resource. To set that name, use the window pane's property inspector.

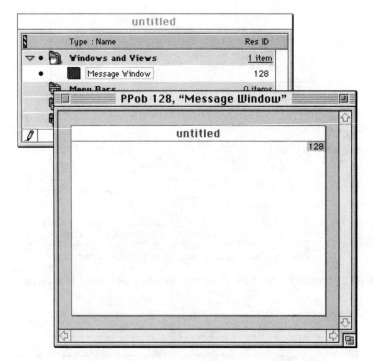

Figure 10.7 *The Constructor layout editor displaying a*
new PPob resource that consists of one pane—an LWindow view.

Unsurprisingly, there are no panes in this new, empty window. To add a
pane, select **Display Classes** from the Window menu. That opens the
window shown back in Figure 10.2. As mentioned by that figure, to add
a pane to a PPob, you simply drag and drop the pane type from the
Display Classes window to the layout editor.

Using Constructor to Gain an Understanding of Panes

One way to explore the relationship of windows, views, and panes is to
compare the look of an existing program that was created using the
PowerPlant framework with the PPob resources that are used by that
program. You can do this by first running a program and taking note of

the contents of one of the program's windows. Then run the Metrowerks Constructor and look at the PPob resource for that same window.

 The full-featured version of CodeWarrior includes several example PowerPlant projects. The electronic documentation *The PowerPlant Book* (on that package's Reference CD) provides a walkthrough of many of the examples.

Examining This Chapter's PowerPlantPane68K Example

Later in this chapter, you'll see the source code for a PowerPlant-created application that displays a single window. Within the window of the PowerPlantPane68K program is a box that can be clicked on and dragged about the window. Figure 10.8 shows the window displayed by that program.

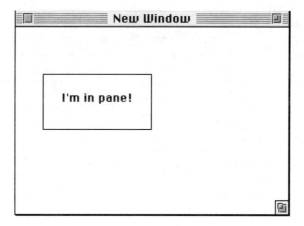

Figure 10.8   *The PowerPlantPane68K program displays a window with a draggable box (a pane) in it.*

The project from which this example program was built includes a resource file—an edited version of the **PP Basic Resource.ppob** file that CodeWarrior adds to each PowerPlant-based project. That file holds a single PPob resource. When this resource is opened with Constructor, I'm able to get a graphical look at the different pane-related components of the program. When I moved the cursor over the layout editor and double-clicked on the white area that represents the window, Constructor displays the property inspector for this pane. You should recognize the inspector in Figure 10.9—it's of a type you saw in Chapter 7.

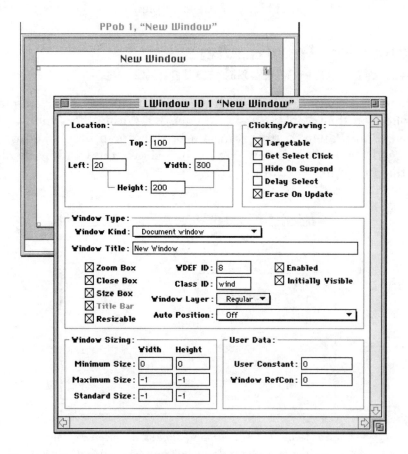

Figure 10.9   *The property inspector for a window—an* LWindow *pane.*

The title bar of the property inspector pictured in Figure 10.9 tells me that this pane has an ID of 1 and holds data that can be used in an object of the PowerPlant class LWindow.

Besides the window itself, the only pane pictured in the layout editor is the outline of a rectangle. When I double-click on that pane, Constructor lets me know that this rectangle is used to hold the data for an LPane object. Constructor shows that this pane has an ID of 2—as shown in Figure 10.10.

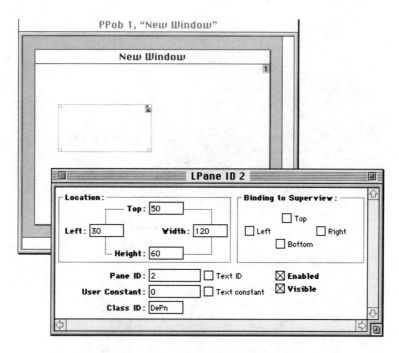

Figure 10.10   *The property inspector for an LPane that is in an LWindow in a PPob resource.*

Figures 10.9 and 10.10 illustrate that the example program I ran consisted of an LWindow object with a single pane object in it. As it turns out, the window's framed rectangle with the text drawn in it is the pane.

Examining the Metrowerks Muscle Demo Example

To really explore the use of panes, consider the Muscle Demo program—one of the many PowerPlant examples that are a part of the

CodeWarrior Gold package. This program has a menu that can be used to display a number of different windows—Figure 10.11 shows one of them. In this figure, I've labeled the three objects that are held in this window. Figure 10.11 shows a window that opens during the running of the Muscle Demo program. Figure 10.12 shows the PPob resource for this same window, as seen in Constructor.

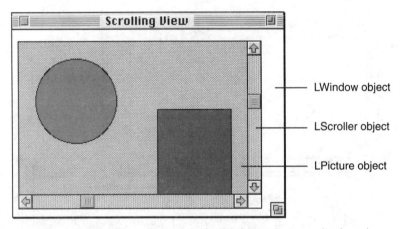

Figure 10.11   *A window with three objects in it, as displayed in the application that creates the window.*

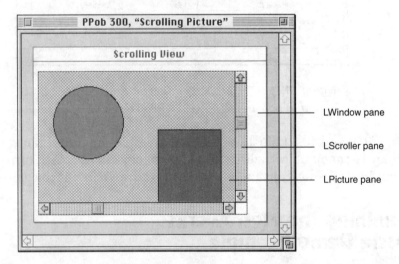

Figure 10.12   *The PPob resource that defines the window of Figure 10.11, as viewed in Constructor.*

Looking at Figures 10.11 and 10.12 it may not be immediately obvious that panes are present in the program's window. If you look at the declarations of the `LWindow`, `LScroller`, and `LPicture` PowerPlant classes, though, you'll see the connection. Each of these three classes is derived from the `LView` class. The `LView` class, in turn, is derived from the `LPane` class. That tells you that in a program, all three of these object types will be able to do the things panes can do (such as draw themselves and respond to mouse clicks).

To learn a little about the relationship of panes, open an existing PowerPlant resource file and then double-click on one of its `PPob` resources to open the layout editor for that `PPob`. Next, choose **Show Hierarchy** from the Layout menu. Figure 10.13 shows the results of doing that for the Muscle Demo `PPob` resource pictured back in Figure 10.12.

NOTE If a program displays different types of windows, its resource file will probably contain a `PPob` resource for each window type. If you open such a file with Constructor, you'll see more than one resource listed under Windows and Views.

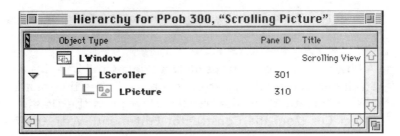

Figure 10.13 *The Hierarchy window helps you visualize the hierarchy of panes in a window.*

The hierarchy in Figure 10.13 shows that for the Muscle Demo `PPob` named Scrolling Picture, the `LScroller` pane lies within the `LWindow` pane, and the `LPicture` pane lies within the `LScroller` pane.

Figure 10.14 shows the results of double-clicking on the vertical scroll bar in the `PPob` resource from the Muscle Demo resource file. In the property inspector, you see that the edit box titled Scrolling View ID holds a value of 310. This number is the ID of a different pane—the pane that holds whatever it is that is to be scrolled within the scroller.

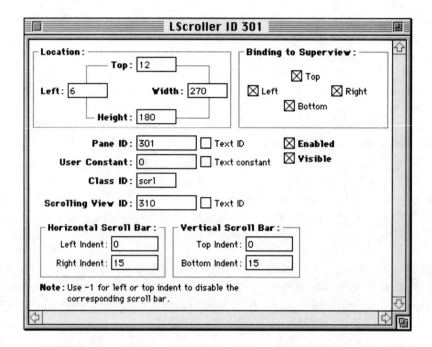

Figure 10.14 *The property inspector for a scroller (an LScroller).*

NOTE A PowerPlant scroller isn't simply a single scroll bar—it's a pair of scroll bars surrounding a scrollable area. To see this, first click on the picture that's in the scroller. Now press the **Delete** key or select **Cut** from the Constructor Edit menu. With the picture gone, you can see the area of the scroller—it encompassed the picture that you just cut. To return the picture to the PPob, either select **Undo** from the Edit menu or make sure you *don't* save any changes you made when you close this file.

Returning to the layout editor and double-clicking on the contents of the scroller—the picture that lies within the scroller—results in the property inspector shown in Figure 10.15. Here, in the Pane ID edit box, you see that the ID value of 310 is what binds this picture to the just-mentioned scroller.

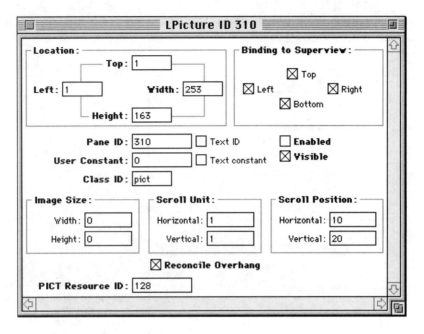

Figure 10.15   *The property inspector for a picture (an* LPicture*).*

To learn more about panes, use Constructor to explore the resource file of any other project that's built using PowerPlant.

A Pane Example

This chapter's PowerPlantPane68K program opens a window that holds a single pane in it. The pane is surrounded by a 1-pixel-wide frame so that you can see it. Inside the pane is a string of text. On its own, this is no spectacular feat. The preceding could be achieved without going through the effort of creating a pane—a call to the Toolbox functions FrameRect() and DrawString() would do the trick. To show off the fact that a pane can do more than hold a simple drawing, PowerPlantPane68K gives its pane the ability to be dragged about the window. When the user clicks the mouse button on the frame and drags the mouse, an outline of the pane follows. When the user releases the mouse button, the pane disappears from its old location and appears at

the new location. The entire pane, including its contents, are moved.
Figure 10.16 illustrates this effect.

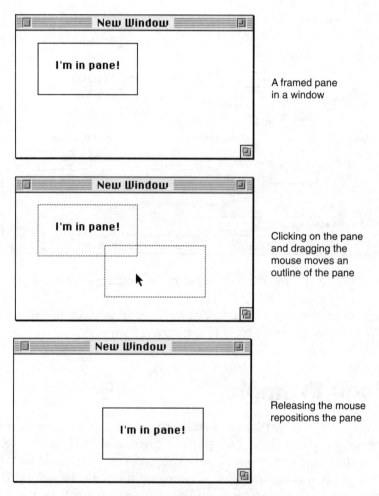

Figure 10.16 *The PowerPlantPane68K program opens
a window that holds a pane that can be dragged.*

The user can even drag the pane partially off the window, as shown in
Figure 10.17. The program will know not to draw any of the pane outside of the window. When the user drags the pane back onto the window, the pane and its contents will be restored.

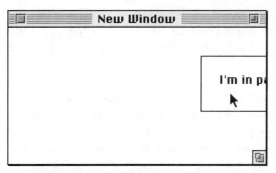

Figure 10.17 *The pane can be dragged beyond the edge of the window.*

Since PowerPlantPane68K exists to demonstrate panes, the program makes minimal use of menus. In fact, the File menu in this program consists of just a single item—the always-present Quit item.

The PowerPlantPane68K Project

In Chapter 9, you read that a PowerPlant project typically includes one source code file for each class declared by the program. That source code file in turn includes a header file. The header file declares the class, and the source code file defines the member functions of that class. The Chapter 9 example PowerPlantMenu68K followed this convention. A header file named **CPPMenuApp.h** held the definition of the example's application class, CPPMenuApp. A source code file named **CPPMenuApp.cp** held the code for the member functions of that class. This source code file also had an #include directive that brought in the class definition from the **CPPMenuApp.h** file. The PowerPlantPane68K example has a similar set up. In brief, here are the steps to setting up the project:

1. Create a new project using PowerPlant project stationery.
2. Rename the **PP Basic Starter.h** header file (to **CPPPane.h** in this case).
3. Rename the **PP Basic Starter.cp** source code file (to **CPPPane.cp** in this example).
4. If the project defines other classes, define each in its own header file (**CTestPane.h** defines a class named CTestPane in this case).

5. If the project defines other classes, define the member functions of each class in its own source code file (**CTestPane.cp** defines the member functions of the CTestPane class in this case).

The PowerPlantPane68K example declares two classes, so its project holds two source code files. The first class is the application class that all PowerPlant programs must have. Its class is declared in the **CPPPaneApp.h** header file, and its member function code appears in **CPPPaneApp.cp**. The second class is a class used to define a pane object. This class is declared in the header file **CTestPane.h**, and its member functions are defined in **CTestPane.cp**. Figure 10.18 shows the two **.cp** files in the **PowerPlantPane68K.µ** project window.

File	Code	Data	
▽ ✹ **Application**	0	0	☑
✹ CPPPaneApp.cp	0	0	• ▶
✹ CTestPane.cp	0	0	• ▶
✹ **PP Basic Resource.rsrc**	n/a	n/a	▶
✹ **PP Basic Resource.ppob**	n/a	n/a	▶
✹ **PP Action Strings.rsrc**	n/a	n/a	▶
✹ **PP DebugAlerts.rsrc**	n/a	n/a	▶
▷ ✹ **Commanders**	0	0	☑
▷ ✹ **Features**	0	0	☑
▷ ✹ **Panes**	0	0	☑
▷ ✹ **File & Stream**	0	0	☑
▷ ✹ **Apple Events**	0	0	☑
▷ ✹ **Lists**	0	0	☑
▷ ✹ **Support**	0	0	☑
▷ ✹ **Utilities**	0	0	☑
▷ ✹ **Libraries**	0	0	☑

PowerPlantPane68K.µ

73 file(s)   0   0

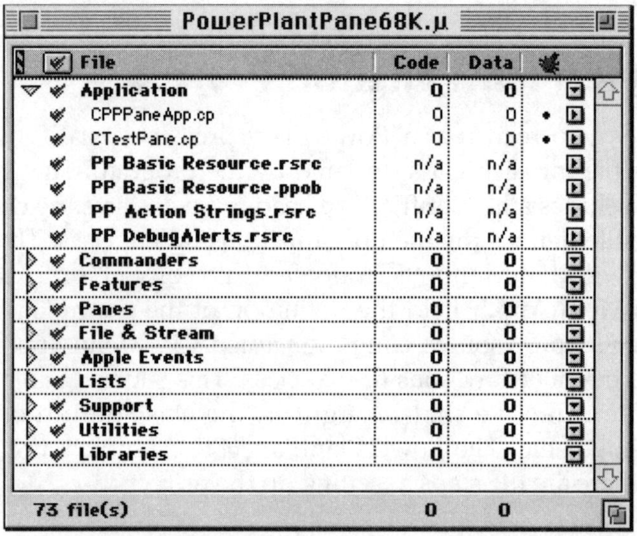

Figure 10.18   The PowerPlantPane68K.µ project window.

Recall that the file name for an application-defined class in a PowerPlant project should be the class name. From Figure 10.18 you can surmise that the PowerPlantPane68K program has a class named CPPPaneApp and a class named CTestPane.

The PowerPlantPane68K Resources

Like the PowerPlant examples in previous chapters, the **PowerPlantPane68K.μ** project holds its application-specific resources in the **PP Basic Resource.ppob** Constructor file.

THE PPOB RESOURCE

The one PPob resource used in the **PowerPlantPane68K.μ** project is a modification of the PPob supplied by CodeWarrior in the **PP Basic Resources.ppob** file. I began by first clicking once on the <replace me> name under the Windows and Views heading in the Constructor project window for this file and then typing in a new name for the resource: **New Window**. Then I double-clicked on that name to open the layout editor. Next, I clicked on the LCaption pane in the window (that is, I clicked on the words **PowerPlant says: hello world**.) and then pressed the **Delete** key to remove the pane.

To establish the window's size, title, and other characteristics, I double-clicked on the window in the layout editor to open the property inspector for this LWindow pane. Unlike previous examples, the window displayed in the PowerPlantPane68K program will be resizable and will have a zoom box. To set these features in this PPob, I checked the three checkboxes shown in Figure 10.19. The other two checkboxes (**Close Box** and **Title Bar**) were already checked in this CodeWarrior-supplied PPob resource.

After closing the LWindow property inspector, it's time to add a new, generic LPane type pane to the window. This will be the pane that will hold some text and will be draggable. To add this pane, I selected **Display Classes** from the Window menu, clicked on the LPane icon at the very top of the Display Classes window, and then dragged the icon over to the window in the layout editor. After releasing the mouse button to drop the new pane, the layout editor looked like the one shown in Figure 10.20.

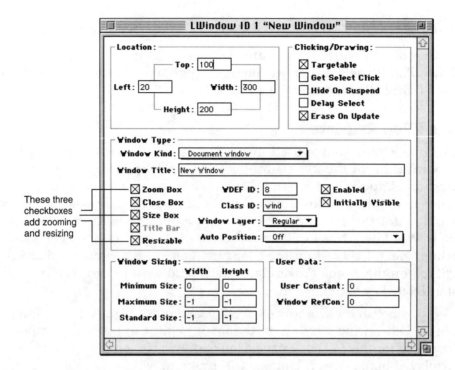

These three checkboxes add zooming and resizing

Figure 10.19   *The property inspector for the window (the* LWindow) *in the one* PPob *resource.*

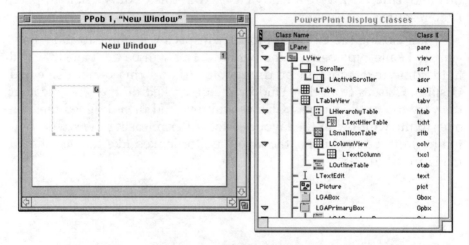

Figure 10.20   *Adding a pane (an* LPane) *to the* PPob *resource.*

Constructor chose the size of the pane and the pane's ID for me. To change both, I double-click on the pane to open its property inspector. There, I type in new values the Location edit boxes. In Figure 10.21, you see that I also changed the value in the Pane ID edit box from 0 to 2. The particular value given to a pane isn't of great importance. I simply prefer to start pane numbering with the LWindow pane given a value of 1, and then give each pane placed in the window a successive ID value.

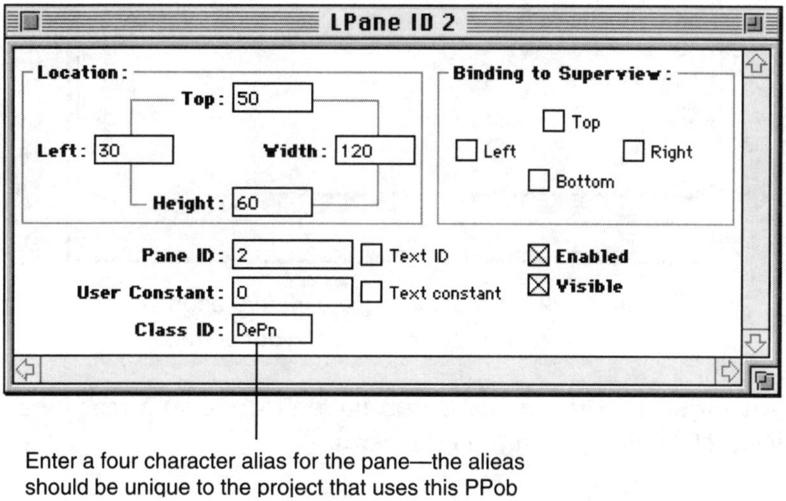

Enter a four character alias for the pane—the alieas
should be unique to the project that uses this PPob

*Figure 10.21   The property inspector for the pane
(the LPane) in the one PPob resource.*

In Figure 10.21, you can see that I've filled in a four-character class ID for the pane. This *class ID* will be used in your source code when you *register* the class that will be associated with this pane. I'll have more to say about this ID, and registering classes, a little later in this chapter. For now, it's enough to know that you can use any four characters, provided they aren't all lowercase characters—strings that are all lowercase are reserved by PowerPlant. You can use the four characters to hint at what the class ID stands for. I've used DePn to stand for "Demo Pane."

When you're finished adding information in the pane editor, close it. In Figure 10.22, you can see that Constructor enlarged the pane in the window because I increased its size in the property inspector.

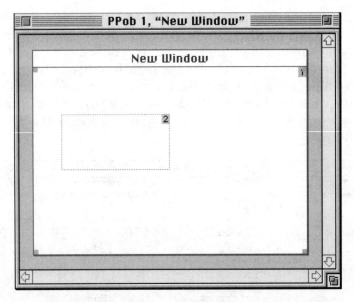

Figure 10.22 *A change of the pane's ID and size is reflected in the Constructor layout editor.*

That's it for adding the pane. If you haven't done so already, save the file by selecting **Save** from the File menu.

THE MENU RESOURCES

The **PP Basic Resources.ppob** file is provided with three Menu resources—resources that define the Apple, File, and Edit menus for an application. In past examples I've left these menus untouched (recall that menu changes in Chapter 10 involved adding a new menu—not altering these three existing menus). To prove that PowerPlant can easily adapt to menu item changes in these existing menus, I've gone ahead and removed all but one menu item from the File menu. To do that, I first double-clicked on the **File name** under the Menus heading in the Constructor project window to display this menu in the menu editor. Then I clicked on the first menu item (the **New** item) to highlight it. Next, I pressed the **Delete** key to remove the item (selecting **Cut** from the Constructor Edit menu would have worked as well). I did the same for each remaining menu item—with the exception of the Quit item. I left that item and its Cmd ID alone. Figure 10.23 shows the results of my menu editing.

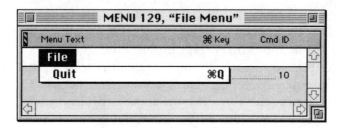

Figure 10.23   *The File menu resource has only a single menu item in it.*

That's it for the changes to the **PP Basic Resources.ppob** file. Again, choose **Save** from the File menu to save the changes. Then return to the CodeWarrior IDE.

The PowerPlantPane68K Source Code

Because this is your first exposure to working with PowerPlant panes, I'll make the walkthrough of this chapter's example source code a long one.

THE PANE CLASS

As an application is represented by an object (derived from the LApplication class), and as a window is represented by an object (of the LWindow class, or a class derived from it), a pane is represented by an object (of the LPane class, or a class derived from it). The pane that I added to the PPob resource in this example will be derived from both the LPane and LCommander classes.

The member functions that will be a part of the pane class depend on the functionality that the pane object is to have. The LPane class consists of about 75 member functions, so there's plenty that you can do with a pane. Your application-defined pane class will of course inherit all of these member functions, so your pane object will have access to each of them. Many work fine as defined in the PowerPlant **LPane.cp** file; others you'll want to override and tailor to the specific needs of your pane. For example, you won't need to override the LPane member functions Show() and Hide(). Another example of an LPane member function that is general enough for use with any pane is ResizeFrame(), which, of course, changes the size of a pane.

Other LPane functions not only should be overridden, they *must* be overridden. In particular, a class derived from LPane must override the DrawSelf() function. PowerPlant invokes the DrawSelf() function to draw the contents of a pane. Because the contents of a pane are specific to an application, PowerPlant can't possibly know what to draw in a pane. For instance, the PowerPlantPane68K program has a pane that has a one-pixel-wide frame drawn along its border, and text that says "I'm in pane!" drawn near its center. This drawing takes place in the overridden version of DrawSelf().

The other function that a class derived from LPane must override is ClickSelf(). This function is called by PowerPlant when the user clicks the mouse on a pane. Again, how a program responds to a mouse click on a pane is an application-specific issue. A program may allow the pane to be dragged, may hide the pane, or may perform any number of other actions to the pane. Or, it might ignore the mouse click altogether. The PowerPlantPane68K program drags its pane in response to a user clicking on it and then dragging the mouse.

Any pane class declared by a program must have its objects built from a stream. In C++, a stream is a general term for a flow of data. The class constructor, along with one other function, takes care of this. You'll read more about streams just ahead.

NOTE

Here's an example of an ANSI C++ line of code that uses a stream:

```
cout << "Enter your age: ";
```

If you've ever used cout in a C++ program, you've used a stream. cout is an object that corresponds to the standard output stream. This stream "flows" data representing text to the monitor. The C++ header file that holds the declaration of cout, **iostream.h**, provides you with a strong hint that cout works with streams.

Now that you know a class derived from LPane must override DrawSelf() and ClickSelf(), and needs to have a function or two for the creation of an object from a stream, you should have a pretty good idea of what a minimal application-defined pane class looks like. Here's the pane class declaration from the PowerPlantPane68K program. Each of the four member functions that are a part of the CTestPane class is discussed in this chapter.

```
class  CTestPane : public LPane, public LCommander
{
   public:
      CTestPane( LStream *inStream );
      static  CTestPane*  CreateTestPaneStream( LStream *inStream );

   protected:
      virtual void  DrawSelf();
      virtual void  ClickSelf( const SMouseDownEvent  &inMouseDown );
};
```

REGISTERING THE PANE

Earlier in this chapter, I said that any pane class declared by a program must have its objects built from a stream, and that a stream is a general term for a flow of data. In a PowerPlant program, this stream of data is the PPob information that was saved to a file by Constructor.

For every pane class in your program, you need to call the PowerPlant function RegisterClass(). This member function of the URegistrar class registers the class. Registering a class consists of pairing the pane's class ID with a function used to create an object of this particular pane class. Recall that the class ID for a pane was set in Constructor. Here's the call to RegisterClass() for the CTestPane class:

```
URegistrar::RegisterClass( 'DePn',
    (ClassCreatorFunc) CTestPane::CreateTestPaneStream);
```

The first parameters in RegisterClass() is the pane's class ID. The second parameter—the one I've devoted an entire line to in the above snippet—is a pointer to the class member function used to create an object of this class type. Figure 10.24 shows where these two parameters come from.

The registering of classes typically takes place in the application's constructor function. Except for this one additional registration, the body of the constructor function for the CPPPaneApp class is the same as that of the Chapter 9 class CPPStarterApp and the Chapter 10 class CPPMenuApp. Those examples used the application class constructor to call RegisterAllPPClasses() to register all of the PowerPlant-defined classes. The CPPPaneApp class constructor does this as well. Additionally, it registers the one application-specific pane.

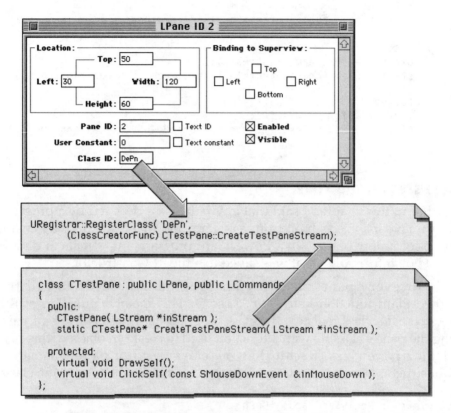

Figure 10.24 Registering a pane in a PowerPlant project.

```
CPPPaneApp::CPPPaneApp( )
{
    RegisterAllPPClasses( );

    URegistrar::RegisterClass( 'DePn',
        (ClassCreatorFunc) CTestPane::CreateTestPaneStream);
}
```

In the preceding example, the class ID DePn is paired with the
CreateTestPaneStream( ) function. When a window that holds a pane
of this type is created (that is, when the PowerPlantPane68K program
opens a window based on the PPob resource that holds this pane),
PowerPlant will be able to match the pane's class ID with the function
that creates the pane, and a new pane object will be created and placed
in the window.

The *pane-creation* function `CreateTestPaneStream()` accepts a pointer to the `LStream` object that holds the `PPob` data, and returns a pointer to the new pane object that gets created. The pane-creation function is called by PowerPlant whenever a new window is opened—your program doesn't have to call it explicitly. That also means your program does not have to be concerned with the `LStream` class—PowerPlant passes in this parameter. The pane-creation function simply calls the pane class constructor, passing along the stream that holds the `PPob` data to read. The *construct-from-stream* constructor function calls the base class constructor—the constructor for `LPane`.

```
CTestPane :: CTestPane( LStream  *inStream ) : LPane( inStream )
{

}
```

If the registering of a class and the subsequent creation of a class object seem a bit confusing, keep the following points in mind:

- For each pane class, call `RegisterClass()`.
- The first parameter to `RegisterClass()` is the pane's class ID, as defined in Constructor.
- The second parameter to `RegisterClass()` is a pointer to the class pane-creation function.
- The pane-creation function name follows this format: `Create[ class name minus leading C]Stream()`. Thus for class `CTestPane`, the function is `CreateTestPaneStream()`.
- The pane-creation function calls the pane's constructor.
- The pane's construct-from-stream constructor calls the `LPane` base class constructor.

Overriding DrawSelf()

When a pane needs updating, PowerPlant will call the pane object's `DrawSelf()` function. That's why your pane class needs to override this `LPane` function. Here's how the `CTestPane` class overrides it:

```
void  CTestPane :: DrawSelf( void )
```

```
{
   Rect   frame;

   CalcLocalFrameRect( frame );
   ::FrameRect( &frame );

   ::TextFont( systemFont );
   ::TextSize( 12 );
   ::MoveTo( frame.left + 20, frame.top + 30 );
   ::DrawString( "\pI'm in pane!" );
}
```

The DrawSelf() function begins by calling CalcLocalFrameRect(). This routine, inherited from the LPane class, returns the location of the rectangle that holds the pane. The coordinates are local to the pane's superview. In this program, the pane's superview is the window. With the boundaries of the pane known, DrawSelf() can frame the pane with a call to the Toolbox function FrameRect().

The superview of a pane could be a view. Recall from the first section in this chapter that a window can hold a view, and the view in turn can hold one or more panes.

DrawSelf() finishes with Toolbox calls that set up and draw the text inside the pane. TextFont() sets the font to the system font, also known as Chicago. TextSize() sets the font to 12 points. A call to MoveTo() sets drawing to begin 20 pixels from the left edge of the pane and 30 pixels from the top of the pane. A call to DrawString() does the drawing.

OVERRIDING CLICKSELF()

When the user clicks on the CTestPane object, PowerPlant calls ClickSelf(). CTestPane overrides the LPane ClickSelf() member function so that PowerPlant calls the program's version of this function. In this version, ClickSelf() responds by dragging the pane as the user drags the mouse. Here's a look at ClickSelf():

```
void  CTestPane :: ClickSelf( const SMouseDownEvent &inMouseDown )
{
   Rect   oldFrame;
   Rect   newFrame;
   Point  oldPoint;
   Point  newPoint;
```

```
Int32   horizChange;
Int32   vertChange;

SwitchTarget( this );
FocusDraw();

::PenNormal();
::PenPat( &qd.gray );
::PenMode( patXor );

oldPoint = newPoint = inMouseDown.whereLocal;
CalcLocalFrameRect( oldFrame );
newFrame = oldFrame;

while ( ::StillDown() )
{
    ::GetMouse( &newPoint );

    if ( ::EqualPt( newPoint, oldPoint ) == false )
    {
        ::FrameRect( &oldFrame );
        ::OffsetRect( &newFrame, newPoint.h - oldPoint.h,
                    newPoint.v - oldPoint.v );
        ::FrameRect( &newFrame );
        oldPoint = newPoint;
        oldFrame = newFrame;
    }
}

horizChange = newPoint.h - inMouseDown.whereLocal.h;
vertChange  = newPoint.v - inMouseDown.whereLocal.v;
if ( horizChange != 0 || vertChange != 0 )
    MoveBy( horizChange, vertChange, true );

::PenNormal();
}
```

ClickSelf() begins by making the pane the target. When the CTestPane object receives a click, it calls SwitchTarget(this) to make itself the target. Next, ClickSelf() prepares for drawing in the pane by calling FocusDraw(). Because a pane doesn't have its own coordinate system, it relies on that of its superview.

The primary task of ClickSelf() is to track the mouse movements for as long as the user holds down the mouse button. A while loop accomplishes this. The Toolbox function StillDown() is at the center of the while test. Before the loop begins, calls to three Toolbox functions set the pen to a dashed gray so that as the pane is dragged, its outline can be dragged about the window. Then, variables representing the old and new mouse location are set up. Finally, variables representing the old and new pane frame are set.

The while loop body offsets the pane rectangle and surrounds it in a dashed gray frame. The loop body draws only this ghost of a frame, not the pane contents. This occurs only once the user has released the mouse button and ended the while loop. When that happens, the change from the final position of the pane to its starting position is calculated. Then a call to the inherited LPane function MoveBy() is made. This function moves the pane by wiping it out at its old, original location, and redrawing it at its new location. Of course, MoveBy() isn't directly doing the drawing—it's the CTestPane DrawSelf() member function that is being invoked by PowerPlant when MoveBy()is called.

THE CTESTPANE.H HEADER LISTING

The declaration of the CTestPane class is made in the **CTestPane.h** header file, which is shown here.

```
#pragma once

#include <LPane.h>
#include <LCommander.h>

class  CTestPane : public LPane, public LCommander
{
    public:
        CTestPane( LStream *inStream );

        static  CTestPane*  CreateTestPaneStream( LStream *inStream );

    protected:
        virtual void  DrawSelf();
        virtual void  ClickSelf( const SMouseDownEvent  &inMouseDown );
};
```

THE CTESTPANE.CP SOURCE CODE LISTING

The **CTestPane.cp** source code file holds the definitions of the CTest Pane class member functions. CreateTestPaneStream() is invoked by

PowerPlant when `CreateWindow()` is called to create a new window. `CreateTestPaneStream()` simply calls the `CTestPane` class construc-tor to create a new pane object. The `CTestPane` calls the `LPane` construc-tor to do the work of getting `PPob` information from the stream.

The `DrawSelf()` function gets called by PowerPlant in response to the update of the window. The `ClickSelf()` function is invoked by PowerPlant in reaction to a click of the mouse on the pane.

```
#include "CTestPane.h"

// ----------------------------------------------------------
//       • CreateTestPaneStream
// ----------------------------------------------------------
//  This function creates a CTestPane pane from a PPob resource.
//

CTestPane*  CTestPane :: CreateTestPaneStream( LStream *inStream )
{
    return ( new CTestPane( inStream ) );
}

// ----------------------------------------------------------
//       • CTestPane
// ----------------------------------------------------------
//  This pane class constructor is the construct-from-stream con-
//    structor.
//

CTestPane :: CTestPane( LStream  *inStream ) : LPane( inStream )
{

}

// ----------------------------------------------------------
//       • DrawSelf
// ----------------------------------------------------------
//  Draws the pane's frame and contents
//

void  CTestPane :: DrawSelf( void )
{
    Rect   frame;

    CalcLocalFrameRect( frame );
    ::FrameRect( &frame );
```

```
   ::TextFont( systemFont );
   ::TextSize( 12 );
   ::MoveTo( frame.left + 20, frame.top + 30 );
   ::DrawString( "\pI'm in pane!" );
}

// --------------------------------------------------------
//      • ClickSelf
// --------------------------------------------------------
//   Responds to a mouse click on the pane
//

void  CTestPane :: ClickSelf( const SMouseDownEvent &inMouseDown )
{
   Rect    oldFrame;
   Rect    newFrame;
   Point   oldPoint;
   Point   newPoint;
   Int32   horizChange;
   Int32   vertChange;

   SwitchTarget( this );
   FocusDraw();

   ::PenNormal();
   ::PenPat( &qd.gray );
   ::PenMode( patXor );

   oldPoint = newPoint = inMouseDown.whereLocal;
   CalcLocalFrameRect( oldFrame );
   newFrame = oldFrame;

   while ( ::StillDown() )
   {
      ::GetMouse( &newPoint );

      if ( ::EqualPt( newPoint, oldPoint ) == false )
      {
         ::FrameRect( &oldFrame );
         ::OffsetRect( &newFrame, newPoint.h - oldPoint.h,
                       newPoint.v - oldPoint.v );
         ::FrameRect( &newFrame );
         oldPoint = newPoint;
         oldFrame = newFrame;
      }
   }

   horizChange = newPoint.h - inMouseDown.whereLocal.h;
```

```
vertChange  = newPoint.v - inMouseDown.whereLocal.v;
if ( horizChange != 0 || vertChange != 0 )
   MoveBy( horizChange, vertChange, true );

   ::PenNormal();
}
```

THE CPPPANEAPP.H HEADER LISTING

The header file for the application class is almost identical to the **PP Basic Starter.h** header file supplied to the project by CodeWarrior. As I did in Chapter 10, I simply opened the **PP Basic Starter.h** file, saved it under a new name (**CPPPaneApp.h**), and then changed each occurrence of CPPStarterApp to CPPPaneApp to reflect the new name I use for the application class.

THE CPPPANEAPP.CP SOURCE CODE LISTING

The **CPPPaneApp.cp** file is a modification of the CodeWarrior-supplied file **PP Basic Starter.cp**. Again, this file was opened and renamed. When I saved it under a new name, CodeWarrior was smart enough to update the **PowerPlantPane68K.μ** project window to reflect this new name.

The changes to the code in this application class source code file are trivial, but I'll describe them here for the sake of completeness. First, all occurrences of CPPStarterApp are changed to CPPPaneApp—that's done using CodeWarrior's Find dialog box.

Next, the #include directive that formerly included the **PP Basic Starter.h** file is changed to now use the file's new name—**CPPPaneApp.h**. One completely new #include directive has been added to the list of #include directives—my own **CTestPane.h** header file is included so that the source code in **CPPPaneApp.cp** recognizes references to the CTestPane class:

```
#include "CPPPaneApp.h"
#include "CTestPane.h"
```

As mentioned earlier, when a PPob defines a new pane, that pane must be registered in the source code. PowerPlantPane68K does that in the application class constructor function:

```
CPPPaneApp::CPPPaneApp()
{
   // Register functions to create core PowerPlant classes

   RegisterAllPPClasses();

   URegistrar::RegisterClass( 'DePn',
      (ClassCreatorFunc) CTestPane::CreateTestPaneStream);
}
```

PowerPlantPane68K opens a new window in the same manner that each preceding example program has—it makes a call to ObeyCommand( ), passing in a value of cmd_New so that ObeyCommand( ) knows that it should execute the code in the cmd_New case section of its switch statement:

```
case cmd_New:
   LWindow   *theWindow;
   theWindow = LWindow::CreateWindow(window_Sample, this);
   theWindow->Show();
   break;
```

The first step in creating a new window is to declare a variable of type LWindow. This is somewhat analogous to declaring a WindowPtr variable in a Mac project that doesn't use PowerPlant. The LWindow member function CreateWindow( ) creates a window. This window is an instance (an object) of the LWindow class and is based on information found in a PPob resource. When completed, the call to CreateWindow( ) returns a pointer to the new window object. Since the LWindow class object doesn't exist before the call to CreateWindow( ) (it is the end result of the call to CreateWindow( ) and thus exists after the call), use the scope resolution operator to call the member function directly:

```
theWindow = LWindow::CreateWindow( window_Sample, this );
```

The first parameter to CreateWindow( ) is the ID of the WIND resource that holds information about this window. Recall that window_Sample is a constant (following the PowerPlant naming convention described earlier in this chapter) that is defined near the start of the program's source code listing:

```
const ResIDT      window_Sample = 1;
```

N O T E If you're paying close attention, you'll recall that earlier I stated that a PPob resource defines a window. It does. A PPob resource consists of more than one part. One of those parts is a WIND resource, the same WIND resource type with which you're familiar.

Once an LWindow object exists, you can access any of its member functions through the object. The constructor function does that when it invokes the Show() member function to display the window:

```
theWindow->Show();
```

N O T E If you programmed in C without the use of an application framework, a very loose translation of the above task might be found in this snippet:

```
#define    kSampleWindow       128

WindowPtr  theWindow;

theWindow = GetNewWindow( kSampleWindow, nil, (WindowPtr)-1L );

ShowWindow( theWindow );
```

Summary

In a PowerPlant-created project, it is the pane that holds a drawing. A pane object is derived (directly or indirectly) from the PowerPlant LPane class. A pane serves as a self-contained drawing area that knows how to respond to mouse clicks and how to redraw, or update, itself.

Panes are created using Constructor, the Metrowerks application that is a graphical editor of PPob resources. You'll save a PPob resource in a Constructor file, include that file in a project, and then write source code that reconstructs a pane object from the data held in the Constructor file.

Chapter 11

ZoneRanger and Macintosh Memory

When a Macintosh application launches, the operating system allocates a section of memory devoted to just that application. This section, or partition, includes an application heap, also called a *heap* or *heap zone*. In this chapter, you'll see just what goes on in the heap—how individual blocks of memory are allocated within this heap and how pointers and handles in your application are used to access these memory blocks.

ZoneRanger is a Macintosh program that is included on the Metrowerks CodeWarrior CD and the CD that accompanies this book.

347

This software utility is used as a memory checker. ZoneRanger "spies" on the heap zone of each application that is running on your Macintosh. There are many difficult-to-grasp concepts included in the theory of how an application is stored in memory. ZoneRanger provides a numerical and graphical look at how each running application is using memory. With this information you'll be able to gain a better understanding of Macintosh memory and, in the process, determine how much memory your application uses, how much free space it leaves unused, and how it can make more efficient use of the memory allocated to it.

Macintosh Memory

Gaining an understanding of how an application uses memory is paramount to developing Macintosh applications that are free of bugs. Knowing how a program is stored in RAM also allows you to reserve just the right amount of memory for it—a practice that end users will appreciate.

 The memory model discussed in this section applies to 68K-based Macintosh computers—Macs that have a microprocessor from the Motorola 680x0 family of CPUs. The memory model for PowerPC-based Macs has many similarities, and some differences, to that of the 680x0 model. If you're programming for 68K-based Macintoshes, all the information in this section applies. If you're creating fat applications, all the information again applies. In the unlikely event that your application will be PowerPC-only, read this section to gain a background on Macintosh memory. After reading about ZoneRanger and walking through a 68K example later in this chapter, you'll be ready for the last section in this chapter, "ZoneRanger and Native PowerPC Programs." It points out some important differences between memory as used in 68K Macs and memory as used in Power Macs. For more Power Macintosh memory details, refer to the *PowerPC System Software* volume of the *Inside Macintosh* series of books.

Memory Overview

When a program is launched, the Macintosh operating system locates a section of free RAM in which to load some or all of the launched application's code. During the entire time that the application is running, the memory that makes up this *application partition* is devoted to that application. When the user quits an application, the partition's memory returns to the pool of free memory and becomes available for use by the next application that is launched.

An application partition consists of four principle sections: an *A5 World*, an *application stack*, an *application heap*, and a section of free memory between the application stack and heap. These four areas of memory can be found in each program that is running. Figure 11.1 illustrates these sections for a Macintosh that has two applications, or *processes*, executing.

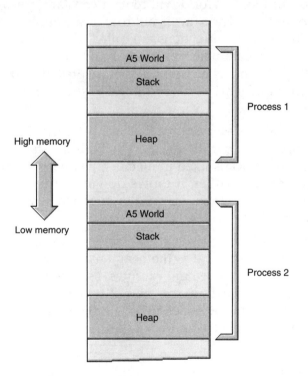

Figure 11.1   *Macintosh RAM with two running applications.*

An application's A5 World is a section of memory that holds that application's global variables. This area of memory is named after the central processing unit register that the operating system uses to track where this memory section starts—the A5 register.

The A5 World holds the values of an application's global variables. The application stack, on the other hand, holds information local to routines in the program. The stack is primarily used to hold parameters, local variables, and return addresses.

The application heap is used to hold the executable code of an application, as well as data structures created as the result of Toolbox calls. Application-created data also get stored in the heap.

When a program is launched, the operating system determines the amount of memory that should be devoted to the application's A5 World. Because the number of global variables in an application is fixed, the size of the A5 World will remain constant during the execution of an application. The same is not true of the application stack and the application heap. As functions are called, the size of the stack will grow and shrink as parameters are passed and local variables are created and destroyed. And as an application executes, the size of the heap will also grow and shrink as code and resources get loaded and unloaded.

The free, unallocated memory that lies between the stack and the heap of an application partition is used by both the stack and the heap. The bottom of the stack is fixed in memory, just beneath the A5 World. As the stack becomes larger, it grows downward in memory. As the heap becomes larger, it grows upward in memory, toward the stack (as shown in Figure 11.2).

While the A5 World, the stack, and the heap are all important areas of an application partition, it is the heap area that ZoneRanger tracks. When an application you've built executes, its code will be in the application heap. As your program executes, it will load resource code into the heap. Before looking at ZoneRanger, a little more background information on the heap will be helpful.

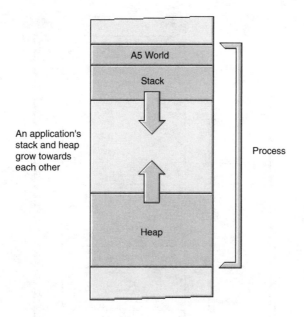

An application's stack and heap grow towards each other

Figure 11.2   An application's heap and stack grow toward one another.

The Application Heap

As your application executes, the Memory Manager will allocate and deallocate blocks of memory in the heap. Each block of memory is a contiguous series of bytes that holds a segment of executable code (a CODE resource), resource data (such as WIND, MENU, or DLOG data), or application data (such as the values in the fields of a struct variable). Each of these blocks has a size and type, and, possibly, one or more attributes. To keep track of this information, each block begins with a block header. Figure 11.3 shows a section of memory with a single process (application) executing. Within this example application heap are three blocks of data, each beginning with a block header.

Because low memory is pictured at the bottom of Figure 11.3, the start of a block of memory is at the bottom of the block.

NOTE

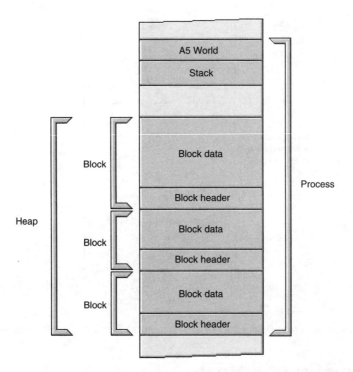

Figure 11.3 *Each block begins with a header that provides descriptive information about the block.*

The size of each block, given in bytes, varies with the block's contents. The type of block can be relocatable, nonrelocatable, or free.

A relocatable block can be moved about in the heap. The Memory Manager will occasionally move relocatable blocks so that it can make the most efficient use of memory. The contents of a relocatable block are accessed by your program through the use of a *handle*.

A nonrelocatable block cannot be moved in memory. The memory location that a nonrelocatable block is originally placed in is the location in which it will remain until the application terminates.

A free block is exactly what its name implies—an unallocated area of memory that is free to accept data and become a relocatable or nonrelocatable block.

Relocatable Blocks

In addition to the size and type of block, the block header for a relocatable block lists the block's three *attributes*. A relocatable block can have the attributes of being locked or unlocked, purgeable or unpurgeable, resource data or nonresource data.

If a relocatable block has its *locked/unlocked* attribute set to **locked**, the block is no longer free to be moved about in memory. A relocatable block may occasionally and temporarily be locked so that the Memory Manager won't move the block while the block's data is being accessed by the application.

If a relocatable block's *purgeable/unpurgeable* attribute is set to **purgeable**, the Memory Manager is given the freedom to purge, or deallocate, the data in the block. This purging won't happen indiscriminately, however. Only when the Memory Manager cannot find free heap memory to satisfy an application's need to load other data will the Memory Manager purge an existing block.

If a relocatable block has its *resource data/nonresource data* attribute set to **resource data**, you know that the block holds the data from a resource.

In Figure 11.3, you saw a heap with three blocks in it. There, no gaps of free memory existed between blocks. The more likely scenario is that during the course of loading and unloading relocatable, purgeable blocks, gaps of free memory will develop, as shown in Figure 11.4. To eliminate these blocks of free memory (which are often too small to be of use when loading other blocks), the Memory Manager will periodically perform *memory compaction*. Memory compaction shuffles relocatable blocks (that are not locked) in an attempt to eliminate as many of the memory gaps as possible.

Your application will always access a relocatable block through a handle. Here's part of a function that uses a local variable to store a picture handle that is returned by the Toolbox function GetPicture():

```
void  GetPictureResource( short pictID )
{
   PicHandle    thePicture;

   thePicture = GetPicture( pictID );
   ...
}
```

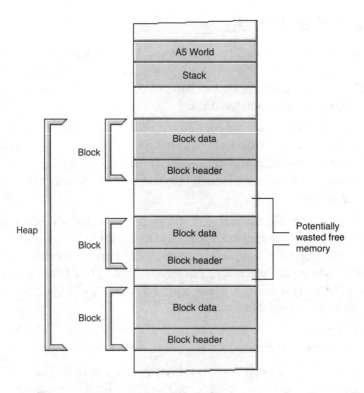

Figure 11.4 *The Memory Manager compacts memory to create one large, free block of memory from other, smaller blocks of free memory.*

While the relocatable block (which holds the PICT resource code) will be in the heap, the handle will be on the stack. That's because in the snippet, the handle is declared to be a local variable.

A *handle* is a program's means of keeping track of a relocatable block of memory. This is done through *double indirection*—also referred to as *double dereferencing*. A handle holds the address of a *master pointer*, and the master pointer in turn holds the starting address of the relocatable block. A master pointer is always in the heap and is always fixed; it cannot be relocated. Figure 11.5 shows a stack with three items in it. One of those items is a handle. In the figure, you can see that the handle points to the master pointer, while the master pointer points to the relocatable block.

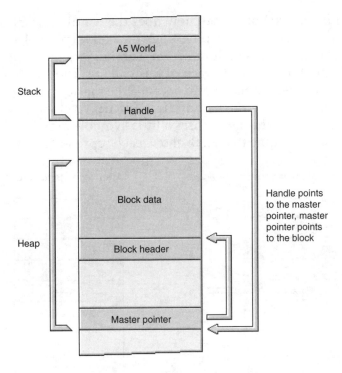

Figure 11.5 *A handle leads to a master pointer,*
which in turn leads to a relocatable block.

Because lower addresses are assumed to be at the bottom of Mac memory illustrations, the start of any area of memory is at the area's bottom. With that in mind, the master pointer in Figure 11.5 is shown pointing to the first address of the block's data, not at the start of the block's header. This is correct. The block header information is used by the Memory Manager. Your application will be interested in the block data.

Keeping Track of Relocatable Blocks

When the Memory Manager moves a relocatable block, the Memory Manager will make note of the block's new starting address by updating the fixed master pointer. Thus the master pointer will always hold the correct address of the relocatable block. The master pointer has the address of the moved block, but how does the handle variable (which is your program's means of keeping track of a relocatable block) become aware of the block's new address? The handle, as it turns out, doesn't have to do anything to keep track of this change. The handle holds the address of the master pointer, and because the master pointer is fixed in the heap, the contents of the handle need never change (see Figure 11.6). For simplicity, this figure uses a little symbolism rather than using real addresses—assume that A, B, and C each represent a RAM address.

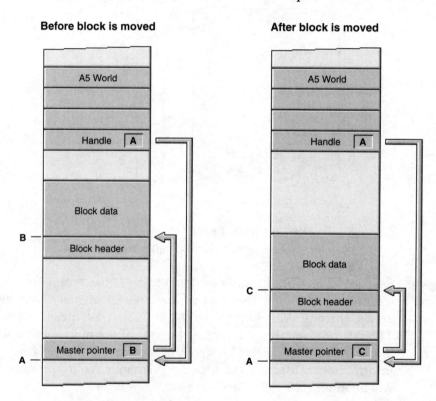

Before block is moved

After block is moved

Figure 11.6 *When a relocatable block moves, its master pointer is updated to hold the new block address.*

In the memory pictured to the left of the figure, the handle holds an address we'll call A. Looking at address A we see that this memory location holds a master pointer, as expected. Examining the contents of the master pointer reveals that it holds an address, B. At address B is a block of data. This is the double-indirection that a handle uses to lead to a block of data.

Now observe the right side of Figure 11.6. Here you can see that the relocatable block has been moved down in memory. When the Memory Manager performed this move, it updated the contents of the block's master pointer. The master pointer now properly holds the new starting address of the block—address C. And the handle? No change to its contents are necessary. It still points to the fixed master pointer. The unchanging handle uses the changing contents of the master pointer to always track down the moving block of data.

In Figure 11.6, note that the handle and the master pointer don't move—even after the block moves. The handle still sits comfortably on the stack, while the master pointer still remains in its original place in the heap.

Nonrelocatable Blocks

A block that is referenced by a handle is *relocatable*. A block that is referenced by a pointer is *nonrelocatable*. A nonrelocatable block never moves about in the heap. Instead, it remains in a fixed location until the program either explicitly disposes of it (as opposed to a relocatable block, which can be purged by the Memory Manager without intervention by your program) or quits.

When the Memory Manager compacts memory, nonrelocatable blocks remain unmoved. Thus a nonrelocatable block has the undesirable side effect of creating an "island" in the middle of free memory. While the free memory on either side of a nonrelocatable block can eventually be used to hold other blocks, they can't be used to hold a single, large block. For the efficient use of memory, it is best to use relocatable blocks, which enables the Memory Manager to use compaction to open large areas of contiguous free space. Occasionally, however, you'll have no choice but to use nonrelocatable blocks. Any time your application uses a pointer variable, it will be working with a nonrelocatable block. Here's an example:

```
void  OpenNewWindow( short windID )
{
   WindowPtr   theWindow;

   theWindow = GetNewWindow( windID, nil, (WindowPtr)-1L );
   ...
}
```

Because a nonrelocatable block won't move in the heap, there's no need to use a double-indirection scheme to keep track of it. Instead, the pointer is enough, as shown in Figure 11.7. In this figure, a pointer variable (such as a variable of type WindowPtr) points to one of the two blocks of data in the heap.

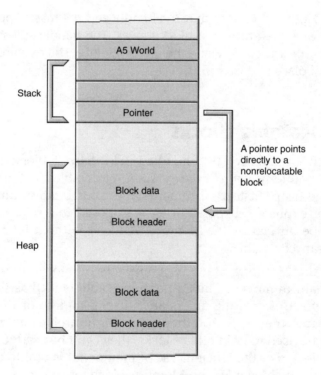

*Figure 11.7   A nonrelocatable block needs only
a pointer to access it—not a handle.*

N O T E A pointer, such as a `WindowPtr`, isn't called a master pointer. While both hold an address that leads to a block of memory, the master pointer is always fixed in the heap. As you can see in Figure 11.7, a "regular" pointer can be outside the heap.

Setting an Application's Heap Size

You'll find projects for two simple Macintosh programs in this chapter's code examples folder on the book's CD. The two programs, PictMemBad68K and PictMemGood68K, are very similar. In fact, the only difference is how they use memory. In this section, you'll see how to make a good first approximation of the heap size needs of PictMemBad68K. Later in this chapter, you'll use ZoneRanger for a better understanding of an application's heap requirements.

What the PictMemBad68K Program Does

Figure 11.8 shows what you'll see as PictMemBad68K runs. This trivial program displays a window but no menu bar. Every time you click the mouse, a picture will be drawn to the window. The resource file for the project holds ten similar `PICT` resources. The only difference between the pictures is in the placement of the cylinder that crosses the Metrowerks logo. As the user repeatedly clicks the mouse, the illusion of a cylinder moving across the logo is created. More important than the simple animation is the fact that you'll get visual feedback confirming that at each of the first ten mouse clicks a different `PICT` is loaded into memory and displayed in the window.

Clicking the mouse button for the eleventh time again displays the first of the ten pictures. Subsequent mouse clicks repeat the animation. A press of any key ends the program.

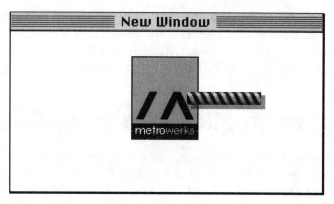

Figure 11.8   *The PictMemBad68K program displays a window with a picture in it.*

 If you have access to a Mac and you run the included
PictMemBad68K program now, don't be surprised if the program
doesn't work properly. The program's name should be a good
N O T E   indication that this is intentional. More on that later. ...

The PictMemBad68K Resources

The **PictMemBad68K.μ** project requires just two resource types—WIND
and PICT. Figure 11.9 shows the resource file.

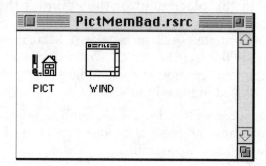

Figure 11.9   *The **PictMemBad68K.μ** project resource
file holds just two types of resources.*

The **PictMemBad.rsrc** resource file includes ten PICT resources, num-
bered 128 through 137. Figure 11.10 shows a few of these pictures, as
viewed from ResEdit.

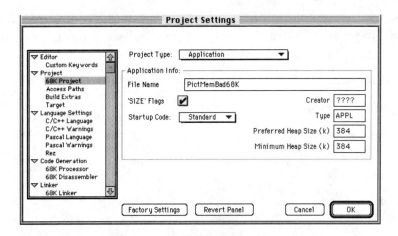

Figure 11.10 The **PictMemBad68K.µ** project
resource file contains ten PICT resources.

The PictMemBad68K.c Source Code

The **PictMemBad68K.µ** project holds a single source code file, the project resource file, and the usual libraries that get added to a project that uses the Basic Toolbox 68k project stationery. Figure 11.11 shows the PictMemBad68K project window.

File	Code	Data	
▽ ✵ **Sources**	0	0	• ▾
✵ PictMemBad.c	0	0	• ▸
▽ ✵ **Resources**	0	0	▾
✵ **PictMemBad.rsrc**	n/a	n/a	▸
▽ ✵ **Mac Libraries**	0	0	▾
✵ **CPlusPlus.lib**	0	0	▸
✵ **MacOS.lib**	0	0	▸
✵ **MathLib68K (2i).Lib**	0	0	▸
▽ ✵ **ANSI Libraries**	0	0	▾
✵ **ANSI (2i) C++.68K.Lib**	0	0	▸
✵ **ANSI (2i) C.68K.Lib**	0	0	▸
✵ **SIOUX.68K.Lib**	0	0	▸

PictMemBad68K.µ

8 file(s) 0 0

Figure 11.11 The PictMemBad68K project window.

The `main()` routine found in the file **PictMemBad.c** begins by initializing the Toolbox and opening an empty window. Then it's off to the main event loop. Here's a look at the `main()` routine:

```
void  main( void )
{
   WindowPtr    theWindow;

   InitializeToolbox();

   theWindow = GetNewWindow( 128, nil, (WindowPtr)-1L );
   SetPort( theWindow );

   MainEventLoop();
}
```

The main event loop looks for just two event types: a key press or a click of the mouse button. When the user presses any key, the global variable gDone is set to `true` and the `while` loop—and program—terminate. If the event is instead a click of the mouse button, the program's `DrawResourcePicture()` routine is invoked.

```
void MainEventLoop( void )
{
   EventRecord    theEvent;

   while ( gDone == false )
   {
      WaitNextEvent( everyEvent, &theFvent, 15L, nil );

      switch ( theEvent.what )
      {
         case keyDown:
            gDone = true;
            break;

         case mouseDown:
            DrawResourcePicture();
            break;
      }
   }
}
```

The purpose of `DrawResourcePicture()` is to load one of the ten PICT resources into memory and draw the picture to the program's window. A call to the Toolbox function `GetPicture()` takes care of the resource loading, while a call to the Toolbox routine DrawPicture() does the drawing. In between these calls, the size of the picture—its bounding rectangle—is determined by examining the picFrame field of the picture's Picture data structure. A rectangle (in window coordinates) in which to display the picture is then set up.

```
void  DrawResourcePicture( void )
{
   static  short  numPICTs;

   Rect          theRect;
   PicHandle     thePicture;
   short         theWidth;
   short         theHeight;
   short         theLeft = 35;
   short         theTop = 20;

   if ( numPICTs < 10 )
      ++numPICTs;
   else
      numPICTs = 1;

   thePicture = GetPicture( 127 + numPICTs );

   theRect = (**(thePicture)).picFrame;
   theWidth  = theRect.right - theRect.left;
   theHeight = theRect.bottom - theRect.top;
   SetRect( &theRect, theLeft, theTop,
            theLeft + theWidth, theTop + theHeight );

   DrawPicture( thePicture, &theRect );
}
```

DrawResourcePicture() uses a static variable named numPICTs to track which PICT resource to load. Recall from your C programming experiences that a variable declared static is not destroyed after the function in which it is declared ends, as is the case with other local variables. Instead, it is initialized to a value of 0 at the first invocation of the function in which it resides and is kept in memory between function calls. Every time it is assigned a new value it retains that new value, even after the function ends. This means that the first time the main event loop invokes DrawResourcePicture(), the variable numPICTs will be initialized to 0 but will quickly be incremented to 1:

```
if ( numPICTs < 10 )
```

```
      numPICTs++;
else
      numPICTs = 1;
```

Next, the call to `GetPicture()` will load `PICT 128` into memory and return a handle to the relocatable block that holds the `PICT` data:

```
thePicture = GetPicture( 127 + numPICTs );
```

After determining the size of the picture and setting a rectangle in which to draw it, a call to `DrawPicture()` does the drawing:

```
DrawPicture( thePicture, &theRect );
```

The first time `DrawResourcePicture()` gets called, `numPICTs` gets incremented from 0 to 1 and `PICT 128` is drawn. The second time, `numPICTs` will be incremented from 1 to 2 and `PICT 129` is drawn. Thus the first ten key presses will result in the display of each of the ten resource pictures. On the eleventh key press, `numPICTs` will have a value of 10 and will get set back to a value of 1 to restart the animation cycle.

Setting the Application's Heap Size

A programming integrated development environment like CodeWarrior lets a programmer easily set the size of an application's heap before building the application. With a project open, select **Project Settings** from the Edit menu, then click on **68K Project** in the dialog box list to display the 68K Project panel (you'll click on **PPC Project** if you're working on a PowerPC project). This panel has two edit boxes that let you set the preferred heap size and the minimum heap size for the application to be built. Figure 11.12 shows that the default values supplied by CodeWarrior are **384K** for both the preferred heap size and the minimum heap size.

 Determining the heap requirements of an application is an inexact science. For determining application heap size, a study like the one done here, along with the use of a memory-watching tool like ZoneRanger, will very often suffice. If you need still more tips on the determination of heap size, refer to the *Memory* volume from the *Inside Macintosh* series of books or to the M&T book *Macintosh Programming Techniques, Second Edition*.

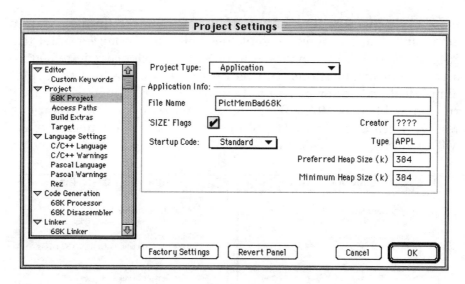

Figure 11.12   *The 68K Project panel in the Project Settings dialog box allows you to set your application's heap size.*

The *preferred heap size* is the number of bytes of RAM that the operating system will attempt to allocate for your application when the program is launched. If that amount of free, contiguous RAM is unavailable on the user's Mac, an amount between the *minimum heap size* and the preferred heap size will be reserved. While the default values of 384 KB often suffice, your application may need more or require less. If it needs more, the application may quit unexpectedly. If it requires less, your application will be consuming more of the user's RAM than necessary, and it may prohibit the user from running another program concurrently with yours.

Estimating an Application's Heap Requirements

If you click once on the icon of any application that is on your hard drive and then select **Get Info** from the File menu in the Finder, you'll set the Info dialog box for that application. There you can see the amount of memory that will be devoted to that one application. While an application may occasionally use the default values of 384 KB, it is more likely that it will request more or less memory (in these days of "monolithic" applications, these values will often be *much* greater than 384 KB). Figure 11.13 provides examples of the memory requirements of a couple of applications. In this figure, you can see that Apple's SimpleText text editor prefers to be given 512 KB of memory (but will run on as little as 192 KB), while the Metrowerks IDE attempts to reserve a heap 3.5 MB (3584 KB) in size (but will still launch if only 2 MB, or 2048 KB, are available).

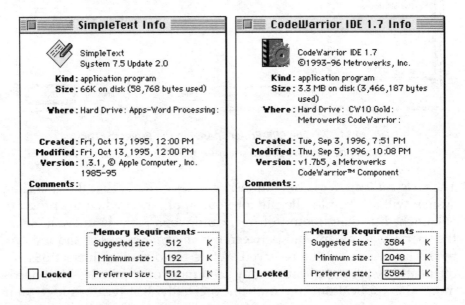

Figure 11.13 *The **Get Info** menu item from the Finder's File menu tells you how much memory an application requires.*

Don't try to make a correlation between the amount of disk space an application occupies and the size of its heap. An application's heap size depends on what the application loads into memory. A small application may be required to load more than just its own executable code into memory. It may need to reserve space for the loading of, say, several large graphics files or resources from an external resource file. Note in Figure 11.13 that SimpleText itself occupies only 66 KB of disk space, yet it needs 192 KB of heap space, and it would prefer half a megabyte (512 KB)!

One means of estimating the minimum amount of heap space an application needs is to look at the application's resources and determine how much memory they will occupy. Here's the quick method to get a rough idea of how much heap space PictMemBad68K will need:

- Add up the size of all `CODE` resources that have their preload attribute set.
- Allow for the loading of some of the other `CODE` resources.
- Add up the size of the largest `PICT` that will be loaded.
- Determine the amount of memory needed for other resources.
- Add an appropriate "buffer" of memory to play it safe.

 Programmers who will be creating fat applications or PowerPC-only applications should read this section for general techniques, then read the last section in this chapter—"ZoneRanger and the **N O T E** Power Mac"—for PowerPC-specific tips.

When your CodeWarrior integrated development environment compiles and links a 68K project, the resulting application consists of all the resources from the project's resource file (or files), as well as two or more `CODE` resources. Each `CODE` resource is a segment of executable code—the 68K instructions that result from compiled source code. Any of these `CODE` resources that are marked as preload will be loaded into the application heap when the application launches. An application's heap must be large enough to accommodate all the `CODE` resources that are marked as preloaded. CodeWarrior will allow you to mark any segment to be preloaded, and it will always mark `CODE` resource 1, which holds the start of your application, as preloaded.

Figure 11.14 shows some of the `CODE` resources for the graphics program MacDraw Pro, as viewed when the application is opened with the resource editor Resorcerer. In this figure, you can see that MacDraw Pro has 20 `CODE` resources, totaling about 330 KB, that will preload when the program is launched. From this, you can safely conclude that the heap size for MacDraw Pro will need to be at *least* 330 KB in size—and more likely much higher. Additional heap space must also be reserved to hold at least some of the other `CODE` resources as well.

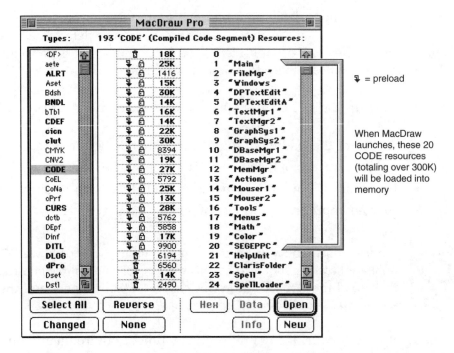

*Figure 11.14   Most commercial applications, such as
Claris MacDraw Pro, have several CODE resources that are marked to preload.*

NOTE   For 68K applications, all the program's executable code need not
be loaded into memory at once; only code marked as preloaded
will be loaded at application startup. Other code will be loaded
as needed and purged (if marked purgeable) when it is not in use
and unavailable memory is being requested by the program.
Again, *Inside Macintosh: Memory* and *Macintosh Programming
Techniques, Second Edition* provides details on memory management for 68K applications.

If you build the PictMemBad68K application and then open it with a
resource editor, you'll see that it has three CODE resources. Figure 11.15
shows the size of each. Because PictMemBad68K is such a trivial pro-

gram, all of its executable code together uses less than 2 KB. Figure 11.15 also takes a closer look at the CODE resource with an ID of 0. The Info dialog box shown in this figure was opened by first double-clicking on the **CODE** icon in the PictMemBad68K window of ResEdit, then clicking on the **CODE 0** resource in the list of CODE resources, and finally selecting **Get Resource Info** from the Resource menu of ResEdit.

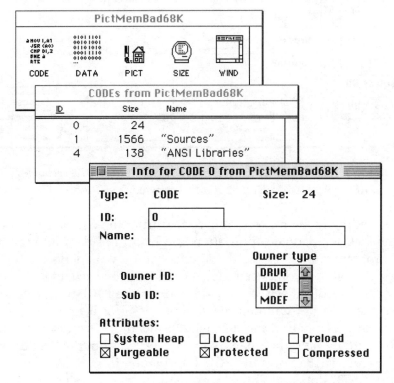

Figure 11.15   *A look at the attributes of one of the CODE resources of the PictMemBad68K application, viewed from ResEdit.*

If you're using Resorcerer rather than ResEdit, refer to Figure 11.16 rather than Figure 11.15—it provides a similar view of CODE 0, this time from Resorcerer. To view the Info window from Resorcerer, select **Resource Info** from the Resource menu.

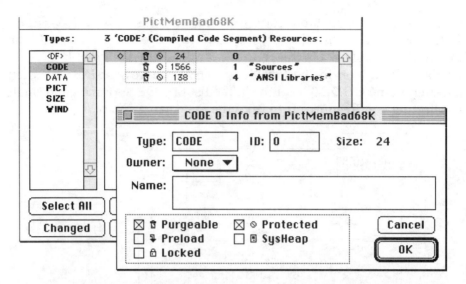

Figure 11.16 *A look at the attributes of one of the CODE resources of the PictMemBad68K application, viewed from Resorcerer.*

Besides loading its own executable code during the course of its execution, the PictMemBad68K application will load PICT data into the heap as the program runs. Because the application only displays one picture at any given time, I won't need to determine the total size of all the PICT resources. Instead, I'll rely on a quick look at the PICT resources to tell me that the program will only need about 5 KB of heap space to hold even the largest picture. Figure 11.17 shows the PICT resources from ResEdit (with by **ID** rather than by **PICT** selected from the ResEdit View menu). Figure 11.18 shows the PICT information from Resorcerer (select the **Hide 'PICT' data** and **Show sizes** items from the View menu).

Another object that will appear in the heap is the data for the one window that PictMemBad68K uses. Opening a new window means a WindowRecord gets loaded into memory, and the WIND resource information gets copied to that record. A window occupies well under 1 KB of memory, so the window is not a concern.

The PictMemBad68K application has less than 2 KB of code, won't display more than 5 KB of picture information at any one time, and will display only one window. Additionally, because PictMemBad68K doesn't work with files, it won't require heap space to hold data from other files. From this information, what can be concluded about the memory requirement of PictMemBad68K? Obviously, it's quite low. If I leave the heap size at the default value of 384 KB, I'll be creating an application that probably wastes about one-third of a megabyte of the user's RAM; so instead, I'll use CodeWarrior to change the heap size.

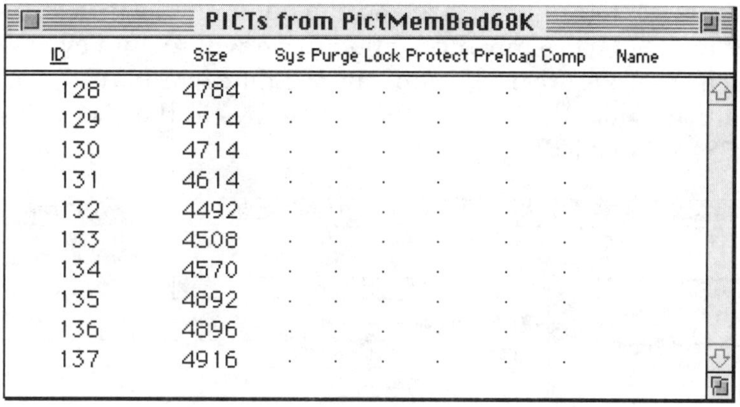

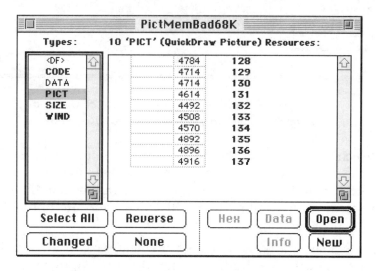

Figure 11.17 *The size of each PictMemBad68K PICT resource, viewed from ResEdit.*

Figure 11.18 *The size of each PictMemBad68K. PICT resource, viewed from Resorcerer.*

372

Metrowerks CodeWarrior Programming, Second Edition

Changing an Application's Heap Size

To tell CodeWarrior to generate a version of PictMemBad68K that uses a smaller heap, I'll select **Project Settings** from the CodeWarrior IDE Edit menu, click the **68K Project** entry in the Project Settings dialog box to display the 68K Project panel, and then enter a much smaller number for both the preferred heap size and the minimum heap size. Though I don't think the PictMemBad68K application will require even 48 KB of heap space, in Figure 11.19 you can see that I've played it safe and entered that value. If I'm right, the net savings to the user is 336 KB of RAM (384 KB – 48 KB).

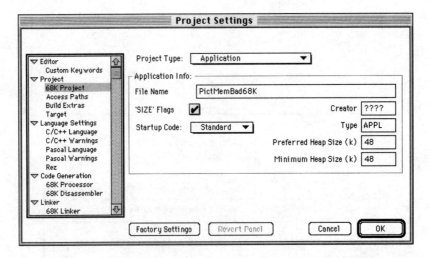

Figure 11.19   An application's heap size can be changed by using the CodeWarrior Project Settings dialog box.

After selecting **Make** from the Project menu, I returned to the Finder. There I clicked once on the new version of **PictMemBad68K** and selected **Get Info** from the Finder's File menu. The numbers in the Info dialog box confirm that the system will indeed allocate only 48 KB to PictMemBad68K, as shown in Figure 11.20.

There's a second way to change the heap size of an application. After the application is built, you can open the application with a resource editor and change the values in the last two fields of the application's SIZE resource.

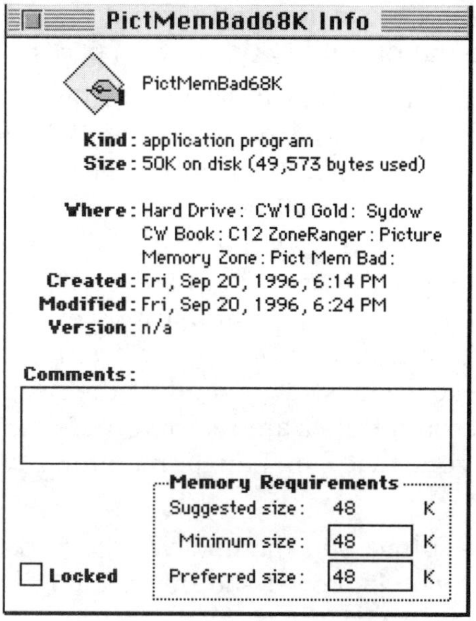

```
┌─────────────────────────────────────────────┐
│ ▣ ▤▤▤ PictMemBad68K Info ▤▤▤                │
├─────────────────────────────────────────────┤
│                                               │
│      ◇─┐                                      │
│     ╱  ╱  PictMemBad68K                       │
│    ╱  ╱                                       │
│                                               │
│       Kind: application program               │
│       Size: 50K on disk (49,573 bytes used)   │
│                                               │
│      Where: Hard Drive: CW10 Gold: Sydow      │
│             CW Book: C12 ZoneRanger: Picture  │
│             Memory Zone: Pict Mem Bad:        │
│    Created: Fri, Sep 20, 1996, 6:14 PM        │
│   Modified: Fri, Sep 20, 1996, 6:24 PM        │
│    Version: n/a                               │
│                                               │
│  Comments:                                    │
│  ┌─────────────────────────────────────────┐ │
│  │                                         │ │
│  │                                         │ │
│  └─────────────────────────────────────────┘ │
│            ┌─ Memory Requirements ─────────┐  │
│            │ Suggested size:   48      K   │  │
│            │                              │  │
│            │ Minimum size:  ┌──48─┐    K   │  │
│  ☐ Locked  │ Preferred size:┌──48─┐    K   │  │
│            └──────────────────────────────┘  │
└─────────────────────────────────────────────┘
```

Figure 11.20   The Finder's Get Info dialog box reflects changes made to an application's heap size in CodeWarrior, after the application is rebuilt in CodeWarrior.

Now it's time for a test run. Double-click on the **PictMemBad68K** icon to launch the application. When the empty window opens, click the mouse button to display the first of the ten pictures. Repeatedly click the mouse to display each picture. What happens after a few clicks? Most likely, some mouse clicks don't display pictures. Keep clicking the mouse. Eventually, the first few pictures may again be displayed—though the ones that should appear at the end of the animation are never drawn. Why? You may have discovered the problem several pages back. But regardless, press any key to end the faulty program and read on to see how ZoneRanger can be used to track down a bug and help determine an appropriate heap zone size.

ZoneRanger Basics

This chapter's Macintosh memory overview provided you with the background you'll need for the use of Metrowerks' impressive memory-watching software tool ZoneRanger. Now it's time to take a look at ZoneRanger and to put this utility through its paces.

You've seen that every application that is running (each process) on a Macintosh has its own application partition. Within this partition is the application heap. As each block in the heap begins with a block header, the application heap itself also begins with a header, called the *zone header*. This header provides the Memory Manager with information about the heap, such as its size in bytes. Because the application heap can expand and shrink as the application executes, the heap ends with a small block of memory, known as the *zone trailer*, which helps the Memory Manager keep track of the end of the heap. Collectively, the heap and its header and trailer are referred to as the *heap zone*. It is an application's heap zone that ZoneRanger monitors.

NOTE

Like all the software in the CodeWarrior package, ZoneRanger is constantly being improved and upgraded. Included on the book's CD is version 1.9 of ZoneRanger, copyright late 1996. If you're going to run ZoneRanger to follow along with the discussions in this chapter and you are an owner of the full-featured Metrowerks CodeWarrior package (which may include a more recent version of ZoneRanger), use this book's version instead. That way, what you see on-screen will match what you read in this book.

The Heap Zones Window

When you launch ZoneRanger, the ZoneRanger Heap Zones (also referred to as the *Open Zone*) window will open. Listed in this window is the name of each application, or *process*, that is currently running. These are the processes that ZoneRanger tracks. Each time you run ZoneRanger you'll notice that the System, Process Manager, and Finder are always listed in this window. That's because as long as your Mac is running, so are these programs. Because ZoneRanger is executing, it too will be listed in the Heap Zones window. If you have any other programs running, their names will also appear in this window. In Figure 11.21, you can see that besides the four applications that will always be named in the Heap Zones window, I have the PictMemBad68K program running.

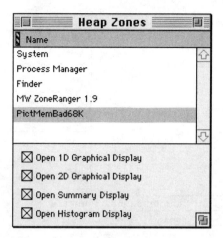

Figure 11.21 *The ZoneRanger Heap Zones window keeps track of all applications that are executing.*

As shown in Figure 11.21, at the bottom of the Heap Zones window are four checkboxes. Each checkbox provides a different way to view the same memory information for any one process. To open one or more of the four display windows, check the appropriate checkbox or checkboxes in the Heap Zones window, then double-click on a process name in the Heap Zones window. A display window for every marked checkbox will then open. In this chapter, we'll take a look at each type of display, starting with the Summary display.

The Summary Display

To explore process heap zones using ZoneRanger, I started out by running a program I'm familiar with—the PictMemBad68K application that I just recently developed. With ZoneRanger running and the Heap Zones window on the screen, I checked the **Open Summary Display** checkbox, unchecked the other three checkboxes, and then double-clicked on the **PictMemBad68K** name in the process list. Figure 11.22 shows the resulting Summary window for this one process—the PictMemBad68K process.

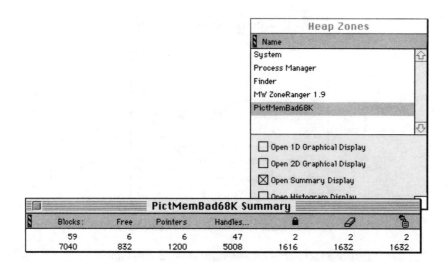

Figure 11.22   *The ZoneRanger Summary window for the PictMemBad68K process.*

Figure 11.23 shows the Summary window and four of the seven pieces of memory-related information that ZoneRanger tracks for the process. From earlier in this chapter you know that a heap, or zone, holds free memory, nonrelocatable blocks, and relocatable blocks. ZoneRanger labels these blocks as Free, Pointers, and Handles, respectively. Within each column appears the number of blocks of one of these types, as well as the number of bytes of memory occupied by those blocks. For example, in Figure 11.23 you can see that at this point in time the PictMemBad68K application's heap zone contains 6 free blocks, 6 nonrelocatable blocks (referenced by pointers), and 47 relocatable blocks (referenced by handles).

Values in your Summary window will differ from the ones shown in mine. Different system configurations will result in different numbers of blocks. Also, Macintosh memory is dynamic—blocks are relocated and purged periodically. As you view the Summary window, don't be surprised to see some of the values changing as the process you're studying executes.

Relocatable blocks have locked, purgeable, and resource attributes. The Summary window reports the number of blocks with each of these attributes for the process being monitored. Figure 11.24 points out the three attributes columns in the Summary window.

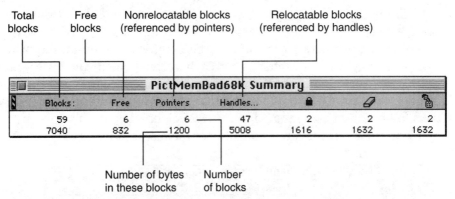

Figure 11.23 *The ZoneRanger Summary window tracks all the free blocks, nonre-locatable blocks, and relocatable blocks in the memory heap of an application.*

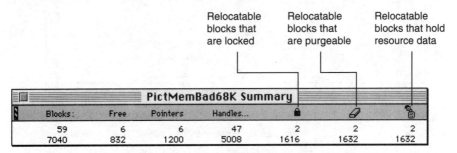

Figure 11.24 *The ZoneRanger Summary window tracks all the attributes of all the relocatable blocks in the monitored process.*

NOTE The blocks in the three rightmost columns are all relocatable blocks referenced by handles. Yet for this process, the total number of blocks in these three columns will not add up to the number of blocks displayed in the Handles column of this same Summary window. That's because many of the application's relocatable blocks may not have any of these three attributes set. That is, a block that is unlocked, unpurgeable, and holds data that isn't from a resource won't appear in the Attributes columns.

The Histogram Display

ZoneRanger provides a few different ways to look at the same information. Rather than displaying just the number of blocks of various types (as the Summary window does), you can choose to view block data in a more graphical way—as a *histogram*. A histogram is a type of chart that uses vertical or horizontal bars of different lengths to represent the distribution of something. In ZoneRanger, each vertical bar in the Histogram window represents a number of blocks in a certain byte range. If one bar is higher than another, that means that a greater number of memory blocks fall into that size range. Figure 11.25 elaborates on this concept by displaying the byte size ranges of some of the histogram bars.

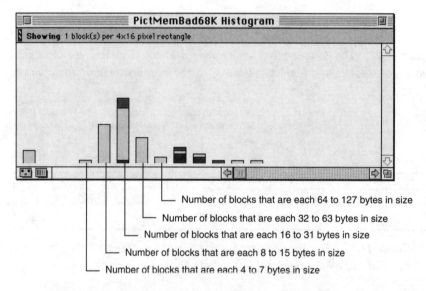

Number of blocks that are each 64 to 127 bytes in size
Number of blocks that are each 32 to 63 bytes in size
Number of blocks that are each 16 to 31 bytes in size
Number of blocks that are each 8 to 15 bytes in size
Number of blocks that are each 4 to 7 bytes in size

Figure 11.25 *The ZoneRanger Histogram window displays the number of blocks in different ranges of sizes in the monitored process.*

To open a Histogram window for an application, check the **Open Histogram Display** checkbox in the Heap Zones window and then double-click on the name of the process to monitor. I did that for the PictMemBad68K program. The resulting Histogram window is shown in Figure 11.25.

NOTE For any one process you can open as many of the four display windows as you want. For example, you can leave open the Summary window for the PictMemBad68K process and still open the Histogram window for this same process.

The Histogram window provides an overview of the block size makeup of a process. To see exactly how many blocks in a given size range are in memory, click on the bar that represents that size range. In Figure 11.26, I clicked on the bar that represents the number of blocks that are at least 16 bytes in size but less than 32 bytes in size. ZoneRanger responds by highlighting the bar and printing the number of blocks (19 in this example) that fall into this size range.

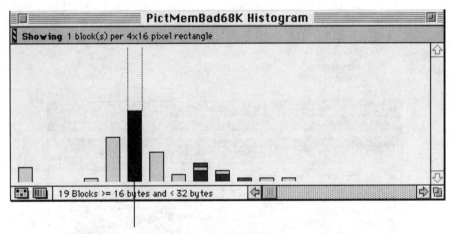

PictMemBad68K uses 19 blocks of memory that
are each in the range of 16 bytes to 31 bytes in size

Figure 11.26   *Clicking on a bar in the Histogram window displays the number of blocks in the size range of that one column.*

In Figure 11.26, I've clicked on the bar that is in the sixth column from the left edge of the window. The PictMemBad68K program isn't currently using any memory blocks of the sizes represented by the second and third columns, so the height of the second and third bars is 0.

The 2D Graphical Display

The Summary window and Histogram window provide two ways of looking at the number of blocks of memory a program is using. However, knowing the *number* of blocks of memory a program is using may or may not answer questions you have about that application. So ZoneRanger provides the 1D Graphical window and 2D Graphical window as ways to provide more information about specific blocks of memory. Here I'll look at the 2D Graphical window—after that I'll open a 1D Graphical window.

To open a 2D Graphical window for an application, check the **Open 2D Graphical Display** checkbox in the Heap Zones window and then double-click on the name of the process to monitor. I did that for the PictMemBad68K program. The resulting 2D Graphical window is shown in Figure 11.27.

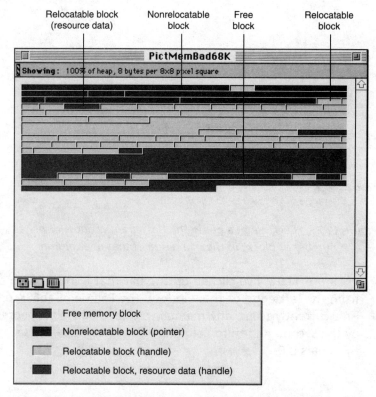

Figure 11.27 *The ZoneRanger 2D Graphical window displays a two-dimensional view of the various types of blocks used by the monitored process.*

Now let's see how the Zone window works. You can determine the type of block by its color. For the figures in this chapter, you can use the grayscale key I've included beneath the 2D Graphical window in Figure 11.27. When running ZoneRanger on your Mac, click on the **Legend Information** pop-up menu—the rightmost of the three small icons in the lower left of the 2D Graphical window—as I'm doing in Figure 11.28. When you do that, you'll see a more comprehensive key that lets you know which colors are used to represent which types of blocks.

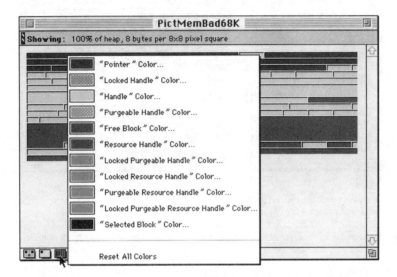

Figure 11.28   *The 2D Graphical window Legend Information menu.*

Back in Figure 11.27 I checked **Show Resource Handles** in the Configure menu so my window displays all relocatable resource blocks in a different color than relocatable blocks that don't hold resource data. You can get still more information about a particular block by clicking on it to select it (the block will change color in the window) and then clicking on the **Block Information** pop-up menu—the middle of the three icons at the bottom left of the window. When you do that, you'll see the Block Information menu, as shown in Figure 11.29.

The Block Information menu in Figure 11.29 shows that the block I've selected is a block of free memory 20 bytes in size. Later in this chapter, I'll use the 2D Graphical window and the Block Information menu to determine why the PictMemBad68K program is failing to properly display the sequence of pictures.

This small block was clicked on once to select it...

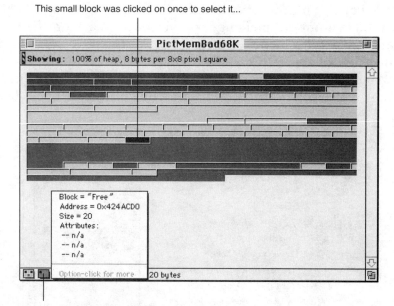

Block = "Free"
Address = 0×424ACD0
Size = 20
Attributes:
-- n/a
-- n/a
-- n/a

...then the Block Information popup menu was
displayed to reveal information about this one block

Figure 11.29   The 2D Graphical window Block Information menu.

The 1D Graphical Display

The last of the four ZoneRanger memory display types is the 1D
Graphical display. To open a 1D Graphical window for a process, check
the **Open 1D Graphical Display** checkbox in the Heap Zones window
and then double-click on the name of the process to monitor.

The 1D Graphical display is similar to the 2D Graphical display in
that blocks of various colors are used to represent different types of
blocks of memory. Unlike a 2D Graphical window, which represents
memory by displaying memory in both the horizontal and vertical
directions, a 1D Graphical window simply displays memory horizon-
tally. The 1D Graphical window also does not place a gray border
around each block, as does the 2D Graphical window. You can, however, select a block by clicking on it (as shown in Figure 11.30), and you
can get more information about a block by selecting the same **Block
Information** pop-up menu that's found in the 2D Graphical window.

Selected block

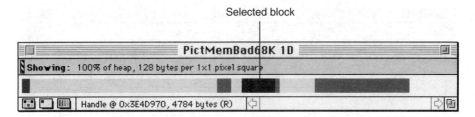

Figure 11.30 *The ZoneRanger 1D Graphical window displays a one-dimensional view of the various types of blocks used by the monitored process.*

Examining a Process Using ZoneRanger

ZoneRanger keeps tabs on the memory usage of all applications that are currently running. ZoneRanger will also monitor any applications you start after ZoneRanger is launched. Earlier in this chapter, you read (or, if you're following along on your Mac, you actually saw) that the PictMemBad68K application had problems displaying the pictures it has stored in its resource fork. Here you'll see how ZoneRanger can help out.

Viewing the PictMemBad68K Heap before Picture Display

To examine how PictMemBad68K uses memory, double-click on the **ZoneRanger** icon to launch the ZoneRanger application. Then launch the application to be examined—PictMemBad68K. If PictMemBad68K has been running and you've clicked the mouse button on its window to view the animation, press any key to quit the program and then launch it again. You'll want to view memory usage from the very start of the program, before pictures have been loaded and displayed.

In the Heap Zones window check any of the four checkboxes—my preference for viewing a heap zone is the 2D Graphical display, so I've checked just the **Open 2D Graphical Display** checkbox. After double-clicking on the name of **PictMemBad68K** in the Heap Zones window list of processes, my screen displayed a ZoneRanger 2D Graphical window like the one pictured in Figure 11.31.

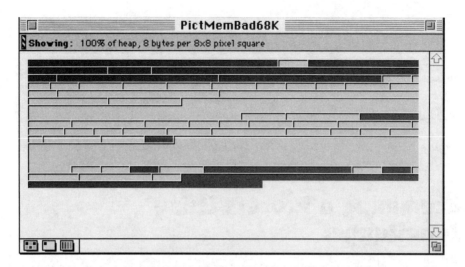

Figure 11.31 *The ZoneRanger 2D Graphical window for the PictMemBad68K application.*

 Remember, if the display of the heap in the 2D Graphical window seems too large or too small, you can increase the area each block occupies by making selections from the Configure menu. You can repeatedly select **Increase Resolution** and **Zoom In** to enlarge the display size of each block or **Decrease Resolution** or **Zoom Out** to decrease the display size of each block.

VIEWING THE PICTMEMBAD68K WIND RESOURCE DATA

To help clarify what's going on in memory as PictMemBad68K runs, you'll want to see which blocks are resource-related. Select **Show Resource Handles** from the Configure menu to make these types of blocks stand out. When I do that, I see that during this running of the PictMemBad68K program, the application's heap zone includes two blocks that hold resource data, as shown in Figure 11.32.

 Don't expect your 2D Graphical window to look just like mine, even if you're running the same PictMemBad68K program. Remember, Macintosh memory is dynamic. The Memory Manager will attempt to make the best use of the memory available on your machine when you run the application and throughout the running of it. What is the same, however, is the size of various blocks of memory. For example, while the same PICT resource may get loaded to a different address each time you run the same program, it will occupy the same amount of memory each time.

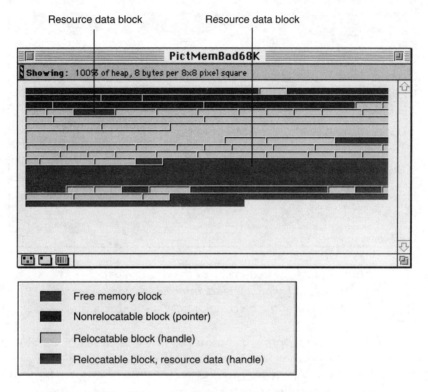

Resource data block   Resource data block

■ Free memory block
■ Nonrelocatable block (pointer)
□ Relocatable block (handle)
■ Relocatable block, resource data (handle)

*Figure 11.32   The two resource data blocks in the heap zone
during this one running of the PictMemBad68K application.*

The resources in the PictMemBad68K program consist of one WIND, ten PICT, and three CODE resources. When the PictMemBad68K is launched, a window opens, so I can assume the WIND resource has been loaded into memory. It's also safe to assume that the Memory Manager has loaded at least some of the executable code of the program into memory, so I know at least one CODE resource will be loaded. Clicking on the smaller resource block and then bringing up the **Block Information** pop-up menu confirms that one of the blocks does in fact hold the data from the program's one WIND resource, as shown in Figure 11.33.

Selected resource data block

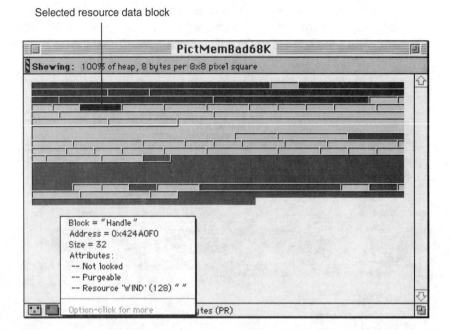

Block = "Handle"
Address = 0x424A0F0
Size = 32
Attributes:
-- Not locked
-- Purgeable
-- Resource "WIND" (128) " "

*Figure 11.33   Selecting one of the resource data blocks
and then displaying the **Block Information** pop-up menu
reveals that the block holds WIND resource data.*

The **Block Information** pop-up menu for the selected block states that this block is 32 bytes in size. If you have any doubts as to the accuracy of ZoneRanger, you can use your resource editor to take a look at the WIND resource in the **PictMemBad.rsrc** file or the PictMemBad68K program. Figure 11.34 saves you this step and lets you see that this is indeed the size of the program's WIND resource.

N O T E

If PictMemBad68K is running, you won't be able to open it with your resource editor. After you're done following along with this experiment, you can quit PictMemBad68K and then open it with ResEdit or Resorcerer.

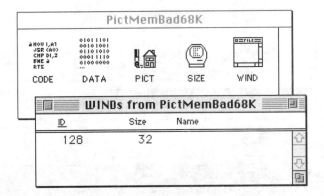

Figure 11.34   *Using ResEdit to check the size of the*
WIND resource in the PictMemBad68K program.

VIEWING THE PICTMEMBAD68K CODE RESOURCE DATA

Selecting the one remaining resource block and then clicking the **Block Information** pop-up menu icon displays the pop-up menu shown in Figure 11.35. The pop-up menu reveals that this block holds the executable code that is kept in one of the CODE resources—the CODE resource with an ID of 1. The menu also lets you know that this block is locked (meaning the Memory Manager can't move it about in memory) and is purgeable (meaning that while the Memory Manager can't move it within memory, it can remove it from memory if none of its code is currently being executed).

N O T E

The more you know about Macintosh memory in general, the more things in particular ZoneRanger will help identify. If you hadn't read about Macintosh memory and CODE resources earlier in this chapter (or if you didn't know about them before you read this book), the fact that there is a block of memory designated as a locked, purgeable, resource block might mean little or nothing to you.

Once again you can gain a little more faith in ZoneRanger by comparing ZoneRanger's report of this block's size with the size stated in a resource editor. Figure 11.36 shows that ResEdit also interprets the CODE 1 resource to be 1566 bytes in size.

Selected resource data block

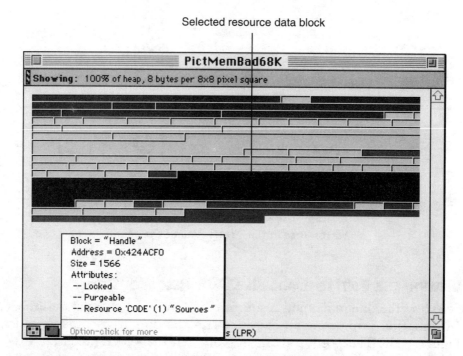

Figure 11.35 *Selecting the second resource data block and then displaying the*
Block Information *pop-up menu reveals that the block holds CODE resource data.*

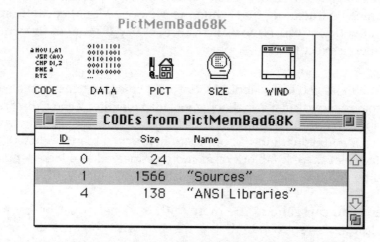

Figure 11.36 *Using ResEdit to check the size of the CODE*
resource in the PictMemBad68K program.

Viewing the PictMemBad68K Heap after Picture Display

As a process runs, ZoneRanger will update any of the ZoneRanger windows that are currently displaying information about the process. The PictMemBad68K has been running this whole time that I've been examining the 2D Graphical window, but the program hasn't been doing anything, so ZoneRanger hasn't had much to do. I'll change that by clicking once on the empty PictMemBad68K program window to make the PictMemBad68K application active (rather than ZoneRanger), and then I'll click again in the program's window to display the first picture.

NOTE

Don't click again in the PictMemBad68K window at this time—you'll want to observe the results in ZoneRanger before displaying the second of the ten pictures that should eventually be drawn.

With the display of the picture, ZoneRanger updates the 2D Graphical window—even though ZoneRanger is now running in the background. Figure 11.37 shows that my mouse click results in a new resource block being added to the 2D Graphical window.

Selecting the new resource block and choosing the **Block Information** pop-up menu reveals that this new block holds the data from a PICT resource—PICT resource 128 to be exact (see Figure 11.38). This is as expected; as written, the first mouse button click to the PictMemBad68K window is supposed to load and display picture data from PICT resource 128.

Clicking in the window of the PictMemBad68K application
causes this picture to appear in the window...

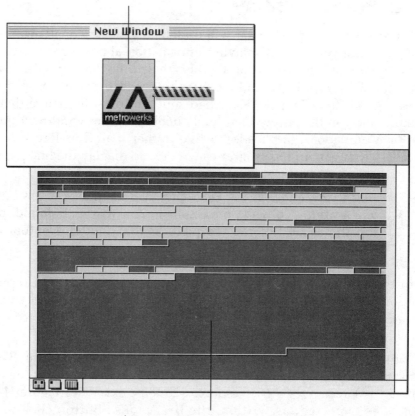

...and causes a new resource data block to appear
in the 2D Graphical window of ZoneRanger

Figure 11.37   *Clicking in the PictMemBad68K program window results in a change
to the display of memory in the ZoneRanger 2D Graphical window.*

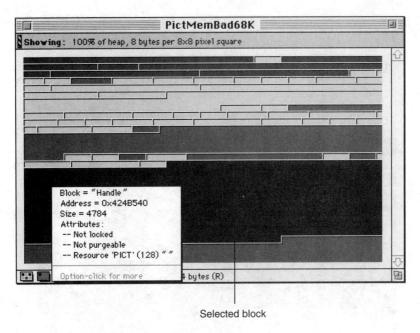

Selected block

Figure 11.38 The **Block Information** *pop-up menu for the selected block shows that the newly added resource block holds the data for PICT resource 128.*

Now, I'll again click on the PictMemBad68K window. Again, a picture is displayed—as expected. And again, a new resource block is added to the PictMemBad68K heap zone. In Figure 11.39, I've resized the 2D Graphical window and popped up the **Block Information** menu to show this new block and reveal that the new block holds the data for PICT 129.

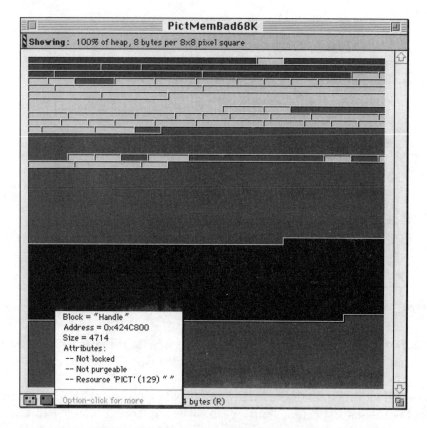

Figure 11.39 The **Block Information** *pop-up menu for the selected block shows that a second click on the PictMemBad68K window results in another resource block being added to memory.*

Discovering the PictMemBad68K Memory Problem

Clicking on the PictMemBad68K window a third time results in a third resource block being added to the heap zone. After each click of the mouse, a new block of about 5 KB in size is added to the PictMemBad68K heap zone. Apparently, each picture that gets drawn is using, and retaining, a part of the application's heap zone. To confirm this finding, I'll use another ZoneRanger window to look at the PictMemBad68K heap zone.

To get a different perspective on the same heap zone, I'll click on the **ZoneRanger Heap Zones** window, check the **Open Summary Display** checkbox, and then double-click on the name of **PictMemBad68K** in the Heap Zones window list of processes. The result is a Summary window like the one shown in Figure 11.40.

PictMemBad68K Summary						
Blocks:	Free	Pointers	Handles...	🔒	✏️	📑
62	6	6	50	2	2	5
56464	36000	1200	19264	1616	1632	15904

Selected column

Figure 11.40   The Summary window for the PictMemBad68K process.

In Figure 11.40, you see that the Handles column is highlighted—clicking once on a column does that. Double-clicking on a column opens a Block List window. A Block List window displays information about all of a heap zone's blocks of a certain type. Double-clicking on the **Handles** column opens a Block List window that holds a list of all the blocks that are referenced by handles. When I examined a block that was added after a picture was drawn, the **Block Information** pop-up listed the block's type as "Handle." You can look at the top of this pop-up menu in Figure 11.38 to confirm this. Because ZoneRanger let me know that pictures are held in memory blocks referenced by handles, I've decided to look at all the handle blocks. Figure 11.41 shows the Block List window for the Handles column of the Summary window.

NOTE Another clue that tells me that picture data is referenced by a handle appears in the source code for PictMemBad68K. There, a call to the Toolbox function GetPicture() returns a PicHandle to the program.

As I scroll through the Block List window, I see that the heap zone for PictMemBad68K does indeed hold three blocks of PICT data—one block for each of the three mouse clicks I've made in the window of PictMemBad68K. Figure 11.41 shows these three blocks at the bottom of the Block List window.

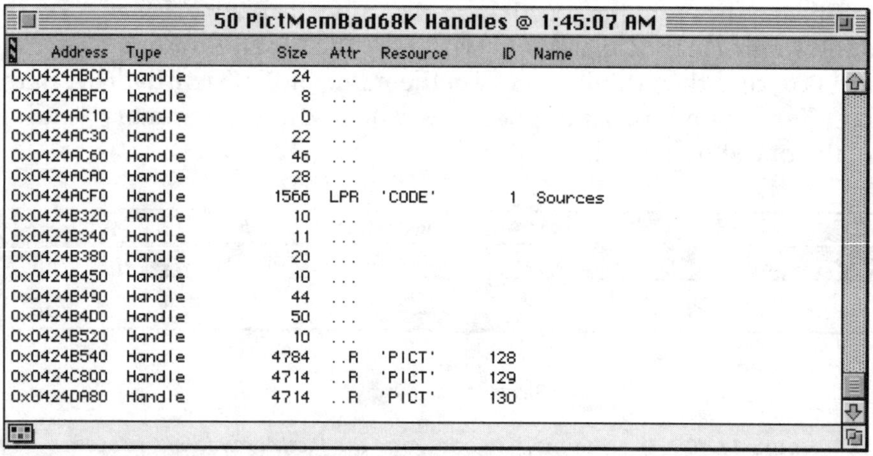

```
        50 PictMemBad68K Handles @ 1:45:07 AM
  Address    Type       Size  Attr  Resource   ID  Name
0x0424ABC0  Handle      24    ...
0x0424ABF0  Handle       8    ...
0x0424AC10  Handle       0    ...
0x0424AC30  Handle      22    ...
0x0424AC60  Handle      46    ...
0x0424ACA0  Handle      28    ...
0x0424ACF0  Handle    1566    LPR  'CODE'      1   Sources
0x0424B320  Handle      10    ...
0x0424B340  Handle      11    ...
0x0424B380  Handle      20    ...
0x0424B450  Handle      10    ...
0x0424B490  Handle      44    ...
0x0424B4D0  Handle      50    ...
0x0424B520  Handle      10    ...
0x0424B540  Handle    4784    ..R  'PICT'    128
0x0424C800  Handle    4714    ..R  'PICT'    129
0x0424DA80  Handle    4714    ..R  'PICT'    130
```

Figure 11.41   *The block list window for the PictMemBad68K process.*

At this point, you should have caught on that something is not right. Though the PictMemBad68K program is displaying only a single picture at a time, it is retaining the PICT data for more than one picture in memory. In fact, if you click the mouse a few more times, you'll see that the zone heap begins to fill with blocks of PICT data.

It should be clear to you that if the heap size of PictMemBad68K is set low, the application will soon run into trouble. Recall that I used CodeWarrior to set the heap size to **48 KB**. At close to 5 KB per displayed picture, the heap will soon become full, and either the program will terminate abruptly or it will simply fail to display each picture.

Correcting the PictMemBad68K Memory Problem

ZoneRanger's ability not only to show memory blocks but also to show the size and type of blocks helps you find memory-related programming bugs. In the case of PictMemBad68K, being able to see that memory blocks holding PICT data remained in memory after the pictures were drawn is what pinpointed the cause of PictMemBad68K's problems. Now, it's up to your Macintosh programming skills to relate this memory problem to the code that needs to be altered.

When a program is finished with a picture, the application should release the memory that was used to hold that picture's PICT data. Let's take a look at the DrawResourcePicture() routine from PictMemBad68K to see if that's being done:

```
void  DrawResourcePicture( void )
{
   static  short  numPICTs;

   Rect        theRect;
   PicHandle   thePicture;
   short       theWidth;
   short       theHeight;
   short       theLeft = 35;
   short       theTop = 20;

   if ( numPICTs < 10 )
      ++numPICTs;
   else
      numPICTs = 1;

   thePicture = GetPicture( 127 + numPICTs );

   theRect = (**(thePicture)).picFrame;
   theWidth  = theRect.right - theRect.left;
   theHeight  = theRect.bottom - theRect.top;
   SetRect( &theRect, theLeft, theTop,
            theLeft + theWidth, theTop + theHeight );

   DrawPicture( thePicture, &theRect );
}
```

You can see that the last line in DrawResourcePicture() is the call to the Toolbox routine DrawPicture(). I never did release the heap memory that was used in the call to GetPicture(). The remedy? I'll simply add a call to ReleaseResource() at the end of the function. ReleaseResource() requires a generic handle as its only parameter, so I'll typecast the PicHandle when I pass it:

```
void  DrawResourcePicture( void )
{
   ...
   ...
   thePicture = GetPicture( 127 + numPICTs );
   ...
```

```
   ...
   DrawPicture( thePicture, &theRect );

   ReleaseResource( (Handle)thePicture );
}
```

Is this really the solution? You can verify that it is by adding the call to `ReleaseResource()` and then selecting **Run** from the Project menu to recompile the code and build a new version of the PictMemBad68K program. Then, again use ZoneRanger to observe the application's memory. This work is already done for you in the form of the PictMemGood68K project and program on the book's CD. The only difference between the PictMemBad68K and PictMemGood68K programs is one line of code—the call to `ReleaseResource()`.

Figure 11.42 is a look at the PictMemGood68K program, along with a ZoneRanger 2D Graphical window. In the figure, you can see that even with the last of the ten PictMemGood68K pictures displayed, there's still plenty of heap space left. The figure also shows that there are only two relocatable resource blocks in the heap (representing the `WIND` and `CODE` resources)—the `PICT` block is released immediately after a picture is drawn.

As you run PictMemGood68K, keep an eye on the amount of free space in the PictMemGood68K Zone window. If, after putting the program through its paces, there is always an ample amount of free memory, you know that you can further reduce the size of the application's heap. Quit PictMemGood68K, click on it once, then select **Get Info** from the Finder's File menu. Lower the minimum size and preferred size values and test the program again. Quit PictMemGood68K, adjust the heap size, and rerun the program several times until you find the optimum heap size. Keep in mind that PictMemGood68K should always have a free block at least the size of the largest `PICT` resource it needs to load.

When you've found the ideal heap size, change the values in the 68K Project panel of the Project Settings dialog box for the **PictMemGood68K.µ** project. Then, each time you make a new version of the program CodeWarrior will give the application the heap size you want. To guarantee that any program you write doesn't use too much of a user's RAM (or so little that it behaves erratically), examine it with ZoneRanger.

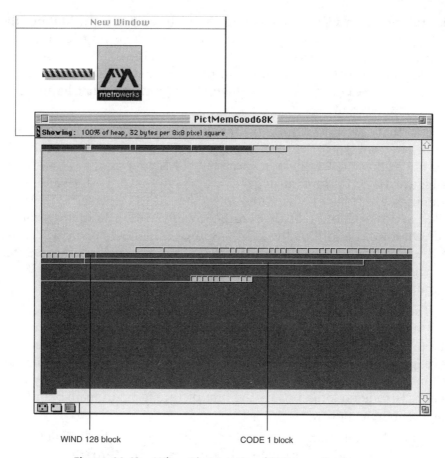

WIND 128 block   CODE 1 block

Figure 11.42   *When PictMemGood68K runs, it releases*
resource blocks immediately after using them.

Why Not Just Use the Debugger?

After using ZoneRanger, you may be wondering if it is really necessary
to use a memory-watching tool like ZoneRanger when you're already
familiar with source-level debugging. After all, a debugger is easy to
use and it too displays the contents of memory. Let's again refer to the
PictMemBad68K application for the answer.

If I wasn't using ZoneRanger and I compiled and ran the
PictMemBad68K program, I would turn to MW Debug when I noticed

that the program wasn't displaying the pictures properly. Making the assumption that perhaps the pictures were not getting loaded into memory, I'd guess that the problem lies in the DrawResourcePicture() routine. In that function, I'd set a breakpoint at the call to GetPicture() and then start watching what happens as the program executes.

The first few times through DrawResourcePicture() I wouldn't notice any problems. Eventually, however, I'd step past GetPicture() and notice that the PicHandle variable thePicture was nil, as shown in Figure 11.43. I'd look at numPICTs and see that it had a value of 7, meaning GetPicture() had attempted to load PICT 134 (127 + 7) but failed to do so. Could it be that I forgot to add PICT 134 to the resource file? Or, if I did add it, is the PICT resource somehow corrupt? Neither of these possibilities would of course be true. A check of the resource file would eliminate the first potential problem, but determining if one or more of the PICT resources was corrupt might be more difficult.

The investigation continues. What happens after the eighth, ninth, and tenth mouse clicks, when each of these pictures fails to be drawn? The program cycles back to the first picture. If it does occur to me that perhaps there is a memory problem, those thoughts might be dashed when I see that the eleventh mouse click does in fact show that thePicture is no longer nil—the first picture is again loaded and displayed in the window.

What did ZoneRanger show that the debugger didn't? ZoneRanger provided a quick, graphical look at the entire heap of PictMemBad68K—not just the values of a few variables. And, because variables reside on the stack, not in the heap, the debugger didn't give the same kind of view of memory as the heap watcher. When watching the PictMemBad68K heap with ZoneRanger, you could easily see that the heap was rapidly filling up, something that the debugger didn't report. And when that eleventh mouse click took place, you already knew from the ZoneRanger 2D Graphical window that PICT 128 had never been released from memory. So even though PictMemBad68K didn't have enough free memory to load another PICT, the call to DrawPicture() still worked.

Like any tool, ZoneRanger isn't to be used for all jobs. But it is helpful for a variety of tasks, such as:

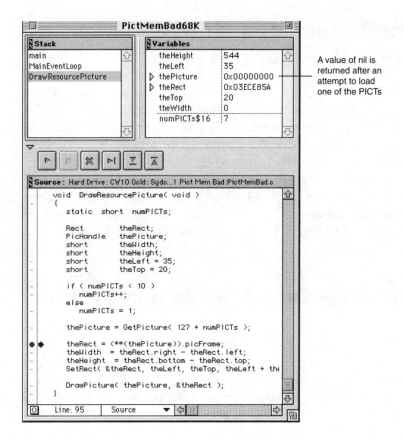

*Figure 11.43 The Metrowerks debugger reports that
a call to* GetPicture() *has failed.*

- To improve your understanding of how Macintosh memory is organized.
- To get a complete, graphical view of what's going on in the heap.
- To help, in conjunction with a debugger, track down memory-related bugs.
- To help determine how large a partition should be devoted to your program.

ZoneRanger and Native PowerPC Programs

Whether you're using a 68K-based Macintosh or a Power Macintosh, if you run a 68K application and ZoneRanger, you'll see results like those shown in the previous sections. If you own a Power Mac, and if you examine a native PowerPC application, however, ZoneRanger will reveal that the contents of the application heap are a little different. When a native PowerPC application is launched, it is given its own application partition in RAM, just as a 68K application is. If you examine this native PowerPC process with ZoneRanger, though, you will notice some differences between the contents of its heap zone and that of a 68K program.

Native PowerPC Applications and Memory

Like a 68K program, a native program is loaded into an application partition that has a stack and a heap. Unlike a 68K program, a native application doesn't use an A5 World; that's shown in Figure 11.44. Information that is held in the A5 World of a 68K application has been either moved or eliminated for native programs. Native application global variables, for example, are all held in a single nonrelocatable block in the application heap.

NOTE The following discussion pertains to applications running on a Power Mac with virtual memory turned off. If you'd like to use ZoneRanger to examine any of your native PowerPC applications, first open the Memory Control Panel from the Apple menu. Click the **Off** radio button in the Virtual Memory section of the Control Panel, as shown in Figure 11.45. Then close the Control Panel and restart your Macintosh.

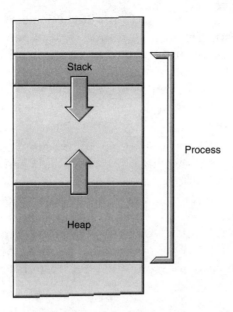

Figure 11.44   *Native applications don't have an A5 World.*

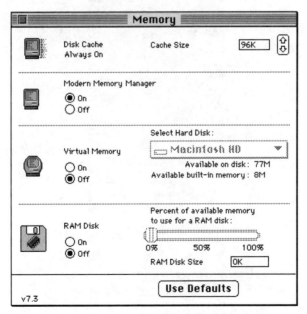

Figure 11.45   *The Memory Control Panel allows you to turn virtual memory on or off.*

As you saw in Chapter 5, a 68K application has its executable code stored in CODE resources in its resource fork. When a 68K application launches, the CODE resources marked as preloaded will be loaded immediately into the application heap. As the program executes, other CODE resources will be loaded as needed (and possibly unloaded when unneeded). As the application needs other types of resources (WIND, MBAR, etc.), they will be loaded into the heap.

A native PowerPC application has its executable code stored in the application's data fork—not in CODE resources. When a native PowerPC application launches, all of its executable code is loaded into one block of nonrelocatable memory in the application's heap—not into several relocatable blocks as it is for a 68K program. Like a 68K application, a native PowerPC application loads and uses all other non-CODE resources as needed. Figure 11.46 provides a look at the heap of a PowerPC application that has its executable code and a few resources loaded.

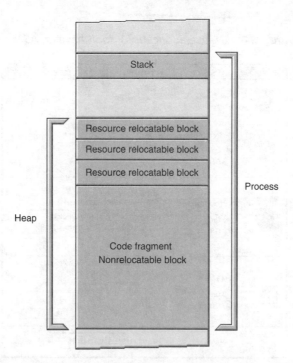

Figure 11.46 *A native application running on a Power Mac keeps its executable code in a nonrelocatable block in the heap.*

I used ZoneRanger to monitor a native application to verify that an application that runs native on a Power Mac does in fact load all its executable code at the low end of its heap at startup. The application I chose to examine was the CodeWarrior IDE itself. With CodeWarrior running, I launched ZoneRanger, made sure the **Open 2D Graphical Display** checkbox was checked, and then double-clicked on the **CodeWarrior IDE 1.7** name in the process list of the ZoneRanger Heap Zones window. When I did that, I saw the 2D Graphical window pictured in Figure 11.47.

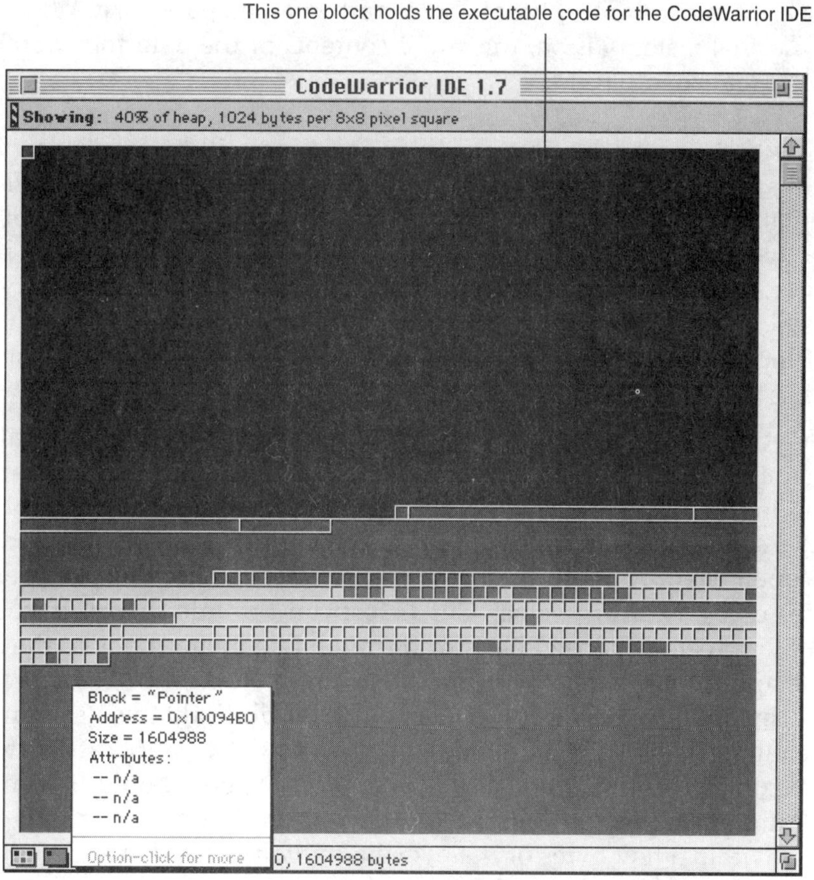

This one block holds the executable code for the CodeWarrior IDE

Figure 11.47 *When a native application runs on a Power Mac, ZoneRanger graphically illustrates that the program's code is stored in a single, nonrelocatable block.*

NOTE Metrowerks distributes the CodeWarrior IDE as a fat application so that you're guaranteed that the IDE will run on your Mac, regardless of whether you're using a 68K-based Mac or a Power Mac. I knew that, so I chose it as the program to monitor. This test will, however, work on any application that is either a fat application or a PowerPC-only program.

 NOTE To see similar results, make sure to turn virtual memory off in the Memory Control Panel and restart your computer first. When virtual memory is on, the entire contents of the data fork won't be loaded into RAM.

I know that one of the first blocks in the zone will be a *nonrelocatable* block (a block referenced by a pointer). Because this block holds *all* the executable code of the application, it may be quite large. Clicking on the block will tell you its size and confirm that it is a block accessed by a pointer, rather than a handle. In Figure 11.47, I've selected the very large block that appears right near the start of the zone and brought up the **Block Information** pop-up menu for it. That menu shows that the block is well over 1 MB in size.

If you're running this test using a different PowerPC application and you'd like further proof that the large, nonrelocatable block you've found in the heap zone is indeed the program's code, make note of the block's size and then quit the application. Launch your resource editor and open the application that you just tested with ZoneRanger. If you're using ResEdit, select **Get Info** from the File menu. If you're using Resorcerer, choose **File Info** from the File menu. Look at the size of the application's data fork (as shown using ResEdit in Figure 11.48) and compare it to the size of the large pointer block that you saw in the ZoneRanger 2D Graphical window. Because a native application stores its executable code in its data fork, these two values should be similar. In Figure 11.48, you can see that the size of the CodeWarrior IDE data fork is within a few bytes of the over 1.6 million bytes that make up the selected block in Figure 11.47.

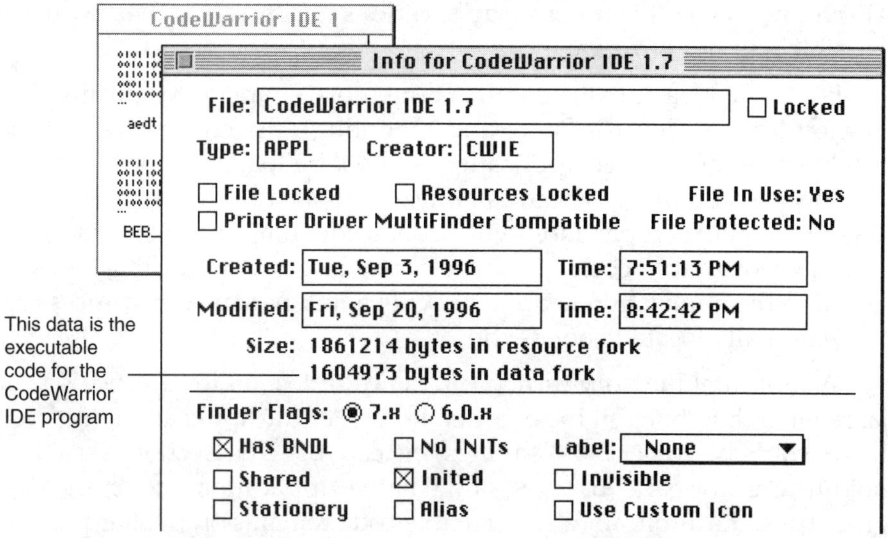

Info for CodeWarrior IDE 1.7

File: CodeWarrior IDE 1.7 ☐ Locked

Type: APPL   Creator: CWIE

☐ File Locked   ☐ Resources Locked   File In Use: Yes
☐ Printer Driver MultiFinder Compatible   File Protected: No

Created: Tue, Sep 3, 1996   Time: 7:51:13 PM

Modified: Fri, Sep 20, 1996   Time: 8:42:42 PM

Size: 1861214 bytes in resource fork
1604973 bytes in data fork

Finder Flags: ◉ 7.x ○ 6.0.x
☒ Has BNDL   ☐ No INITs   Label: None ▼
☐ Shared   ☒ Inited   ☐ Invisible
☐ Stationery   ☐ Alias   ☐ Use Custom Icon

CodeWarrior IDE 1

aedt

BEB

This data is the executable code for the CodeWarrior IDE program

Figure 11.48   *The size of an application's data fork can be*
found by opening the application with either ResEdit or Resorcerer.

If you specify a heap size that is too small to hold the code for your native application, the operating system will automatically enlarge the heap to accommodate the code. Don't rely on this operating system service when establishing a heap size for your native application, though. You should take note of your native application's data fork size and include that value in the heap size. Remember, the application code won't be the only block in the heap; you should allow room for resources and any other data that your application will need.

NOTE

Native PowerPC Applications and Virtual Memory

Macintosh computers equipped with a 68030, 68040, or a PowerPC processor and running a version of system software 7.0 or later, can use *virtual memory*. Virtual memory allows the operating system to use memory other than the Mac's physical RAM. To do this, the operating system views a part of the hard drive memory as an extension of RAM.

This allows a user to run more applications concurrently than would be possible without virtual memory.

If a Power Macintosh has virtual memory enabled (by turning it on in the Memory Control Panel and rebooting), the entire block of executable code of a native application will *not* be loaded into the application heap when the program is launched. Instead, a part of RAM outside the application partition will be set aside to hold some of the application's executable code. A nonrelocatable block will then be established in the application heap to provide a link between the process and this externally located code section.

With virtual memory turned on, the code section for a process is not large enough to hold all the executable code of the application. If it were, there would be no net RAM savings. Instead, the code section is used as a holding area for parts, or *pages*, of the native application's code. As a program runs, the application's executable code remains on the hard drive—in the data fork of the application. When a part of an application's code needs to be executed, it is loaded into the code section of the process. When a different part of the application's code needs to run, the code currently in the code section is swapped with it. Figure 11.49 illustrates how a native application runs on a Power Mac with virtual memory enabled.

The fact that your native application may not need any heap space for your application's code may tempt you to consider decreasing the size of your application's heap; don't do it. While many users of your PowerPC program may have virtual memory enabled, you can't make the assumption that all users will. You'll want to estimate your application's heap size with virtual memory turned off.

While the use of virtual memory is transparent to the end user (except for a slowdown in program execution in some cases), it will be noticeable to you, the programmer, if you run ZoneRanger. Figure 11.50 shows the 2D Graphical window for the CodeWarrior IDE—this time running on a Power Mac that has virtual memory turned on. If you compare Figure 11.50 with Figure 11.47, you'll see that the large nonrelocatable block found in Figure 11.47 is not present in Figure 11.50. In Figure 11.50, the size of the largest block of memory is far smaller than the 1.6 MB of the CodeWarrior IDE data fork. That's because with virtual memory on, the CodeWarrior IDE application code is now located outside the application's heap zone.

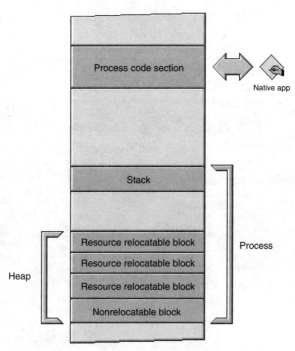

Figure 11.49   *A native application running on a Power Mac*
with virtual memory turned on will have its executable code stored
in RAM outside of the heap, and in the application itself.

Because virtual memory is implemented in a way that makes its details
transparent to the user, you won't have to consider any special virtual
memory programming concerns when writing a native application.
Your application will run whether or not virtual memory is enabled.
Still, it's a good idea to be familiar with how virtual memory works, if
for no other reason than to avoid the confusion of assuming code is
missing from the heap when you examine your application with
ZoneRanger!

The largest block of non-free memory is much smaller
than the size of the CodeWarrior IDE data fork

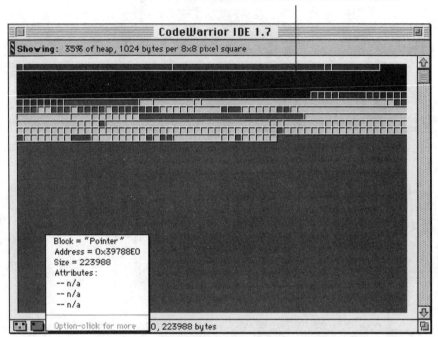

Figure 11.50 *ZoneRanger demonstrates that a native application running on a Power Mac with virtual memory on will not have its code stored in its heap zone.*

Fat Binary Applications and RAM

While a fat binary application holds twice the code of either a 680x0 version or a PowerPC-only version of the same application, a fat app doesn't need a partition size twice as big as either of those versions. That's because no matter which of the two environments the fat app runs in (680x0 or PowerPC), only one of the two code versions (resource fork or data fork) will execute at any one time.

When a fat application is launched on a Power Mac that has virtual memory turned off, all the application's executable code will be loaded into memory. You saw that happen when I monitored the CodeWarrior IDE from ZoneRanger. For that reason, you'll want to determine the application's heap size based on the PowerPC version of the code. For a fat application, there's one additional consideration. Any CODE resources that are marked as preload and locked will be loaded into the heap and remain there, even though the application will use instead the native code from the application's data fork.

In Figure 11.51, you can see that a fat binary named VMtestFat was launched on a Power Macintosh. ZoneRanger shows that the 68K CODE 1 resource has been loaded just before the PowerPC data fork code. This figure shows the heap with virtual memory turned off. Figure 11.52 shows the same application in a Power Mac's memory, this time with virtual memory enabled. For VMtestFat, it would be wise to add the byte size of the CODE 1 resource to the heap size of the VMtestFat application.

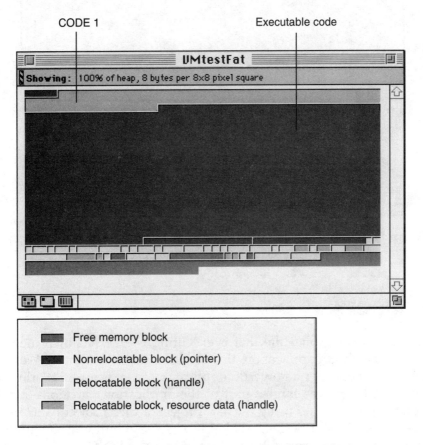

Figure 11.51 *A fat application running on a Power Mac with virtual memory turned off will have* CODE 1 *in its application heap.*

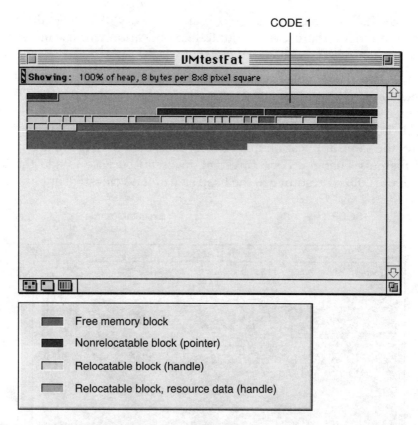

Figure 11.52   A fat application running on a Power Mac with virtual memory enabled will also have CODE 1 in its application heap.

Summary

Each Macintosh application that is executing is given its own memory partition. For a 68K application, this partition consists of an A5 World, a stack, and a heap. For a PowerPC application, there is no A5 World. The size of the heap—the largest part of the application partition—can be set by the programmer using the 68K Project or PPC Project panel in the CodeWarrior Project Settings dialog box. After rebuilding the application, the new heap size can be confirmed by selecting **Get Info** from the Finder's File menu.

An application's heap, or heap zone, holds blocks of memory. Each block is nonrelocatable (it can't be moved by the Memory Manager), relocatable (it can be moved), or free (it is available to hold a nonrelocatable or relocatable block). Nonrelocatable blocks are accessed via pointers. Relocatable blocks are accessed using handles. A relocatable block may have (but doesn't have to have) any of the following three attributes: purgeable (it can be removed from memory by the Memory Manager), locked (it cannot be moved or purged), or resource (it holds data obtained from a resource).

ZoneRanger is a software utility that is used as a memory checker. ZoneRanger is used to examine the heap zone of any application that is running on a Mac. ZoneRanger is useful because it provides a numerical and graphical look at how applications use memory.

Chapter 12

Profiler and
Program Timing

As you write a Mac program, you may have concerns about its execution speed—especially if it makes extensive use of graphics. If this is the case, you'll want to devote programming time and effort to optimizing your code, thereby eliminating unneeded code and replacing sluggish routines with faster ones. To handle this fine-tuning, you'll want to rely on more than guesswork. Enter the CodeWarrior Profiler.

By adding a few Profiler function calls to your source code, you tell the Mac to keep track of processor timing information as your program executes. The Profiler monitors the amount of time spent in each function and saves this data to a file. This information is vital to determining which of your application-defined routines are the slowest. After quickly isolating the time-consuming functions, you'll know where to devote your optimization energies. And when you rewrite a function in the hopes of speeding it up, you'll be able to again use the Profiler to verify that your efforts did in fact improve your program's performance.

Using the CodeWarrior Profiler

The CodeWarrior Profiler makes monitoring a program's execution speed simple. In short, you'll add a single library to your existing CodeWarrior project, include a few extra function calls in your source code, and then build an application. After you do that, each time you run your program the timing results will be saved to a file that can be viewed using the CodeWarrior Profiler viewing application.

The CodeWarrior Profiler

The CodeWarrior Profiler consists of a library you add to your CodeWarrior project, a number of Profiler function calls you can add to your own source code, and a viewer application named MW Profiler. The library holds the compiled code for the handful of Profiler functions that you invoke from the source code file that is a part of whatever project you're working on.

The Profiler functions will monitor your program as it runs and will track and save information about the time your program spends performing various tasks. They'll also create a file and save this information in it. When you quit your program, you'll run the CodeWarrior Profiler viewer application to open this file and view the results.

Figure 12.1 shows the Profiler file that is the result of profiling a simple Macintosh program—a program named ProfilerIntro68K, covered later in this chapter. The figure shows the file as viewed from the MW Profiler application. The figure points out information that can be garnished from the profile.

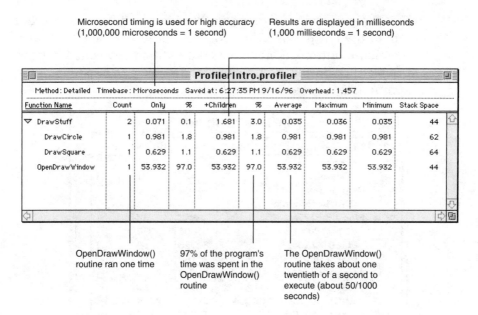

Figure showing callout text:

Microsecond timing is used for high accuracy (1,000,000 microseconds = 1 second)

Results are displayed in milliseconds (1,000 milliseconds = 1 second)

ProfilerIntro.profiler

Method : Detailed   Timebase : Microseconds   Saved at : 6 :27 :35 PM 9/16/96   Overhead : 1.457

Function Name	Count	Only	%	+Children	%	Average	Maximum	Minimum	Stack Space
▽ DrawStuff	2	0.071	0.1	1.681	3.0	0.035	0.036	0.035	44
DrawCircle	1	0.981	1.8	0.981	1.8	0.981	0.981	0.981	62
DrawSquare	1	0.629	1.1	0.629	1.1	0.629	0.629	0.629	64
OpenDrawWindow	1	53.932	97.0	53.932	97.0	53.932	53.932	53.932	44

OpenDrawWindow() routine ran one time

97% of the program's time was spent in the OpenDrawWindow() routine

The OpenDrawWindow() routine takes about one twentieth of a second to execute (about 50/1000 seconds)

Figure 12.1   *Some of the information that can be found in a Profiler output file.*

Adding Profiling to a Project

As mentioned, the Profiler isn't just an application; it's also code stored in a several libraries—only one of which you'll need to add to your project. When you link this library of code with the rest of a project's code, your program will be able to use the Profiler functions that monitor processing time. That means you'll be able to determine how much time a program spends in each of your own application-defined functions. In Figure 12.2, you can see that a 68K version of the Profiler library has been added to the first example project found in this book—the Chapter 2 example **MyFirstMacApp.μ**. Since that project was created from the Basic Toolbox 68 project stationery, one of the 68k Profiler libraries was added to the project.

NOTE

Recall that project groups exist for organizational purposes only. There is no right or wrong group to add the profiler library to. In fact, being the organized programmer that you are, you might want to place the library in its own new group. After adding the Profiler library to a project, you can do that by clicking on the library name and then dragging the file name beneath the bottom of the last group. When you then drop the file (by releasing the mouse button), a brand new group titled **Segment 5** appears. Double-click on this group name and rename it something more appropriate, such as **Profiler Library**.

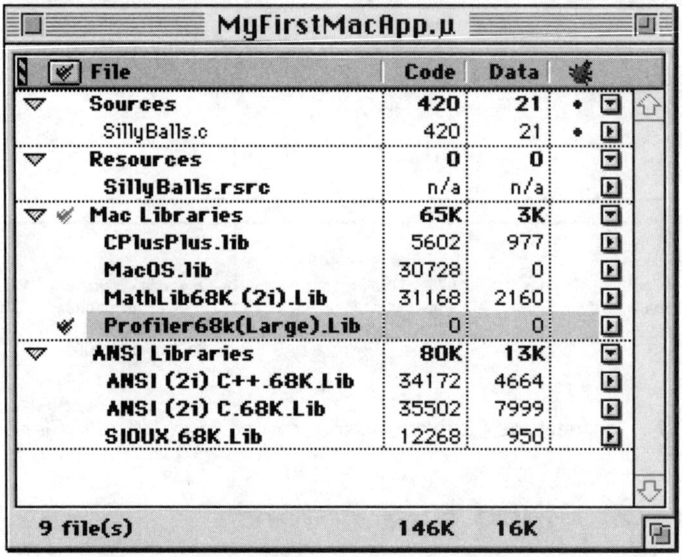

File	Code	Data	
▽ **Sources**	**420**	**21**	
SillyBalls.c	420	21	
▽ **Resources**	**0**	**0**	
SillyBalls.rsrc	n/a	n/a	
▽ ✔ **Mac Libraries**	**65K**	**3K**	
CPlusPlus.lib	5602	977	
MacOS.lib	30728	0	
MathLib68K (2i).Lib	31168	2160	
✔ Profiler68k(Large).Lib	0	0	
▽ **ANSI Libraries**	**80K**	**13K**	
ANSI (2i) C++.68K.Lib	34172	4664	
ANSI (2i) C.68K.Lib	35502	7999	
SIOUX.68K.Lib	12268	950	
9 file(s)	146K	16K	

MyFirstMacApp.µ

*Figure 12.2 To add profiling capabilities to a
68K project, add one of the Profiler68k libraries to it.*

You add a Profiler library to a project as you would any other library:

1. Click on a group name in the project window.

2. Select **Add Files** from the Project menu.

3. Move to the folder that holds the file to add.

4. Click on the file name and then click the **Add** button.

5. Click the **Done** button.

SELECTING A PROFILER LIBRARY FOR A 68K PROJECT

The Profiler libraries are located in three separate folders in the **Libraries** folder in the MacOS Support folders. That folder is in turn found in the **Metrowerks CodeWarrior** folder. For 68K projects the libraries are in a folder titled **Profiler 68K**. Figure 12.3 shows the path to traverse to reach the Profiler libraries used in 68K projects.

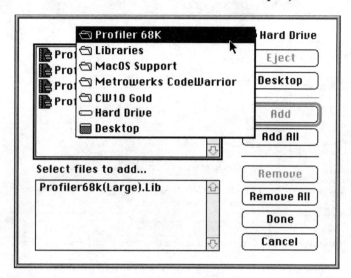

Figure 12.3   *The path to the Profiler libraries used in 68K projects.*

Figure 12.3 shows that the Profiler library named **Profiler68k(Large).Lib** appears in the bottom list of the Add Files dialog box, meaning that I've selected it to be added to the current project—a click on the **Done** button will do that.

For 68K projects, Profiler offers five different libraries. In almost all cases you'll use the **Profiler68k(Large).Lib** library. If you've created your project from the Basic Toolbox 68k project stationery and you're using the processor settings supplied by CodeWarrior (which is most likely the case), then this is the Profiler library to add. If you'd like to ensure that you're using the proper library, select **Project Settings** from the Edit menu and then bring up the 68K Processor panel, as shown in Figure 12.4. If the Code Model pop-up menu is displaying the Smart code model, then the **Profiler68k(Large).Lib** is the library to use.

The *Profiler Manual* electronic documentation that is a part of the full-featured editions of CodeWarrior describes the uses for the other Profiler libraries.

N O T E

Use the Profiler68k(Large).Lib library for a
project that uses the Smart code model

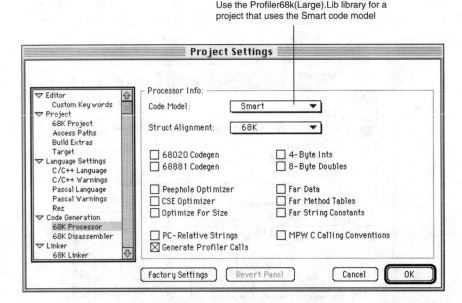

*Figure 12.4   Confirming that the **Profiler68k(Large).Lib**
is the Profiler library to add to a 68K project.*

SELECTING A PROFILER LIBRARY FOR A POWERPC PROJECT

For PowerPC projects, your choice of Profiler libraries is straightforward—always use the **ProfilerPPC.Lib** library located in the **Profiler PPC** folder. That folder is in the same folder as the **Profiler 68K** folder—the folder named **Libraries**. Figure 12.3 shows the path to the **Libraries** folder.

GENERATING PROFILER CALLS

The CodeWarrior IDE includes an easy means to turn on and off the generation of Profiler calls. When you're testing your code, you'll turn the generation of Profiler calls on so that your program calls the Profiler library routines that time your program and write the results to an output file. When you're satisfied with the results of your testing and are ready to build a final application, you can easily remove the Profiler calls and recompile your code one last time.

After adding a Profiler library to a project, you'll need to make sure the CodeWarrior option for generating Profiler calls is turned on. If you're working with a 68K project, choose **Project Settings** from the Edit menu and click on the **68K Processor** panel in the Code Generation group in the list in the Project Settings dialog box. Then check the **Generate Profiler Calls** checkbox if it isn't already checked. Figure 12.5 illustrates.

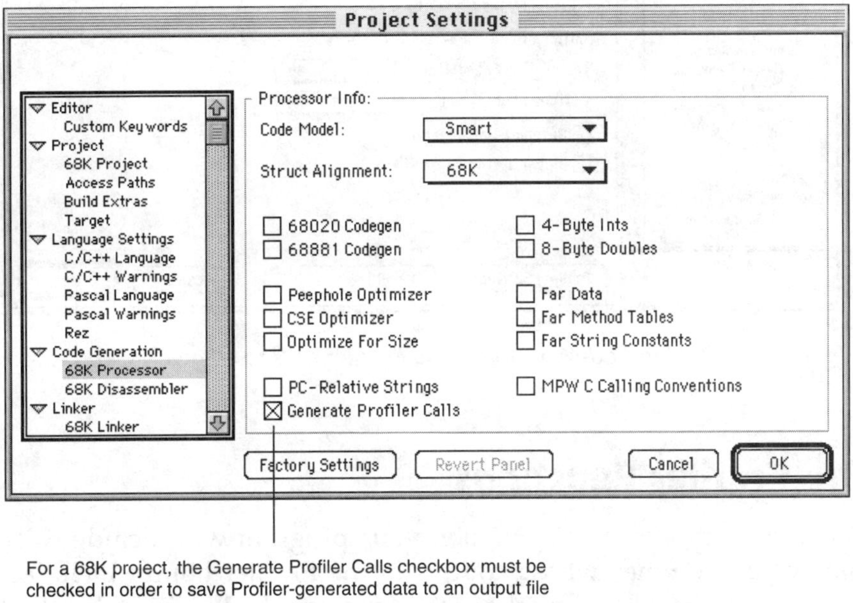

For a 68K project, the Generate Profiler Calls checkbox must be checked in order to save Profiler-generated data to an output file

Figure 12.5   Telling CodeWarrior to add Profiler calls to a 68K application.

If you're working instead with a PowerPC project, choose **Project Settings** from the Edit menu and bring up the **PPC Processor** panel by clicking on its name in the Code Generation group in the list in the Project Settings dialog box. Now check the **Emit Profiler Calls** checkbox if it is unchecked, as shown in Figure 12.6.

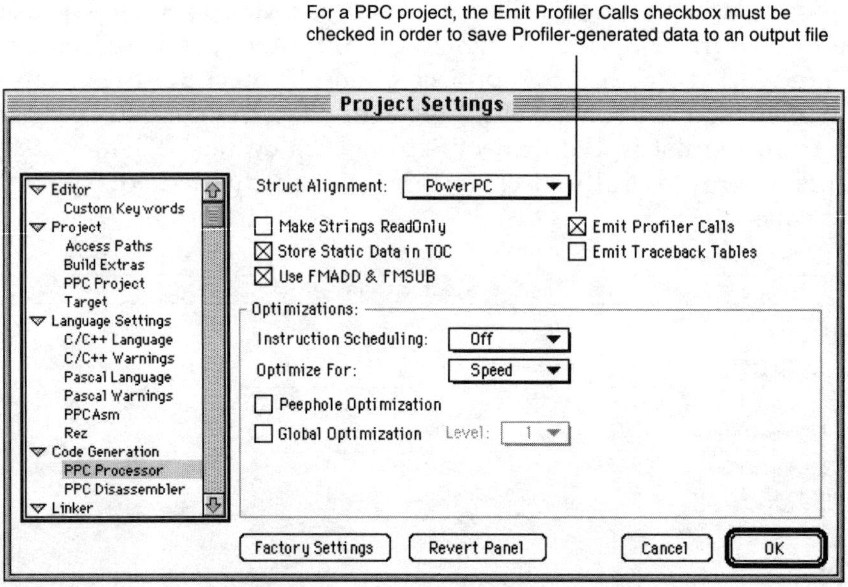

For a PPC project, the Emit Profiler Calls checkbox must be
checked in order to save Profiler-generated data to an output file

Project Settings

Struct Alignment: | PowerPC ▼

- [ ] Make Strings ReadOnly   [X] Emit Profiler Calls
- [X] Store Static Data in TOC   [ ] Emit Traceback Tables
- [X] Use FMADD & FMSUB

Optimizations:

Instruction Scheduling: | Off ▼

Optimize For: | Speed ▼

- [ ] Peephole Optimization
- [ ] Global Optimization   Level: | 1 ▼

Tree list (left panel):

- ▽ Editor
  - Custom Keywords
- ▽ Project
  - Access Paths
  - Build Extras
  - PPC Project
  - Target
- ▽ Language Settings
  - C/C++ Language
  - C/C++ Warnings
  - Pascal Language
  - Pascal Warnings
  - PPCAsm
  - Rez
- ▽ Code Generation
  - PPC Processor
  - PPC Disassembler
- ▽ Linker

[Factory Settings] [Revert Panel]   [Cancel] [OK]

Figure 12.6   Telling CodeWarrior to add Profiler calls to a PowerPC application.

The Profiler Functions

To communicate with the Profiler, your program will include calls to
some of the routines whose code is in the Profiler library included in
your project. Before adding these calls, include the **Profiler.h** header file
at the top your source code listing so that the function definitions are
known to the compiler:

```
#include <Profiler.h>
```

Your source code will typically rely on just three of the Profiler functions:

ProfilerInit()	Prepares the Profiler for use and turns it on
ProfilerDump()	Creates a file and dumps the stored Profiler information to it
ProfilerTerm()	Turns the Profiler off

A few pages ahead you'll look at an example of how to add these calls to a Mac program. For now, here's a quick, abbreviated look at how they'll be used:

```
ProfilerInit( collectDetailed, bestTimeBase, 10, 10 );

// Your program's source code, which will now be
// monitored by the Profiler - can be any number of
// calls to the functions that make up your program

ProfilerDump("\pProfilerIntro.profiler");
ProfilerTerm();
```

The `ProfilerInit()` function has four parameters. The first parameter is a constant that tells the Profiler whether to collect detailed (`collectDetailed`) or summary (`collectSummary`) timing information.

The second parameter to `ProfilerInit()` is a constant that tells the Profiler which timebase to use. A *timebase* is the means the Profiler uses to keep track of time. The four available timebases range from somewhat crude (using the sixtieth second tick count available on all Macintoshes) to extremely accurate (using the built-in timing facilities found only on the PowerPC chip of a Power Mac). Typically you'll use the constant `bestTimeBase` to let the Profiler select the most accurate timebase available on the host machine.

The Profiler allocates memory for its own use—memory it uses to store timing information as your program runs. The third parameter to `ProfilerInit()` is used by the Profiler in its calculations of an appropriate buffer size. This parameter is the number of functions that will be profiled. If the Profiler will be watching your entire program and your program defines 20 functions, this parameter should have a value of "at least" 20. Why "at least" 20? Because the Profiler may count a single function more than one time. If a function is called from within two functions, Profiler views it as two separate functions. In this snippet, Profiler would assume it is to profile four functions: `DrawLargeShape()`, `DrawSmallShape()`, and `RequestShapeSize()`—twice:

```
void DrawLargeShape( void )
{
   RequestShapeSize( LARGE_SHAPE );
```

```
    // draw the large shape
}

void DrawSmallShape( void )
{
    RequestShapeSize( SMALL_SHAPE );

    // draw the small shape
}
```

Multiple calls to a routine, when made within the same function, aren't counted as separate functions by the Profiler. Thus RequestShapeSize() would only be considered one function in this next snippet:

```
void DrawShapes( void )
{
    int  i;

    for ( i = 0; i < 10; i++ )
    {
        RequestShapeSize( UNKNOWN_SHAPE );

        // draw the shape
    }
}
```

The value of this third parameter does not have to be an exact match to the number of functions in your program. If you're profiling a large program, you can easily count the number of functions your program uses by counting the number of function prototypes, then adding a little to that value. Your best bet is to play it safe and use a value you feel is somewhat higher than the actual number of functions. It's better to have the Profiler allocate its buffer too big than too small.

The fourth parameter to ProfilerInit() is also used by the Profiler for allocating its own buffer. This parameter is the greatest number of functions that may be on the stack at any one time. This is the greatest length call chain, or call tree, in your program. For example, if function A calls function B, which in turn calls function C, the call chain is 3. If this is the longest chain in your program, then this final ProfilerInit() parameter should have a value of 3. Like the third parameter to ProfilerInit(), it's better to have this value too large rather than too small.

NOTE

If your values for either the third or fourth parameters to `ProfilerInit()` are too small, don't panic. Profiler will report this fact in the output file it generates. If the output file states that Profiler ran out of memory and lost data, you'll know that you should go back to your source code, boost the value of the third and fourth parameters, and then recompile and rerun your project.

The second Profiler function you'll rely on is `ProfilerDump()`. When you're done profiling, call `ProfilerDump()` to send the collected timing information to a file. The only parameter to `ProfilerDump()` is a Pascal string that establishes the name of the file. While this can be any valid file name, you may want to consider including an extension of **prof** or **profiler** to make this file's identity obvious.

The last of the three commonly used Profiler routines is `ProfilerTerm()`. Before your program quits, call `ProfilerTerm()` to terminate profiling. Don't assume that quitting the program is enough to end profiling. A program that calls `ProfilerInit()` must also call `ProfilerTerm()`. If it doesn't, timers created by the Profiler may continue to run in the background and may eventually crash the user's Mac.

Adding Profiling to a Project

Checking **Generate Profiler Calls** for a 68K project or **Emit Profiler Calls** for a PPC project sets a preprocessor variable named __profile__ to **1**, or on. Unless your code explicitly changes the value of this variable, the Profiler will be considered on for every file in the current project. While you'll most likely be profiling your entire project, if you do want to turn profiling off for a section of code, do so by using the following #pragmas to toggle the value of the __profile__ variable:

```
#pragma profile off    // disables  calls to the profiler

// the code that won't be profiled is here

#pragma profile on    // enables calls to the profiler
```

To begin profiling, call `ProfilerInit()`. Before doing so, verify that the project is set up to be profiled by using the __profile__ variable with the #if preprocessor directive. If profiling is enabled, call ProfilerInit(). Then check to see if the call was successful by comparing the function's return value to the Apple-defined constant noErr. If there was an error, you'll want to exit the program or post an alert. If there was no error, it's on to the code to profile:

```
OSErr   theErr;

#if __profile__
   theErr = ProfilerInit( collectDetailed, bestTimeBase, 10, 10 );
   if ( theErr != noErr )
     ExitToShell();
#endif

// your function calls here
```

The __profile__ preprocessor variable begins with *two* under-scores and ends with two underscores.

NOTE

When profiling is complete, again use the __profile__ variable in a check to ensure that profiling was turned on for this code. If it was, call ProfilerDump() and ProfilerTerm(). Here's how calls to the three Profiler routines you'll be using should look:

```
OSErr   theErr;

#if __profile__
   theErr = ProfilerInit( collectDetailed, bestTimeBase, 10, 10 );
   if ( theErr != noErr )
     ExitToShell();
#endif

// code to monitor

#if __profile__
   ProfilerDump("\pProfilerIntro.profiler");
   ProfilerTerm();
#endif
```

A Profiler Example

With the preliminaries out of the way, it's on to an example. The ProfilerIntro68K program found on the included CD is a simple application that opens a window and then draws a rectangle and circle in that window. Clicking the mouse button ends the program. The result of running ProfilerIntro68K is shown in Figure 12.7. The **ProfilerIntro68K.µ** project—with the **Profiler68k(Large).Lib** library—is shown in Figure 12.8.

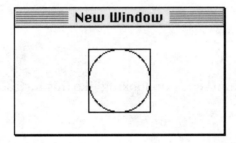

Figure 12.7   *Result of running the ProfilerIntro68K program.*

🖉	☑	File	Code	Data	🐞	
▽	🖋	**Sources**	**0**	**0**	•	▼
	🖋	ProfilerIntro.c	0	0	•	▶
▽	🖋	**Resources**	**0**	**0**		▼
	🖋	**ProfilerIntro.rsrc**	n/a	n/a		▶
▽	🖋	**Mac Libraries**	**0**	**0**		▼
	🖋	CPlusPlus.lib	0	0		▶
	🖋	MacOS.lib	0	0		▶
	🖋	MathLib68K (2i).Lib	0	0		▶
	🖋	Profiler68k(Large).Lib	0	0		▶
▽	🖋	**ANSI Libraries**	**0**	**0**		▼
	🖋	ANSI (2i) C++.68K.Lib	0	0		▶
	🖋	ANSI (2i) C.68K.Lib	0	0		▶
	🖋	SIOUX.68K.Lib	0	0		▶
9 file(s)			**0**	**0**		

Figure 12.8   *The ProfilerIntro68K project.*

The ProfilerIntro68K Source Code

ProfilerIntro68K consists of main() and five other application-defined functions—four of which will be profiled. Here's how the program's main() function would look if *no* profiling code was to be included:

```
void  main( void )
{
    InitializeToolbox();

    OpenDrawWindow();
    DrawStuff( 1 );
    DrawStuff( 2 );

    while ( !Button() )
        ;
}
```

With profiling, main() ends up looking like this instead:

```
void  main( void )
{
    OSErr  theErr;

    InitializeToolbox();

#if __profile__
    theErr = ProfilerInit( collectDetailed, bestTimeBase, 10, 10 );
    if ( theErr != noErr )
        ExitToShell();
#endif

    OpenDrawWindow();
    DrawStuff( 1 );
    DrawStuff( 2 );

#if __profile__
    ProfilerDump("\pProfilerIntro.profiler");
    ProfilerTerm();
#endif

    while ( !Button() )
        ;
}
```

Between the calls to ProfilerInit() and ProfilerTerm() lie two application-defined routines: OpenDrawWindow() and DrawStuff(). DrawStuff() itself invokes two other application-defined routines—

DrawCircle() and DrawSquare()—bringing the total number of profiled functions to four. Figure 12.9 shows the functions that make up ProfilerIntro68K and highlights the four functions that will be profiled.

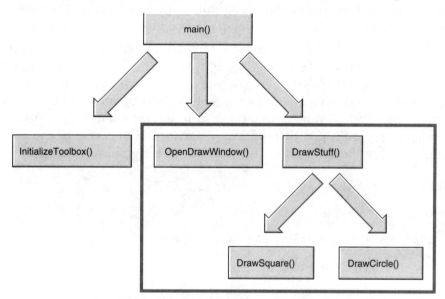

Figure 12.9 *The function hierarchy of ProfilerIntro68K with emphasis on the functions to profile.*

The InitializeToolbox() function includes the standard Toolbox initialization code found in all Mac programs. There's little room for variance in this routine, so there's not much point in profiling it. It's here to stay, without change, so there's little need to see how much time is spent in the function. Remember, you don't have to profile your entire application—only the parts of interest to you.

Looking at Figure 12.9 you can see that four functions will be profiled, and the largest call tree is two: DrawStuff() invoking DrawSquare(), or DrawStuff() invoking DrawCircle(). That means I could pass ProfilerInit() the following parameters:

```
theErr = ProfilerInit( collectDetailed, bestTimeBase, 4, 2 );
```

Instead, I chose to call it as follows:

```
theErr = ProfilerInit( collectDetailed, bestTimeBase, 10, 10 );
```

As stated earlier, it's OK to have the Profiler allocate a little extra memory for its own buffer. In doing so, I also avoid having to keep careful track of how many functions my program calls as I add and modify routines in the ProfilerIntro68K program. If my program grows considerably, I'll reevaluate the values that get passed to ProfilerInit().

Before examining the Profiler output file, take a look at the code for the four functions that will be profiled. OpenDrawWindow() makes a call to the Toolbox routine GetNewWindow() to load the program's only resource—a WIND—into memory. DrawStuff() accepts a short parameter that determines which of two application-defined functions should be invoked. DrawSquare() does just that—draws a square in the center of the program's window. DrawCircle() draws a circle in the window's center.

```
void  OpenDrawWindow( void )
{
   WindowPtr  theWindow;

   theWindow = GetNewWindow( 128, nil, (WindowPtr)-1L );

   SetPort( theWindow );
}

void  DrawStuff( short shape )
{
   if ( shape == 1 )
      DrawCircle();
   else if ( shape == 2 )
      DrawSquare();
}

void  DrawSquare( void )
{
   Rect  theRect;

   SetRect( &theRect, 70, 20, 130, 80 );
   FrameRect( &theRect );
}

void  DrawCircle( void )
{
   Rect  theRect;

   SetRect( &theRect, 70, 20, 130, 80 );
   FrameOval( &theRect );
}
```

The Profiler Output File

After running ProfilerIntro68K, a new file will appear in the folder that holds the ProfilerIntro68K application—a file named **ProfilerIntro.profiler**. This file was created by the call to `ProfilerDump()` in the ProfilerIntro68K program:

```
ProfilerDump("\pProfilerIntro.profiler");
```

To open the file, double-click on its icon. That will launch the MW Profiler application—the program used to display and analyze Profiler files. Double-clicking the **ProfilerIntro.profiler** file will result in a window that looks like the one in Figure 12.10.

Function Name	Count	Only	%	+Children	%	Average	Maximum	Minimum	Stack Space
▷ DrawStuff	2	0.088	0.2	1.682	2.9	0.044	0.054	0.034	44
OpenDrawWindow	1	55.627	97.1	55.627	97.1	55.627	55.627	55.627	44

Method: Detailed Timebase: Microseconds Saved at: 1:22:47 AM 9/18/96 Overhead: 1.444

ProfilerIntro.profiler

Figure 12.10 *The Profiler file generated by the ProfilerIntro 68K program, as opened with the MW Profiler application.*

If you run the ProfilerIntro68K program and then open the resulting Profiler file, you'll notice that the values in your file don't match the values shown here. Values vary depending on factors such as the speed of your machine and whether virtual memory is turned on.

You can vary the width of any column in the Profiler window by clicking on one of the column's vertical lines and dragging the mouse.

ProfilerIntro68K consists of four application-defined routines that get profiled (`InitializeToolbox()` being the fifth routine, and the one function not profiled). Yet the Profiler window lists only two of the functions—DrawStuff() and OpenDrawWindow(). From the Profiler's point of view, these are first-level, or level 1 functions—the functions that appear directly between the calls to ProfilerInit() and ProfilerDump():

```
// ProfilerInit() called here

    OpenDrawWindow();
    DrawStuff( 1 );
    DrawStuff( 2 );

// ProfilerDump() called here
```

When you open a Profiler file that holds detailed information (created using collectDetailed as the first parameter in the program's call to ProfilerInit()), the function hierarchy will be preserved. While only the names of the first-level functions will be displayed upon opening the file, you'll be able to see information about the functions that these first-level routines invoke. Back in Figure 12.10 you can see that DrawStuff(), which calls two other application-defined functions, has a small triangle, or arrow, icon to the left of its name. Clicking on this icon displays the names of each application-defined function that DrawStuff() invokes, as shown in Figure 12.11.

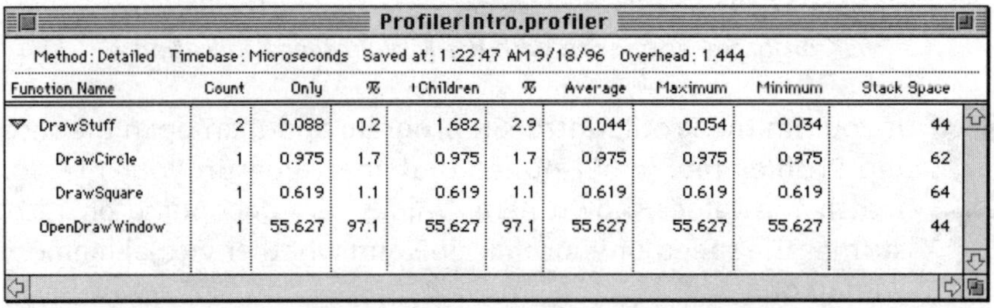

Function Name	Count	Only	%	Children	%	Average	Maximum	Minimum	Stack Space
▽ DrawStuff	2	0.088	0.2	1.682	2.9	0.044	0.054	0.034	44
DrawCircle	1	0.975	1.7	0.975	1.7	0.975	0.975	0.975	62
DrawSquare	1	0.619	1.1	0.619	1.1	0.619	0.619	0.619	64
OpenDrawWindow	1	55.627	97.1	55.627	97.1	55.627	55.627	55.627	44

ProfilerIntro.profiler

Method: Detailed Timebase: Microseconds Saved at: 1:22:47 AM 9/18/96 Overhead: 1.444

Figure 12.11 Clicking on a triangle by a function's name results in a display of that function's subordinate routines.

Examining the Profiler Output File

After the function name column, a Profiler file has nine other columns. The first, *Count*, gives the number of times each function was invoked during the execution of the program.

The next column, *Only*, tells the amount of time spent in each function. The word *only* is used to denote that this value includes only the time spent in the one function listed in each row; it doesn't include any time spent in application-defined routines invoked by the function. To find out how much time was spent in a first-level function and all its children, or subordinate, functions, look to the +*Children* column. In Figure 12.12, you can see that when the times spent in each of the two children functions of DrawStuff() (0.975 and 0.619 milliseconds) are added to the time spent in DrawStuff() itself (0.088 milliseconds), the total (1.682) is the same as the value listed in the +*Children* column for the DrawStuff() row.

Time spent *only* in the function named in each row—does *not* include time spent in subordinate functions

Time spent in the function named in this row, plus the time spent in this function's subordinate, or children, functions

ProfilerIntro.profiler									
Method: Detailed Timebase: Microseconds Saved at: 1:22:47 AM 9/18/96 Overhead: 1.444									
Function Name	Count	Only	%	+Children	%	Average	Maximum	Minimum	Stack Space
▽ DrawStuff	2	0.088	0.2	1.682	2.9	0.044	0.054	0.034	44
DrawCircle	1	0.975	1.7	0.975	1.7	0.975	0.975	0.975	62
DrawSquare	1	0.619	1.1	0.619	1.1	0.619	0.619	0.619	64
OpenDrawWindow	1	55.627	97.1	55.627	97.1	55.627	55.627	55.627	44

Figure 12.12   *The sum of the times for a function and the routines it invokes can be found in the function's +Children column.*

Because the same routine can be called from more than one other function, a function can be a child of more than one first-level function. For example, if DrawCircle() was also called from OpenDrawWindow(), it would be considered a child of both DrawStuff() and OpenDrawWindow(). It would also appear indented, in its own row, under each of those first-level functions.

The two percentage columns in the Profiler window report information in the same manner as the *Only* and +*Children* columns. The first percent column gives the percent of the time a program spends in the one function listed in a row. The second percent column—the one after the +*Children* column—gives the percent of the time a program spends in a function and all the function's children. In Figure 12.13, you can see that the DrawStuff() function, less the calls to DrawCircle() and DrawSquare(), account for just 0.2% of the program's time. When the times spent in DrawCircle() and DrawSquare() (1.7% and 1.1%) are added to this value, the result is the time spent in DrawStuff() and its children (2.9%).

Like the Only column, the % column refers to only the function named in each row—not to children functions

The percentage of time spent in the function named in a row, *plus* the percentage of time spent in that function's children, appears in this column

				ProfilerIntro.profiler					
Method: Detailed	Timebase: Microseconds	Saved at: 1:22:47 AM	9/18/96	Overhead: 1.444					
Function Name	Count	Only	%	+Children	%	Average	Maximum	Minimum	Stack Space
▽ DrawStuff	2	0.088	0.2	1.682	2.9	0.044	0.054	0.034	44
DrawCircle	1	0.975	1.7	0.975	1.7	0.975	0.975	0.975	62
DrawSquare	1	0.619	1.1	0.619	1.1	0.619	0.619	0.619	64
OpenDrawWindow	1	55.627	97.1	55.627	97.1	55.627	55.627	55.627	44

Figure 12.13 *The sum of the percentages for a function and the routines it invokes can be found in the function's second % column.*

NOTE The Profiler output file makes it clear that the vast majority of the ProfilerIntro68K program's time is spent in the one execution of the OpenDrawWindow() function. More on this later. ...

The next three columns in the Profiler window display the average, maximum, and minimum times spent in each function. If a function is executed only a single time, all three of these values will be the same for that one function.

The last column indicates the stack space—the largest size of the stack when the routine is called. This value is listed in bytes.

A Further Look at the Profiler Output File

You can change the way information is displayed in a Profiler window by selecting menu items from the MW Profiler View menu. If your program used the `collectDetailed` parameter in its call to `ProfilerInit()`, the resulting Profiler file will open with the **Detailed** menu item checked in the View menu. This item displays the application-defined functions with their hierarchy preserved. If you'd rather see all of your program's functions listed without regard for their function relationships, select **Summary** from the View menu. For the ProfilerIntro68K Profile file, the result would be as shown in Figure 12.14.

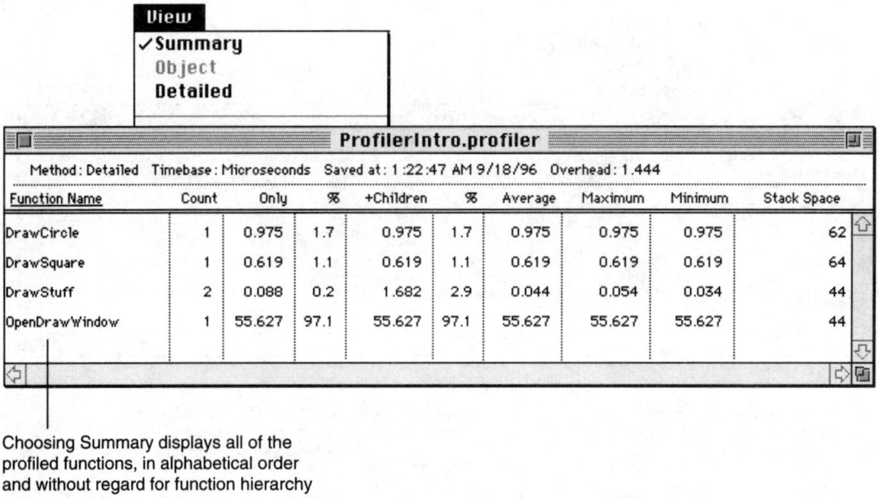

View								
✓Summary								
Object								
Detailed								

ProfilerIntro.profiler

Method: Detailed   Timebase: Microseconds   Saved at: 1:22:47 AM 9/18/96   Overhead: 1.444

Function Name	Count	Only	%	+Children	%	Average	Maximum	Minimum	Stack Space
DrawCircle	1	0.975	1.7	0.975	1.7	0.975	0.975	0.975	62
DrawSquare	1	0.619	1.1	0.619	1.1	0.619	0.619	0.619	64
DrawStuff	2	0.088	0.2	1.682	2.9	0.044	0.054	0.034	44
OpenDrawWindow	1	55.627	97.1	55.627	97.1	55.627	55.627	55.627	44

Choosing Summary displays all of the profiled functions, in alphabetical order and without regard for function hierarchy

Figure 12.14   *A Summary view shows all of a program's application-defined routines, without regard for hierarchy.*

By default, Profiler lists functions in alphabetical order. If you'd rather use a different criterion, choose one of the other **Sort** options in the View menu. When you do, the functions will be rearranged in the window, and the column used as the basis for the sort will be underlined. In Figure 12.15, the **by Maximum** menu item has been selected. This is a good way to sort the functions if you're working with a larger program and are interested in finding its slowest functions.

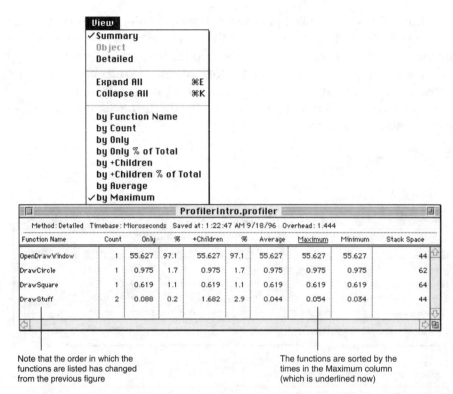

Note that the order in which the functions are listed has changed from the previous figure

The functions are sorted by the times in the Maximum column (which is underlined now)

Figure 12.15   *Functions in a Profiler file can be sorted by any column.*

Speeding Up a Function

The four profiled functions in the ProfilerIntro68K program execute in a total time of about a twentieth of a second—not an ideal candidate for a program to devote time to fine-tuning. But then, ProfilerIntro68K is simply a vehicle to demonstrate how Profiler works, it's not a real-world application. However, since it is a simple program, and one you're familiar with, I'll ignore its impractical nature and continue to use it in the following discussions. The techniques described on the following pages apply equally to your own much larger applications.

Getting a Sampling of a Function's Execution Time

One execution of a function may not provide an accurate representation of how long that function takes to execute. Why? There are several factors that can change the speed at which a function executes, including virtual memory. If you're going to make changes to a function in the hopes of speeding it up, you'll want to get an accurate idea of how long the original version of the function takes to run. Only then will you know if your changes have improved or diminished the function's speed.

Because a function's execution time can vary from one running to the next, you might want to place a call to the function in a loop. Then, compile and run the program. When complete, view the resulting Profiler file and look at the average time the function took to execute. I've done that for the `OpenDrawWindow()` function in the ProfilerIntro68K program. To preserve my original program, I've copied the entire folder that houses the ProfilerIntro68K project and renamed the files. The new program, called WindowResource68K, can be found on this book's CD.

NOTE

If you can stand the suspense, the reasoning behind this new version's name will be evident in just a bit. ...

The source code for WindowResource68K is the same as that of ProfilerIntro68K except for the addition of two lines of code and the changing of one in the `main()` function. The additions include a declaration of an `int` variable and a `for` loop that invokes `OpenDrawWindow()` 20 times. The one change consists of a new Profiler file name in the `ProfilerDump()` function. Here's the new version of `main()`—the additions are shown in underlined type:

```
void  main( void )
{
   int    i;
   OSErr  theErr;

   InitializeToolbox();
```

```
#if __profile__
    theErr = ProfilerInit( collectDetailed, bestTimeBase, 10, 10 );
    if ( theErr != noErr )
        ExitToShell();
#endif

for ( i = 0; i < 20; i++ )
    OpenDrawWindow();

DrawStuff( 1 );
DrawStuff( 2 );

#if __profile__
    ProfilerDump("\pWindowRes.profiler");
    ProfilerTerm();
#endif

while ( !Button() )
    ;
}
```

The third parameter to `ProfilerInit()`—the number of functions called—hasn't changed. My overestimate of 10 is still valid. Though `OpenDrawWindow()` is called 10 times, the Profiler views it as only one function. That's because all 10 calls are made from the same routine—`main()`.

Recall that earlier I found that `OpenDrawWindow()` took about 55 milliseconds, or just over a twentieth of a second, to execute on my Macintosh (the time it takes to run on *your* Mac may differ). After running the WindowResource68K program, I now see that on average, this function takes closer to a twelfth of a second to run. This value of about 80 milliseconds (shown in Figure 12.16) is the number I'll use in comparisons to subsequent versions of the `OpenDrawWindow()` function.

The looping method is a good way to compare an average time of one version of a function to the average time of another version of that same function. That's a good use of the Profiler, and something you'll probably be interested in doing. However, if you aren't interested in which version of a function is quicker, but instead want to know the execution time of a function "as is," you might want to reconsider putting it in a loop. If the function won't appear in a loop in the actual program, then don't place it in a loop during testing. Why? The same code is repeatedly being executed, so it may end up in fast cache memory. Thus the average time would be lower than the time for a single execution of the same function.

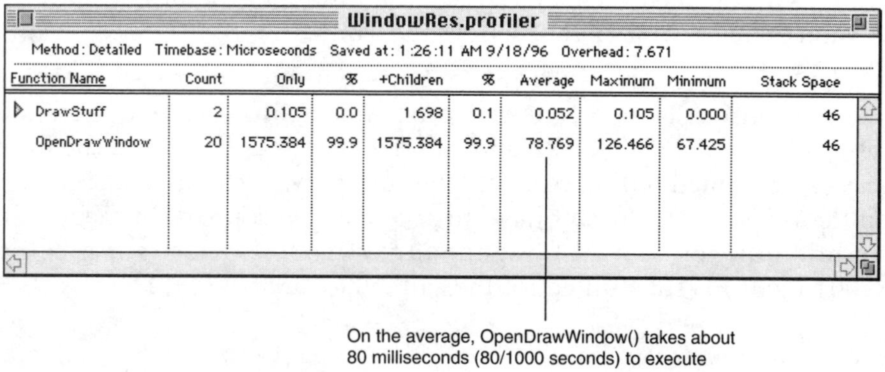

WindowRes.profiler

Method: Detailed Timebase: Microseconds Saved at: 1:26:11 AM 9/18/96 Overhead: 7.671

Function Name	Count	Only	%	+Children	%	Average	Maximum	Minimum	Stack Space
▷ DrawStuff	2	0.105	0.0	1.698	0.1	0.052	0.105	0.000	46
OpenDrawWindow	20	1575.384	99.9	1575.384	99.9	78.769	126.466	67.425	46

On the average, OpenDrawWindow() takes about
80 milliseconds (80/1000 seconds) to execute

Figure 12.16   The Profiler file shows that the OpenDrawWindow()
function takes a quarter of a second to run.

Improving the OpenDrawWindow() Function?

Why the question mark in this section's heading? When you attempt to fine-tune a function, there's no guarantee that your improved version will be just that—improved. But it never hurts to try.

OpenDrawWindow() consists of just three lines of code. Your own functions will of course be larger and will afford you more opportunities (and challenges) for fine-tuning. Still, even this short piece of code, shown below, may be open to improvement.

```
void  OpenDrawWindow( void )
{
   WindowPtr  theWindow;

   theWindow = GetNewWindow( 128, nil, (WindowPtr)-1L );

   SetPort( theWindow );
}
```

In a Macintosh program, there are two ways to open a window. You can use a call to the Toolbox function GetNewWindow() to load window information from a WIND resource into memory, or you can use a call to the Toolbox function NewWindow(), passing in the window information as parameters to the function. ProfilerIntro68K uses GetNewWindow(). WindowResource68K, created to test the timing of the ProfilerIntro68K version of OpenDrawWindow(), does the same.

As written, ProfilerIntro68K gets its window information from a WIND resource. That means the program has to locate a particular resource (WIND 128) on disk and call GetResource() to load the information contained in that resource into memory. A call to NewWindow(), on the other hand, doesn't have to access any resources. In theory, this sounds quicker. Here's how OpenDrawWindow() looks if a call to NewWindow() is substituted for the call to GetNewWindow():

```
void  OpenDrawWindow( void )
{
    WindowPtr    theWindow;
    Rect         theRect;

    SetRect( &theRect, 10, 40, 210, 140 );
    theWindow = NewWindow( nil, &theRect, "\pNew Window", true,
    documentProc, (WindowPtr)-1L, false, nil );

    SetPort( theWindow );
}
```

Does the theory hold up in practice? To see, I've copied the entire folder that holds the WindowResource68K files to create a new set of files for a new CodeWarrior project. Then I made a couple of small changes to the source code file. The source code for this project has the same for loop found in the WindowResource68K source code—the loop that executes OpenDrawWindow() 20 times. The difference is in the OpenDrawWindow() routines. The new program, named WindowCode68K, uses NewWindow().

After compiling and running the WindowCode68K program, it's time to examine the Profiler file. Figure 12.17 shows that this new version of OpenDrawWindow() takes an average of about 40 milliseconds to run—half the time of the original version of the function.

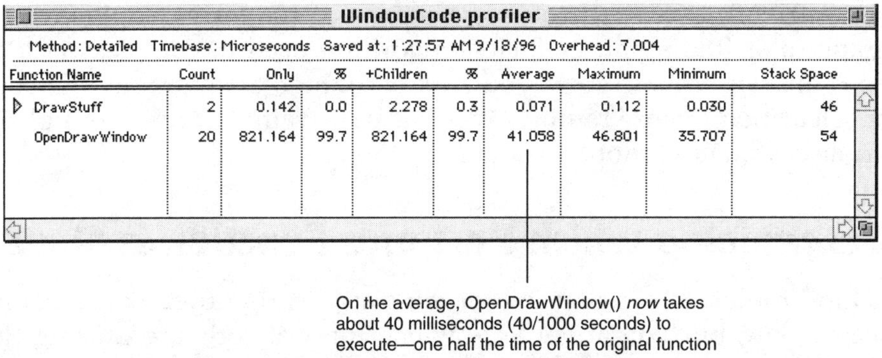

Function Name	Count	Only	%	+Children	%	Average	Maximum	Minimum	Stack Space
▷ DrawStuff	2	0.142	0.0	2.278	0.3	0.071	0.112	0.030	46
OpenDrawWindow	20	821.164	99.7	821.164	99.7	41.058	46.801	35.707	54

WindowCode.profiler

Method: Detailed   Timebase: Microseconds   Saved at: 1:27:57 AM 9/18/96   Overhead: 7.004

On the average, OpenDrawWindow() *now* takes about 40 milliseconds (40/1000 seconds) to execute—one half the time of the original function

Figure 12.17   *After making changes to the* OpenDrawWindow() *function, its execution time is decreased.*

Is a potential savings of less than a twentieth of a second (40 milliseconds from 80 milliseconds) worth the abandonment of my practice of using a resource editor to create easily modifiable windows? Probably not. But then, the true purpose of this exercise wasn't really to dramatically speed up the ProfilerIntro68K program; it was to see the steps to take to speed up a function. Those same steps can be applied to routines that *will* really benefit from time savings. Here are the steps you'll want to follow when using Profiler to help speed up your program:

- Profile the functions in your application.
- Determine the average execution time of a function you feel is slowing down your program.
- Analyze the function to see where improvements might be made.
- Make the change or changes and determine the average execution time of the new version of the function.
- Compare the execution times of the two versions of the function and decide if the time savings justify the changes.

Your program will benefit by even a small savings in a routine, if that routine is called *iteratively* (several times in succession, as in a loop). The cumulative effect of the small savings will be noticeable by the user. Your program can also benefit by reducing the execution time of a routine that is only called once, or infrequently—provided the time savings is nontrivial. Discovering a slow means of rendering sophisticated graphics or finding an inefficient algorithm used in complex calculations are two trouble spots you may encounter. Such graphics-intense or calculation-intense routines keep the user waiting for results and are prime candidates for optimization.

Determining which Part of a Function Is Slow

If the Profiler shows that one of your application-defined functions seems slow, but you aren't sure which lines of code are causing the sluggish performance, move the contents of the one function into two or more new functions. Then call these new routines from the original function. Consider a program that has a function named DrawObjects(). This routine draws two objects in a window. For this hypothetical example the specific code used to perform the drawing isn't important, so I'll show the DrawObjects() routine as follows:

```
void DrawObjects( void )
{
   // code to draw 1st object
   // code to draw 2nd object
}
```

Profiling the DrawObjects() function shows that the routine takes more than 1500 milliseconds to execute. That's longer than a second and a half—a time period that's too long for the quick updating of a window. Figure 12.18 shows that by profiling DrawObjects() I can find the time this routine takes to run, but no details of where the time-consuming code lies is revealed.

To confine my fine-tuning efforts to the slow code, I'll break up the DrawObjects() code into two new functions: DrawObjectOne() and DrawObjectTwo(). Then I'll have DrawObjects() call both these new routines, as shown here:

```
void DrawObjects( void )
{
   DrawObjectOne();
   DrawObjectTwo();
}

void DrawObjectOne( void )
```

```
{
    // code to draw 1st object
}

void DrawObjectTwo( void )
{
    // code to draw 2nd object
}
```

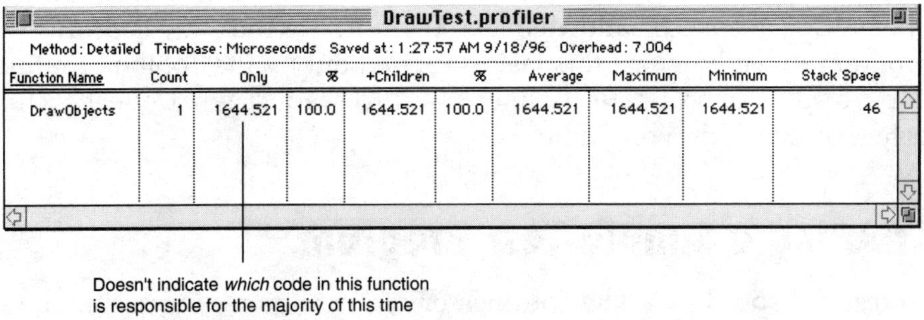

Method: Detailed Timebase: Microseconds Saved at: 1:27:57 AM 9/18/96 Overhead: 7.004 DrawTest.profiler									
Function Name	Count	Only	%	+Children	%	Average	Maximum	Minimum	Stack Space
DrawObjects	1	1644.521	100.0	1644.521	100.0	1644.521	1644.521	1644.521	46

Doesn't indicate *which* code in this function
is responsible for the majority of this time

Figure 12.18 *The Profiler gives the total execution time for a function.*

As far as program execution, the end result will be the same as the original version of `DrawObjects()`. With the new version, however, the Profiler will be able to report the execution time in a more helpful manner. As shown in Figure 12.19, it's the code that draws the first object that takes the most time. This is the code I'll want to expend the greatest effort on improving. After I've sped up `DrawObjectOne()`, I can move the code from `DrawObjectOne()` and `DrawObjectTwo()` back into `DrawObjects()`.

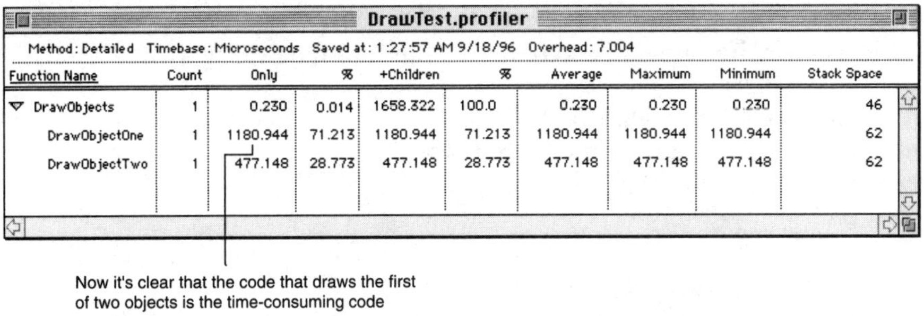

Method: Detailed Timebase: Microseconds Saved at: 1:27:57 AM 9/18/96 Overhead: 7.004 DrawTest.profiler									
Function Name	Count	Only	%	+Children	%	Average	Maximum	Minimum	Stack Space
▽ DrawObjects	1	0.230	0.014	1658.322	100.0	0.230	0.230	0.230	46
DrawObjectOne	1	1180.944	71.213	1180.944	71.213	1180.944	1180.944	1180.944	62
DrawObjectTwo	1	477.148	28.773	477.148	28.773	477.148	477.148	477.148	62

Now it's clear that the code that draws the first
of two objects is the time-consuming code

Figure 12.19 *Dividing the contents of a single function into two separate functions helps determine where the slow code is located.*

Analyzing the Drawing Time of PICTs

The Profiler is a great utility for examining an existing Mac project and determining where speed enhancements can be made. But it's also a good code exploration tool. For example, you can write a short test program that performs one task, and then profile it to see if your way of doing things is efficient. In this section, I'll profile a test program that opens PICT resources and displays them in a window. I'll profile the program to see how fast this task is carried out by the Toolbox routines GetPicture() and DrawPicture() and to see just what effect picture byte size has on drawing time.

Creating a Simple Test Program

To test the speed of a few routines or of a programming technique of yours, you don't need to write a full-blown Macintosh application. Instead, quickly set up a simple project that forgoes the event loop and terminates with the click of a mouse button—a technique a few of this book's example programs (such as EmptyWindow in Chapter 2) have used. You can use the Toolbox routine Button() to check to see if the mouse button is down. If it's not (!), then carry on with the loop (;):

```
while ( !Button() )
    ;
```

If the code you'll be testing uses the mouse button, the preceding strategy won't work—the mouse button click will instead end your test program. In that case you can replace the preceding while loop with a loop that looks for the press of a particular key, such as **q** for **quit**:

```
unsigned char    theKeyMap[16];
Boolean          quitKeyPressed = false;
short            keyNum = 12;

while ( quitKeyPressed == false )
{
   GetKeys( (long *)theKeyMap );
   quitKeyPressed = (theKeyMap[keyNum >> 3] >> (keyNum & 7)) & 1;
}
```

N O T E   Yes, it does look ugly. Briefly, here's what's going on. The Toolbox function GetKeys() fills 16 bytes (128 bits) with information about the current state of the keyboard. Each bit tells whether one particular key is pressed (bit equals 1) or not pressed (bit equals 0). The C language can be used to readily access bytes, but not bits. So a little bit shifting and bit masking need to be done to examine any single bit. The above code is looking to see if the **q** key is pressed. On a Macintosh keyboard, the key number of the **q** key is $0C, or 12. Each pass through the while loop checks the state of the keyboard to see if the **q** key has been pressed. For more information on keyboard key numbering, refer to the *Macintosh Toolbox Essentials* volume from the *Inside Macintosh* series of books.

Next, write the function to be tested and then invoke it. Place the call to it between the calls to ProfilerInit() and ProfilerDump(). Run the program, and then examine the Profiler file to see how fast your code executes.

The PictureResource68K Test Program

You might guess that DrawPicture() will take longer to draw a larger picture to a window than a smaller picture. But how much longer? Will a picture that is twice as large in pixel size take twice as long to draw? What about a picture that is twice as large in byte size? To answer these questions, I've written a short program named PictureResource68K that loads two PICT resources and draws them to a window.

PictureResource68K loads two pictures, PICT resources with IDs of 128 and 129, into memory and draws them to the same window, one on top of the other. Figure 12.20 shows the two PICT resources in the ResEdit. In Figure 12.21, you can see that the PictureResource68K program draws picture 129 (the small Metrowerks logo) over picture 128 (the larger airplane picture).

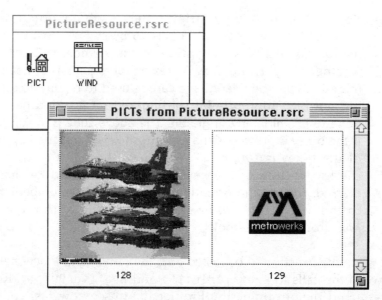

Figure 12.20   *The two PICT resources used by the PictureResource68K project.*

Figure 12.21   *The result of running the PictureResource68K program.*

NOTE If your program works with large `PICT` resources, don't forget to set your application's heap accordingly, as discussed in Chapter 12. The largest PICT resource in the Picture Resource68K program is about 225K, so the 384K heap that CodeWarrior defaults to is large enough.

To profile my code, I've written a single function named `DrawStuff()` and placed it between the three standard Profiler functions. Following is a look at the PictureResource68K program's `main()` routine. Notice that I've kept the program simple by using the `Button()` routine to end the program at the first click of the mouse button.

```
void  main( void )
{
    WindowPtr    theWindow;
    OSErr        theErr;

    InitializeToolbox();

    theWindow = GetNewWindow( 128, nil, (WindowPtr)-1L );

    SetPort( theWindow );

    #if __profile__
        theErr = ProfilerInit( collectDetailed, bestTimeBase, 10, 10 );
        if ( theErr != noErr )
            ExitToShell();
    #endif

    DrawStuff();

    #if __profile__
        ProfilerDump("\pPictRes.profiler");
        ProfilerTerm();
    #endif

    while ( !Button() )
        ;
}
```

`DrawStuff()` calls an application-defined routine named `GetPictureResource()` to load a single picture into memory and to obtain the rectangle that holds the picture's boundary. `GetPictureResource()` accepts a `PICT` ID and a pointer to a rectangle as its two arguments, and it returns a handle to the loaded picture. A second application-defined routine, DrawPicture128(), uses the returned picture handle and rectangle to draw the picture to a window. These steps are repeated for a second picture—one with an ID of 129.

```
void  DrawStuff( void )
{
   PicHandle    thePicture;
   Rect         pictRect;

   thePicture = GetPictureResource( 128, &pictRect );
   DrawPicture128( thePicture, pictRect );

   thePicture = GetPictureResource( 129, &pictRect);
   DrawPicture129( thePicture, pictRect );

   ReleaseResource( (Handle)thePicture );
}
```

Next is a look at GetPictureResource(). I'm not concerned with the four boundaries of the rectangle parameter as the routine is entered. Instead, I'm counting on GetPictureResource() to fill this pictRect variable with the loaded picture's boundaries. Notice that a pointer to a rectangle is passed to the routine rather than a rectangle. That way, the changes made to the rectangle's boundaries will show up back in the calling routine, DrawStuff().

```
PicHandle  GetPictureResource( short pictID, Rect *pictRect )
{
   Rect         theRect;
   PicHandle    thePicture;
   short        theWidth;
   short        theHeight;

   thePicture = GetPicture( pictID );

   theRect = (**(thePicture)).picFrame;
   theWidth  = theRect.right - theRect.left;
   theHeight = theRect.bottom - theRect.top;
   SetRect( pictRect, 0, 0, theWidth, theHeight );

   return ( thePicture );
}
```

After GetPictureResource() returns the picture handle and picture boundary rectangle, a call is made to DrawPicture128() to draw the

picture to the window. After `DrawStuff()` calls
`GetPictureResource()` and `DrawPicture128()` to draw the first picture, it calls `GetPictureResource()` and `DrawPicture129()` to draw
the second picture.

```
void  DrawPicture128( PicHandle thePicture, Rect pictRect )
{
    DrawPicture( thePicture, &pictRect );
}

void  DrawPicture129( PicHandle thePicture, Rect pictRect )
{
    DrawPicture( thePicture, &pictRect );
}
```

Figure 12.22 shows how `DrawStuff()`, `DrawPictureResource()`, and
`DrawPicture128()` work together to draw a picture with resource ID
128.

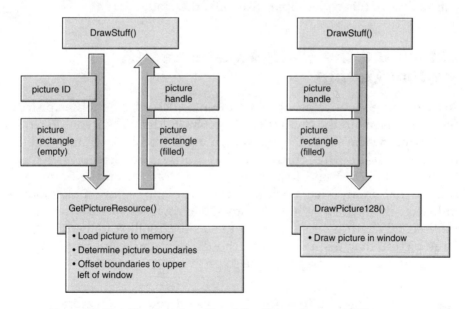

Figure 12.22   *The functionality of the PictureResource68K program.*

The two drawing routines, `DrawPicture128()` and
`DrawPicture129()`, are identical, so I could easily have used a single
function. But that would have defeated the point of the program. I'm

using the Profiler to compare the time it takes to draw two different-sized pictures. When the program completes, I'll be looking at the timing information for the two functions.

Since `DrawPicture128()` consists of nothing more than a call to the Toolbox routine `DrawPicture()`, I could also have omitted the `DrawPicture128()` function altogether and just included the call to `DrawPicture()` in `DrawStuff()`, like this, right?

```
thePicture = GetPictureResource( 128, &pictRect );
DrawPicture( thePicture, &pictRect );
```

Wrong! Sure, the program would work. But since the picture-drawing code would now be buried in the `DrawStuff()` routine, along with other code, the Profiler wouldn't be able to profile how long the drawing of `PICT` 128 took. I've intentionally isolated the picture-drawing code in its own routine so that the Profiler could keep track of the execution time of this code—apart from all other code.

Examining the PictureResource68K Profiler Output

After running PictureResource68K, double-click on the **PictRes.profiler** file that appears in the **PictureResource68K** folder. When you do, you'll see a window similar to the one shown in Figure 12.23. Of most interest to you will be the columns that show the speed at which `DrawPicture128()` and `DrawPicture129()` ran. From the figure, you can see that on my Macintosh the larger airplane picture took about 80 milliseconds to draw, while the small Metrowerks picture took just 4 milliseconds to draw. As guessed, it takes the Toolbox longer to draw a large picture than a small picture, though you might not have suspected the difference in time would be so great.

The "great" difference is relative, of course. While drawing the larger picture takes 20 times longer than drawing the smaller picture, the time it takes to draw the larger picture is still less than a twelfth of a second (80 milliseconds is 80 thousands of a second, or 8 hundredths of a second, or about a twelfth of a second).

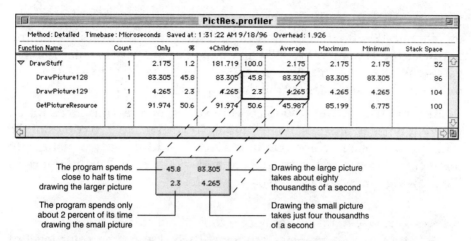

		PictRes.profiler							
Method: Detailed Timebase: Microseconds Saved at: 1:31:22 AM 9/18/96 Overhead: 1.926									
Function Name	Count	Only	%	+Children	%	Average	Maximum	Minimum	Stack Space
▽ DrawStuff	1	2.175	1.2	181.719	100.0	2.175	2.175	2.175	52
DrawPicture128	1	83.305	45.8	83.305	45.8	83.305	83.305	83.305	86
DrawPicture129	1	4.265	2.3	4.265	2.3	4.265	4.265	4.265	104
GetPictureResource	2	91.974	50.6	91.974	50.6	45.987	85.199	6.775	100

The program spends close to half its time drawing the larger picture — 45.8 / 83.305 — Drawing the large picture takes about eighty thousandths of a second

The program spends only about 2 percent of its time drawing the small picture — 2.3 / 4.265 — Drawing the small picture takes just four thousandths of a second

Figure 12.23 *The Profiler clearly shows the speed at which each function runs.*

Also of interest in Figure 12.23 is the timing of the GetPictureResource() function. This function executes twice—one time to load each of the two PICT resources. By looking at the *Maximum* and *Minimum* columns, you can see that it took much longer for GetPictureResource() to load one of the two pictures. While you might have a pretty good idea which picture took longer to load, you'd need to break up the one GetPictureResource() into two separate functions (such as a GetPictureResource128() and a GetPictureResource129() function) to verify your suspicions.

NOTE What would happen if you put a call to GetPictureResource() inside a loop to get an average execution time? The result might surprise you. While the *Maximum* column might show a value such as 85 milliseconds, the *Minimum* column would show a value much smaller, perhaps 1 millisecond or less. That's because of how the GetPicture() Toolbox function works. If the PICT resource GetPicture() is to load is already in memory (as it would be after the first iteration of the loop), GetPicture() doesn't reload it—it just returns the handle to the picture.

To get timing information for two different pictures, just open the PictureResource68K program (*not* the project resource file) with a resource editor and either cut out the original two pictures or renumber them. Then paste in the new PICT resources. Give the new pictures IDs of 128 and 129, then save the program and quit the resource editor. Rerun PictureResource68K. When you look at the new Profiler file that gets generated, the DrawPicture128() and DrawPicture129() routines will show the times for the drawing of these two pictures.

You can use PictureResource68K to study the drawing times for all different types of pictures. For example, you can make two copies of the same picture: one in color, one in grayscale. Add these two pictures to the PictureResource68K resource file and see if there is a difference in the drawing times of color versus grayscale.

One way to make a grayscale copy of a picture is to open the picture using a graphics program. Then change the color level of your monitor from color to gray using the Monitors Control Panel. Next, do a screen dump (**Command-Shift-3**). Open the resulting PICT file with your graphics program and select and copy the area that holds your picture.

Profiler and the Event Loop

All the Profiler examples to this point have been short, simple programs that end when the user clicks the mouse button. This is adequate for the purpose of demonstrating how the Profiler works and for short test programs like the PICT resource timer program PictureResource68K. But your Mac applications will of course be larger and, more importantly, won't end when the user clicks the mouse button. That doesn't present a problem for the Profiler. In fact, profiling an event-driven Mac application is quite simple.

The EventLoop68K Program

On this book's CD you'll find a program named EventLoop68K. The program displays two menus—the Apple and File menus. The Apple menu holds the **About** menu item, as well as all the user's **Apple Menu Item** folder items. The File menu has a single item—**Quit**. When you run EventLoop68K, an empty, draggable window will open. Figure

12.24 shows the program's menus and window. The program watches for update events (events of type updateEvt) and mouse down events (mouseDown events) and responds to each. EventLoop68K is a small, standard event-driven Mac program that takes up a couple of pages of source code.

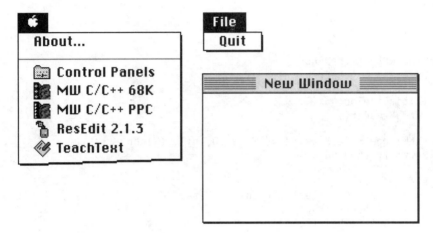

Figure 12.24   *The menus and window of the EventLoop68K program.*

 The intent of this section isn't to discuss in detail the code that makes up a basic Mac program, but rather to find out how the Profiler can be used to gain an understanding of an event-driven program. For that reason the entire listing of EventLoop68K isn't given here. If you're interested, open the **EventLoop.c** source code file on the included CD.

EventLoop68K consists of a main() function and eight other application-defined routines. Their function prototypes are listed as follows:

```
void   InitializeToolbox( void );
void   SetUpMenuBar( void );
void   EventLoop( void );
void   HandleUpdate( void );
void   HandleMouseDown( void );
void   HandleMenuChoice ( long );
void   HandleAppleChoice( short );
void   HandleFileChoice( short );
```

The main() function initializes the Toolbox, sets up the menu bar, opens a window, and then jumps into the main event loop. To profile an event-driven program, you can use the same three Profiler functions that have been used throughout this chapter. Now, just place the call to the event loop routine between them. Here's how EventLoop68K does that:

```
void  main( void )
{
   WindowPtr    theWindow;
   OSErr        theErr;

   InitializeToolbox();
   SetUpMenuBar();

   theWindow = GetNewWindow( WIND_ID, nil, (WindowPtr)-1L );
   SetPort( theWindow );

   #if __profile__
      theErr = ProfilerInit( collectDetailed, bestTimeBase, 10, 10 );
      if ( theErr != noErr )
         ExitToShell();
   #endif

   EventLoop();

   #if __profile__
      ProfilerDump("\pEventLoop.profiler");
      ProfilerTerm();
   #endif
}
```

Function Dependencies and the Profiler

To test the profiling, I ran EventLoop68K and put the program through its paces. I clicked on the window, dragged it, and released the mouse button. I did that a second time. Then I selected the **About** menu item from the Apple menu. Next, I selected the **Scrapbook** from the Apple menu. Finally, I chose **Quit** from the File menu. All of this action was followed by the Profiler and saved to a file named **EventLoop.profiler**. Figure 12.25 shows what that file looks like for my sample running of EventLoop68K.

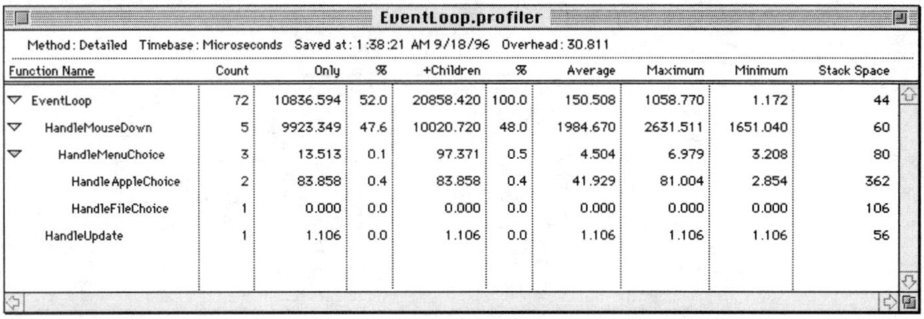

EventLoop.profiler

Method: Detailed Timebase: Microseconds Saved at: 1:38:21 AM 9/18/96 Overhead: 30.811

Function Name	Count	Only	%	+Children	%	Average	Maximum	Minimum	Stack Space
EventLoop	72	10836.594	52.0	20858.420	100.0	150.508	1058.770	1.172	44
HandleMouseDown	5	9923.349	47.6	10020.720	48.0	1984.670	2631.511	1651.040	60
HandleMenuChoice	3	13.513	0.1	97.371	0.5	4.504	6.979	3.208	80
HandleAppleChoice	2	83.858	0.4	83.858	0.4	41.929	81.004	2.854	362
HandleFileChoice	1	0.000	0.0	0.000	0.0	0.000	0.000	0.000	106
HandleUpdate	1	1.106	0.0	1.106	0.0	1.106	1.106	1.106	56

Figure 12.25 *The Profiler output file for the EventLoop68K program.*

Before looking at the values in the columns of the Profiler window, take notice of the levels at which the EventLoop68K application-defined functions are listed under *Function Name*. At the first level is the `EventLoop()` function. At the second level are `HandleMouseDown()` and `HandleUpdate()`. The third level lists `HandleMenuChoice()`, while the fourth level shows `HandleAppleChoice()` and `HandleFileChoice()`. Figure 12.26 emphasizes how the Profiler displays a program's functional hierarchy. Figure 12.27 gives you another way of viewing the hierarchy.

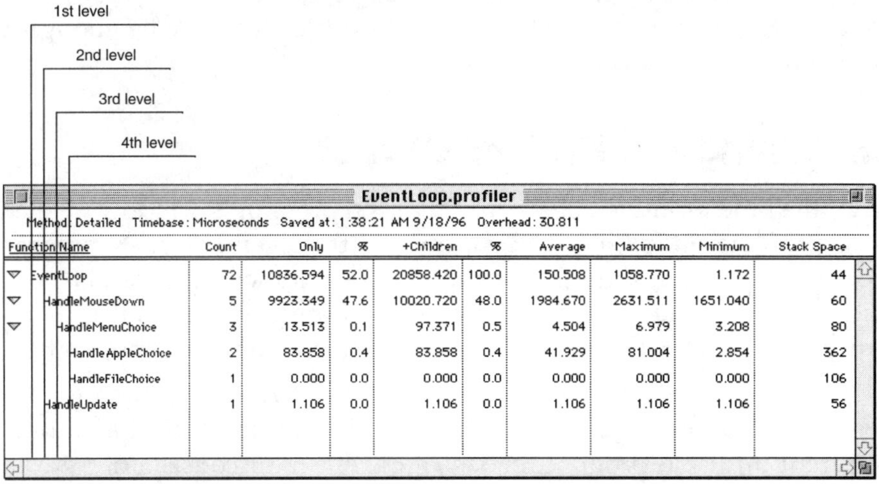

EventLoop.profiler

Method: Detailed Timebase: Microseconds Saved at: 1:38:21 AM 9/18/96 Overhead: 30.811

Function Name	Count	Only	%	+Children	%	Average	Maximum	Minimum	Stack Space
EventLoop	72	10836.594	52.0	20858.420	100.0	150.508	1058.770	1.172	44
HandleMouseDown	5	9923.349	47.6	10020.720	48.0	1984.670	2631.511	1651.040	60
HandleMenuChoice	3	13.513	0.1	97.371	0.5	4.504	6.979	3.208	80
HandleAppleChoice	2	83.858	0.4	83.858	0.4	41.929	81.004	2.854	362
HandleFileChoice	1	0.000	0.0	0.000	0.0	0.000	0.000	0.000	106
HandleUpdate	1	1.106	0.0	1.106	0.0	1.106	1.106	1.106	56

Figure 12.26 *Profiler displays functions by hierarchy, or level.*

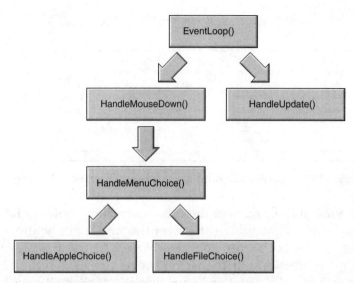

Figure 12.27   Another way of displaying a program's function hierarchy.

The functional hierarchy displayed in the Profiler window is itself a good tool for analyzing a large program. It clearly shows a program's flow of control as well as its function dependencies. If one of your programs isn't behaving as expected, simply profiling it and looking at the *Function Name* column of the generated Profiler file may be enough to help you find any flaws in your logic.

Examining the Profiler Output

From the time profiling began (just after the program's window opened) until profiling ended, my test running of the EventLoop68K program took about 21 seconds. In this section, I'll look at those 21 seconds, not to find a way to reduce the execution time of any routines, but rather to gain a better understanding of how an event-driven program operates.

Once the EventLoop68K program invokes EventLoop()—the main event loop routine—the program stays in this routine (and the routine's children) until the program ends. The event loop consists of a while loop that cycles continuously until a global variable named gAllDone is set to **true** (by the user selecting **Quit** from the File menu). Even when no action is taking place, the program is still running the event loop, waiting for a new event to take place. This means that as long as the program is running, the Profiler will be logging time to the EventLoop() routine and its children. For example, if the user runs EventLoop68K for 60 seconds before quitting, the EventLoop() routine's *+Children* column will have a value of 60,000 milliseconds.

Just as the time in the EventLoop() *+Children* column will be high, so will the time spent in the EventLoop() routine itself (as logged in the EventLoop() *Only* column). This long period of time in the EventLoop() routine doesn't mean the routine is flawed—it's just the nature of an event-driven program. If you want to reduce the execution time of a program, you'll look at routines other than the event loop. Figure 12.28 shows that for the 21 seconds I ran the EventLoop68K program (see the value of close to 21,000 in the *+Children* column in the *EventLoop* row), the program spent about 11 seconds cycling through the while loop in the EventLoop() routine (see the value of a little under 11,000 in the *Only* column of the *EventLoop* row).

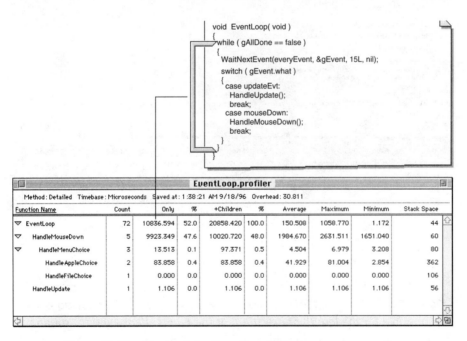

Figure 12.28 *Much of the EventLoop68K program's execution time is spent cycling through the event loop.*

The Profiler output file shows that HandleMouseDown() takes about 10 seconds to execute (9923 milliseconds) five times. This relatively long period of time isn't due to a poorly written function, though. Instead, the time is dependent on how long the user holds down the mouse button when making a menu selection and when dragging a window. When the user clicks on a menu, HandleMouseDown() calls the Toolbox function MenuSelect(). This routine gains and maintains control of the program until the user releases the mouse button, whether that's a half second or a hundred seconds. The same is true of the Toolbox function DragWindow(). When the user clicks on a window's title bar and drags a window, DragWindow() executes until the user releases the mouse button.

Figure 12.29 shows what HandleMouseDown() looks like and serves as a reminder that it is this routine's calls to the two Toolbox functions that are responsible for the routine's execution time.

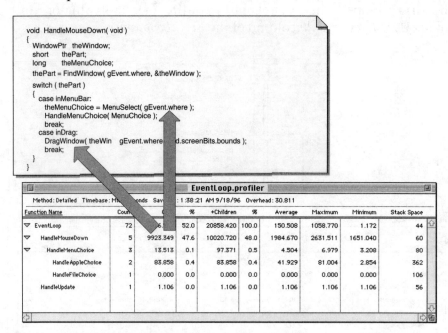

Figure 12.29 *The MenuSelect() and DragWindow() Toolbox functions are responsible for the length of execution of the HandleMouseDown() routine.*

When running EventLoop68K, I clicked the mouse button five times. Three of the five executions of HandleMouseDown() are devoted to

457

menu item selections (mouseDown events with a part code of inMenuBar), while the other two executions handle window dragging (mouseDown events with a part code of inDrag).

Looking at the *Only* column for the HandleMenuChoice() function shows that this routine uses only about 13.5 milliseconds of CPU time to execute three times. That's because there's not much to HandleMenuChoice(). The bulk of the work is done using the Toolbox routines HiWord() and LoWord() to extract the menu and menu item from the one long variable menuChoice. The Profiler file shows that *excluding* the time spent in subordinate functions, HandleMenuChoice() took about 13.5 milliseconds to run, while the function *and* its children routines together took about 97 milliseconds. This should cause you to guess that it must be the children functions of HandleMenuChoice() that do the real work. Figure 12.30 adds emphasis to this point.

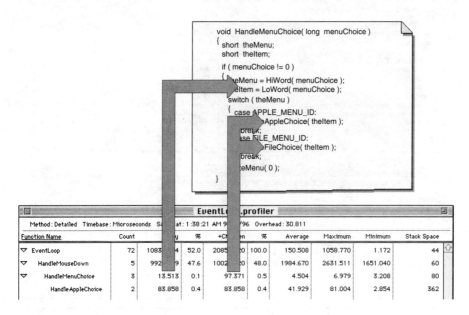

Figure 12.30   *The HandleMenuChoice() function does little work; instead, its subordinate routines take care of menu selections.*

HandleMenuChoice() takes very little time to run; it's the routine's children that take time. Actually, as you can see in Figure 12.31, only one of its two children functions uses much time. The `HandleAppleChoice()` executes two times, at a cost of about 84 milliseconds (three-fourths of a second) each time. Looking at the *Maximum* and *Minimum* columns for this function you see that one execution takes about 81 milliseconds while the other takes only about 3. Recall that the first selection I made from the Apple menu was the **About** item and the second selection was the **Scrapbook**. It's a safe guess that the time to open the **Scrapbook** file is the time that appears in the *Maximum* column.

The other child function of `HandleMenuChoice()`, the `HandleFileChoice()` function, appears to take zero time! In fact, it executes so quickly that its execution time is less than the accuracy at which Profiler can measure, so Profiler simply enters 0.0 for the timing (see Figure 12.31).

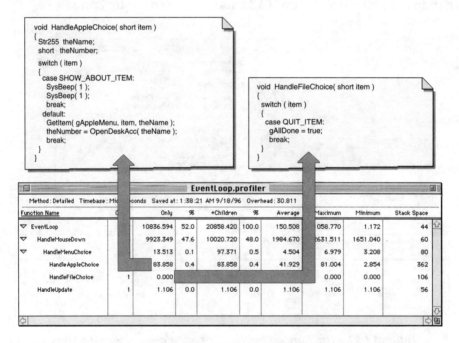

Figure 12.31 `HandleAppleChoice()` uses CPU time, while `HandleFileChoice()` uses almost none.

Finally, you can see from Figure 12.32 that the `HandleUpdate()` function takes just 1 millisecond to run. That's because this function is set up for updating a window but doesn't do any drawing. If `HandleUpdate()` *did* redraw a window's contents, the single comment would be replaced with the drawing code or a call to an application-defined routine that did the drawing. Figure 12.32 shows the code for the EventLoop68K version of `HandleUpdate()`. If you'd like to modify it so that it draws a picture to the window, replace the commented line with a call to a routine like `UpdatePictureWindow()`, as shown here:

```
void  HandleUpdate( void )
{
    WindowPtr    theWindow;

    theWindow = ( WindowPtr )gEvent.message;

    BeginUpdate( theWindow );
        EraseRgn( theWindow->visRgn );
        UpdatePictureWindow();    // call routine to draw picture
    EndUpdate( theWindow );
}

void  UpdatePictureWindow( void )
{
    PicHandle    thePicture;
    Rect         theRect;
    short        theWidth;
    short        theHeight;

    thePicture = GetPicture( 128 );
    theRect = (**(thePicture)).picFrame;
    theWidth = theRect.right - theRect.left;
    theHeight = theRect.bottom - theRect.top;
    SetRect( &theRect, 0, 0, theWidth, theHeight );
    DrawPicture( thePicture, &theRect );
    ReleaseResource( (Handle)thePicture );
}
```

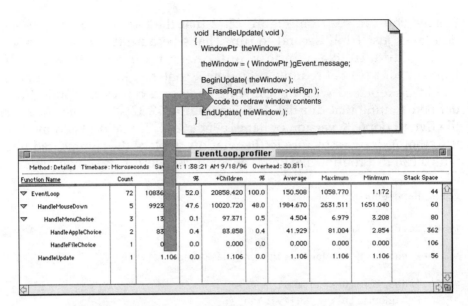

Figure 12.32 *If HandleUpdate() included code to redraw a window's contents, its execution time could be much higher.*

Summary

The time that each application-defined routine takes to execute can easily be determined for any program. To do so, follow these steps:

1. Add the appropriate Profiler library (**Profiler68k(Large).Lib** or **ProfilerPPC.Lib**) to the project to profile.

2. Make sure the **Generate Profiler Calls** (or **Emit Profiler Calls** for a PowerPC project) checkbox is checked in the Code Generation panel of the Project Settings dialog box.

3. Include the profiler header file **Profiler.h** in the project's source code.

4. Call ProfilerInit() before any calls are made to the functions to profile.

5. Call ProfilerDump() and ProfilerTerm() after all functions are profiled.

6. Open the resulting Profiler file with the MW Profiler application.

The output file generated from profiling your code reveals much about how processor time is being spent in an application. The *Count* column indicates how many times a function was called during the running of the program. The *Only* column tells the time, in milliseconds (1000 milliseconds equals one second), that a function took to execute. This time is the total time spent in the function, regardless of how many times the function executed. This time doesn't include the time spent in any of the other application-defined routines. To find out the total time spent in a function, including time spent in all the function's subordinate, or children, functions, look to the *+Children* column. Both the *Only* and *+Children* times can be viewed as percentages of the overall time spent in the program—look at the % columns for this information. The next three columns of the Profiler file—*Average*, *Maximum*, and *Minimum*— are self-explanatory. The stack column lists the number of bytes in the stack at the time of the call to a function.

Appendix A

Introduction to the C Language

The source code for many of this book's example programs is listed in the C language. If you aren't well versed in C, read this appendix to get a much-needed overview of this language. If you have used C in the past, but only sparingly, you might want to check in on this appendix throughout the reading of this book.

If you know C, but don't know C++, jump to Appendix B. If you've programmed in these languages, but not on a Macintosh, take a look at Appendix C and Appendix D to get up to speed on Macintosh programming.

Anatomy of a C Program

Looking at the source code for a very simple program is a good way to learn about the basics of any language, including the C language. Over the next several pages, I'll take a close look at the source code for a program that simply writes a single line of text to a window. Figure A.1 shows the output of the MyFirstCProgram application.

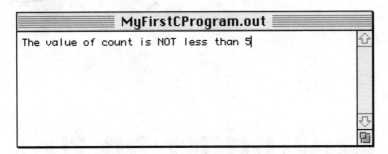

Figure A.1   The results of running MyFirstCProgram.

CodeWarrior and IBM-Compatible C Code

A simple DOS program that runs on an IBM-compatible writes text to the monitor. A Macintosh program, on the other hand, never writes directly to the screen—that would be writing on the desktop! Instead, a Mac program always writes (or draws) to a window. The source code for a Macintosh program typically includes code that creates and displays at least one window (or dialog box) so that the user and program can communicate with one another.

When learning C, you might want to rely on simple C source code examples written by programmers working on IBM-compatible computers. You might also learn from a book that isn't "Macintosh-specific." That is, you might have access to a C programming tutorial that was aimed at people running DOS on their IBM-compatibles. Metrowerks understands that this learning scenario might apply to you—so they've implemented an easy way for you to take source code that was designed to run on an IBM-compatible and use it in a CodeWarrior project. Such a project is created using the ANSI Console 68k or ANSI Console PPC project stationery. When you base a project on one of these two project stationeries, you can compile and execute DOS code without modification. That is, you won't have to add any code to create a dialog box to accept user input, or to create a window that displays output.

NOTE You don't have to learn C by first examining source code written for DOS programs. However, because you can run very short, simple programs that don't rely on windows, dialog boxes, or menus, it is a good way to learn the very basics of the language.

The Example Project

Using one of the two ANSI Console project stationeries allows you to compile standard C code and then execute the resulting application without adding any new window-related source code. It does that by inserting a little code within your program—code that does in fact open a window. This handy feature allows you to learn C from books normally written for people using IBM-compatible computers running DOS. To create such a project, use the ANSI Console 68k project stationery—as I did for the **MyFirstCProgram.µ** project used in this appendix.

NOTE When you create a project based on ANSI Console project stationery, a source code file named **HelloWorld.c** will appear in the project. You can then double-click on this file name in the project window, select **Save As** from the File menu, and enter a new name in the dialog box that appears. In Figure A.2, you can see that I did exactly that so the name of the source code file more closely matches the project I'm working on.

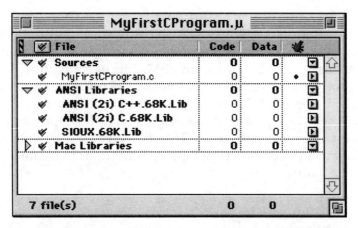

Figure A.2 *The project window for the **MyFirstCProgram.μ** project.*

The Example Source Code Listing

Figure A.3 shows the entire source code listing for a simple C language program. While only about a dozen lines in length, the code in this listing demonstrates a number of features that you'll see again and again in your dealings with C.

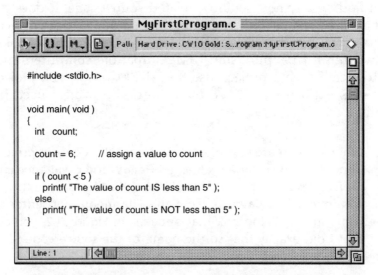

Figure A.3 *The complete source code listing for **MyFirstCProgram**.*

Walking Through the Source Code

Over the next several pages, I'll break down the code shown in the listing in Figure A.3 to see what is really going on.

THE MAIN() FUNCTION

Functions are the building blocks of a C program. A function is one or more lines of C code grouped together and given a name. Functions are also called routines—the terms are interchangeable. The function name is followed by parentheses to identify it as a function. The **MyFirstCProgram.c** listing groups several lines of code together into a single function—a function named main(). When you write functions for your own programs, you'll be able to give them just about any name you want. However, every C language program *must* have one function called main(). When a program written in C is launched, the operating system looks for a function named main()—the system considers that function as the starting point from which it should begin executing the program.

BRACES

After the parentheses that follow the name of a function comes an opening brace, and after the last line of code in the body of the function comes a closing brace. Braces mark the beginning and end of a block of code. A block of code is one or more lines of related code that are grouped together. The body of a function, as you may have just surmised, is a block of code that makes up the function itself.

NOTE
Some other computer languages, such as Pascal, use the words begin and end for the same purpose as C braces.

VARIABLES, DATA TYPES, AND DECLARATION STATEMENTS

This line of code from **MyFirstCProgram.c** is a declaration statement:

```
int    count;
```

A *declaration statement* lets the compiler know that a variable is being created—it *declares* that this is what is taking place. A *variable* is used to keep track of a value of some kind. The kind, or *type*, of the data that the variable keeps track of is listed first in the declaration. The variable name is listed next.

In the preceding example, the variable named `count` holds a value of type `int`. The name `count` was of my own choosing—I could have made up just about any name I wanted. The word `int` isn't entirely of my own choosing—it is one of several standard C data types available.

A variable name can be almost any combination of lowercase letters, uppercase letters, digits, and the underscore character. However, the first character of your variable name cannot be a digit. When choosing variable names, keep in mind that the C language is case-sensitive. A case-sensitive language is one that makes a distinction between lowercase and uppercase letters. That means, for instance, your program could have a variable named `count` and another variable named `Count`.

The CodeWarrior C compiler needs to know the data type of a variable so it can allocate, or reserve, the proper amount of memory to hold whatever value the variable will eventually have. In the case of a variable declared to be of type `int`, four bytes of memory need to be reserved. The compiler also needs to know the data type of a variable so that it can verify that this variable is used properly elsewhere in your source code. In the case of a variable of type `int`, CodeWarrior will be expecting that the variable will be used only for the purpose of holding an integer—a whole number that contains no decimal point.

Words that are a defined part of the C language, like `int`, are referred to as *keywords*. Such keywords can only be used as intended by the C language. For instance, the keyword int is used in a declaration statement to specify the type of data a variable will hold. Because it's meant to be a designator of a data type, I can't name a variable `int`.

A declaration statement, like most C language statements, ends with a semicolon. The semicolon lets the CodeWarrior compiler know that the line is a C statement. In C, a statement is a complete instruction to the computer.

Assignment Statements

This line of code from **MyFirstCProgram.c** is an assignment statement:

```
count = 6;
```

An *assignment statement* gives a previously declared variable a value—it *assigns* a variable a value. The declaration statement declared an integer variable named `count`. The above assignment statement assigns this variable a value of 6. An assignment statement, like a declaration statement, ends with a semicolon.

 NOTE Recall that because count was declared to be a variable of type int—an integer—this variable is capable of holding only a whole number. Attempting to assign data of one type to a variable declared to be of a different type will result in either an error during compilation or a variable that holds an unpredictable or undesirable value.

Comments

Text that occupies part or all of a single line, and is preceded by a double slash, is a comment. This code from the **MyFirstCProgram.c** listing is a comment:

```
// assign a value to count
```

A *comment* is text that appears within source code, but isn't treated by the compiler as source code. Instead, a comment is simply ignored by the compiler. So, what good is a comment if it doesn't have any meaning to the compiler or to the computer? The benefit of a comment is to you—or to anyone reading and trying to understand your source code. You add comments to your code to describe the purpose of a function or the purpose of a single line of code.

It's not necessary for a comment to accompany every line of code you write—hopefully the intent of much of your source code will be apparent to any programmer views it. Occasionally, though, the purpose of your code may not be intuitive. In such a case, add a comment to offer insight by adding one or more comments.

You can put a comment on the same line as code, as is done in the **MyFirstCProgram.c** listing:

```
count = 6;          // assign a value to count
```

You can also devote an entire line to a comment. The above could also be written like this:

```
// This next line assigns a value to count:
count = 6;
```

Function Calls

Not all of the code your program will rely on will have been written by you. Your code is free to *call*, or *invoke*, functions that were written by other programmers. Your program must, of course, have access to the code that makes up these functions. Metrowerks includes several libraries of such code as a part of the CodeWarrior programming environment. As discussed in Chapter 2, any time you create a new project, CodeWarrior includes one or more such libraries in that project.

Back in Figure A.2, you see that for a project based on the ANSI Console 68k project stationery includes three libraries in a group named ANSI Libraries. These libraries hold the code for standard functions that are a part of any implementation of the C language. An example of one such function is `printf()`. The `printf()` routine handles the task of writing text to the screen

Include Directives and Function Prototypes

When you write your own function, the compiler knows what that function looks like—it discovers the details of the function as it compiles it. When your program makes use of a function that you haven't written—like the `printf()` function discussed above—it doesn't know what to expect. That's because the code that makes up the function exits in a separate file, and in a precompiled state (again, as mentioned in Chapter 2). To give the compiler an indication of what such a function looks like, you supply the compiler with a prototype of the function.

A *function prototype* allows the compiler to determine if your program's use of the function is correct. You don't need to include function prototypes in your source code. Instead, they've been written for you and included in a number of header files. For instance, one of the many function prototypes in a header file named **stdio.h** (for *standard input/output*) is the prototype for the printf() routine. By naming the **stdio.h** file in an #include directive, you tell the compiler what to expect of the function named printf(). By including the proper library in your project you supply the linker with the already-compiled code for the printf() function.

CONDITIONAL STATEMENTS

Decision making is an important part of all but the most trivial programs. In C, decision making is achieved by using one of several different *conditional statements*. One such statement is the if-else statement. In effect, the if-else tells your program that one block of code should be executed if a certain condition is true, but a different block of code should be executed if that same condition is false.

The **MyFirstCProgram.c** listing includes the following if-else statement:

```
if ( count < 5 )
   printf( "The value of count IS less than 5" );
else
   printf( "The value of count is NOT less than 5" );
```

In the above snippet, the condition that is tested is whether variable count has a value that is less than five. Because the program assigns this variable a value of 6, you know that the result of this comparison will be false—count isn't less than 5. Because the test is said to have failed, the block under the else executes. In the example, the block under the else consists of only a single line of code—a call to the printf() function. A block can consist of any number of lines of code.

Summing Up What a Program Consists of

The structure of a typical C program can be described by the following points:

- A program consists of one or more functions. The main() function is the starting point of the program, and must be a part of every program.

- A function is a collection of C statements grouped together between a pair of braces.

- A function consists of a number of different statements including: declaration statements, assignment statements, and conditional statements.

Data Types and Operators

Data is categorized into different types. Numbers that don't include a decimal point, numbers that do include a decimal point, characters—each is a separate type of data. C provides different names, and different memory storage sizes, for these different types of data.

Data is stored in variables. After that, your program uses these variables to manipulate the data. This manipulation could include multiplying two numbers together, adding a series of numbers, comparing the value of one number to another, or sorting a list of words. This manipulation, or processing, of data is accomplished through the use of operators.

C Data Types

The most commonly used data types are the ones that holds integers, floating-point numbers, and characters.

NOTE

In Macintosh programming, there are other data types you'll encounter—types that exist to hold the kind of data not found in simple programs that weren't designed to run on a computer that uses a graphical user interface. For instance, a Mac program may need to store the data that makes up a graphical image or a sound.

Integer Data Types

An *integer* is a whole number—a number that doesn't include a decimal point. In C, you use the short, int, or long data types to hold an integer.

To store a number that is in the range of -32,768 to +32,767, use a variable declared to be of type `short`. For larger numbers, use a `long` variable. In Macintosh programming, the `int` type is seldom used—typically it's used only for a variable that serves as a loop counter (loops are discussed later in this appendix). Here's a snippet that uses each integer type:

```
short    theShort;
long     theLong;
int      theInt;

theShort = -27;
theLong = 2500000;
theInt = 5;
```

FLOATING-POINT DATA TYPES

If your program needs to work with floating-point numbers—numbers that include a decimal point—you'll use the `float` data type. Here are a few examples of assignments and declarations of `float` variables:

```
float    verySmall;
float    veryBig;

verySmall = 0.00045;
veryBig = 654334430504.5;
```

CHARACTER DATA TYPE

To store characters C uses the `char` type. The Mac, like many computers, uses the ASCII code to map each character to a number. While each character has a numerical representation, you'll typically work with just the character. To assign a character to a variable of type `char`, enclose the character in single quotes:

```
char    firstLetter;

firstLetter = 'A';
```

C Operators

The C language provides a great many ways in which you can process your program's data. Operators are key to working with variables.

ASSIGNMENT OPERATOR

The most familiar of operators, the assignment operator (=) allows you to assign a variable a value. Here are two examples of its use:

```
short   theShort;
char    theChar;

theShort = 5;
theChar = 'b';
```

MATH OPERATORS

To add the values in two variables, you'll use the addition operator (+). The following snippet results in variable total having a value of 12:

```
short   num1;
short   num2;
short   total;

num1 = 5;
num2 = 7;
total = num1 + num2;
```

Subtraction involves the subtraction operator (-), multiplication uses the multiplication operator (*), and division makes use of the division operator (/).

INCREMENT AND DECREMENT OPERATORS

Programs often involve the incrementing of the value of a variable. In C, to increment a variable is to increase its value by 1. To do that, use the increment operator (++) either before or after the variable name. In this snippet, the increment operator is used to change the value of count from 9 to 10:

```
short   count;

count = 9;
count++;
```

Decreasing a variable's value by 1—decrementing the variable—is accomplished in a similar fashion by using the decrement operator (–).

COMPARISON OPERATORS

To compare the value of one variable to another, use one of the comparison, or comparative operators. To see if the value of one variable is less than another, use the less than operator (<). To see if the value of the variable is greater than another, use the greater than operator (>). There's also a less than or equal to operator (<=) and a greater than or equal to operator (>=). To see if the value of one variable is equal to the value of another, use the equality operator (==). Typically such operators are used in conditional statement tests—an example of which you saw in the MyFirstCProgram example in this appendix. In that program, the less than operator was used to see if the value of variable count was less than the number 5:

```
if ( count < 5 )
    // do something
```

Control Statements

The flow of execution of a program is determined by the use of control statements. To make a decision—to lead the flow down one path or another—use a branching statement. To repeat a block of code, use a looping statement.

Branching Statements

For decision making, use the if-else statement or the switch statement.

IF-ELSE STATEMENT

From the MyFirstCProgram example, you're already familiar with the if-else branch. Again, the format of that type of branch is:

```
if ( test expression is true )
{
    // do something
}
```

```
else
{
   // do something else
}
```

If more than one line of code makes up the block that appears under the if or else, then that code must be enclosed in braces. If a block consists of only one line of code, then the braces shown above are optional. An example of an if-else statement is:

```
short    score1;
short    score2;
short    highScore;

// assign values to score1 and score2 somewhere in the program

if ( score1 > score2 )
   highScore = score1;
else
   highScore = score2;
```

Switch Statement

If your program is to choose between many paths, use a switch statement rather than the if-else statement. The format of the switch is:

```
switch ( variable to test )
{
   case constant1:
      // do one thing
      break;
   case constant2:
      // do one thing
      break;
   case constant3:
      // do one thing
      break;
   and so forth
}
```

The break keyword is required at the end of each block of code under each case *label*—it tells the compiler where the block ends.

An example of a switch statement follows. In this example, the number of guesses the user of a guessing game took to answer a question determines the size of a bonus that is to be added to the user's score.

```
short    guesses;
short    bonus;

// assign a value to guesses somewhere in the program

switch ( guesses )
{
   case 1:
      bonus = 10;
      break;
   case 2:
      bonus = 5;
      break;
   case 3;
      bonus = 0;
      break;
}
```

Looping Statements

To repeat a block of code, use a `for` loop. The first line of a `for` loop actually performs three tasks: It initializes a variable that is used as a loop counter; it compares the value of this loop counter to an end value; and it increments the value of the loop counter. If the middle task—the comparison of the loop counter to the end value—passes, then the body of the loop executes. Here's the format:

```
for ( initialize counter; compare counter; increment counter )
{
   // do something
}
```

The first task, the initialization of the loop counter, is performed only once—when the for loop is encountered. The other two tasks are performed repeatedly until the second task, the comparison of the loop counter to a final value, fails. An example helps to clarify:

```
int    index;

for ( index = 1; index <= 3; index++ )
   // do something
```

In this next snippet, the loop counter is a variable named index. When the program encounters this `for` loop, the `for` loop initializes this variable to a value of 1. It then compares the value of index to the number 3. If index is less than or equal to 3 (it is—it was just initialized to a value of 1), then the body of the loop executes. Before executing the loop body, the value of index is incremented from 1 to 2.

After the body of the loop executes, the program returns to the for statement to again make the comparison of the value of the loop counter to the end value. The value of index is now 2, which is still less than or equal to 3. So the comparison test again passes and the body of the loop again executes. Once again, before the loop body executes, the value of index is incremented—this time from 2 to 3. By now you should see that the body of the loop will execute one more time—index having a value of 3 qualifies as being less than or equal to 3. The next time the test is performed, however, the for loop body will not execute—index will have a value of 4.

Appendix B

Introduction to the C++ Language

The source code that makes up the PowerPlant application framework, as well as the source code for the examples in this book's four PowerPlant chapters, is written in C++. You don't need to be a master of the C++ language to work with PowerPlant—but you do need to know at least the basics. If you don't know C++, read this appendix. If you don't know C++ or C, first read Appendix A, then read this appendix—C++ takes up where C leaves off.

Finally, if you don't know C++ or the Java language but want to read this book's Java chapter, read this appendix. Java can be considered an offshoot of C++. Once you know C++, Java will quickly make sense to you.

NOTE If you've programmed in C++, but not on a Macintosh, take a look at Appendix C and Appendix D to get up to speed on Macintosh programming.

Anatomy of a C++ Program

Looking at the source code for a short, simple program provides a good introduction to the language the program was written in. Here, I'll present the source code for a little program written in the C++ language. You can assume that this program is the beginnings of an inventory program that the Ace Widget Company is developing to keep track of its large variety of world-class widgets. Over the next several pages, I'll take a close look at the source code for a program that writes a single line of text to a window. Figure B.1 shows the output of the MyFirstC++Program application.

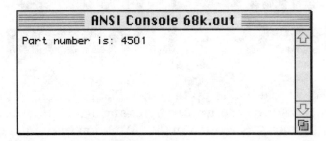

Figure B.1   *The result of running MyFirstC++Program.*

CodeWarrior and IBM-compatible C++ Code

The MyFirstC++Program doesn't include any code that opens a window—yet it does display one. This slight of hand is accomplished by including a little Metrowerks-written code in the **MyFirstC++Program.µ** project. By leaving out Mac-specific code from MyFirstC++Program, you're free to test out source code from C++ examples listed in books that might not have been written with the Macintosh in mind. To read a little bit more on this idea, refer to the CodeWarrior and IBM-compatible C Code section in Appendix A.

The Example Project

The example project uses the ANSI Console 68k project stationery. This project stationery allows you to compile standard C++ code and then execute the resulting application without adding any new window-related source code. That allows for short, simple examples.

When you create a project based on ANSI Console 68k project stationery, a source code file named **HelloWorld.c** will appear in the project. You can then double-click on this file name in the project window, select **Save As** from the File menu, and enter a new name in the dialog box that appears. In Figure B.2, you can see that I did exactly that so the name of the source code file more closely matches the project I'm working on.

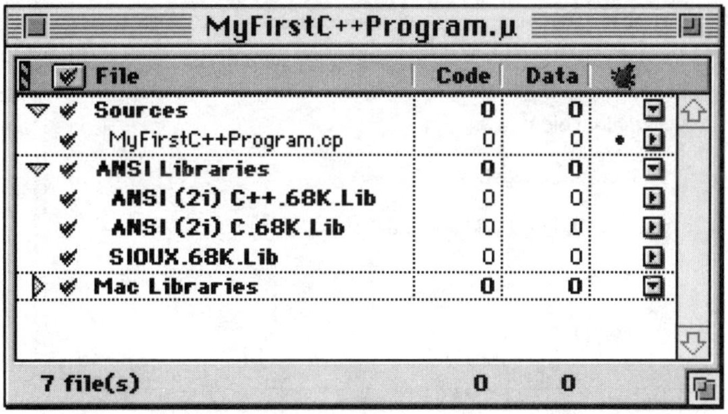

Figure B.2   *The project window for the **MyFirstC++Program.µ** project.*

The Example Source Code Listing

Figure B.3 shows the entire source code listing for a simple C++ language program. While only about a couple of dozen lines in length, the code in this listing demonstrates a number of object-oriented concepts that you'll see in all your dealings with C++.

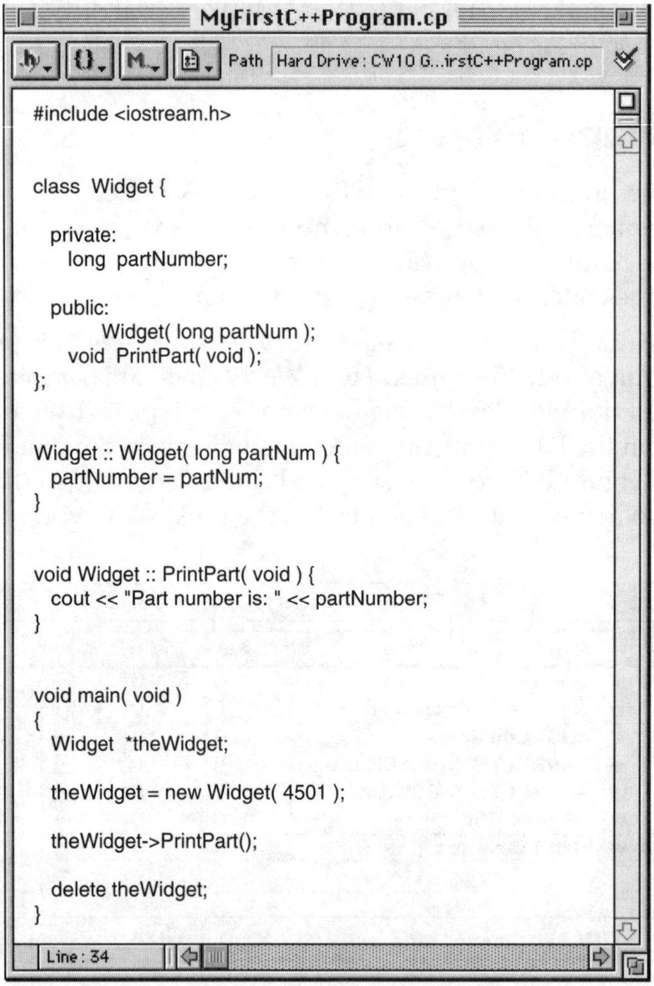

```
MyFirstC++Program.cp

Path Hard Drive : CW10 G...irstC++Program.cp

#include <iostream.h>


class  Widget {

  private:
    long  partNumber;

  public:
        Widget( long partNum );
      void  PrintPart( void );
};


Widget :: Widget( long partNum ) {
  partNumber = partNum;
}


void Widget :: PrintPart( void ) {
  cout << "Part number is: " << partNumber;
}


void main( void )
{
  Widget  *theWidget;

  theWidget = new Widget( 4501 );

  theWidget->PrintPart();

  delete theWidget;
}

Line : 34
```

Figure B.3   *The complete source code listing for MyFirstC++Program.*

Walking Through the Source Code

Over the next several pages, I'll examine the code shown in the listing in Figure B.3. Here you'll see the importance of the class in a C++ program. A class is a data structure that encapsulates, or groups together, both data and the functions that operate on, or work with, that data. In C++, you first declare a class—you define the name of the class, the data that will be kept track of, and the functions that will be used to manipulate that data. In effect, the declaration of a class is the defining of a new data type.

Like a data type, a class itself isn't used to store data. Instead, a class serves as a sort of template from which objects, or instances, of the class are defined. Just as you can declare any number of variables of a data type such as, say, type `short`, so too can you declare any number of objects of a specific class type.

DEFINING A CLASS

The **MyFirstC++Program.cp** listing defines a single class—the class named `Widget`. As shown in Figure B.4, this class consists of one data member and two member functions.

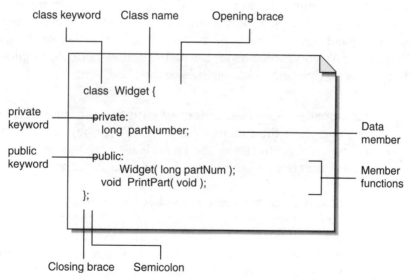

Figure B.4   *The format of a class definition.*

Figure B.4 shows that a class begins with the `class` keyword, followed by the name of the class. The contents of the class—the data members and member functions—lie between a pair of braces. The class definition ends with a semicolon.

Each *data member* can be of any C++ type—pick a type appropriate for the data that is to be stored. The one data member of the Widget class, partNumber, will hold a part number that may consist of a number of digits, so partNumber is declared to be of type long.

Before listing the data member or members of a class, a keyword is used to limit the level of access to the data members. Typically, the private keyword is used. By declaring data members to be private, you tell your program that only *member functions*—the functions that are listed within this class definition—of this class can access or modify the values in these data members. For instance, in the Widget class, only the member functions named Widget() and PrintPart() "know about" the data member partNumber. If the program were to define other classes (a C++ program usually consists of several class types), the member functions of those classes could not work with the Widget class partNumber data member.

After the data members are declared, the member functions are listed. As shown in Figure B.4, only a function prototype for each member function is listed here—there is no body defined for either of the member functions. As you'll see ahead, the actual source code that makes up the body of each function exists outside of the class definition.

 Traditionally, a C++ class is defined with the data members listed first, and then the member functions. This doesn't have to be, however. As you'll see in the PowerPlant chapters of this book, **NOTE** PowerPlant class definitions list the member functions first.

Specifying that the data members of a class be private "hides" the data of a class from other classes. In effect, it protects the integrity of the data—data members can't be indiscriminately assigned values from anyplace within your program. That becomes especially important in large programs written by more than one programmer. Member functions, on the other hand, are usually specified to be public. Since a member function holds no data of its own (it only works on, or manipulates, class data), there's no reason to shield member functions from the rest of your program. By specifying that a member function be public, your program can readily make use of the member function.

If a member function can alter a data member, and the member function can be used anywhere in the program, is the data really protected at all? Yes. A `private` data member can't just simply be assigned a value, like this:

```
void main( void )
{
   ...
   partNumber = 52240;    // invalid - won't compile
   ...
}
```

You'll have to be familiar with the member functions of a class in order to use them to alter data member values. Forcing you to be knowledgeable of the member functions of a class is the security measure that affords the data protection.

DEFINING MEMBER FUNCTIONS

Member functions listed in a class declaration represent only prototypes of the functions. That is, they provide the compiler with information about each function, such as its return type, its name, and the types of parameters the function accepts. The code that makes up each function is included elsewhere in the listing.

The Widget class names two member functions. That tells you that the **MyFirstC++Program.cp** listing must include the source code for two functions. Here's the code for one of those two functions—the `PrintPart()` member function:

```
void Widget :: PrintPart( void ) {
   cout << "Part number is: " << partNumber;
}
```

With one exception (a constructor function—which is discussed ahead), the first line of a member function definition begins with the function's return type. The `PrintPart()` function doesn't return a value, so the `void` keyword is used here. Next, comes the name of the class to which the function belongs. After the class name comes the scope resolution operator (`::`). This operator, along with the class name, lets the compiler know which class this function is a member of. Your source code may consist of several classes, so it could include source code for several—perhaps dozens of—member functions. After the scope resolution operator comes the function name followed by a list of parameters, if any. The PrintPart() function has no parameters, so again the void keyword is used.

The body of the member function lies between a pair of braces. Note that the function definition does not end with a semicolon (while the class definition itself does). The body of a member function is written in the same manner as a C function—to perform some specific task. In the case of the PrintPart() function, the purpose is to write out the value of the partNumber data member. To do this, the C++ operator cout is used. The C++ cout works much like the C printf()—you can print out both text (by surrounding it in quotes) and numbers (by naming a variable). For each entity that is to be written, use the << operator. In the PrintPart() function, both a string and a value are being written:

```
cout << "Part number is: " << partNumber;
```

NOTE Because a member function can act on the data of its class, a member function can freely use the names of data members—such as partNumber. A function that isn't a member of the Widget class couldn't reference the partNumber data member in this way.

A special type of member function that a class can optionally define is a constructor. This function is useful for supplying initial values to data members. A *constructor* function must have the same name as the class itself, and it must *not* have a return type (all other member functions must list a return type—even if the type is void). The Widgets class defines a constructor member function:

```
Widget :: Widget( long partNum ) {
    partNumber = partNum;
}
```

Aside from the fact that no return type is given in the first line of the function definition, a constructor has the same form as any other member function. Just ahead you'll see how a constructor is used.

THE MAIN() FUNCTION

Like a C program, a C++ program must have a main() function. The main() function for MyFirstC++Program performs the following tasks:

- Declares a variable of the Widget class type.
- Uses the new keyword to allocate memory for an instance of the Widget class—it creates an object of type Widget.
- Invokes the Widget object's PrintPart() member function.
- Deletes the Widget object when done with it.

DECLARING A CLASS VARIABLE

The definition of a class (such as the definition of the Widget class) does not reserve memory for a variable of that class type. Instead, it simply serves as a template for variables of this class type. The first step to doing that is to declare a pointer to the class—as done in the main() function of **MyFirstC++Program.cp**:

```
Widget    *theWidget;
```

CREATING AN OBJECT

Declaring a pointer to a class readies the compiler for what's about to come—the allocation of memory for a new object. Here's how MyFirstC++Program does that:

```
theWidget = new Widget( 4501 );
```

To allocate memory, you need to create an instance, or object, of the class. The new operator does that. If you're well versed in C, you can liken the use of new in C++ to the use of malloc() in C. As shown above, you follow the new keyword with the name of the class from which an object is to be created. If the class doesn't define a constructor function, then a pair of empty parentheses follow the class name. If the class does define a constructor, then arguments need to be place between the parentheses. The new keyword returns a pointer to the allocated memory. This returned pointer is considered the object. In the above snippet, theWidget would be called a Widget object. Figure B.5 shows that the above snippet causes an object to appear in memory.

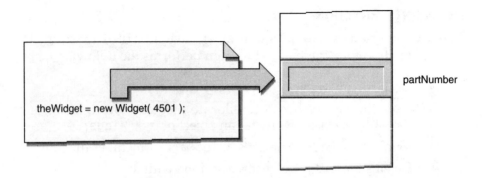

theWidget = new Widget(4501);

partNumber

Figure B.5 *The new operator allocates memory for a new object.*

When an object is created, it gets one copy of each of the data members defined in the object's class. In general, the size of an object is the size of the memory needed to hold a single copy of each of its data members. For the Widget example, an object would consist of just the memory necessary to hold a single long—as shown in Figure B.5.

NOTE Each object gets its own private copy of each data member. That allows a program to have any number of objects, each independent of all other objects. For example, if MyFirstC++Program created three Widget objects, each would have its own partNumber data member. It's worth noting that each object *doesn't* store its own copy of each member function in memory. Only one version of a member function needs to be in memory. Because the member function itself doesn't store data, all objects can share it.

If the class from which the object is being created defines a constructor function, then the use of new automatically triggers the execution of this constructor. The Widget class does in fact define a constructor, so the above snippet will invoke it. Here's another look at that function's definition:

```
Widget :: Widget( long partNum ) {
    partNumber = partNum;
}
```

The Widget constructor accepts a single parameter. The body of the constructor assigns this value to the one data member of the Widget class. Thus the constructor serves as a means of providing the new Widget object with an initial value. In Figure B.5, you saw that new allocated memory for an object—but didn't supply any value for its one data member. In Figure B.6, you see that the Widget class constructor takes care of placing an initial value in the partNumber data member.

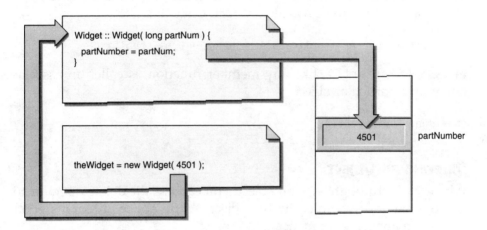

Figure B.6   Creating a new object invokes the constructor member function of that object's class type.

INVOKING AN OBJECT'S MEMBER FUNCTION

When a new object is created, its constructor function is automatically invoked. Your program has control over when any other member functions execute. To call a function, first name the object, then use the -> operator, and finally list the function name. MyFirstC++Program does that when it has the object theWidget invoke the PrintPart() member function:

```
theWidget->PrintPart();
```

Here's another look at the definition of the PrintPart() member function:

```
void Widget :: PrintPart( void ) {
    cout << "Part number is: " << partNumber;
}
```

MyFirstC++Program creates only one Widget object—but it could be very easily modified to create more. Notice that the PrintPart() member function makes no mention of a particular Widget object. Any object of the Widget class type can invoke this routine. And no matter which object does, PrintPart() will print out the value of the partNumber data member for the correct object. This happens because the PrintPart() function isn't called directly, like this:

```
PrintPart();     // invalid call - no object is specified
```

Instead, PrintPart(), like any member function, is called in association with a particular object:

```
theWidget->PrintPart();
```

DELETING AN OBJECT

When you're through with an object, you can use the delete operator to free the memory occupied by the object. While not required, it's good memory management practice to do so:

```
delete theWidget;
```

Appendix C

Introduction to Mac Programming

If you're new to CodeWarrior, you might just be new to Macintosh programming as well. If you've never programmed, look over Appendix A and Appendix B to get overviews of the C and C++ languages—then jump back here. If you've programmed in C or C++, but not on the Mac, you're at the right place. Read this appendix to get an overview of Mac programming.

491

If you become serious about Mac programming, you'll need a good reference to programming with the Toolbox — the thousands of functions built into the Mac and available for use by all programs and all programmers. Consider the M&T Books text *Macintosh Programming Techniques, Second Edition*, or some of the books that are a part of the *Inside Macintosh* series.

Bitmapped Graphics

Graphical user interfaces like the one found on the Macintosh use bitmapped graphics. *Bitmapped* means that every pixel (each display dot on the monitor) has a corresponding bit (or corresponding bits), in memory. A pixel on a monochrome monitor has a single memory bit associated with it, and that bit controls whether that one pixel is on or off. A pixel on a color monitor has several memory bits associated with it, and those bits control the color displayed by that one pixel.

In a bitmapped system, each pixel can be referenced by a pair of numbers. This pair of numbers describes the pixel's horizontal and vertical position on the monitor. Giving each pixel an exact reference allows a programmer to accurately and predictably draw graphics and display images.

Event-Driven Programming

When a program runs on a Macintosh, it is ever watchful for events. An *event* is the occurrence of something that the program may want to respond to. Events are typically initiated by the program's user. A click of the mouse button, a press of a keyboard key, or the insertion of a disk in a floppy drive each produce an event. Some user actions produce events indirectly. For instance, when a user clicks on a partially obscured window, that window moves to the forefront—and an update event is generated. The occurrence of an update event lets the program know that a window needs to be updated—its contents need to be redrawn.

When an event occurs, the Macintosh system software saves information about the event in an event record. The event record consists of fields that contain information about an event. The event, and the fields of event information, are accessible by the program.

At the heart of a Mac program is an event loop. The event loop is a block of code that executes over and over from the time the program starts to the time it ends. Each pass through the event loop results in a check to see if an event has occurred. If it has, code within the program handles the event as the program deems appropriate.

Resources

Each element of a Mac program's interface is based on one or more resources. Windows, menus, and dialog boxes all make use of resources. A *resource* is code, but not source code. Instead, a resource is code that can be displayed in a visual manner. Resources are kept in their own file—one that can be opened and edited using a special type of editor called a *resource editor*. A resource editor consists of a number of built-in editors, each designed to display and edit the data from a particular type of resource. For instance, the menu editor of the resource editor program ResEdit displays a menu as shown in Figure C.1.

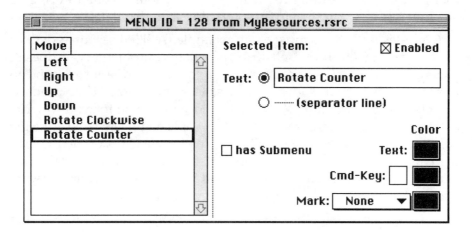

Figure C.1   *A MENU resource being edited in the menu editor of ResEdit.*

A CodeWarrior project generally consists of both a source code file and a resource file (though it can hold more than one file of either of these types). When you build a program from the files in a project,

CodeWarrior compiles the source code in any source code files and links the resulting object code with the resource code in any resource files in the project. In that way, source code and resources merge into a single file—the application file. So while resources are not part of your source code, your source code will be aware of them, use them, and eventually become linked with them.

Different elements of a program's interface have different resource types. Each resource type has a four-letter, case-sensitive name. The resource type of a menu is MENU, for example. Appendix D discusses resources in more depth and mentions a few of the most commonly used resource types.

The Toolbox

Resources provide a programmer with an easy, intuitive way to work with the elements of a graphical user interface. A resource, however, contains only a description of an element of a program's interface. The resource doesn't "stand on its own"—it needs source code to bring its data into memory and then to do something with that data.

Consider a MENU resource as an example. A MENU resource defines the look of a menu. It doesn't load that menu into memory, it doesn't display the menu in a program's menu bar, and it doesn't respond to user mouse clicks in it. For each of these tasks, traditional code needs to be included in a program. While it would be possible for you to write all this code yourself, there's no need to. Apple engineers have done the work for you—and they've provided you with the fruits of their labors. The code for the thousands of routines that are readily available for your program's use are included in the ROM chips and system software of every Macintosh. Including, of course, your Mac.

An example of a Toolbox routine is GetNewWindow(). The code that makes up this function is responsible for loading the data from a window resource—a resource of type WIND—into memory. Once in memory, your program can work with the window. Your program can call the Toolbox routine ShowWindow() to display the window or the Toolbox routine HideWindow() to make the window invisible. Your program can call the Toolbox function DragWindow() to respond to a user's mouse click on the window's title bar and to drag the window about the screen. In each of these examples, your program needs to only make calls to these functions—your program isn't responsible for providing the code that makes up the functions themselves.

Introduction to Resources

If you're new to Macintosh programming, you're probably new to the idea of resources as well. Almost every Macintosh program makes use of resources—code that defines the look of user interface items like menus and windows, yet is easily editable in a visual manner. If you've never programmed, look over Appendix A and Appendix B to get overviews of the C and C++ languages. Then move on to Appendix C for a brief overview of what Macintosh programming is all about. Finally, return to this appendix for a little extra information on resources.

NOTE For a complete reference on Macintosh programming using C or C++, consider either *Macintosh Programming Techniques, Second Edition*, also by M&T Books, or some of the books that are a part of the *Inside Macintosh* series.

Resources and the GUI

When you look at your Macintosh screen, everything you see originated as a resource:

- A menu bar has an MBAR resource that specifies which individual menus are in it.
- Each individual menu has its own MENU resource that defines the items in that menu.
- A window has a WIND resource that defines its size and initial position on the screen.
- A dialog box has a DLOG resource that defines its size and initial position.
- A dialog box has a second resource, the DITL, that defines the items, such as buttons, that are to appear in the dialog box.

There are about 100 different resource types. You'll probably only find the need to use fewer than a dozen types in your programs. Here's a list of some of the more commonly used resource types.

ALRT	Defines the look of an alert box
BNDL	Relates an icon to a program
CODE	All the instructions of a program
DITL	Contents of a dialog box
DLOG	Defines the look of a dialog box
DRVR	Desk accessory—a driver
ICN#	List of icons
PICT	Picture
SIZE	Partition size of a program
STR#	List of strings
WIND	Defines the look of a window
snd	Sound

Resources and Source Code

Appendix C mentioned that there is a relationship between a resource and source code. A resource holds the data that defines the look of an interface element of a program—such as the size, initial screen placement, and look of a window. Source code then allows a program to make use of this resource by loading its data into memory.

A specific example will go far to illustrate the connection between a resource and source code. To define the look of a resource, you can create a WIND resource using a resource editor. Figure D.1 shows such a resource as it is being edited in Apple's resource editor ResEdit.

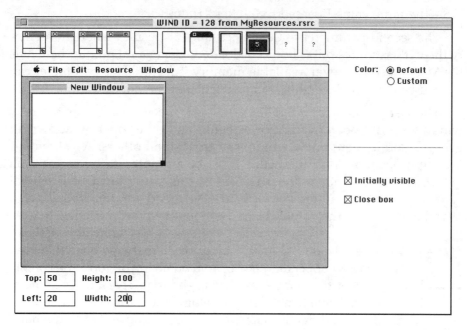

Figure D.1 *A WIND resource being edited in the window editor of ResEdit.*

After creating, editing, and saving the resource to a resource file, it's on to the source code. At the appropriate place in your program's source code listing (typically in response to a user's selection of the **New** item from the File menu), you'll make a call to GetNewWindow(). This Toolbox function returns to your program a pointer to the area in memory that holds this data. Such a returned value has a data type of its own—the WindowPtr data type:

```
WindowPtr    theWindow;

theWindow = GetNewWindow( 128, nil, (WindowPtr)-1L  );
```

The GetNewWindow() function loads into memory the data that makes up a WIND resource. Because a resource file may hold more than one resource of a resource type, the call to GetNewWindow() must specify which resource is to be loaded into memory. The first parameter is used for this purpose—here you pass the ID of the WIND resource to use. You can look back at the title bar of the ResEdit window editor pictured in Figure D.1 to see that the ID of the WIND resource I created has an ID of 128—the same value I passed to GetNewWindow().

The second parameter to GetNewWindow() specifies where in memory the WIND resource data should be loaded. Using a nil pointer here tells the Mac to use whatever available memory it wants. This parameter can instead be used to place the data in a particular memory location.

The last parameter to GetNewWindow() specifies whether the new window should open in front of or behind all other open windows. In general, you'll open a new window in front of all others. A value of -1 accomplishes this. Also, this value must be a pointer, so by convention we make it -1L. And, more particularly, this value must be a special type of pointer—a window pointer. Preceding the value with (WindowPtr) casts the value -1L to a WindowPtr type.

N O T E A pointer always occupies 4 bytes of memory, as does the long data type. By appending an "L" to a number, you force the compiler to look at the number as a long, and to reserve 4 bytes of memory for that number. *Casting* a value temporarily turns that value into one of a different data type. So appending an "L" to the number 1 causes the compiler to use 4 bytes of memory to hold this number, while casting the number 1 to a WindowPtr causes the compiler to view the number as a pointer to a window. If that all seems somewhat confusing, don't become too alarmed. You'll almost always make a call to GetNewWindow() as shown. While you might use a different WIND resource ID for the first parameter, you won't have to modify the second or third parameter.

When you create a `WIND` resource in ResEdit, you have the option of specifying whether the window should be visible or hidden when this call is made. If you examine the `WIND` resource in Figure D.1, you'll see that the checkbox labeled Initially visible is checked. That means that when the call to `GetNewWindow()` is made and the call is complete, a window will appear on the screen. If the Initially visible checkbox hadn't been checked, that information would have been a part of the `WIND` resource data. In such a case `GetNewWindow()` would still load the `WIND` resource data into memory, but it wouldn't display the window on screen. To do that, your source code would make a call to another Toolbox function—`ShowWindow()`.

Appendix E

Using Resorcerer As Your Resource Editor

When you double-click on the name of a resource file in a project window, CodeWarrior launches the resource editor ResEdit and then opens the resource file from within that editor. If you use Resorcerer by Mathemaesthetics, you'll want to set up CodeWarrior such that it launches this resource editor rather than ResEdit.

In order to start up the proper program, CodeWarrior examines the file type of the file name you've double-clicked on. When you create a new project using one of the Basic Toolbox project stationeries, the

SillyBalls.rsrc file is included. Metrowerks has created this file using Apple's ResEdit, so double-clicking on this file name in a project window will result in CodeWarrior attempting to run ResEdit. If your preference in resource editors is the more sophisticated Resorcerer by Mathemaesthetics, you'll need to change the file type of the resource files that CodeWarrior uses when it creates a new project.

First, launch Resorcerer. Do this by double-clicking on the icon of your Resorcerer application—don't try to launch it from a project file just yet. The Open File dialog box will appear. Use the pop-up menu at the top of this dialog box to work your way into the folder that holds the **SillyBalls.rsrc** file used by the Basic Toolbox PPC project stationery. Figure E.1 shows the path to traverse to get to this file.

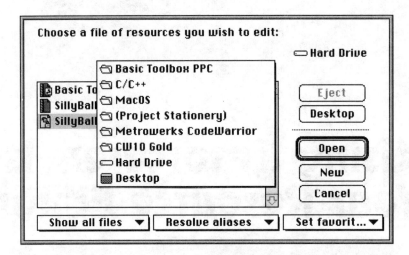

Figure E.1   Moving to the folder that holds the SillyBalls.rsrc resource file.

 Here you're going to make a change to the **SillyBalls.rsrc** file that is used by the Basic Toolbox PPC project stationery. If you have a new project started, note that you're *not* working with that version of the file.

With the **SillyBalls.rsrc** file open, choose **File Info** from the File menu. In the lower left of the file's window you'll see two edit boxes. Change the contents of the Type edit box from **rsrc** to **RSRC**. Next, change the contents of the Creator edit box from **RSED** to **Doug**. These changes are shown in Figure E.2. Now choose **Save** from the File menu to save the file, then click on the **SillyBalls.rsrc** window to close the file.

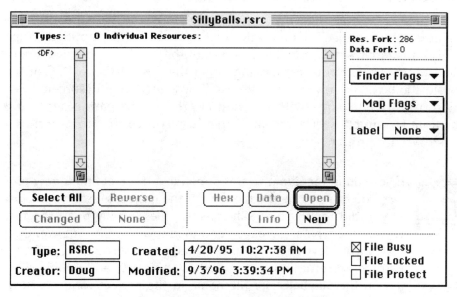

Figure E.2   *Changing the Type and Creator strings in the SillyBalls.rsrc resource file.*

By making this change, every time you create a new project based on the Basic Toolbox PPC project stationery, the copy of **SillyBalls.rsrc** that ends up in the new project will be a Resorcerer file rather than a ResEdit file. What if you create a project using the Basic Toolbox 68k project stationery, you ask? That stationery uses a different version of the **SillyBalls.rsrc** file, so you'll need to change the type and creator of that version as well.

From within Resorcerer, select **Open File** from the File menu. Back your way out of the **Basic Toolbox PPC** folder into the **C/C++** folder, then move into the **Basic Toolbox 68k** folder—the folder that holds the **SillyBalls.rsrc** file for the Basic Toolbox 68k stationary. Starting from the main CodeWarrior folder on your hard drive, here's the complete path to this version of the **SillyBalls.rsrc** file:

```
Metrowerks CodeWarrior:(Project Stationery):MacOS:C/C++:Basic Toolbox
   68k
```

Make the same changes to this file as you did for the other version of **SillyBalls.rsrc**, then save and close the file.

Since I'm supplying you with this tip after you may already have created a new project, it's too late for the change to be applied to the **SillyBalls.rsrc** resource file that is a part of that project. However, every subsequent project you create using either the **Basic** Toolbox PPC or the Basic Toolbox 68k project stationery will now include a Resorcerer version of **SillyBalls.rsrc**—with no extra effort on your part. Now, you'll be able to launch Resorcerer and open a resource file from within a CodeWarrior project.

N O T E If you did in fact jump to this appendix after creating a new project, you can change the file type of the project's resource file just as you did for the two **SillyBalls.rsrc** files. Simply open the file, change the type and creator, and then save the file. You can then test out CodeWarrior's ability to launch Resorcerer by quitting Resorcerer, returning to the CodeWarrior IDE, and double-clicking on the **SillyBalls.rsrc** file name in the project window. Now, Resorcerer rather than ResEdit should launch.

Appendix F

Mcmd Resources and Resource Editors

PowerPlant uses a few resource types that aren't common to other Mac applications. As you read in Chapter 7, the Mcmd is one of them. To make editing resources of these new types easier, use Constructor—Metrowerks own PowerPlant resource editor. If for some reason you'd like to view or work with Mcmd resources in either ResEdit or Resorcerer rather than Constructor, you'll need to add the appropriate template to your resource editor so that it can properly display Mcmd resources. Metrowerks has included TMPL resources for both of these popular resource editors. Without these templates, editing Mcmd resources in either ResEdit or

Resorcerer would require that you use the resource editor's hex editor—definitely not an easy task. With these templates, PowerPlant resources such as the Mcmd can be opened in an easy-to-edit format.

If you use Resorcerer as your resource editor, read the next section. If you're a ResEdit user, skip the following section and move on to *The Mcmd Resource and ResEdit* section.

The Mcmd Resource and Resorcerer

If you're a Resorcerer user, copy the file named **PowerPlant Resorcerer TMPLs** into the **Private Templates** folder in your Resorcerer folder (if you don't have a **Private Templates** folder, create a new untitled folder and give it this name). Refer to Figure F.1. The **PowerPlant Resorcerer TMPLs** file can be found on this book's CD. If you own the full version of Metrowerks CodeWarrior, you'll find it on that CD as well (search from the Finder to find out exactly where this file is on the CD).

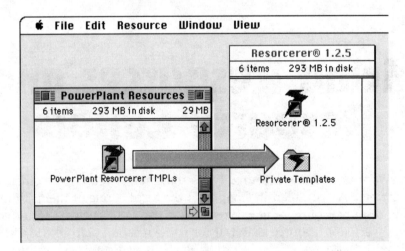

Figure F.1 *Resorcerer users should make sure the PowerPlant Resorcerer TMPLs file is in the Private Templates folder.*

If you'd like to get a little practice working with Mcmd resources in Resorcerer, create a new, empty Resorcerer file in a scratch folder. I've named mine **PPIntro.rsrc**, but you can give your file any name you want. The next several pages will describe how to add three Mcmd resources to this file. The result will be Mcmd resources for the menus shown in Figure F.2.

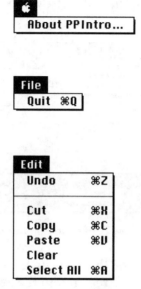

Figure F.2   *The three menus for which Mcmd resources will be created.*

With an open Resorcerer file, select New Resource from the Resource menu. Resorcerer's New Resource dialog box, pictured in Figure F.3, will open. Scroll to **Mcmd** and click on it.

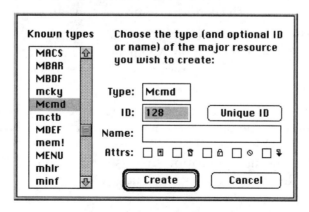

Figure F.3   *Resorcerer's New Resource dialog box, with the Mcmd type selected.*

After clicking the **Create** button, Resorcerer creates a new Mcmd resource, gives it an ID of 128, and opens the Mcmd editor. Initially the Mcmd has no items in it. Click the **New** button to add an item. Figure F.4 shows that Resorcerer gives new items a value of 0.

Figure F.4   *Adding a new command number to an Mcmd resource.*

You can change the value of the new item to any of the PowerPlant-defined Mcmd constants—they're listed in the arrow pop-up menu that's located to the left of the new item. Figure F.5 shows that the menu item is being given the value represented by the constant cmd_About.

In Figure F.6, you can see that the menu item now has a value of 1. Recall from Table 10.1 that cmd_About is a constant that represents the number 1. Figure F.7 shows the relationship between a MENU resource, an Mcmd resource, and the command number constants.

The Apple menu for the hypothetical program I'm creating the resources for has just this single About item, so the Mcmd resource for MENU 128 is complete. You can save the changed resource and click in the close box of the Mcmd editor.

Next, give the Mcmd a descriptive name by selecting **Resource Info** from the Resource menu. Type the name "Apple" in the **Name** field, as shown in Figure F.8. This name will be displayed in Resorcerer, but won't be used by the application that uses the resource. Save the file and close the Resource Information dialog box.

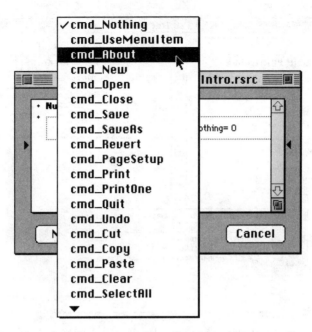

Figure F.5 *Changing the command number of an item in an Mcmd resource.*

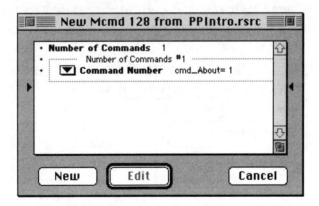

Figure F.6 *The Mcmd resource with one menu command number.*

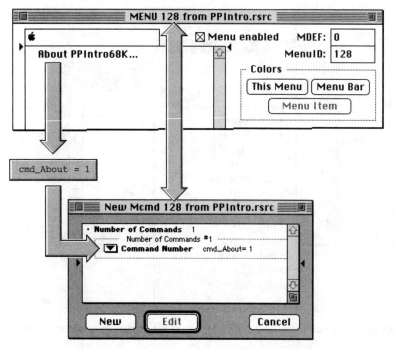

Figure F.7   *The Mcmd resource ID matches the ID of a MENU resource, and its command numbers correspond to menu items.*

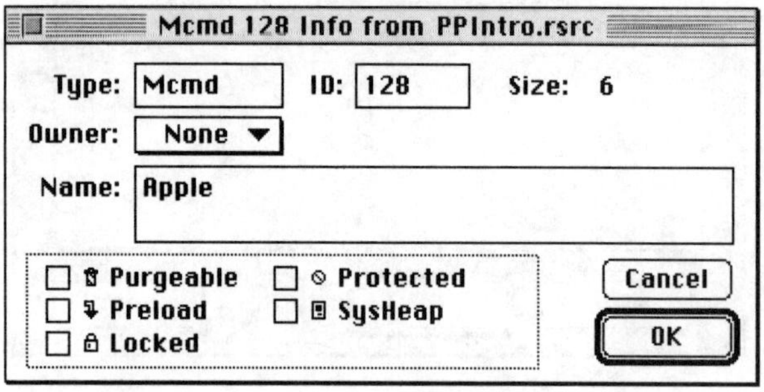

Figure F.8   *Naming the Mcmd resource.*

Now create the Mcmd for the File menu. Click the **New** button in the File window—as is being done in Figure F.9. Resorcerer will create a new Mcmd resource with an ID of 129. You can click on the **Info** button in the File window to give this new resource the name "File."

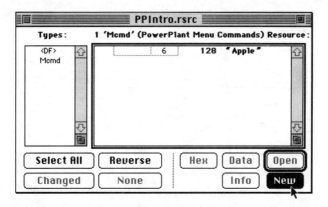

Figure F.9   *Adding a new Mcmd resource to a resource file.*

Click the **New** button to add an item. Like this example's Apple menu, the File menu has only one menu item—here it's the Quit item. PowerPlant defines `cmd_Quit` to have a value of 10, so that's the command number to enter in the File menu's `Mcmd` resource. If you didn't remember that a Quit menu item should have an `Mcmd` command number of 10 (or you didn't care to look it up), simply use the pop-up menu to select **cmd_Quit**, as was done for the About menu item in the Apple menu. Figure F.10 shows the `Mcmd` resource for the File menu.

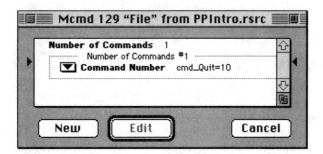

Figure F.10   *The Mcmd resource for the PPIntro68K File menu.*

Next, create an `Mcmd` resource for the Edit menu. Again click the **New** button in the File window, as shown back in Figure F.9. Then click the **New** button in the `Mcmd` editor and use the pop-up menu to add the **Undo** menu command number. Insert each of the Edit menu's seven command numbers in this way. Figure F.11 shows the Mcmd resource that is used for the Edit menu.

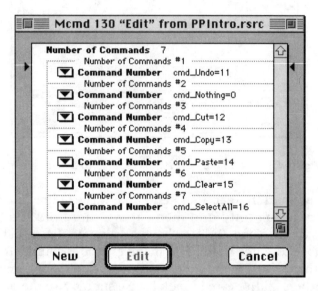

Figure F.11 *The Mcmd resource for the PPIntro68K Edit menu.*

Note that the IDs of the three Mcmd resources match the IDs of the three MENU resources.

The Mcmd Resource and ResEdit

If you're a Resorcerer user, skip this section since it covers the material you just read, from a ResEdit-user point of view. If you use ResEdit, launch ResEdit now. Then open the **PowerPlant ResEdit TMPLs** file that's found on this book's CD. If you own the complete version of Metrowerks CodeWarrior, you'll notice that this file also appears on that CD; either version will work. Next, open the **ResEdit Preferences** file that's found in the Preferences folder in the System Folder of your Mac's hard drive. Click once on the **TMPL** icon in the **PowerPlant ResEdit TMPLs** file and select **Copy** from the Edit menu. Now click on the window that displays the resources in the **ResEdit Preferences** file and then select **Paste** from the Edit menu, as shown in Figure F.12. You've just copied all of the PowerPlant templates to the **ResEdit Preferences** file.

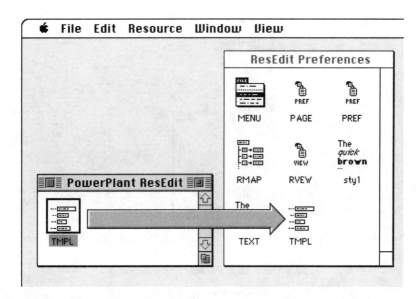

Figure F.12 *ResEdit users should make sure the TMPL resources from the PowerPlant ResEdit file are copied to the ResEdit Preferences file.*

If you'd like to get a little practice working with Mcmd resources in ResEdit, create a new, empty ResEdit file in a scratch folder. I've named mine **PPIntro.rsrc**, but you can give your file any name you want. The next several pages will describe how to add three Mcmd resources to this file. The result will be Mcmd resources for the menus shown in Figure F.13.

With a ResEdit file open, select **Create New Resource** from the Resource menu. In the Select New Type dialog box (shown in Figure F.14), scroll down to the **Mcmd** resource. Any resource that appears in this list has an editor associated with it. Before adding the PowerPlant TMPL resources to the **ResEdit Preferences** file, the Mcmd resource type would not have appeared in this list. Now, ResEdit knows about this new template and will use it whenever you add a new Mcmd resource to any ResEdit file. After clicking on the **Mcmd** resource in the list, click the **OK** button.

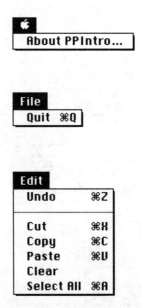

Figure F.13   *The three menus for which Mcmd resources will be created.*

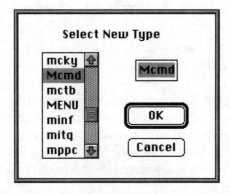

Figure F.14   *ResEdit's Select New Type dialog box, with the Mcmd type selected.*

You'll see that a new Mcmd resource editing window has opened. ResEdit has given this resource an ID of 128, as it does with most new resources. Since the MENU resource for the Apple menu has an ID of 128—and because the Mcmd resource is paired by ID with a MENU resource—this Mcmd resource should be used to hold the command numbers of the Apple menu items.

Click once on the row of asterisks, then select **Insert New Field(s)** from the Resource menu. In the edit box that appears, type in the number 1. Recall from Table 10.1 that the number 1 is always used for the About menu item in the Apple menu. Because there's only one item in the Apple menu for the hypothetical program I'm creating, the Mcmd resource for this menu will have only one command number in it. Figure F.15 shows the completed Mcmd 128 resource. Figure F.16 shows the relationship between a MENU resource, an Mcmd resource, and the command number constants.

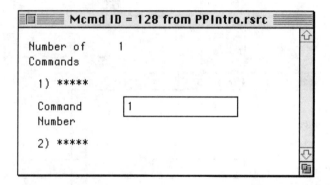

Figure F.15 *The Mcmd resource with one menu command number.*

Next, select **Get Resource Info** from the Resource menu. Give this resource the name "Apple" so that you'll be able to quickly identify this Mcmd resource from the others that you'll be creating. This name will be displayed in ResEdit but won't be used by the application that uses the resource. Figure F.17 shows the ResEdit Get Resource Info dialog box.

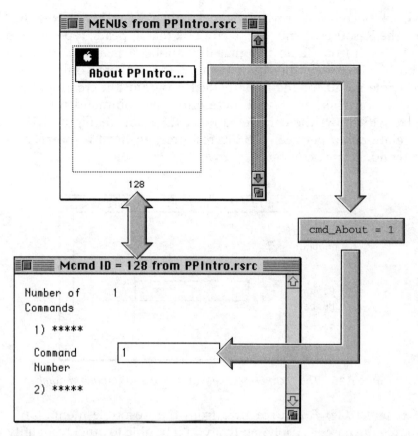

Figure F.16 *The Mcmd resource ID matches the ID of a MENU resource,
and its command numbers correspond to menu items.*

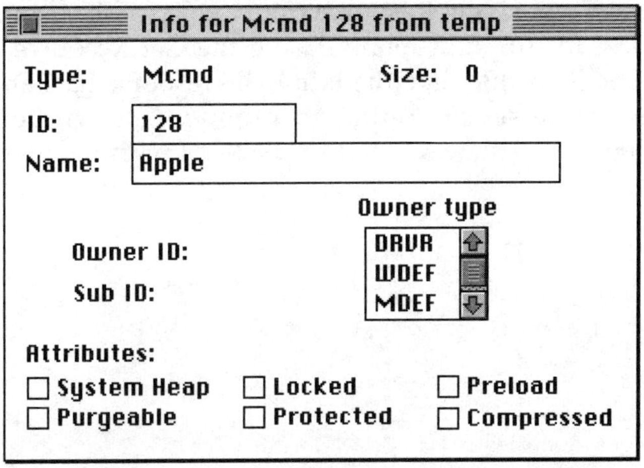

```
┌─────────────────────────────────────────────────┐
│ ▦▦▦▦▦▦▦▦  Info for Mcmd 128 from temp  ▦▦▦▦▦▦ │
├─────────────────────────────────────────────────┤
│                                                   │
│  Type:      Mcmd              Size:    0          │
│                                                   │
│  ID:      ┌──────────┐                            │
│           │ 128      │                            │
│  Name:    │ Apple    │                            │
│           └──────────┘                            │
│                                                   │
│                             Owner type            │
│                           ┌─────────┐ ┌─┐         │
│        Owner ID:          │ DRUR    │ │⬆│         │
│                           │ WDEF    │ │▓│         │
│        Sub ID:            │ MDEF    │ │⬇│         │
│                           └─────────┘ └─┘         │
│                                                   │
│  Attributes:                                      │
│   ☐ System Heap    ☐ Locked      ☐ Preload       │
│   ☐ Purgeable      ☐ Protected   ☐ Compressed    │
└─────────────────────────────────────────────────┘
```

Figure F.17   Naming the Mcmd resource.

Now create the Mcmd for the File menu. Again select **Create New Resource** from the Resource menu. Use the Get Resource Info dialog box to give the Mcmd resource the name "File." If the Mcmd doesn't have an ID of 129 (to match the File MENU resource ID), give it that ID now. The File menu for this example has just a single menu item—the **Quit** item. PowerPlant defines cmd_Quit to have a value of 10, so that's the command number to enter in the File menu's Mcmd resource, as shown in Figure F.18. Remember to click on the row of asterisks and then select **Insert New Field(s)** from the Resource menu to add an edit text box to the Mcmd editor.

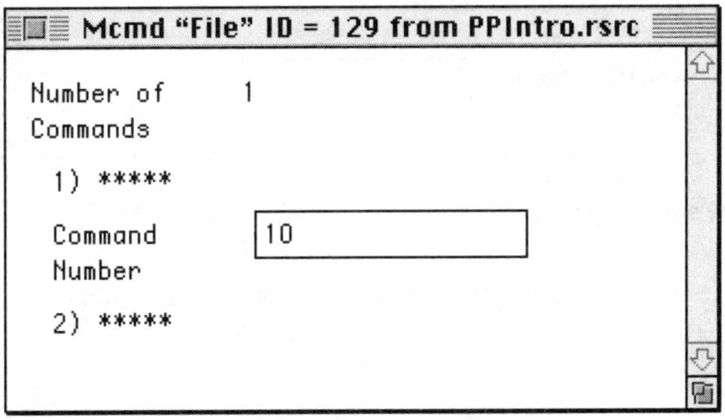

```
┌─────────────────────────────────────────────────┐
│ ▦▦▦ Mcmd "File" ID = 129 from PPIntro.rsrc ▦▦▦ │⬆│
├─────────────────────────────────────────────────┤─┤
│                                                   │ │
│   Number of      1                                │ │
│   Commands                                        │ │
│                                                   │ │
│    1) *****                                       │ │
│                                                   │ │
│   Command     ┌──────────────────┐                │ │
│   Number      │ 10               │                │ │
│               └──────────────────┘                │ │
│                                                   │ │
│    2) *****                                       │⬇│
│                                                   │▣│
└─────────────────────────────────────────────────┘─┘
```

Figure F.18   The Mcmd resource for the PPIntro68K File menu.

Finally, select **Create New Resource** from the Resource menu to add the Mcmd resource for the Edit menu. Using the Get Resource Info dialog box, give it an ID of 130 (like the Edit MENU resource has) and the name "Edit." Insert the seven command numbers shown below in this resource. Figure F.19 shows a part of the Mcmd resource that is used for the Edit menu.

```
cmd_Undo       =    11
cmd_Nothing    =     0
cmd_Cut        =    12
cmd_Copy       =    13
cmd_Paste      =    14
cmd_Clear      =    15
cmd_SelectAll  =    16
```

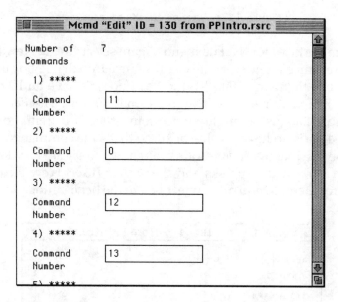

Figure F.19   *The Mcmd resource for the PPIntro68K Edit menu.*

Note that the IDs of the three Mcmd resources match the IDs of the three MENU resources.

Index

Warranty & Support

Free technical support from Metrowerks is provided by acquiring any of Metrowerks' commercial products. You can upgrade from this limited version of CodeWarrior to a commercial product and thereby benefit from this technical support. For more information, contact Metrowerks at 1-800-377-5416, or via email at sales@metrowerks.com.

About The CD

The CD that accompanies this book contains a limited version of the CodeWarrior integrated development environment (IDE). "Limited" means that while this version of CodeWarrior can be used to work with any of the more than twenty example projects that are also on the CD, you won't be able to create new projects of your own. To get the full-featured version of CodeWarrior—as well as numerous programming tools, extensive documentation, and technical support—you'll want to purchase the complete Metrowerks CodeWarrior Gold package. Until then, you can use this version to compile and modify the supplied examples, experiment with different compiler features, and learn more about Macintosh programming.

The CodeWarrior Lite IDE on this CD run on either a 68K Mac (a Macintosh driven by either a Motorola 68020, 68030, or 68040 processor) or any Macintosh that has a PowerPC processor. So it doesn't matter what kind of Mac you have—as long as you have several megabytes of free RAM and System 7.1.2 or later installed.

Once you've popped the CD into your CD-ROM drive, read Chapter 1 of this book to get an idea of what the many programs and files on the CD are for. Then move on to Chapter 2 to see how to write a Macintosh program using CodeWarrior!